Global Capital's 21st Century Repositioning:
Between COVID-19 and the Fourth Industrial Revolution on Africa

Edited by

Rewai Makamani, Artwell Nhemachena & Oliver Mtapuri

Langaa Research & Publishing CIG
Mankon, Bamenda

Publisher:
Langaa RPCIG
Langaa Research & Publishing Common Initiative Group
P.O. Box 902 Mankon
Bamenda
North West Region
Cameroon
Langaagrp@gmail.com
www.langaa-rpcig.net

Distributed in and outside N. America by African Books Collective
orders@africanbookscollective.com
www.africanbookscollective.com

ISBN-10: 9956-551-80-5

ISBN-13: 978-9956-551-80-4

About the Authors

Rewai Makamani is Associate Professor, Head of Department, and former Associate Dean: Research and Innovation at the Namibia University of Science and Technology (NUST), and a Research Fellow of the University of South Africa (UNISA). He has taught at the University of Zimbabwe among others. He holds a PhD degree from UNISA (AFL: Specializing in Applied Linguistics and Communication) and a Master of Arts in African Languages and Literature, Master of Arts in Language for Specific Purposes, Bachelor of Arts Honours and Graduate Certificate in Education from the University of Zimbabwe including a number of professional qualifications. He has supervised and examined students' research projects in Language, Literature and Communication. He has published book chapters and articles in peer reviewed journals. His research interests are in Text Linguistics, Critical Discourse Analysis of land, cultural, courtroom, parliamentary, media and healthcare communication discourses.

Artwell Nhemachena holds a PhD in Social Anthropology, MSc in Sociology and Social Anthropology, BSc Honours Degree in Sociology. In addition to having a good mix of social science and law courses in his undergraduate studies, he also has a Certificate in Law and a Diploma in Education. He has lectured in Zimbabwe before pursuing his PhD studies in South Africa. His current areas of research interest are Knowledge Studies; Development Studies; Environment; Resilience; Food Security and Food Sovereignty; Industrial Sociology; Agnotology, Sociology and Social Anthropology of Conflict and Peace; Transformation; Sociology and Social Anthropology of Science and Technology Studies, Democracy and Governance; Relational Ontologies; Decoloniality and Anthropological/Sociological Jurisprudence. He has published over 80 book chapters and journal articles in accredited and peer-reviewed platforms. He has also published over eighteen books in accredited and peer reviewed platforms. At the University of Namibia, he chairs the Faculty of Humanities and Social Sciences Seminar Series on Researching, Writing and Publishing. Artwell Nhemachena is also a Research Fellow in the College of Humanities of the University of South Africa. He has also been appointed a visiting Professor at Kobe University, Japan.

Oliver Mtapuri is a Professor in Development Studies at the School of Built Environment and Development in the College of Humanities, University of KwaZulu-Natal in Durban, South Africa. Oliver is also the Interim South African Research Chairs Initiative (SARChI) chair in Applied Poverty Reduction Assessment, funded by the National Research Foundation (Grant no. 71220) and the Department of Science and Innovation. His areas of research interest include poverty, inequality, redistribution, public employment programmes, community-based tourism, research methodologies, climate change and project management.

Christopher Chikandiwa obtained his PhD (Leadership Studies) from the University of KwaZulu-Natal, MBA (Operations, Entrepreneurship & Innovation) from WHU (Germany), M.Com (Business Economics) from the University of Fort Hare, as well as the Bachelor of Business Studies (Hons) from the University of Zimbabwe. He is a Lecturer in Operations and Supply Chain Management at the Graduate School of Business and Leadership, University of KwaZulu-Natal. He also taught Purchasing and Operations Management at the University of Fort Hare. Dr Chikandiwa has vast experience and research interest in supply chain management, operations research, project management, project planning, real options analysis, innovation management and entrepreneurship.

Anthony Chirimuuta holds an M.Phil. in Curriculum Policy, Planning and Management from Nelson Mandela Metropolitan University, South Africa, an M.Ed. in (Physics) from the University of Zimbabwe, a B.Ed. in Physics from the University of Zimbabwe and a Certificate in Education, majoring in Biology, Chemistry and Physics, from the University of Zimbabwe. He has published papers and chapters in refereed platforms. Above all he has written a book entitled *Systematic Approach to Curriculum Planning: Curriculum Planning, Implementation, Evaluation and Quality Control*. His research interests are in the interface of Indigenous Knowledge systems, Science and Technology.

Chipo Chirimuuta holds a PhD from The University of South Africa (UNISA), an MA in African Languages and Literature degree from the University of Zimbabwe, a BA Special Honours degree in

African Languages from the University of Zimbabwe, a BA general degree (majoring in English, Ndebele, and History) from the University of Zimbabwe, a Post-Graduate Diploma in Media and Society Studies from the Midlands State University and a Post-Graduate Certificate in Education from the University of Zimbabwe. She is an Associate Professor and Chairperson of the Department of Culture and Heritage Studies at the Zimbabwe Open University. Her research work is centred on indigenous knowledge systems, indigenous languages, culture and gender, culture and heritage, language and the media vis-à-vis their contribution to the development of the people's understanding of themselves, their historical experience, and their spaces on the global world as well as their self-identity.

Aaron Rwodzi holds a PhD in History. He is currently a lecturer in the Department of History under the Faculty of Humanities and Social Sciences at the Catholic University of Zimbabwe. His areas of research interest include political and social history, democracy, ethnicity, and culture.

Edmore Dube holds a PhD and he is a Senior Lecturer in the Department of Philosophy and Religious Studies, Great Zimbabwe University. His research interests are in the areas of religion, health and justice resonating with the common good, and mediated by religio-cultural processes. His publications include, *The Great Zimbabwe Monuments and Challenges in African Heritage Management;* and *Enhancing Human Flourishing: Reflections on the Zimbabwe Catholic Bishops' Conference as an Enduring Prophetic Voice (1957-2017)*, both published by African Sun Media; *The Search for Justice and Peace: Reflections on the Jambanja Discourse as an Articulation of Justice Foreshadowing Peace* published by Routledge; *The Ass-load: A Symbolic Re-appraisal of the Bible and Gender Troubles in Africa,* published by the University of Bamberg Press; and *Zimbabwe Land Tenure Impact on Development and Justice Delivery* published by Langaa. His current chapter on *Inclusive contextual approach in the fight against the COVID-19 pandemic,* which observes the communitarian nature of African health systems and African solutions to African problems, falls perfectly into the general schema.

Enna Sukutai Gudhlanga holds a holds a Doctor of Literature and Philosophy in African Languages from the University of South Africa. She is an Associate Professor and Chairperson of the

Department of Languages and Literature at Zimbabwe Open University. Her research interests are gender in literary and cultural studies. Enna holds certificates in Gender Mainstreaming from OSSREA, CODESRIA and UNIDEP. She is also a research fellow at the University of South Africa and is a rising star of the Circle of the Concerned African Women Theologians. Enna is interested in the study of Africa and the development of its literatures, cultures, and world outlooks. Her main concern is the ultimate self-definition and complete mastery of the African people's own life. Enna has consistently researched and published on gender and literature. Her publications include: *Gender, Politics and Land Use in Zimbabwe, 1980-2012* (Dakar: CODESRIA, 2015). She has presented papers on gender issues at many international conferences and been awarded research grants by several organisations to research on gender issues in Zimbabwe. Enna is also interested in socio-linguistic issues like democracy, language rights, planning and policy.

Angeline Mavis Madongonda is a holder of a Master of Arts degree in English and is a senior lecturer in the Department of Languages and Literature at the Zimbabwe Open University. Currently she is the Programme Leader for the Bachelor of Arts in English and Communication Studies. She is an accomplished researcher and academic and she has authored a number of journal articles which include "'Knock Knock Knock' The paradox of the Music genre and Serious Discourse in HIV and AIDS Communication" (2019) in *African Journal of Rhetoric* and "Surviving a rabid economy: The current cash crisis and its threat to security and governance in the monetary sector in Zimbabwe" (2019) in *Journal Africa Development,* with E S Gudhlanga. Her research interests include Postcolonial Studies, Corpus Linguistics and Ecocriticism. Her current research focus is on marginalised voices in both traditional and contemporary writings in Zimbabwe and Africa. Angeline is a doctoral candidate at the Zimbabwe Open University.

Hatikanganwi Mapudzi holds a PhD in Communication from the University of Fort Hare, Postgraduate Diploma in Media Management and the Master of Arts in Journalism and Media Studies, both from Rhodes University. She has also successfully completed the Postgraduate Certificate in Higher Education with the Namibia University of Science and Technology. She is a lecturer in the Department of Communication, Faculty of Human Sciences at the Namibia University of Science and Technology. She teaches various courses which include Research Methods, Gender Studies, Advertising and Public Relations. She also supervises postgraduate students in the Department of Communication. Her research interests are in the areas of journalism, ICTs and democracy, higher education in the fourth industrial revolution, health communication, indigenous languages, as well as gender issues. She is also a member of the Professional Editors' Guild.

Collin Kamalizeni is an educationist and researcher in Business and sociology and is involved in the field of gender equality and advocates against gender-based violence. He has also researched extensively on the role of women leadership in public enterprises, earning a PhD in Business Administration and gender from the University of KwaZulu-Natal. Collin has also been actively involved in educational leadership helping out young female leaders to courageously enter into the male dominated managerial and leadership positions. He also holds an MBA, focusing on strategic planning and management and a Bachelor's degree majoring in Economics and Education.

Ntandokazulu Siwela holds a Master's in Development Studies from the University of Fort Hare, where her thesis focused on curriculum relevance to societal needs. A member of the Public Relations Institute of South Africa, she started her career as a Sports Journalist for the Beats Magazine and later became the magazine's editor. She also worked as the Alumni Relations Officer for the University of Fort Hare, a role that saw her doing a lot of research to ensure the publishing of *The Fort Harian* magazine. Further, she was involved in research across countries to enable the university to set up Alumni chapters in various provinces and countries. She has tutored at the University of Fort Hare in various Communications related subjects. She also lectured at the MSC college where she taught Public Relations, Business Communication, Research Methods, Marketing, Office Secretarial Techniques and HIV/Counselling. Miss Siwela has a passion for research and her interests include communication for development, health communication, the use of ICTs for development, Advertising, and the role of religion in community development.

Memory Muteeri graduated with a PhD in Communications from the North West University, a Master of Media Studies from the Nelson Mandela Metropolitan University, South Africa. Currently, she is a freelance communication Consultant and Researcher. She has previously worked as a Research Monitor for Regional Mixed Migration Secretariat (RMMS), carrying out interviews with adult and child migrants along the southern Africa route. She was a Tutor in the Department of Communication, Nelson Mandela Metropolitan University and a Communication and Marketing Coordinator for the Community Veterinary Clinic in Port Elizabeth. Her research focuses on ICTs and Social Media.

Peter Masvotore is an ordained Minister of the Methodist Church in Zimbabwe and a part time tutor with the Zimbabwe Open University (ZOU). He has published articles in peer reviewed journals, wrote books and presented papers at international Conferences. Contact number +263774958353 email masvotorep@gmail.com

Rumbidzai E. Makamani is a teacher. She holds a Masters' in Education (Adult Education) Degree, Bachelor of Adult Education Honours from the University of South Africa, Bachelor of Education (Special Needs) Degree from Great Zimbabwe University, Executive Certificate in Strategic HIV/AIDS Project Management from the University of Zimbabwe, and a Diploma in Education. Her research interest are vested in education matters in schools and issues of the vulnerable societies.

Susan Shamaoma Katowa holds a Master of Education Degree in Curriculum Studies and Honours Bachelor of Education with Specialisation in Inclusive Education. Her current writing is an expression of the emerging 4IR and wreaked havoc of the novel coronavirus pandemic in the education system. She is passionate about knowledge sharing which prompts her interest in conducting educational research.

Ndinaani Mwashita is a PhD candidate with the University of South Africa (UNISA). She obtained an Honours degree in Teaching and Learning from North West University (South Africa) and went on to complete her Master of Education degree in Curriculum Studies with the Midlands State University (Zimbabwe). Her area of research is Social Science and Curriculum Development.

Lizazi Eugene Libebe is a former Magistrate and lectures in the Faculty of Law University of Namibia Department of Public Law and Jurisprudence. He holds a B-juris degree & LLB (UNAM); LMM in

International Law (UCT). His areas of interest and publications include public international law, natural resources law, economic law, environmental law and policy, African jurisprudence, decolonization, criminal law and procedure, law of evidence, family law, legislative drafting, sociology, philosophy, management, higher education, and multi-disciplinary research.

Pilisano Masake is an international law scholar. He holds an LLD – public law: international criminal law (Stellenbosch University), LLM (Stellenbosch University), Masters in Policing Practice (Southern Business School), LLB and B-Juris (UNAM), a Lecturer and Acting Head of Department in the Department of Social Sciences, the Faculty of Human Sciences at the Namibia University of Science and Technology. A former police officer with the rank of Detective Chief Inspector – Namibian Police Force. The co-founder of the *Unam Law Review* and serving as Head Articles Editor till 2013. A co-author of various articles and book chapters. Further, co-authored a book *"The Law of Pre-Trial Criminal Procedure in Namibia"*. Serving, – community engagement, with the Namibia Red Cross Society a non-profit humanitarian-based institution. Further, serving as a Listed Professional Investigator for the International Criminal Court (ICC) – duties, including, investigating core international crimes, such as: genocide, crime against humanity, war crimes, and crime of aggression – crimes that are punishable by the ICC. Pilisano's areas of expertise include – international law, niche: international criminal law, with a particular interest in corporate criminal liability for international crimes.

Munyaradzi Mukesi is a Senior Lecturer and Associate Dean of Teaching and Learning in the Faculty of Health and Applied Sciences at the Namibia University of Science and Technology (NUST). He is a registered Medical Laboratory Scientist in clinical and chemical pathology with the Health Professions Council of Namibia and has extensive experience in laboratory diagnostics. His research focuses on maternal and neonatal issues and laboratory diagnostics in general and has published several papers and book chapters. He holds a PhD (Microbiology) from the University of Fort Hare, Master of Medicine degree in Biochemistry from the University of Zimbabwe and a Post graduate Certificate in Higher Education from NUST. He teaches clinical chemistry, immunology, research methodology, and integrated clinical pathophysiology. He has successfully supervised and graduated several honours and masters students. Currently, he is supervising several honours, masters and PhD students researching on maternal and neonatal issues and various aspects of diagnostics in infectious diseases.

Emmy Wabomba is a Lecturer at Namibia University of Science and Technology, Department of Social Sciences. Over several years, in her career, she has served on various panels on issues concerning different Acts of Parliament in Namibia such as the review of the Electoral act and the symposium of the Draft Use of Electronic Transactions and Communication Bill of Namibia. She participated in the research on the establishment of a capacity building institution in the energy sector in Namibia and in the APEDIA, an academic partnership for environmental and development innovations in Africa. She also participated in a seminar that was held in China, on the University Teachers from Developing countries sponsored by the Ministry of Commerce in China and organised by North-West University in Changchun People's Republic of China. In 2012 she presented a paper at the fourth APEDIA Conference in Ethiopia which discussed the importance of policies in preserving soil as an important component of food security in Africa. In 2014, she carried out a research on behalf of the Anti-corruption Commission to establish whether the private entities have any legal policies in place to curb corruption in their organisations. In 2018 Emmy carried out a research, as co-researcher on Contemporary land discourses in Namibia: A critical analysis of newspaper reports and views from select information rich informants. The paper was published in The African Association for Rhetoric journal and presented a paper at 8th International Conference on the theme: "The Rhetoric and Language of Decolonisation in Africa: Challenges and Prospects. The African Association for Rhetoric in collaboration with the Faculty of Arts & Design-DUT. Emmy holds: B Juris, LLB & LLM (International Economic Law) and is an Admitted Legal Practitioner of the High Court of Namibia, Court Accredited Mediator of the High Court of Namibia, and Member of the Law Society of Namibia.

Table of Contents

Preface

Little recognition is made in scholarship and thought that Africans do not necessarily need revolutions against their own institutions and leaders for them to develop and prosper: they may, however, need revolutions to recover material resources looted during the colonial era. Europe and America did not develop because of revolutions but because they enslaved and colonised Africans for centuries. Similarly, Europeans and Americans did not develop because of political revolutions against their own institutions and leaders but they developed and prospered by enslaving and colonising Africans for centuries. Equally, Europeans and Americans did not develop and prosper because of democracy and good governance but they prospered and developed through enslaving and colonising Africans and other peoples in the world. Yet Africans are made to believe that they can only develop through revolutions, through revolting against their own institutions and leaders and through the so-called industrial revolutions. Africans are made to believe that they can only develop through liberal democracy and through the so-called good governance realised by desisting from restitution and reparations for crimes of enslavement and colonisation. Once Africans start to demand restitution and reparations for enslavement and colonisation, they are quickly described as violating democracy, human rights, and good governance. If democracy, human rights, good governance, and industrial revolutions really explain progress and development in the world, then Euro-Americans would not have enslaved, colonised, dispossessed, and exploited other people in the world.

In spite of such brute facts of history relating to development through enslaving, colonising, dispossessing, and exploiting other people, we still witness a lot of literature uncritically celebrating industrial revolutions as the supposed motors of development, productivity, and growth. Of course, Ngugi wa Thiongo would argue that Africans, including some academics, are suffering colonised minds which explains the apparent lack of imagination beyond mimicry of what is given in Eurocentric literature. Material privation has destroyed African senses of self-worth, self-respect, and self-confidence to the point where even some academics are afraid of exercising academic freedom, beyond parrotry. Also, anxious to win grants and other forms of funding from Western institutions, some

African academic institutions directly or indirectly censor staff members who seek to exercise academic freedom, ostensibly because they dampen chances of getting coveted grants. Put differently, the paradox is that some Africans celebrate the Fourth Industrial Revolution even as they suppress decolonial revolutions that would set the minds free from Eurocentric parrotry and mimesis. It would not be surprising that even some African institutions that may not be favourable to decolonial revolutions would mimetically celebrate the Fourth Industrial Revolution and other revolutions associated with the disruptive technologies. In such cases, all that matters is what parrotry and mimesis yield – the indignity of the process notwithstanding. This book is an exercise beyond parrotry and mimesis; it is a book that foregrounds decolonial revolutions and uses decolonial thought to interrogate the Fourth Industrial Revolution. The book unflinchingly asks why the Fourth Industrial Revolution appears to be celebrated and sponsored much more than decolonial revolutions on the continent of Africa. The book also asks African scholars and academies to stop prioritising funding over their self-respect and self-worth as Africans: drawing from the Shona term *chihure* (prostitution), the book dissuades African scholars and academies from recklessly singing and dancing to the tunes of those that supposedly pay such African pipers. The Shona term *chihure* underlines recklessness and abandoning the African self to the material benefit of the moment. In this regard, there is need for Africans to meticulously unpack and carefully consider the costs and benefits of the Fourth Industrial Revolution, from an African locus on enunciation – and not from an African locus of enunciation of global capital.

Artwell Nhemachena, Rewai Makamani
& Oliver Mtapuri

Chapter One

"Nature's" Role in 21st Century Revolutions? COVID-19, the Fourth Industrial Revolution and the Repositioning of Global Capital

Artwell Nhemachena, Rewai Makamani & Oliver Mtapuri

Introduction

The metaphysical dance of global capital is being felt and experienced as COVID-19 and as the Fourth Industrial Revolution in the twenty first century. Seeking to achieve full spectrum dominance from the twenty-first century onwards, global capital is engaging in its rituals of renewal that are being theorised in Eurocentric scholarship as postcapitalism – a period when the economic system is supposedly no longer considered to be capitalism. However, it is important to notice that capitalist rituals of renewal do not imply the end of capitalism. Capitalism is simply moulting and renewing itself; it is gunning for full spectrum dominance in which it destroys peripheral states and borders that prevent it from openly exploiting the entire planet. Global capital is destroying peripheral states in order to create a borderless world open for global capitalist exploitation. Global capital is invading human bodies using invasive new technologies including nanobots, nanovaccines or nanomedicines – and it is microchipping human bodies and brains so that it can collect Big Data from human bodies connected in the Internet of Things, Internet of Battlefield Things and Internet of Humans. Empire is creating cloud computing so that it usurps data from peripheral states whose citizens are set to be governed more by global capital than by their own states. The peripheral states are being leapfrogged through new digital technologies and digital economies that facilitate the transgression of borders and boundaries in ways that make such states otiose. Through massive retrenchments of billions of human workers that are replaced by robots, the peripheral states are set up for revolutions and massive conflagrations as billions of unemployed youths are set to blow up their own states in lieu of blowing up global capital. To destroy peripheral states or to set the states up for destruction through revolutions by billions of unemployed human

1

workers, global capital has to first of all destroy economies in such states – already the process of destroying economies in such peripheral states started with the Economic Structural Adjustment Programmes. COVID-19 and the Fourth Industrial Revolution are simply fast-tracking the process of destroying economies in peripheral states. They are part of the metaphysical dance of global capital – a process wherein global capital is moulting and digging its heels further in under the façade of transformation and the industrial revolutions.

Global capital is squeezing and destroying its opponents: The metaphysical dance of global capital

To squeeze African states to ultimate destruction, global capital has refused to return land and other resources that were stolen by colonialists during the colonial era – at the same time, global capital has started squeezing out African youths out of employment by replacing them with robots. Also, to squeeze African states to ultimate destruction, global capital is in the 21st century new scramble for Africa where it is grabbing land from African peasants. At the same time, the same global capital is replacing billions of human workers with robots which will create massive unemployment that will serve as tinder for the oncoming revolutions against African states. In this way, African states are set up for revolutions worse than what happened during the Arab Spring in Libya, Tunisia and Egypt (Robinson 2020; Wolfsfeld, Segev & Sheafer 2013; Lanchovichina 2018; Drine 2012; Wilson & Corey 2012). The postMarxist era that neo-imperialism and global capital are gunning for is achieved by replacing billions of workers with robots thereby rendering them useless and disorganised. The postMarxist era is also achieved by destroying those states that could possibly assist the retrenched and demobilised workers remobilise and fight against global capital. Already African states are losing their sovereignty to transnational institutions and transnational corporations in the logics of the withering away of the state and the eternal recurrence of global capitalism and imperialism. Already COVID-19 regulations on social distancing have yielded to global capital's plan to demobilise billions of global workers through online work and working from home: this destroys workers' collective consciousness and abilities to organise and to strike. Already COVID-19 is demobilising African states that have already been captured and are writhing and responding to the 21st century metaphysical dance of global capital.

Having retained land and other material resources stolen during the colonial era, global capital is simply repositioning itself for greater unopposed dominance in the world. Resuming dispossession by grabbing land from African peasants in the 21st century new scramble for Africa, global capital is repositioning itself for unopposed dominance in the world – it is not necessarily a postcapitalist dispensation that global capital is seeking. Having dispossessed Africans of their land and other resources, global capital is also grabbing and monopolising African seeds systems such that African farmers will become even more dependent on the transnational corporations that are grabbing the African seeds systems and patenting the seeds (Shiva & Shiva 2019). Having mastered the art of biotechnologically producing meat in factories through genetic modification, global capital is now seeking to intensify its control over economies in Africa by preventing Africans from surviving on their wildlife or their farm animals. This is meant to force Africans and the rest of the world to begin to depend utterly on genetically engineered or factory produced meat that global capital controls. Having mastered the art of biotechnologically producing meat and other food stuff from factories rather than on the farms, global capital is now mounting discourses on climate change, environmental catastrophism/apocalypse and animal rights so that it forces Africans and the rest of the world from producing food on farms. This way the rest of the world will be forced to depend on biotechnologically produced food which global capital monopolises. Having squeezed African states out of industrial manufacturing and having destroyed economies in Africa, global capital is setting out to force African states to accede to harvesting Big Data from their citizens and trade the data for humanitarian aid from the transnational corporations that are beginning to mine Big data from forcibly microchipped Africans who are then connected in the global Internet of Things for purposes of global surveillance, sousveillance, uberveillance and remote control (Nhemachena, Hlabangane & Kaundjua 2020).

Global capital knows that if Africans get back their land which was stolen during colonialism, then they will be able to effectively resist genetically modified food that transnational corporations are producing. Global capital knows that if Africans retain the small farms which they have, then they will be able to resist consuming genetically modified food which global capital is producing for them

3

in spite of the dangers of consuming such genetically modified food (Lovelock 2006; Mawere & Nhemachena 2017). Global capital knows that if Africans retain ownership and control over their environment and animals then they will be able to effectively resist consuming the genetically modified meat which is being produced in factories [rather than on farms] for them. Thus, through excessive animal rights and excessive environmental protection, global capital seeks to leave Africans with no options but to yield to genetically modified food, including meat produced in factories rather than on farms. Similarly, because global capital knows that if Africans retain their jobs then they will be able to effectively resist microchipping and the mining of Big Data from their bodies, brains and environments – global capital seeks to first of all destroy economies in Africa so that it becomes easier to force Africans to yield to mining of Big Data from their brains, bodies and environments (Nhemachena, Hlabangane & Kaundjua 2020). The point here is that what is currently happening in the world cannot be understood outside the context of the metaphysical dance of global capital and the attendant rituals of its renewal and moulting. When global capital dances, everyone is forced to dance along; when global capital sneezes everyone is forced to sneeze; when global capital engages in rituals of renewal, everyone is forced to engage in rituals of renewal; when global capital moults, everyone is forced to moult. Global capital has become a god that assumes immanence in nature and so the global capital can manifest as and become indistinct from "natural" viruses, bacteria, animal forms, typhoons, droughts, floods etc. In this regard, COVID-19 can be understood as an obligatory passage point (Callon 1984; Latour 2005) meant to force the world to transition in terms of global capital's rituals of renewal.

COVID-19 arrived at a time when "nature" or "Gaia" has been gaining ascendancy as a revered actor in Eurocentric scholarship (Lovelock 2006; Latour 2005) – and indeed "nature" has finally acted, in COVID-19, by not only making humanity sick and dead but also by catalysing the Fourth Industrial Revolution. It is as if Eurocentric scholarship has for the past decades not only been invoking but also conjurating "nature" to act as is evident in scholarship writing on animism, actor-networks, agency, performativity and so on. It is in this context that some thinkers and scholars have argued that the COVID-19 pandemic is in fact a plandemic appearing at the behest and instance of those that stand to benefit from the emerging Fourth Industrial Revolution, the information society, the emergent biotechnology revolution, the emergent nanotechnological revolution, the emergent Internet of Things, the emergent Internet of Battlefield and the associated Big Data regimes which are set to transform society and indeed the entire world. Naturally the emergent information society and associated Big Data will and are already benefiting global elites who own and control the transnational corporations that are reaping profits from the shifts to e-commerce, digital economies, the shift to online work and the shift to smart factories where human workers are already being replaced by industrial robots. The point here is that COVID-19 has been understood by some as not merely a freak of nature, coinciding as it did with the global *zeitgeist* marking the various revolutions – the Fourth Industrial Revolution, information technology revolution, biotechnology revolution, nanotechnological revolution, posthumanist and transhumanist revolution and so on. The thesis of this book therefore is that COVID-19 is an enabler of the repositioning of global capital such that it resets and launches the world into an information society/economy and the Fourth Industrial Revolution. In such a society, retrenched human workers will increasingly become mines for Big Data that will drive the global economy in the context of the creepy information and communicative capitalism (Nhemachena, Hlabangane & Kaundjua 2020; Dean & Passavant 2004) .

Global capital has for a long time suffered challenges from Marxism and Marxist-inclined organisations, global capital has similarly suffered challenges and hurdles from indigenous states seeking to protect their citizens from exploitation and from the looting by global capitalists that siphon resources away from indigenous peoples of the world. Now global capital is repositioning itself such that it finally destroys Marxist organisations such as trade unions and workers' organisations, more generally, by replacing human workers with industrial robots. By so doing, global capital permanently demobilises trade unions and workers' organisations because when human workers are replaced with industrial robots it means trade unions become moribund and so instead of capitalism becoming moribund, global capitalism is rendering Marxism moribund in its place. Instead of global capital becoming moribund, what we are set to witness is human workers, and the Marxism buttressing them, becoming moribund. While indigenous states have historically protected their citizens from the ravages of colonialism, global capital and COVID-19, the 21st century revolutions are set to render the indigenous states moribund, particularly as global transnational corporations are usurping the functions of indigenous states in relation to governance of indigenous populations. E-commerce retrenches indigenous states which are being leap-frogged by deterritorialised transnational commerce beyond the control of the states. Digital economies also leap-frog indigenous states and thus rendering them moribund as their jurisdictional economies are usurped by the transnational corporations that own and control digital economies. Similarly, cryptocurrencies and bitcoins are leap-frogging indigenous states and therefore rendering them moribund and desovereignised (Georgiou 2020; Diwakar 10 August 2020; Huang 23 September 2020). In these senses, global capital is repositioning itself by dealing mortal blows to its historical opponents in the form of the trade unions and indigenous states that have historically prevented the free mobility of capital which has always sought the liberty to loot and exploit resources across the planet. Of course, global capital erroneously assumes that what is good for it is good for everybody.

Which humanity will benefit after humans have been turned into transhumans and posthumans?

Because global capital controls global media – including the social media – brainwashed sections of humanity now uncritically believe that what is good for global capital is necessarily good for them as well. Sections of humanity now uncritically believe that the Fourth Industrial Revolution which is good for global capital is good for them also; they believe that cryptocurrencies which are good for global capital are necessarily also good for them; they believe that undoing their states' sovereignty which is good for global capital is also good for them. In this regard, addressing "social media" as social erroneously presupposes that global capitalism – which owns and controls such media is social when in fact it is antisocial, in a Marxist sense. In this sense social media hides the antisociality of global capital that owns and controls it and uses it to churn out ideologies supporting, for instance, the repositioning of global capital. Thus, it is not surprising that, in the context of COVID-19, the global media owners responded to critical popular clips by labelling them as fake news, disinformation, misinformation and so on. Historically capitalism has condemned and dismissed everything that is critical of its telos and trappings. Capitalism has historically been about

6

sacrificing humanity for the sake of profits. From the enslavement era to the colonial era, we witness how capitalism sacrificed sections of humanity for the sake of profits. In the contemporary era, we witness the sacrificing of sections of humanity who are constituted and engaged as global capital's sources of cheap labour. For this reason, it is not surprising that some people have interpreted COVID-19 as another instance of global sacrifice of the sections of humanity that global capital is keen to dispose of while it also resets the world to suit its postMarxist dispensation. In the emergent postMarxist dispensation, humanity will not necessarily be defined in terms of Marxist logics of exploitation of the working class by global capital – rather humanity will be retrenched, dispossessed and left to wither away or die.

In fact, the postMarxist world order into which global capital is resetting the world will be a posthumanitarian world order undergirded by the emergent Eurocentric ideologies of posthumanism and transhumanism (Duffield 2018; 2019; Nhemachena & Mawere 2020). It is not surprising that humanism is currently being deconstructed by posthumanist and transhumanist scholarship, which is gaining traction in Eurocentric thought. In such posthumanitarian, posthumanistic and transhumanistic world order, human rights will become moribund because the category of humans will be replaced by the category of transhumans and posthumans. The point is that while some scholars argue that the Fourth Industrial Revolution is good for humanity and will benefit humanity by increasing productivity and efficiency, the irony is that the category of humanity and human beings itself is becoming moribund. The same Eurocentric scholarship that celebrates the emergence of the Fourth Industrial Revolution, as beneficial to humanity, is paradoxically also celebrating the posthumanism and transhumanism which are supplanting humanism and humanity. The point is that if human beings are being turned into posthumans and transhumans who do we refer to when we argue that the Fourth Industrial Revolution will benefit humanity. Who is this humanity that survives the onslaught of transhumanism and posthumanism which Eurocentric scholarship is already celebrating and supporting? If transhumanism and posthumanism are occurring at the same time with the Fourth Industrial Revolution, the question is which humans will remain human enough to benefit from the Fourth Industrial Revolution? The point is that the Fourth Industrial Revolution will not and is not meant to benefit all of humanity because some section(s) of humanity are being turned – through nanotechnology and biotechnology – into posthumans and transhumans (Flores 2018). They will not remain human for long to benefit from the Fourth Industrial Revolution.

Of course, when imperial capitalism was inserting itself into the colonial territories, even the victims of colonial capitalism were promised that they would benefit from the process of colonisation that was disguised as civilisation and modernisation. It is inherent in capitalism to promise heaven and paradise even for those that it would be disposing and dispossessing. In this regard, it is cause for wonder whether everyone will benefit from the Fourth Industrial Revolution that is so much glorified in Eurocentric scholarship. Of course, academies are also funded by global capital which uses the academies to propagate its ideologies and evangelise to its victims. The point we are making here is that when global capital repositions itself, it always employs its evangelists who propagate its capitalist ideologies which may be presented in various shades and guises including appearances of humanitarianism and philanthropy, including in a world that is increasingly becoming antihumanist, posthumanist and posthumanitarian. For humanity to believe that the Fourth Industrial Revolution would be philanthropic, and humanitarian is to stretch imagination too far in a world where evidence abounds that capitalism is not about philanthropy and humanitarianism but exploitation, dispossession and profits.

The biggest façade is arguably that humanity is fooled to believe that the West developed or industrialised due to industrial revolutions when in fact there is a lot of evidence that the West developed and industrialised through enslaving and colonising other people in the world. In the matrix of Western industrialisation and development, there is hardly any mention of the realities of enslavement and colonisation of other people. Similarly, in the matrix of the Fourth Industrial Revolution, there is hardly any mention of the sacrifices, including disposability, that some sections of humanity are forced to take. Those that were enslaved and colonised are ignored in the historiography of Western industrialisation and development. Those that died while on the colonial cheap labour regimes are ignored and those that were dispossessed and exploited are ignored. All credit is given to the global elites who now own and control global capital and transnational corporations. The problem in much scholarship is that there is glorification even over-glorification of those that have benefited from dispossessing, enslaving, colonising and exploiting others. It is not surprising that in the contemporary hype about the Fourth Industrial Revolution, there is glorification of those that will benefit from dispossessing, retrenching and sacrificing others. Eurocentric scholarship hardly tells the stories from the vantage points of the vanquished and sacrificed. In this vein, we argue that there is a need to critically analyse the contemporary revolutions from the sacrificed people's locus of enunciation.

Whereas African peasants would want revolutions that enhance the restitution of their resources that were stolen during the colonial era, global capital and global elites prioritise revolutions that ensure that the dispossessed Africans further lose their jobs to industrial robots – and this is called the Fourth Industrial Revolution. Whereas dispossessed African peasants would desire revolutions that enhance their chances of getting reparations for enslavement and colonisation, global capital and elites are obsessed with nanotechnological revolutions that destroy the human identities of the Africans. Put differently, the revolutions sponsored by global capital and global elites are not meant to make right the enslavement and colonial crimes on Africans and other peoples of the Global South. When Africans and other peoples of the Global South embark on revolutions to repossess their resources stolen during the colonial era, global media which are owned and controlled by global elites demonise such African revolutions as disruptive and as causing crises supposedly warranting indictment at the International Criminal Court or at the Hague. However, when global capital and global elites induce their revolutions, they are celebrated as beneficial revolutions even if they are disruptive and destructive to sections of humanity in the Global South. Thus, when Africans embark on land redistribution, they are demonised and condemned as disruptive to the economies and jobs but when global capital and global elites embark on the disruptive Fourth Industrial Revolution and on nanotechnological, biotechnological and posthumanist revolutions, all we witness are glorifications and celebrations of such revolutions as beneficial to humanity even as billions of human workers are losing jobs to industrial robots. The point is that when African leaders embark on land redistribution, they are condemned and demonised as disruptive and destructive but when global capital and global elites embark on their revolutions, they are protected from criticisms. In fact, those that criticise the global capital and global elites are condemned as conspiracy theorists, as post-truthers, as propagating disinformation, misinformation and so on. When global capital and global elites embark on their revolutions, we are informed that humanity must not be critical about them because in times of crises, humanity needs global cooperation rather than conflicts supposedly arising from criticisms directed at global elites. However, when it is Africans who have embarked on their own revolutions to repossess their resources, the global media does not hesitate to criticise, condemn and demonise including in ways that generate animosity among Africans themselves.

Building on contemporary discourses about degrowth, postgrowth and postdevelopment, this book challenges the Eurocentric assertions that the Fourth Industrial Revolution is meant to enhance growth and development. If, as is evident in Eurocentric scholarship, the world is moving towards degrowth and postgrowth wherein economic growth is deemphasised and scaled-down (Nhemachena, Warikandwa, Mpofu & Chitimira 2019), the question is, what then is the essence of the Fourth Industrial Revolution? Given the proliferation of the degrowth and postgrowth movements and associated discourses about biocentrism, earthcentrism and ecocentrism, there is evidence that the Fourth Industrial Revolution is not meant to raise productivity and enhance development and growth for the entirety of humanity. In this regard, the major problem with Africans, particularly academics, is that many suffer from misrecognition in the sense that when they read about the benefits of the Fourth Industrial Revolution, they think such benefits apply to them when in fact they are meant to apply to sections of humanity that own and control global capital. Thus, much as some Africans, during colonialism, thought that colonialists' allusions to civilisation, development and progress referred to Africans, some contemporary Africans still suffer similar misrecognition. When sections of humanity that own and control global capital speak about development, progress, growth, security and well-being, they naturally will be referring to their own situations, yet some Africans mistakenly think they are the reference points in such discourses. The situation is more like that of victims of sacrifice who listen to discussions of life after the sacrifice and they mistakenly believe that such discourses about life postsacrifice refer to them as well. Or more graphically a dog hears its master speak about sumptuous dinner and then it also mistakenly believes that the dinner belongs to it as well.

The point in the foregoing is that the Fourth Industrial Revolution must be understood in the context of emergent discourses on postsustainability wherein growth and sustainable development are losing traction. They must also be understood in the context of the emergent posthumanitarianism and antihumanism. Increasingly the idea in global governance discourses is to abandon the notion of sustainable development and to embrace discourses on postsustainability including sacrifice, austerity and letting some humans die off supposedly so as to save the environment and the global spaceship. Similarly, discourses about COVID-19 need to be understood in the context of postsustainability and not in the context of the waning notion of sustainable development. If the contemporary era is increasingly marked by postsustainability, voluntary extinction, Anthropocene, degrowth, postgrowth, postdevelopment, posthumanism, posthumanitarianism, ethics of vulnerability and so on, why then must we believe that global capitalism and global academies sponsored by global capital are acting out of philanthropy and humanitarianism? The point we are making here is that it is the same global capital that is sponsoring the ideas about postsustainability, degrowth, postgrowth, postdevelopment, posthumanism, transhumanism, voluntary extinction and so on. Similarly, and ironically, it is the same global capital that is marketing its nanovaccines, nanomedicines, nanobots and so on as beneficial to humanity (Flores 2018; Nhemachena, Hlabangane & Kaundjua 2020). Put differently, global capital and global elites are sponsoring projects and ideas to turn human beings into posthumans and transhumans yet, paradoxically, they want to justify the same projects as beneficial to humanity. The question is who is this humanity that benefits from the Fourth Industrial Revolution after humans have been turned into posthumans and transhumans?

Chapter outlines

Chipo Chirimuuta and Antony Chirimuuta's chapter two argues that the African continent cannot afford to ignore the 4th Industrial Revolution and the various implications that it has to the developmental trajectory of its people. The duo argue that while it is good to acknowledge the advantaged position of continents such as Europe, Australia, USA among many others, it is high time Africans realise that the revolution at hand was never designed to benefit them, but the conglomerates, the global elite and the imperialists. As such, African survival in this revolution is not derivable from parroting the neo-imperialists. Africans need to advance the uniqueness of Africa. Africans will then be better placed to curve their own spaces on the global terrain and claim their position on the global marketplace of ideas. It is high time Africans concentrate on inventing, researching and coming up with innovations that are peculiar to their situation rather than blindly attempting to fit in or to access what the neo-imperialist communities would have designed. Innovations from these countries are never meant to change the status quo vis-à-vis their relationship with Africa but to advance the neo-imperialist agenda.

In chapter three, Munyaradzi Mukesi and Emmy Wabomba note that the West is not keen to embrace inventions from Africa, opting to cast a suspicious look and at times outright rejection of African inventions. The authors observe that some African governments do not promote their own knowledge systems in human health, preferring to play second fiddle to Western medicine. Mukesi and Wabomba argue that the recent stance by African countries which threw their weight behind Madagascar is laudable although they still need to do more to support and use their own African knowledge systems in medical inventions. It is further argued that while the majority of African countries are signatories to countless declarations and conventions on health, health systems on the continent have remained an eyesore facing continued underfunding, dilapidation, human resource flight and a perennial inability to service the African population. In the majority of cases, African health systems rely on funding from multilateral organisations such as WHO and other development partners to supplement their national budgets and be able to run crucial programmes, thus they remain vulnerable to external influence.

In chapter four, Aaron Rwodzi notes that like elsewhere in the world, the COVID-19 pandemic has had so many ramifications in the socio-economic, political, religious, cultural and even ideological dimensions of SADC member states. This chapter demonstrates that despite the willingness of the member states to collaborate by pooling their resources together towards the elimination of the pandemic, most, if not all, member states are financially and materially handicapped to deal with the pandemic. The high mobility that characterised the region in terms of cross-border movements either by individuals migrating to their countries or by truck drivers made containment of the pandemic untenable and infection high. In the context, the Zimbabwean government has been abusing human rights in its efforts to contain the virus. At the time of writing this chapter, there is pressure on the Zimbabwean government from the AU Chairman, President Ramaphosa, Human Rights Groups, and the Zimbabwe Council of Bishops Conference (ZCBC) among others. The sanctions imposed by the USA and the European Union on Zimbabwe impact negatively on the government's efforts to fight the pandemic and save lives. The sanctions are incompatible with regional efforts to pursue WHO protocols on the containment of the pandemic.

In chapter five, Edmore Dube argues for *ubuntu*-driven responses to COVID-19. He further argues that associating a condition with particular groups of people has a tendency of endangering them by creating xenophobic spirit among the population. The chapter further contends that the *unhu/ubuntu* philosophy that is operational among the Karanga people and their Bantu counterparts, does not give room for segregation on account of age or health condition. Segregating the old among the Karanga people is particularly difficult, because the elderly are the knowledge reservoirs in charge of communal justice and ritual cleansing. Dube contends that a disrespectful community also opens itself to avenging spirits called *botso*, and epidemic lockdowns must avoid such dissentious approaches. Among the Karanga people, curing of the sick is a function of the whole society, at the invitation of the *bembera* announcer. Thus, for the COVID-19 lockdowns to be effective they must not disrupt respected unitary local perceptions and procedures.

In chapter six, Rumbidzi E. Makamani, Susan Shamaoma-Katowa and Ndinaani Mwashita explore the implications of the 4IR and the readiness of African countries to adopt it, if at all. As the world moves towards the new industrial era, Africans may participate in it, but they have to become innovative and empower themselves to become masters of their economies. It should be noted that the 4IR technologies need to benefit people globally. It is therefore imperative to structure the African education system in line with digital industry demands if they cater for African interests. The education system in Africa has already been altered in many ways due to the outbreak of the COVID-19 pandemic. The Namibian education system, in particular, was also affected by the COVID-19 pandemic, hence, some rural schools were unable to migrate to the new modes of learning.

In chapter seven, Enna Sukutai Gudhlanga and Angela Mavis Madongonda discuss the history of COVID-19, contextualising it in Zimbabwe. They interrogate popular knowledge on the origins of the virus. They note that biomedical strategies used to combat COVID-19 have created some fissures in African culture, threatening African traditional beliefs and practices. The chapter has also demonstrated that in order to win the war against COVID-19, there is need to contextualise it in traditional African beliefs and practices rather than head for a collision course that results in culture conflict and hence adverse effects on the people. If *ubuntu/unhu* is used in the fight against COVID-19, it would go a long way in combatting current fissures that seem to be widening with the use of bio-security measures that disregard cultural practices and values. With statistics in Africa proving to the world that it has its own unique ways of combatting the virus, it can be deduced that Africa has lessons that could save the world from the devastation it is facing.

Angeline Mavis Madongonda and Enna Sukutai Gudhlanga's chapter eight focuses on humour in the era of a global COVID-19 pandemic. While the pandemic and its effects are harmful, people take time to share lighter moments. However, the chapter has established that humour during dark times is critical but emphasises that the laughter should not be fleeting and short-lived. A deeper reflection on the messages offers some solutions to the challenges that are bantered about. A semiotic analysis of the messages gave room for the scrutiny of both what is present and that which is absent, the abundance and the lack; binary oppositions that are meant to unpack hidden meanings in seemingly just jocular messages. However, it takes a trained eye to unearth many of the media messages that may be communicated overtly or covertly by those messages. It becomes the privilege of the semioticians to delve into the messages enshrined in visual messages. The same needs to be done by consumers of humorous messages when they take time to reflect on the messages and possibly offer solutions to challenges hidden within such messages.

In chapter nine, Rewai Makamani focuses on how African languages can be deployed to ward-off vicissitudes of digital capitalism in Africa. The chapter unravels the discourses on the 4IR and the COVID-19 pandemic within a historical context and everyday life reality. The chapter navigates through the real and perceived effects of 4IR and the COVID-19 pandemic on African people and how they can use their local languages to resist the negative effects of digital capitalism. The chapter's main rendition is that African languages need to be utilised to provide local solutions to challenges of the 21st century which are products of human activities and well-orchestrated manoeuvrings as dictated by social, economic and political interests of dominant digital capitalist forces. African people can mobilise local languages to cushion citizens against job losses, fear, anxiety, psychological trauma, and physical harm experienced as a result of 4IR and the COVID-19 pandemic.

Peter Masvotore's chapter ten addresses the relevance of the healing practitioner and the church's healing modes in the wake of COVID-19. The chapter discusses Covid-19 in a context where churches are being closed forcing practitioners to retreat back to the trenches without performing healing and deliverance in sanctuaries. The chapter also demonstrated that in taking heed of the government's call for social distancing and lockdown, the church did not err, but it was guided by Luther's call never to tempt God by endangering others. Further, the chapter raised ethical issues in the production of vaccines using human foetuses and concluded that it is veiled cannibalism into which everyone is being recruited using vile means. The chapter contends that it is inhuman when animal lives are deemed sacred at the expense of unborn human foetuses/lives.

In chapter eleven, Hatikanganwi Mapudzi, Collin Kamalizeni, Ntandokazulu Siwela and Memory Muteeri focus on the economic value of women and their deteriorating conditions in the face of the COVID-19 pandemic. They note that the pandemic has created profound socio-economic challenges. The authors recommend that since the pandemic has been universally experienced, robust efforts and resources should be invested into regional and national research to collectively establish relevant strategies for addressing the harm being caused by the pandemic. The chapter advocates for a Public-Private-Partnership (PPP) approach to be employed to lobby international/regional and inter-sectoral stakeholders to play a synergistic role against the pandemic. The authors note that the pandemic is not gender neutral as such, as both men and women are affected, with women who nurture mankind being hardest hit.

In chapter twelve, Pilisano H. Masake and Lizazi E. Libebe note that the convergence of ICT in financial sectors has boosted e-commerce particularly in industrialised nations. While e-commerce makes provision for opportunities, for various developing economies, the benefits of e-commerce have not fully penetrated many African economies like in the West. This chapter explored some jurisdictional challenges in e-commerce and the implications of internet jurisdiction on e-commerce. It examines regulatory frameworks, efforts, and constraints in e-commerce in Africa, the US and EU, and the role of the AU, African states, and regional organisations. Given its travails, Africa must support and develop an inclusive Pan-African paradigm or framework for e-commerce and the digital economy. It is argued that the role of the AU, African states and regional organisations is vital for transforming and contextualising e-commerce in Africa. E-commerce in Africa cannot simply involve the application of e-commerce and information technology diffusion principles developed in the Western context – rather, the e-commerce legal framework should be adopted taking cognisance of the independent sovereignty, social, economic and political context of Africa.

In chapter thirteen Oliver Mtapuri examines COVID-19 and 4IR and their effects on the workplace and workforce. Both assumed revolutionary omnipresence with severe disruptive effects to the status quo by dislodging, displacing, and destroying the old order as a new order emerges. Both phenomena make planning increasingly difficult because of these disruptions and they increase the precarity and vulnerability of workers and jobs. With unemployment comes destitution and desperation as indicative of a dual blow inflicted on society by 4IR and COVID-19. It is argued that this is pertinent in developing countries where poverty, inequality and unemployment rates are already relatively high. Some of the effects of the two phenomena include helplessness effects; hopelessness effects, stress effects, depression effects, inequality effects, poverty effects, paralysis effects, corruption effects, uncertainty effects and others. The chapter also posited a Hierarchy of Vulnerabilities Framework as well as some properties of vulnerabilities as its key contribution to knowledge.

In chapter fourteen, Hatikanganwi Mapudzi, Christopher Chikandiwa and Memory Muteeri highlight how the COVID-19 pandemic has disrupted the Higher Education Institutions (HEIs) life. They indicate the unique challenges posed by the pandemic to different stakeholders of the HEIs. The authors further contend that the COVID-19 pandemic intensely underlined the need for change in HEIs, by exposing the fragility of the education system, as well as their inherent inequalities. It is noted that the closure of institutions was a way of managing the spread of the pandemic but then the closures resulted in greater exclusion and inequality for the marginalised and vulnerable groups. The investments that have so far been made in remote learning should be a launchpad for better and more personalised, as well as sustainable way of education provision.

This entails the need for effective online learning strategies to provide continuity in learning even when institutions open their doors for face to face teaching and learning.

References

Callon, M. (1984) 'Some elements of a sociology of translation: Domestication of the scallops and the fishermen of St Brieuc Bay', *The Sociological Review*, Vol 32 (1): 196-233.

Dean, J. and Passavant, P. (2004) *Empire's New Clothes*. Routledge.

Diwakar, A. (10 August 2020) 'States, sovereignty and the Brave New World of cryptocurrencies'. Retrieved from https://www.trtworld.com/magazine/states-sovereignty-and-.

Drine, I. (2012) 'Youth unemployment and the Arab Spring'. Retrieved from https://www.wider.unu.edu/publication/youth-unemployment.

Duffied, M. (2019) 'Post-Humanitarianism: Governing precarity through adaptive design', *Journal of Humanitarian Affairs*, Vol 1 (1): 15-27.

Duffield, M. (2018) *Post-Humanitarianism: Governing Precarity in the Digital World*. Wiley.

Flores, D. S. (2018) 'Transhumanism: the big fraud-towards digital slavery', *International Physical Medicine & Rehabilitation Journal*, Vol 3 (5): 381-392.

Georgiou, G. C. (2020) 'Cryptocurrency challenges sovereign currency', *World Economics*, Vol 21 (1): 117-141.

Huang, R. (23 September 2020) 'The coming sovereign debt crisis will boost cryptocurrencies'. Retrieved from https://www.forbes.com/sites/rogerhuang/2020/09/23/the-com.

Lanchovichina, E. (2018) *Eruptions of Popular Anger: The Economics of the Arab Spring and its Aftermath*. Washington: The World Bank.

Latour, B. (2005) *Reassembling the Social: An Introduction to Actor-Network-Theory*. Oxford University Press.

Lovelock, J. (2006) *The Revenge of Gaia*. Penguin Books.

Mawere, M. and Nhemachena, A. (eds.). (2017) *GMOs, Consumerism and the Global Politics of Biotechnology: Rethinking Food, Bodies and Identities in Africa's 21st Century*. Bamenda: Langaa RPCIG.

Nhemachena, A. and Mawere, M. (eds.). (2020) *Securitising Monstrous Bottoms in the Age of Posthuman Carnivalesque? Decolonising the*

Environment, Human Beings and African Heritages. Bamenda: Langaa RPCIG.

Nhemachena, A., Hlabangane, N. and Kaundjua, M. (2020) 'Relationality or hospitality in twenty-first century research? Big Data, Internet of Things, and the resilience of coloniality on Africa', *Modern Africa: Politics, History and Society*, Vol 8(1): 105-139.

Nhemachena, A., Warikandwa, T. V., Mpofu, N. and Chitimira, H. (2019) 'Explosive economic minefields in invisible neo-imperial force-fields: An introduction to decolonising economies in Africa', in T. V. Warikandwa., A. Nhemachena., N. Mpofu. and H. Chitimira (eds.). *Grid-Locked African Economic Sovereignty; Decolonising the Neo-Imperial Socio-Economic and Legal Force-Fields in the 21st Century.* Bamenda: Langaa RPCIG.

Robinson, K. (3 December 2020) 'The Arab Spring at ten years: What's the legacy of the uprising', *Council on Foreign Relations.* Retrieved from https://www.cfr.org/article/arab-spring-ten-years-whats-legacy.

Shiva, V. and Shiva, K. (2019) *One Earth, One Humanity vs. the 1%.* PM Press.

Wilson, M. I. and Corey, K. E. (2012) 'The role of ICT in Arab Spring movements', *NETCOM,* Vol 26 (3/4), 343-356.

Chapter Two

The Preparedness of Africans for the Fourth Industrial Revolution and for COVID-19

Chirimuuta Chipo & Chirimuuta Antony

Introduction

Before the African continent has exhausted discoursing on pertinent issues of slavery, colonialism, neo-colonialism and globalisation paying great attention to their negative impact on the African people's ownership and control of both the natural and human resources, their developmental trajectory, the brainwashing of indigenous people that culminated in their abandoning of their culture, religion, medicines and medical practices; a new revolution is knocking at their doors. This is the 4th Industrial Revolution. It is digital and would definitely affect the way individuals, communities and nations relate. Coupled with the new revolution is the COVID-19 pandemic which again, has affected every single nation on the globe. The major question being raised in this chapter is the readiness of African societies and the feasibility of them being equal participants and beneficiaries in this revolution. Are the African communities going to benefit more by being assertive and demonstrating their individuality and uniqueness on the global terrain or by continuously parroting the imperialist nations? Could these twin challenges be a blessing in disguise that will see Africa's societies emerging with their heads above the tide of these stormy waves? For purposes of carrying out this research, the authors were guided by Afrocentricity. This paradigm focuses on the history of people of African descent and asserts that Africans must re-assert themselves and be agents in their destinies. Data were collected through documentary analysis, interviews with informed Pan-Africanists and questionnaires distributed to find out how the Africans themselves feel about their preparedness for the twin challenges of the 4th Industrial Revolution and the COVID-19 pandemic. Conclusions are deduced from the general trends emerging from the collected information.

The 4th industrial revolution has announced itself and can never be wished away. Being a revolution that is technologically driven, it demands that the continent be on its toes technologically to ensure that it moves at the same wavelength with the rest on the globe. The unfortunate part, however, is that the revolution is being ushered against a backdrop of African underdevelopment that has resulted from many incidents that range from effects of the Trans-Atlantic slave trade, colonialism and even the neo-colonial systems that continue to grip the so-called independent African nations. This chapter attempts to highlight the challenges that Africa as a continent finds herself in and the nature of the damage that was caused by the centuries of exploitation and uprooting of labour force as it grapples with fitting into the new revolution that is both technologically and imperially driven. The worst part of it, which makes navigating through the new revolution challenging and boggling, is that Africa is not part of the driving forces.

Theoretical framework

This chapter is guided and given impetus by the Afrocentricity perspectives to viewing the world and all the activities that characterise it. According to Asante (2002: 97):

> Afrocentricity is the conscious process by which a person locates or relocates African phenomena within an African subject content or agency and action. It is therefore location as opposed to dislocation; centeredness as opposed to marginality... The objective of such a critical process is to determine the degree to which a writer or speaker, from a rhetorical point of view, demonstrates centeredness within the African or African American cultural experience.

In examining the pertinent issues of the day, Afrocentricity demands that researchers be guided by the principle of centeredness and grounded-ness within the intellectual and cultural ambits of the African people's way of life. Afrocentricity as a theory, targets at making the African scholars better placed to ask the right questions as well as use the proper methods of collecting data that would ultimately be interpreted in ways that best "make cultural, psychological, and literary liberation more certain" (Asante 2002: 98). The thrust of this theory is breaking the mental and culture prisons, making a breakthrough into the African people's cultural realities. Afrocentric theory, drives us closer to explaining how conceptual distance from our own centres leaves us on the margins of the European reality (Asante 2002: 98).

The critical position that Afrocentricity emphasise on is the question of investment in African agency, and it proclaims that this agency is premised on the best practices derived from the wisdom embedded in the rich African historical experiences. For this theory, instead of parroting the English, French, Portuguese and many other cultures from the former colonial masters, the progressive African scholars have to resuscitate and reinvigorate the functional past experiences that have since been swept to the doldrums of epistemology by the hash experiences of slave trade, colonialism and neo-colonialism.

Afrocentricity recommends that Africans, both within and without the continent have a mandate to view knowledge using African lenses. The point is that whenever critics, scholars and even political leaders look at pertinent issues, they must do so from an African point of view because:

> ...we misunderstand Africa when we use viewpoints and terms other than that of the African... When Africans view themselves as centred and central in their own history, they see themselves as agents, actors, and participants rather than as marginal and on the periphery of political or economic experience (Chawane 2016: 79).

In a nutshell, Afrocentricity is intended as an answer to the intellectual colonialism that girds Africa and serves to validate political and economic colonialism. The theory places African people at the centre of any analysis of African phenomena in terms of action and behaviour.

As an ideology it embodies the continued African respect for philosophies that unite them as a community and offer some alternative ways of accomplishing goals in life which would otherwise be dismissed by the Europeans. In short this is a philosophy that advocates for 'a true connectedness to an African heritage' (Jackson 2003). The vital proposition of Afrocentricity is that all relationships are viewed in terms of the centre and margin dynamics. As such when African people perceive themselves as being grounded, centred and central to their own historical existence, they see themselves as

21

agents, actors and active participants rather than marginals on the periphery of the global political or economic experiences (Asante 2002).

The relationship between revolutions and pandemics

History is awash with examples of situations in which pandemics coincide with the occurrence of revolutions, be they economic or political revolutions (wars), in societies. De Waitte (2020) confirms that the most trying periods of human existence such as economic revolutions, wars, (world wars, wars of conquest, economic wars and liberation struggles, in the case of former colonised people), are paradoxically sources of pandemics. The mass movement of human beings that is characteristic of such incidents often fashion central avenues by which diseases spread from one individual to the next (Evans 1988). In some cases, war situation, through the exploitation of biological warfare, become sources of pandemics (Ellert 1989 cited in Mahamba 2018).

The 1918-1920 Spanish flu also known as influenza or swine flu became one of the most known pandemics that hit the world and changed the socio-economic status of the globe. According to Saunders-Hastings and Krewski (2016), the origins of this pandemic is subject to debate with propositions pointing to the United States and China as the sources. This pandemic has been recorded as the "greatest medical holocaust in history', 'the greatest public health disaster in recorded history' (Saunders-Hastings & Krewski 2016) that claimed the lives of approximately 39.5 million people globally (Potter 2001). For Potter (2001), the virus infected approximately more than half of the world's population between 1918 and 1920, resulting in the shutting down of schools, businesses and leading to economic meltdown. Saunders-Hastings and Krewski (2016), have pointed out that the First World War greatly contributed to the spread of influenza since the war created an environment that facilitated human mobility creating a high level of contacts within and among people. The war brought a lot of people into contact with one another making it possible for carriers to spread the virus. Furthermore, the trenches that characterised the warfare is believed to have provided an ideal environment for the spread of the pandemic (Saunders-Hastings & Krewski 2016).

In Africa most of the pandemics were experienced as a result of the mass movement of settlers in the continent. With colonialism came the sexually transmitted infections (STI) such as gonorrhoea, syphilis chancroid and herpes genitalia among many others. Like in the case of other already mentioned pandemics, colonialism witnessed movement of people from Europe to Africa resulting in carriers of certain infections transporting the bacteria or viruses into the continent. Sexually transmitted infections (STIs) across Africa were "branded as the foreigners' diseases" which developed within the "special context of colonial confrontation between Europeans and Africans" (Becker & Collignon (nd): 65). The urban settlements that resulted from colonialism became epicentres of sexually transmitted infections with the majority of the affected people comprising of prostitutes and the military personnel. "French soldiers in Madagascar were promoting syphilization in Madagascar... civilisation [became] syphilization" (nd: 65-66). The prostitutes, that emerged out of the urbanized settlement characteristic of colonial systems in Africa, were also carriers of pathogens that caused the STIs.

There are some pandemics that are believed to have resulted from biological warfare during the liberation war. In Zimbabwe, in addition to other irritating chemicals, bacteria that caused cholera-like symptoms were used to subdue the liberation war fighters (Mahamba 2018). The cholera causing bacteria were deposited into water sources which were obviously used by the fighters engaged in guerrilla warfare in the forests. The pandemic that ensued took its toll on both the liberation fighters and the innocent and defenceless masses.

Like the other pandemics that have come in the background of revolutions, COVID-19 has also been linked to the ushering in of the 4th Industrial Revolution. The origins of the pandemic, like that of influenza, is subject to debate. There is one theory that points to China as being the source of the devastating virus and another point at USA. This argument points to the idea that COVID-19 might be a product of biological warfare between the global superpowers that are fighting for global economic supremacy. However, there has also been another hypothesis that circulated at the peak of the pandemic that linked COVID-19 to a New World Order that is propelled by high speed technologies. In this new world order, there has to be one system of governance, one currency, one religion and a manageable population that is far less than the people currently existing on the planet. For this to be achieved, the hypothesis argued high speed network has to be used, 5G technology (Ahmed, Vadal-Alaball,

Downing & Segnis 2020). The theory proposes that 5G network is believed to have radiation effects on human beings, unfortunately none of the imperialist nation could ascertain the extent of the damage that the network could cause on humans. To find out, 5G network is believed to have been rolled out in Wuhan (a city in China), USA, France, Italy, UK, Iran and many other selected cities across the globe as a stratagem to test the extent to which it affected humanity after which technological interventions to stop the human body from reacting to the high speed technology would be designed, developed and rolled out (Ahmed, Vadal-Alaball, Downing & Segnis 2020). The dying of people, the theory posits, is just the collateral damage that has to take place before the vaccine is ready. One could conclude that it could be a way of reducing the population so that the density suits the desired one economy population. According to this 5G technology theory, this vaccine is believed to be in fact a microchip that is programmed to 'power the next generation of artificial intelligence' (Ahmed, Vadal-Alaball, Downing & Segnis 2020). The hypothesis goes on to say that in addition to extensive and intensive exposure to 5G technology the victims were introduced to Corona Virus (a common flue under normal circumstances) and the combination of the two became drastic. The gravity of the situation and the alarming death toll, according to the proposition was believed to force the shock-stricken people into becoming willing recipients of the microchip disguised as a vaccine. All the information about the recipients of the microchip is believed to be stored in the chip. The recipients will not need to carry identity cards, bank cards, passports, or even keys with them, they will be connected digitally to the server of the one world government, one world economy and one world religion. The proposal finally concludes that the deaths that were experienced in Africa are the ones that were a result of Corona Virus and they were minimal and lots of people are recovering.

The 4th Industrial Revolution

The 4th Industrial Revolution is driven by trailblazing digital technologies. These technological developments are creating a convergence between the physical and the digital spaces in human existence in ways that have potential advantages as well as potential hazards to humanity. The digital change demands a re-orientation of focus within all nations globally and movement to harnessing the converging technologies in ways that would positively impact societies. The unfortunate thing about the ushering in of this revolution is that it is coming in when Africa has barely embraced or even invested in the digital technologies that were characteristic of the 21st century. Africa still has a long way to go to demonstrate readiness for this new development. With limited access to western driven advanced technology as a result of compromised infrastructure such as lack of electricity, lack of internet connectivity, inadequate bandwidth and inaccessible costs of the gadgets with which to get connected on internet, Africa stands very little chances of managing to keep her head above the fast tides of this revolution. In fact, one is persuaded to conclude that this 4th Industrial Revolution was never designed to help Africans, but the global elites and owners of transnational corporations. The problem that we are running into, once again, is being naïve and misconstruing the technological revolution as an all-embracing development which is meant to benefit the entire world population. Technology has never been neutral force (Krenzberg 1986). It is designed to accomplish set goals and push certain agenda.

The internet connectivity and access gap that exist between Africa and fellow players in the revolution will surely militate against her benefiting from the opportunities that are bound to be opened by the new digital developments (Goodman 2020). As already highlighted, the million-dollar question for Africa in this fast-moving digital revolution is whether to parrot the Americans, Arabs or Europeans as they try to navigate their way through, or retain their individuality as they grope through the dark pages created by the abrupt digital change.

Africa's preparedness for the 4th Industrial Revolution

Africa's preparedness for the new industrial revolution is a major question that needs to be addressed. Taking cognisance of the level of technological development in Africa in comparison to what has already been experienced in the imperialist nations, one is persuaded to believe that Africa will never be given the latitude and space to enter into the 4th Industrial Revolution as an equal partner. There is so much that has happened in the lives of the Africans that makes them lag behind all other continents. Continents such as Europe, North America and the Arab Countries in Asia, with which Africa has to co-exist within the context of the revolution, have experienced many revolutions that were driven by resources for which they either paid less or got free of charge.

The research discovered that when it comes to this technological revolution, African communities are beaten all systems out because some of these continents have benefited immensely from the inhuman development strategies that are no longer applicable in the new world order that is characterised by human rights, freedom and democracy. During the transatlantic slave trade, European, American and even Arab countries immensely benefited from slavery (African forced labour) from which they developed their industries, economies, wealth and societies at large using African free labour. The use of free labour resulted in milestones in their favour, which African countries can no longer achieve in the present circumstances without enslaving other races. It is thus, worth noting that the kind of development that was achieved is not comparable – it was actually asymmetrical. In fact, the development that was being experienced in the benefiting nations resulted in underdevelopment in Africa (Rodney 1973) as the physically fit elements within most parts of the continent were uprooted from Africa to develop other societies.

Effects of the Atlantic Slave trade and colonialism and the development of the capitalist nations

According to Pheko (2012) up until the14th century AD, Africa was ahead of or even at par with Europe with regards military dexterity. Pheko posits that the Romans used spears just like the Africans did and for him this explains why: "...famous Roman Emperor, Julius Caesar in adoration and admiration of the advanced Africa exclaimed, "ex Africa semper aliquid novi!" (Out of Africa always something new!)

With regards to education, Pheko (2012), again postulates that Africa also had the best kind of education ever. He highlights the fact that the earliest crop of educated Greeks received their education in Africa, in ancient Egypt.

The slave trade exposed Africa to unprecedented exploitation by the imperialist nations that happen to be in the fore front of the 4th Industrial Revolution. With the coming of the slave trade, Africa suffered the worst genocide and holocaust at the hands of these engineers of slavery. Human cargo, comprising of able-bodied, skilled and economically active people, was transported to Europe and America to provide labour in the cotton and sugar plantations.

According to Pheko (2012) historical evidence point to the fact that present day Ghana (then known as the Gold Coast) lost approximately six thousand people to slavery every year for four hundred years. In 1700, the estimated number of slaves produced and transported across the Atlantic Ocean in the region of Africa was 28 million people (McEverdy & Jones 1978: 241-249). About 4 million people were transported out of Congo through the Congo River in English ships to Britain, where Britain and the British merchants heavily benefited from the Congolese resources (BBC News 2013).

Slave labour helped boost the economies of these so-called developed countries and when the architects realised that it was no longer profitable to trade in humans as well as to sustain their lives in the plantations, some of their kith masqueraded as humanitarians and lobbied for the abolition of the human trade. Regarding the effects of slave trade on the African continent, Rodney (1973) questions what the level of Britain's development would have been had her people been forcibly moved to provide slave labour outside their country for a period of more than four centuries. Furthermore, the international demand for enslaved Africans induced a reallocation of resources in Africa towards slave production and away from other economic pursuits (Witney & Gillezeau (2011: 17).

Before Africa had come to grips with the reality of the abolition of the slave trade, her tears of joy were abruptly wiped off when the Berlin Conference, hosted by Bismarck in Germany, with the sole purpose of, to use King Leopold II's words, finding the best ways to "…divide among ourselves this magnificent African cake" (Davison 1992: 77). At this conference it was agreed that any nation that had developed an interest in a territory in Africa had to demonstrate effective occupation to prevent incidents of clashes among the major powers. This saw the member states rushing for those territories that best saved their economic interests. Portuguese, who had established themselves as traders, having traded with the African communities from as far back as prior to slave trade, found themselves occupying regions in the coastal areas. This explains why Portugal had to grab Mozambique, Guinea Bissau, the islands of Sao Tome and Principles, Cape Verde and Angola (Richard 2019). While countries like France, Britain, Italy, Germany and Spain went in-land in search of the unexplored resources, the hidden treasure as well as favourable climatic conditions in the continent. Because of colonialism;

Europeans own almost all the land in the Americas, almost all the good land in Australia, New Zealand and Tasmania and most of the best land in African countries like South Africa, Zimbabwe, Namibia and Kenya. To acquire this land outside Europe, Europeans did not use law, justice or money. They took the land and its riches with the gun.... Europeans continue to own millions and millions of hectares of the best land in Africa... (Koigi Mamwere 2000, cited in Mpeko 2012: 65).

What is of critical importance in this chapter is not the process and procedures of the partitioning of Africa amongst the imperialists, but the fact that this landmark in the lives of Africans gave yet another blow to the continent, leaving her in a position where she could neither compete nor compare herself with any other continent on the globe with regards technological advancement or even population density.

Unlike during the slave trade, colonialism came and dispossessed the Africans of their land, their mineral resources, and above all distorted their historical trajectory in a bid to create a reservoir for cheap or even free labour for the established imperialists economies. Just like during the period of slavery, colonialism, the imperialist nations got free natural resources, free labour, cheap labour, looted the heritage from the African communities. This implies that once again the population in the continent was forced to neglect its own developmental flight to respond to the demands of the settler systems and their imperial enterprise. When the African men failed to provide the required labour or resources that would have been demanded by the settlers, they were abused or even killed. "Troops were sent to the village to spread terror, if necessary, by killing some of the men...they were ordered to bring one right hand amputated from an African victim for every cartridge used" (Jackson 2015: 310-311). As a result of such atrocities, in Congo the population was reduced from twenty million to nine million people in a period of fifteen years (Mpheko 2012). In Namibia, the Germany pushed the Herero off their land and quarantined them in the desert where 70% of the population perished from dehydration and starvation, while in South Africa they hunted down and exterminated the Khoisan and took over their land (Mpheko 2012).

To put the icing on the cake, the colonialists destroyed the socio-cultural systems in the continent to create a vacuum into which they deposited their own culture and belief systems. The settlers brainwashed the indigenous people so that they abandoned their culture, religion, medicines, medical practices and traditions. An education system was introduced to instil in the indigenous people a slave mentality. The education system alienated the African from his community (Fanon 1963) and "misled him by showing him the greener pastures of European society where he is not allowed to graze" (Pheko 1984:150). There was further underdevelopment of the African societies. There was disorientation that resulted in confusion and it is that same disorientation that African societies are battling with to find their feet and re-direct themselves to be better placed to develop their development strategies or trajectories.

The bottom-line of slavery and colonialism in light of Africa's technological development is that the adventurers syphoned resources from Africa to imperialists nations leaving the continent drastically impoverished (Rodney 1978). The education and religious systems that were forced upon the continent left it with no referral point to allow them to get their bearing on the technological advancement course. A continent that is still groping to find its bearing can surely not be in a position to enter the 4th Industrial Revolution with the confidence and the energy that the said revolution demands of it.

The neo-colonial era

The struggle and attainment of independence in all the African countries has not helped much in creating an environment conducive for Africa's so-called lip-frogging in the digital era. In Africa, independence was attained during the Cold War period when the Eastern and Western giants were clashing for supremacy. African countries attained independence through the assistance of the Eastern European nations, getting handouts, training assistance and ammunition from the then 'friendly' countries, the communist and socialist nations (Sousa 2016). As such independent African countries found themselves being over dependent on their sympathisers from Eastern Europe. Upon attainment of "independence", through armed liberation struggles, African nations were faced with a cosmetic form of freedom, where "…an end of colonial rule [was] not synonymous with independence" (Philby 1961, cited in Coetzee & Roux 2005: 619). The "new" nations had to contend with "indirect political and; economic manipulation, designed to perpetuate external control in Africa in more subtle ways" (Coetzee & Roux 2005: 619), neocolonialism.

In the same vein, former colonisers could not let African countries go, they started state-funding donor organisations who made an influx into the newly independent African countries so as to maintain their grip on the African leaders, people and the natural resources (Mann 2011; Burgis 2015). Donations poured into the continent creating an environment where the African people's need to effectively tap and use their natural resource became minimal, creating a situation where the natural resources were preserved and probably left for the imperialist countries to come and exploit. The donations that were rolled out into Africa reduced the population to mere consumers and not producers of what they consumed. Through the funding independent African countries were reduced to gullible entities by the former colonialists – *kuvumbamirwa nemuroyi*. This Shona expression literally means being placed under the seemingly "protective" wings of a witch or sorcerer. The pseudo comfort they got from the assistance removed the creative and innovative ingenuity among the Africans. Even to this day, most African countries are suffering from the hangover of donor-funding (Burgis 2015), since they were never able to design as well as roll out policies that promote autonomy, empowering them to be active agents in determining the nature of their relations with the former colonial metropolitan states.

Then came democracy, the form of multiparty democracy, the strategy was to weaken revolutionary parties, the imperialists would identify opposition leaders who would receive heavy funding not for the development of their respective countries, but just to create an impression that the opposition is better than the revolutionary parties (Mann 2011). The opposition parties were heavily funded. It is through the opposition parties that they would smuggle their governance, legal, political, economic, religious and cultural systems that continue to derail the African people from their genuine development paths. Furthermore, through scholarships and lucrative job opportunities, African intellectuals were and still continue to be looted. They are syphoned from their respective countries to the already imperialist societies, either through scholarships (Burgis 2015) or enticing job offers in comparison to what they will be getting in their home countries (even though they might be getting less than what nationals in those countries will be getting) leading to further underdevelopment of the African societies (Rodney 1978).

The 4th Industrial Revolution, is being ushered to the African societies against the highlighted background, with COVID-19 sneaking in, at a time when Africa is in the process of trying to rediscover their feet, their development path, their culture, their indigenous knowledge system (heritage), that includes the indigenous medicines (De Waitte 2000). In a nutshell, Africa is very underdeveloped to cope with the 4th Industrial Revolution and pandemics such as COVID-19, however, despite the fact that the continent is lagging behind in terms of the much-needed technology, Africa can still derive sustenance from its indigenous knowledge system as the continent strives to develop its own relevant technologies.

Africa in the 4th Industrial Revolution

The 4th Industrial Revolution has come, and it cannot be wished away, the million-dollar question is: Whither Africa in this revolution? As Asante (2002) has posited that the objective of the continent must never be to catch-up with the so-called developed nation, but rather to retain its unique individuality amid the global changes and work towards moving from the global peripheries where the imperialist enterprises have left the continent. Asante (2002: 110), has this to say: The aim of Africa should not be to catch up with Europe, but to be Africa...the only way to return from the margins of history, literature, culture, economics, or any other sector or sphere of life is to reassert a centred place within one's own experiences."

The unique 'place within the people' experience' in the continent is embedded in the culture. For Cabral (1990: 142), "culture... at every stage of history represents the result of a ceaseless search for a dynamic equilibrium between levels of productive forces and the system of social utilisation of these forces, indicate the status reached by a given society and each of its components before itself and before history."

The African people's creativity and innovation within the 4th Industrial Revolution must be propelled by their culture. This culture must be envisaged as a record of the traditions, discoveries and innovations that a society would have made in its developmental course. The new forms of innovation must not, therefore, be parroting the former colonial masters, it must always derive from the indigenous traditions to ensure sustainability and stability, "there is nothing easier or more consistent than the elasticity within one's own culture (Asante 2002: 110). What Asante might be positing is that there is need to let the digital technologies take over in those societies that have benefited from free and cheap labour, and let Africa maintain the use of human capital as it develops its digital technologies. The 4th Industrial Revolution, however, will remain the interface between the developed and developing countries through educational institutions and some industrial sectors where such technologies can be employed without necessarily disrupting employment opportunities for the majority of people who may not be ready for such advanced technologies.

Africa and its preparedness for disease control and management

In as far as Africa would be using 'conventional' medicinal system, many nations may argue that they have functional health systems in place. However, a closer look at the systems will demonstrate that everything in place is imported stuff, right from the machinery that is used in the laboratories to the syringes and needles that are used for administering the medication. There is virtually nothing that is African about the medical systems in Africa. This explains why when developed nations pull out of a nation, everything crumbles. A good example is what happened in the Zimbabwean situation, as a result of the political wrangles between the ruling party and the former colonial master that saw white farmers losing farms to the indigenous people in a campaign code named fast track land redistribution. (Muchemwa 2015). Investors pulled out of the nation and sanctions were imposed. At the moment the medical system in Zimbabwe is shattered with most public hospitals failing to service the ordinary people in the nation. This explains why political leaders and 'the haves' decide to go out of the country to seek medication when their health is compromised (Liedong 2017). However, under normal circumstances, when we talk about Africa's preparedness to any given pandemic, we are trying to find out what responses are in place, from the historical referent points for African people, regardless of whether there have been any intervention of colonialism or enslavement on not.

As already stated in the discussion on the devastating effects of slave trade and colonialism, COVID-19 is coming against a backdrop of a situation where indigenous medicines and medical processes in

Africa were demonised, castigated and shoved to the doldrums of human existence as the newly introduced colonial system paved way for the complete subjugation of the colonised people through the imposition of western systems, industrial finished goods including pharmaceutical products among other things (Ashcroft, Griffiths & Tiffin 1989). The imperial system through its acculturation strategies challenged indigenous ways and this translated to the shunning of everything local including the medicines. The colonial system, with the assistance of the missionaries invigorated stereotypes about indigenous institutions, particularly the local medicine and its practitioners (Bourdillon 1989). Thus, defying the healing power embedded in the African medicinal institution.

With brainwashing, most indigenous people began to view indigenous medicines and indigenous medicinal practices with disparagement and dismissing them as antique. As a result, literature about indigenous medicinal knowledge and other systems ended up being written by foreigners, creating room for them to define and give meaning to the systems even from an uninformed position (Bourdillon 1989). However, in spite of being presented as tantamount to evil, indigenous medicines remained very vibrant and effectively used by some locals behind the western created medical fraternity façade, of course secretively being used. Unfortunately, the secrecy that shrouded the practice of indigenous medicinal practices and the use of the medicines resulted in the knowledge being left as a preserve of a few.

Africa's preparedness for COVID-19

From the survey that was carried out it emerged that Africa is not very much ready for the COVID-19 pandemic. To use the most pessimistic word, Africa appears helpless in the face of this problem. This may probably help explain why African countries had to emulate what nations like China, USA, France, Italy and many other so-called developed countries did to mitigate the spread of COVID-19, imposing lockdowns. Many countries which include Zimbabwe, South Africa and Botswana among others, imposed lockdowns and closed their borders (Kaplan, Frias & McFall-Johnsen 2020). Countries like Tanzania and Madagascar that had delayed were severely hit as the pandemic took its toll on the people. Like other disease that came, wreaked havoc and almost left the populations decimated, COVID-19 is leaving a landmark on the African society leaving its indigenous medical systems under the spotlight.

The politics of medical approval

In cases where pandemics hit the world or communities, the 'norm' has been that any medication that passes as therapy for the epidemics must pass the tests of scientists in advanced laboratories in the so-called developed nations (Bourdillon 1989). In most cases, medicinal interventions from the African continent have hit a brick wall as they are expected to pass the tests. The situation at hand, however, demands a totally new approach that takes cognisance of the fact that:

> so much of the African people's civilisations were intentionally destroyed or distorted by invaders, interrupted by the transatlantic slave trade, or not written or codified. Furthermore ... for decades much Western scholarship was subverted by racism and cultural arrogance (Boyd & Lenix-Hooker 1992: 47).

When HIV and AIDS made its impression on the global terrain, Africa was also among the continents that presented its possible remedy for the pandemic, Kenya presented her drug, Kemron, for trial (Thepharmaletter 1992). This drug was taken for trial by the World Health Organisation and resultantly short down as failing to live up to the expected medical standards. The US Institute of Health's AIDS Research Advisory Committee (ARAC) took it to the laboratory and condemned it. ARAC, reported that the drastic benefits that had been attributed to the drug were minimal (Kamau, 2020) and therefore not a reliable remedy for the pandemic.

When COVID-19 started in Madagascar in early 2020, the people resorted to their indigenous knowledge system to find a remedy for the problem (Sheridan 2020). However, because of the politics of inventions and epistemology, the remedy, the organic therapy, was shot in the air before landing. The World Health Organisation pointed out that it was not scientifically proven and demanded that it goes through scientific enquiry before being accepted into the conventional medical fraternity. The brushing aside of the Madagascar initiative is just but one other example of ways by which the capitalist system would keep Africans out of the critical domains of life. This act must be viewed as "the result of peripherisation due to a knowledge market controlled by the metropolitan worlds" (Hountondji 1995: 3). It is yet another way of removing the agency from the African people, to ensure that they sit like ducks waiting for solutions to come from the already established nations in the pharmaceutical industries. The ultimate result has been buttressing "Africa's knowledge dependency on Europe", European monopoly of intelligence (Coetzee and Roux 2005: 645) and incubation of poverty in Africa (Burgis 2015). One can posit that denying the Madagascar remedy a space on the various attempts to addressing the problem of Africa was denying them their entitled right to their own perspective on the African experience. The emphasis was on the Madagascar therapy as a way by which the global medical fraternity was meant to tap from a new perspective, exposing an opportunity to explore different views and bring new perspectives to the challenge bedevilling the world.

What we see in this case is a continuation of the 'slave mentality' that was instilled during the colonial system through the colonial education systems, where what passed for knowledge and deserving to be studied was that which was captured in the texts of the imperialists' tenet (Bourdillon 1989). And, "any attempt to articulate one's own native wisdom or tradition, if it was allowed at all, had to be by reference to European concepts, thinkers, and texts and always, of course, still in the colonisers' language" (Chawane 2016: 89)

What this amounted to was the undermining of the continent as potential contributor or erasing any traces of its rich contributions to the global pool of knowledge and innovation in order to sustain white supremacy. And in 2020, when Madagascar talks of indigenous organic therapy to a new challenge on the global medical fraternity, she has to talk about it making reference from the texts and documented medical philosophies of the established 'conventional' canons (Akisanya, 1969 cited in Bourdillon 1989). She has to take the organic therapy to the laboratory, yet in Africa the lives in the natural ecosystem, society itself, has been the laboratory in which experiments have been carried out and results published, and practices being refined from time immemorial.

Africa, represented by Madagascar has made her contribution to the global system of ideas, asserting Africans as "subjects and human agents, rather than objects in a European frame of reference" (Asante 2002: 32). The African Union mobilised resources to mitigate the effects of COVID-19 and in a teleconference voiced the need to unite in finding a solution to the pandemic (African Union 2020). The call for a concerted effort to address the problem alludes to the re-awakening and assertiveness of the continent amid the background of the wrecking COVID-19. Whether this is political rhetoric or not, at grassroots level, Africans may not be quietly waiting for a panacea to come from the laboratories of the so-called developed nations. People may not be waiting for the pandemic to wipe their families from the surface of the planet, they may be using the little that has been left of the indigenous knowledge systems to wad the ferocious effects of COVID-19 because right from the period of colonialism the health delivery system that was in place was mostly meant to cater for the settler community and Africans continued to rely on their indigenous knowledge systems (De Waite 2000). In Zimbabwe, in particular, people resorted to their home remedies, which are locally available and accessible either at no cost or at low cost, from the natural ecosystem, especially those that address the problem of chest infections, irritation of nasal passages or irritation of the respiration tracts. These home remedies include *Zumbani*, pure honey, peppermint, garlic, ginger mint, among other indigenous therapies as prophylaxis in the face of COVID-19. Zimbabwean philosophy of life emphasises human agency in situations of crises and this is summarised in the Shona proverb that say, *Zvinhu zviyedzwa, chembere yekwaChivi yakabika mabwe ikape muto.* Literally this proverb means that 'trials must be done, the old woman of Chivi community cooked stones and added soup to the meal'. What this implies is that when faced with a problem, we cannot watch people die, and in the absence of a conventional cure, indigenous Africans have to resort to their traditional remedies and medical practices as professionals in the conventional medical fraternity are engaging in scientific enquiries aimed at finding a lasting medical solution to the pandemic. As the proverb proclaims, people need to seek recourse from their knowledge archives, search for all possible remedies instead of just folding hands and watch problems wreak havoc among the people. In other words, African nations have to go to their archives, dig into the indigenous medicinal knowledge and therapies as they allow the World Health Organisation and its funders to continue on the quest for a scientific solution. A whole giant continent cannot surely flinch from the dreadful effects and wait for solutions from other nations. It is true that even the World Health Organisation and its funders are declaring that there is no cure as yet to the COVID-19 pandemic (WHO 2020). Going for the indigenous remedies even before they have been scientifically proven, as WHO and those who are funding it would argue, is a way of standing at the centre of Africa to find possible solutions, this must not be construed as a confrontation of the World Health Organisation as such, but an articulation of the "harmonious coexistence of an endless variety of cultures" Chukwuokolo (2009: 32) and ways of grappling with this challenge that is causing sleepless nights globally. Chukwuokolo (2009: 33) further proclaims that looking inward for home-grown solutions: "…does not [imply] violently confront any person or any people, but a resolution to attempt to put the records right, it is about placing African people within their own historical framework, it demands that the contribution of Africa in all areas of civilization be reflected in world history."

In fact, such an intervention would result in what Verharen (2000) has described as the reconstruction of post-colonial African cultures through a synthesis of both African and European contributions to humanity.

Even if Africa cannot find indigenous remedies that can completely eradicate the COVID-19, Africa must find remedies to address the symptoms of the pandemic such as, severe fever, itching of nasal passages, chest pains, headache, breathing difficulties, loss of sense of taste, body weakness among many other symptoms of COVID-19. Communities are baffled by the waiting stance that most African communities have adopted, for most of the countries, prevention, staying safe has been the order of the day, we are not hearing much about researches to come up with globally acknowledged remedies. Africa must be seen to be taking action, because even on issues that may appear natural, Africans normally take action, for instance, people in Africa do not even wait for rains to come, they perform rituals and prayers for the rains to come *(mukwerera/chipwa)*, popularly known by the settler communities as rain-making ceremonies. Africans invest in agency. It is surprising when Africa finds itself having to be recipients of everything. For the majority of the African-centred minded people, the whole idea of denying the efficacy of indigenous approaches to medical problems is a manifestation of Europe's insatiable desire to dominate the world, control knowledge and be the anchor of the destiny of the globe. Solutions to global problems that come from Africa make them jittery and agitated because they have never dreamt of Africans as agents in the global matrix and canons of knowledge. It therefore calls for the rigorous interrogation and unmasking of the demand for laboratory tests. This demand may be what Asante, (2009) has termed the rhetoric of power, privilege and position.

Therefore, if Africa can find therapies that can mitigate or even lessen the wrath of the pandemic on the population of the continent, there is no reason why they should not make use of them. Waiting for solutions has never been part of the African people's philosophy, there is always an intervention that is performed by the human race.

What is the way forward for the Africans?

As has already been stated, the slave trade, colonialism and neo-colonialism all had their fair share in convincing Africans that their local medical systems were useless. However, taking a leaf from the various responses that we have seen being taken to respond to different ailments in the 21st century Zimbabwe, there has been more of emphasis on the natural remedies. After HIV and AIDS had taken its toll on Zimbabwe, the nation found itself being asked to revert to the traditional foods and herbs that we had long thrown away. Many people had to regress to traditional foods such as the blackjack, *mufushwa, nyevhe/ulude, ishwa/izinhlwa,* small grains, indigenous fruits among many other food stuffs that enhanced the immune system of the human body. Furthermore, society was also forced to revert to the indigenous ailments management strategies that placed emphasis on the critical role of the families and the community in the recovery of a patient. This witnessed the encouragement of the concept of home-based care which resulted in hospitals transferring patients to their homes for care. Subsequently, the overwhelmed conventional health systems relieved themselves of the unmanageable burden of the high rates of AIDS patients as families took over the caring of their relatives, of course with the assistants of trained professionals. However, it has to be remembered that this care giving model was not new to Africa. Traditionally ailing Africans members of the family have always been taken care of in their homes/families. Even with the COVID-19 scenario, aspects of home-based care have been used to cater for the needs of the patients in spite of it being viewed as highly infectious. Home-based care (self-quarantine in the context of COVID-19), within the family set-up, has been recommended as opposed to hospitalisation or quarantine centres. In the case of self-isolation, family members are requested to provide a room, separate from the main house, where the rest of the family members will be living. Members of the family, would then frequently provide food, and medication to the patient under the guidance and regular visits of the medical practitioners. In a way, this roping in of the family and community demonstrates the fact that the so-called advanced societies outsource solutions to emerging problems from African indigenous people when their systems are under pressure.

The answer for Africa is not in toeing the lines of the former imperialist states, but in going back into history and see 'where the rain began to beat us' (Achebe 1975). It is in digging into the wisdom of the African populations to get even the remnants of the knowledge on medicine so that we can bail the continent out of the quagmire that it finds itself in. Africa has to go back to its source (indigenous knowledge systems), even though the continent has lost a lot of knowledge as a result of brainwashing through colonial education and foreign religions, death of the elderly members who were the custodians of indigenous knowledge, climate change which could have led to the extinction of some plant species, the setting up of colonial systems that led to the clearing of large areas for the establishment of farms, urban centres, mission centres, mining communities and the communal areas which eventually became overpopulated, congested, overgrazed and deforested. More than a century of losing knowledge while the custodians of indigenous knowledge systems are dying demands a high level of commitment towards research in IKS for the continent to recover some of the lost knowledge for the benefit of the indigenous people. Otherwise, Africa will continue to be a laboratory for developed nations for testing their vaccines, other medicinal substances and even technologies.

Education to support Africa amid the 4th Industrial Revolution

To swim above the tide of the 4th Industrial Revolution, Africa needs a diverse education system that is tailor-made to satisfy the economic needs of her people. As well as destroy the colonial education structures whose goal was to deprive the African people of critical skills that promote creativity and industrialisation. The education system has to move from the route learning that demanded the regurgitation of information deposited into the learners to skills bused, hands-on-mind-on type of education. This education must be the type that capacitates Africans with the knowledge and skills to process their own mineral resources into finished goods and products. This way, the continent will no longer be compelled to sell mineral ore to the so -called developed countries for peanuts. Such that the tantalum, cobalt, cadmium, cooper, zinc, nickel, lead, aluminium, lithium and gold among many other minerals used for the designing and construction (manufacturing) of electronic gadgets that are the key drivers in the revolution (Brown 2017) can be developed in Africa for both the local and global market. According to Brown, cobalt is essential for the manufacture of lithium-ion batteries that are used in smartphones and laptops. This implies that the curriculum must be designed in such a way that it gives the learners adequate knowledge and skills for value addition with respect to all the mineral resources that are found in the continent. It has to capacitate the Africans with skills to turn their renewable energy such as the solar energy into commodities that make them compete favourably in the industrial revolution where solar systems are developed to power the African continent, leaving excess that can be exported. The uranium that is found in abundance in Africa has to be made maximum use of in the generation of electricity in nuclear reactors.

Conclusion

The African continent cannot afford to ignore the 4th Industrial Revolution and the various implications that it has to the developmental trajectory of its people. While it is good to acknowledge the advantaged position of continents such as Europe, Australia, USA among many others, it is high time Africa realises that the revolution at hand was never designed to benefit her, but the conglomerates, the elite as well as propagate the imperialist agenda. As such, survival in this revolution is not in parroting the imperialists, but in being unique and advancing the African uniqueness, that way Africa will be better placed to curve her own space on the global terrain and claim her position on the global marketplace of ideas. It is high time Africa concentrates on inventing, researching and coming up with innovations that are peculiar to her situation than blindly attempting to fit in or accessing what the imperialist communities would have designed. Innovations from these countries are never meant to change the status quo vis-à-vis their relationship with Africa but to advance the imperialist agenda.

References

Achebe, C. (1975) *Morning Yet on Creation day: Essays*. New York: Doubleday.

Ahmed, W. Vadal-Alaball, J., Downing, J. and Segnis, F. L. (2020) COVID-19 and the 5G Conspiracy Theory: Social Network Analysis of Twitter Data. Retrieved 2 September 2020 from https://www.jmir.org/2020/5/e19458/.

Asante, M. K. (2002) 'Intellectual Dislocation: Applying Analytic Afrocentricity to Narratives of Identity', *The Howard Journal of Communications*, (13), 977-110.

Ashcroft, B., Griffiths, G and Tiffin, H. (1989). *The Empire Writes Back: Theory and Practice in Postcolonial literatures*. London: Routledge.

Becker, C. and Collignon, R. (nd) 'A History of Sexually transmitted Diseases and AIDS in Senegal: Difficulties in Accounting for Social Logistics in Health Policies.'
Retrieved 2 September 2020 from https://horizon.documentation.ird.fr/exl-doc/pleins_textes/pleins_textes_7/b_fdi_51-52/010019077.pdf.

BBC News. (2013) 'DR Congo: Cursed by its natural wealth.' Retrieved 16 May 2020 from https://www.bbc.com/news/magazine-24396390.

Birgis, T. (2015) *The looting machines, Warlords, tycoons, smugglers and the systematic theft of Africa's wealth*. New York: Public Affairs.

Bourdillion, M.F.C. (1989) 'Medicines and Symbols', *Zambezia*, XVI(i), 29-65.

Brown, R. (2017) 'Descending into conflict: tech minerals finance war'. Retrieved on 1 September 2020 from https://www.raconteur.net/business-innovation/future-proofing-procurement-2017/descending-into-conflict-tech-minerals-finance-war.

Boyd, A. and Lenix-Hooker, C.J. (1992) 'Afrocentricism', *Library Journal*, 117 (18), 46-49.

Cabral, A. (1980) *Unity and Struggle*. London: Heinemann.

Coetzee, P.H., and A.P.J., Roux, (ed.) (2005) *The African Philosophy Reader Second edition: A text with Readings*. London: Routledge.

Chiwane, M. (2016) 'The development of Afrocentricity: A historical survey'. Retrieved 1 September 2020 from https://www.researchgate.net/publication/312477184_The_development_of_Afrocentricity_a_historical_survey.

Chukwuokolo, J. C. (2009) 'Afrocentrism Or Eurocentrism: The Dilemma of African Development'. *OGIRISI: A New Journal of African Studies*. 6, 24-38.

Davison, B. (1992) *The Black Man's Burden: Africa and the curse of the nation-state*. London: James Currey.

De Waitte, G. (2000) 'Traditional Medicine and the Quest for National identity in Zimbabwe', *Zambezia*, XXVII (ii), 235-268.

Evans, R. J. (1988) 'Epidemics and Revolutions: Cholera in Nineteenth-Century Europe', *Past & Present*, 120, 123-146.

Fanon, F. (1963) *The Wretched of the Earth*. New York: Grove Press.

Goodman, P. (2020) '16 Advantages of Digital Technology'. Retrieved 16 May 2020 from https://turbofuture.com/computers/Advantages-of-Digital-Technology.

Hountondji, P. J. (1995) 'Producing knowledge in Africa Today the Second Bashorun M.K.O Abiola Distinguished Lecture', *African Studies Review*, 38 (3), 1-10.

Jackson, J. G. (2015) *Introduction to African Civilisations*. Harmondworth: Penguin.

Jackson, R. L. (2003) 'Afrocentricity as metatheory: A dialogic exploration of its principles', in R. L. Jackson and E.B. Richardson (eds.), *Understanding African American rhetoric: Classical origins to contemporary innovations*. New York: Routledge.

Kamau. J. (2020) 'Kemron: the HIV/AIDS cure that never was'. Retrieved 28 May 2020 from https://nation.africa/kenya/news/kemron-the-hiv-aids-cure-that-never-was-287542

Kranzberg, M. (1986) 'Technology and History: Kreuzberg's Laws', *Technology and Culture*. (27)3, 547.

Liedong, T. A. (2017) 'African politicians seeking medical help abroad is shameful, and harms health care'. Retrieved 16 May 2020 from https://theconversation.com/african-politicians-seeking-medical-help-abroad-is-shameful-and-harms-health-care-82771.

Mahamba, I. (2018) 'Clothes and water bodies poisoned', *The Patriot*. Retrieved 3 September 2020 from https://www.thepatriot.co.zw/old_posts/clothes-and-water-bodies-poisoned/.

Mann. S. (2011) *Cry Havoc*. London: John Black Publishers.

McEvedy, C. and Jones, R (1978) *Atlas of World Population*. London: Penguin Books.

Muchemwa, F. (2015) *The Struggle for Land in Zimbabwe*. Harare: Heritage Trust.

Potter, C. (2001) 'A history of influenza', *Journal of Applied Microbiology*, (91), 572–579.

Pheko, M. (1984) *Apartheid: The Story of a Dispossessed People*. London: Marram Books.

Pheko, M. (2012) 'Effects of colonialism on Africa's past and present'. Retrieved 17 June 2020 from https://www.pambazuka.org/global-south/effects-colonialism-africas-past-and-present.

Richard, K.S. (2019) 'The Portuguese Colonial Empire'. Retrieved 20 July 2020 from https://www.thoughtco.com/the-portuguese-empire-1435004.

Rodney, W. (1973) *How Europe Underdeveloped Africa*. Dar-Es-Salaam: Tanzanian Publishing House.

Saunders-Hastings, P. R. and Krewski, D. (2016) 'Reviewing the History of Pandemic Influenza: Understanding Patterns of Emergence and Transmission' *Pathogens*, (5)4, 66.

Sheridan, R. (2020) 'Does Madagascar's herbal remedy, COVID-Organics work?' Retrieved from https://www.researchgate.net/publication/342654901_Does_Madagascar%27s_herbal_remedy_COVID-Organics_work.

Sousa, A.N. (2016) 'Between East and West: The Cold War's legacy in Africa: 'Red Africa': From a generation of cinematographers to the end of Apartheid- Africa, Cuba and the Soviet Union'. Retrieved from https://www.aljazeera.com/indepth/features/2016/02/east-west-cold-war-legacy-africa-160214113015863.html.

The pharmaletter, (1992) 'Kemron comes under attack'. Retrieved from https://www.thepharmaletter.com/article/kemron-comes-under-attack.

Verharen, C. C. (2000) 'Molefi Asante', *The Western Journal of Black Studies*, (24)4, 223-238.

Witney, W. and Gillezeau, R. (2011) 'The impact of slave trade on African Economies'. Retrieved from https://www.researchgate.net/publication/254432065.

World Health Africa, (2020) 'WHO to study Madagascar's drug to treat COVID-19? Who gets in touch with Madagascar, after country's president slammed global health body for not endorsing?'

Retrieved from https://www.aa.com.tr/en/africa/who-to-study-madagascars-drug-to-treat-covid-19-/1840971.

World Health Organisation, (2020) 'Coronavirus Cure: What progress are we making on treatment?' Retrieved from https://www.bbc.com/news/health-52354520.

Chapter Three

Vaccinations in Africa: The Paradox of Human Rights and Human Experiments

Munyaradzi Mukesi & Emmy Wabomba

Introduction

Immunisation is a key component of primary health in which a person is made resistant to infection usually through deliberate administration of a vaccine which contains among other things, an attenuated form of the microorganism which is known to cause the infection in question. Immunization was practiced in Africa and Asia long before its introduction in Europe in the 18th century (Riedel 2005) and medicine was taught in Africa from as far back as the 12th century at the University of Timbuktu which is cited as one of the oldest universities in the world. It offered all disciplines, ranging from History, Religion, Mathematics, Medicine and Law (Khair 2003). Immunization is touted as the greatest health investment money can buy and is largely perceived as an undisputable human right. However, with the rise of the contemporary post human and post-anthropocene discourse terms such human right may see profound changes in their definition. Since the inception of vaccines, a lot of lives have been saved through the prevention and control of infectious disease outbreaks. A right to life cannot be alluded to, without the mention of good health. In their paper, Obradovic, Balta, Obradovic and Mesic (2014), reported that almost 11 million children died from preventable diseases and the World Health organization (WHO) (2018) reported that an estimated 6.2 million children and adolescents died from preventable diseases. Most of these deaths are recorded in resource limited countries that are unable to distribute or make vaccines available to their citizens (Obradovic *et al.* 2014). Although millions of children still remain without access to vaccines, immunization has contributed tremendously in reducing infant and child mortality which aligns with the fourth Millennium Development Goal (MDG-4). In order to realize the MDGs, policies and funding, need to augment efforts to reduce mortality rates among children from vaccine preventable diseases by increasing coverage (Mhatre & Schryer-Roy 2009).

Obligation to international instruments

The United Nations Human Rights Office of the Commissioner outlines nine core international human rights instruments for the protection of human rights. If a country ratifies an international instrument, it is obliged to adhere to it. The enforcement of these instruments largely depends on other factors such as the penalties that are imposed for non-compliance. It is in that dimension that richer countries are more likely to comply than the poor ones (Gauri 2011). This is critical as, a right to life is synonymous to health. For instance, in article 6 (2) of the Centre for Civil and Political Rights (CCPR) (1948) the state parties to the convention should make sure that a child's survival and development is guaranteed. That will include, immunization especially at the early years of a child, on preventable diseases. There are several international instruments that speak to the right of life. Countries that are state parties to these conventions are therefore obligated to comply with the requirements as provided in the instruments. Giving a boarder interpretation of these instruments means a right to life includes a right of access to medical care including vaccines on preventable diseases. The following are some of the instruments that grant a right to life. Convention on the Rights of the Child (CRC) (1989) – Article 6(1), CCPR (1948) - Article 6, Convention on the Rights of People with Disabilities (2008) - Article 10.

The Universal Declaration of Human Rights (UDHR) is a crucial instrument because it provides a common standard of achievement for all people and all nations. And every individual and nation is expected to respect the rights as provided in the instrument, universal and effective recognition and observance is the ultimate goal. Article 25 of UDHR states that everyone has a right to a standard of living adequate for the health and well-being of himself and of his family, including food, clothing, housing and medical care and necessary social services. Medical care will include a right to a vaccine to prevent attacks from preventable diseases and WHO now recognizes the role played by traditional or complementary medicine in health care (WHO 2015). These sentiments are also held in Article 25 of the Covenant on The Rights of People with Disabilities (2008).

The law and protection of human rights

Article 16 of CRC (1989) states that a child should not be subjected to arbitrary or unlawful interference with his or her privacy, or unlawful attack on his or her honour and reputation. The child should be protected against such interference or attacks. The same sentiments are in Article 12 UDHR. In Article 1 of UDHR all human beings are born free and equal in dignity and rights. They are endowed with reason and conscience and should act towards one another in a spirit of brotherhood. Article 7 of CCPR stipulates that no one shall be subjected to torture or cruel, inhuman degrading treatment or punishment. In Particular, no one shall be subjected without his free consent to medical or scientific experimentation. Article 17 adds that no one should be subjected to arbitrary or unlawful interference with his or her privacy, or unlawful attack on his or her honour and reputation. These laws imply that everyone should be protected against such interference or attacks.

Although there are numerous declarations to protect the dignity and life of human beings, some which have been revised and continue to be revised to tighten restrictions on the use of human subjects for testing purposes, clinical trials have continued to perform experiments on humans in many cases in a manner which can only be regarded as cruel and dehumanizing. Historic studies which fit such a description include: the Tuskegee study (1932-1972) whereby black men were injected with syphilis and left untreated while being offered 'free' medical examinations, free meals and burial insurance; the Thalidomide study (1957-1962), rolled out in 46 countries and resulting in several hundreds of children being born with deformed limbs and in some cases without limbs; and more recently clinical trials at AIIMS, New Dehli, India (2006-2008) where mortality rate in infants during the study was reported as 1.18% and the polio vaccine programme (2011) which aimed to eradicate polio, but reported non polio acute flaccid paralysis (NPAFP) which was more severe than polio infection resulting in morbidity and mortality of 47500 and 540 respectively (Bhatt 2010). A vaccine campaign in 2015 in Busia County, Kenya left 28 children crippled. The county (Busia) was ordered by the courts to pay the children Sh 40 million in compensation.

While medical experiments continue to be problematic around the world, the vulnerability of participants in African countries or resource limited settings even in the same geographic location is profound when compared to wealthier environments. Although most experiments in Africa are conducted either in South Africa or Egypt, the rest of the continent has had its share of experiments gone badly. Tuskegee-like experiments include the Development of Antiretroviral Therapy (DART) trials in Zimbabwe and Uganda, Pfizer's Trovan clinical trials in Kano (Nigeria) and several other studies in Kenya, Uganda, Ethiopia, Burkina Faso and South Africa. All these experiments were cited for human rights violations through failure to get patient consent when changing the experiment, administering wrong doses of drugs, delays in reporting the harmful effects of drugs and in some cases destroying relevant research reports. In these experiments several hundreds of pregnant women, infants, children, men and women suffered long term problems including damage to the brain and other organs in some cases even death (Shehata 2017).

Vaccines may have detrimental consequences in humans which can be medical, religious or personal. Obligatory vaccinations cause conflicts between individuals and the public health systems. Although informed consent was first described in 1900, most vaccines do not allow for it such as the case of vaccinations in children which is not based on informed consent but coercion as the child can only be admitted into school upon producing a medical report or proving that a child received all the necessary vaccines (Ciolli 2008). In the case of COVID-19, the coercion is based on denial of entry to certain places, if one does not have a certificate to show that the test was done and is negative or you have been treated as is currently the practice in most African countries such as Kenya, Rwanda, Namibia, Zambia, Botswana and South Africa with long distance or cross-border truck drivers IOM, 2020). This current practice, if it is allowed to continue will develop into a trend which will be inclined towards expecting one to be vaccinated before travelling from one place to another, as is the practice with yellow fever.

A lot of legislation has been put in place to safeguard the human rights of individuals during medical experiments, but a lot more still has to be done to change the mindset of researchers especially those from western countries who view Africa as a testing ground for their medical inventions. Mira and Locht (French doctors) recently suggested that the trials of COVID-19 vaccines be done in Africa because of the prevailing conditions in Africa that is highly exposed people, with no protection but due to global outrage they have since rendered an apology (BBC 2020c). This case looks like, was just one of those extended traditions, where Africans have been subjected to experimental projects. Between 1921 and 1956, millions of Africans were coerced to take part in questionable experiments and trials some which were orchestrated by western governments with these people suffering severe adverse reactions and sometimes even death (Lowes & Montero 2020). The unfortunate utterances of Mira and Locht were not only poorly timed but were but to undo the argument that since COVID-19 represents a threat to global public health, it requires a global solution. This means that vaccines should be tested in populations were the disease has had considerable impact. Consideration should be given to affordability, availability and adoption to the health-care system in each country or population that they serve. If the call was made by WHO, then that would have been received differently. Resistance by African countries could have been minimal if other countries had been receptive to African initiatives and detailed and transparent guidelines were provided through a multilateral organisation such as the WHO. This would have been beneficial to all especially in a situation where social distancing is proving to be difficult to achieve.

Although Africans have their misgivings concerning human experiments such as vaccine trials, several aspects need to be considered in developing vaccines such as immunogenicity, tolerability, and appropriate dosing schedule for vaccines. It is believed that most of these infectious diseases occur in Africa or resource-constrained countries and therefore the vaccines need to be tested in such countries. However, classification of countries into groups based on resources is biased, favouring certain resources and not others. It should be understood that for a license to be issued within a certain region, tolerance and effectiveness should take centre stage. To test a vaccine in Africa at late stage clinical trials may pose unique challenges. There should be adequate measures put in place to safeguard the relationship between the sponsors and partners involved in the evaluation of the investigational products. The appointed investigation authority becomes a link between the sponsors and the community. Such interactions can be complex causing challenges to the community or the testing process. This complexity may undermine the intended objectives especially if the major players in the partnership or collaboration fail to capture the prevailing circumstances in the chosen region (Idoko *et al.* 2013).

Another foreseeable challenge is community dependence. The chosen community may depend on initiatives by development partners for healthcare. Sometimes the community, especially donor driven economies, may see the research project as a cheaper option in meeting health needs. They lack the understanding to differentiate between research and development projects. They would therefore expect it to be long time healthcare. The health facilities and governments also tend to rely on such services and therefore neglect to plan appropriately for healthcare human resource, medication, laboratory facilities and other consumables. In some cases, the interventions given during clinical trials are the only therapeutic options for patients, limiting their options in decision making (Shehata *et al.* 2017). This leads to a rapid decrease in the performance of the healthcare system on key areas which could have been doing well during the active phase of clinical trials.

The involvement of donor agencies or development partners as they prefer to be called now, albeit the irony in the phrase and the lack of understanding in African communities between research and development has created a new type of colonization where these communities are only good for providing raw data which is only synthesized and processed in the west and the finished product sold back to Africa at an unaffordable price. The west is once again being accused of using African raw materials in developing their economies, just as what happened with minerals and other raw materials during the industrial revolution. Glaringly, the lack of a defined Africa agenda is difficult to ignore, resulting in apparent epistemological colonization with Africa still supplying raw data, raw materials and being a field for research as the western countries seek to develop their economies, which they have now transformed into knowledge economies.

Knowledge gathering and the African quagmire in health

The industrial revolution was a major turning point in human history which focused on mechanizing manufacturing processes. After this revolution, future development of countries centred on knowledge and innovation-based development processes. This knowledge is used to accelerate and deepen development of new technologies generating wealth and creating a huge job market in western countries with little or no financial benefit to the countries from which knowledge was acquired. Countries which have emerged as champions of what is referred to as knowledge economies such as Finland and Republic of Korea have been known to use specific industries to advance the growth of their economies. Businesses have been known to exploit knowledge from activities by individuals to develop new platforms, strategize and ensure sustainability (World Bank 2007). This knowledge can be obtained from the countries of origin or from markets around the world to gain a global view of potential and emerging trends and needs. This system of knowledge hunting and gathering is now hugely funded by governments as knowledge has become an important ingredient in gaining a competitive edge over rivals in the global economy, expanding economies and creating wealth and employment (World Bank 2007).

Information from nomads has been used to develop telecommunication technologies and expand tourism, understanding languages has been used to inform marketing strategies while traditional remedies have been used for production of pharmaceuticals (World Bank 2007). Meanwhile developments in genetics and biotechnologies have been key in huge advances witnessed in life sciences and their applications. The focus in the health sector is now shifting to information sharing and knowledge acquisition and management to create efficient health processes, reduce costs, increase customer satisfaction and improve patient outcomes (UN 2020).

Despite the availability of overwhelming evidence showing that the difference between development in Africa and developed countries is knowledge, the concept of knowledge economies is poorly adopted by the former. The African continent which is much endowed with natural resources is lagging behind in development and still relies on exporting raw resources and importing finished products. Developed countries create effective innovation systems which tap into the growing stock of global knowledge and adapt them to the needs of African countries and people. These innovation systems include research programmes, universities and multinational corporations which are running massive research initiatives in Africa and other developing countries, gathering crucial knowledge for innovation of new platforms. These programmes offer the much-needed foreign direct investment (FDI) to African economies but obscure and marginalize the continent's own knowledge assets (World Bank 2007). The use of African knowledge by western countries has always been controversial to say the least and researchers have coined the name biopiracy to it. The commercialization and patenting of *Hoodia gorginni* in southern Africa was a classic case of biopiracy among the many other examples (Amusan 2017).

Developed countries use as much as 3% of their GDP on research and development, focusing on increasing awareness of global developments, identifying and importing relevant technologies and fostering interaction between universities and industries (World Bank 2017). These activities are given government support, with governments facilitating bilateral agreements with potential markets in instances as developmental aid. However, sociocultural issues and differences have implications in how the developmental agenda is accepted whether it is locally or foreign driven. These disparities are evident in medicine and science in which the Western world views addressing medical problems as being based on scientific research to determine the cause and potential treatment avenues. Meanwhile, much of Asia just like Africa relies on a holistic approach of existing knowledge and commonly used technologies derived from tradition than new developments. The acceptance of new knowledge or that which is packaged in the west especially when it is viewed as foreign is also affected by the unresolved trauma of colonialism or history of exploitation. Advancement of medicine in Africa is affected by the perception that western medicine is meant to harm Africans, even reducing the population (New York Times 2007). History is littered with cases of Western doctors and nurses who have voluntarily and knowingly harmed Africans in unsanctioned, uncouth and unethical experiments and research. These cases are spread across the length and breadth of the continent from South Africa to Libya. Notable cases are those of intentional injection of the Human Immunodeficiency Virus (HIV) in children to study its progression (Libya), administering excessive doses of chemotherapy to breast cancer patients (South Africa), injection of lethal doses of anaesthesia (Zimbabwe) and injection of excessive potassium, a cardio active substance (Zimbabwe & Zambia), resulting in harm and deaths to countless patients. The sale of fake drugs has been another challenge, with 42% of fake drugs in the world being sold to Africa and in areas like sub Saharan Africa the cases going up to 70% (The New York Times 2007; BBC 2020a).

In 1955 a senior British physician at Oxford University professed that Africa offered an unlimited field for clinical research (Tiley 2016). He made this statement after witnessing years of unethical researches which were conducted in Africa at the turn of the 19th century with no agreed upon ethical standards for human subjects and researchers did not get informed consent from subjects. There were no treatment protocols for infections, with no demarcation of acceptable and unacceptable practices. Trials were conducted using coercive means such as quarantine of subjects against their will and at times lacing the drugs and vaccines with harmful chemicals such as arsenic. These vaccine and drug trials were seen as a conquest for Africa after the scramble for Africa and partition, a dark continent where people were viewed as being infested with diseases caused by microorganisms. During that time, Africa was only seen as a supply of human subjects, with the Western countries collecting all the useful knowledge gathered from these researches to advance their health systems back home. This view has been widely condemned and numerous protocols have been put in place to safeguard the dignity of human subjects. However, during this COVID-19 pandemic and the ensuing clinical trials, questions from the experiences of yester-year are coming back to haunt current research. Critical questions are centred on how the continent benefits from the knowledge apart from just supplying human subjects for clinical trials and how is it different from the clinical trials at the turn of the 19th century (Tiley 2016; The East African 2020).

Western organisations and universities continue to play centre stage in research conducted in Africa, raising a critical question of the role of African universities in generating knowledge, resulting in them being viewed as a means in perpetuating colonial philosophies (Angu 2018). Universities should be playing a leading role in repudiation of the subordination of African forms of knowledge, thereby disrupting western epistemic hegemonies. Regrettably, this failure viewed by many as catastrophic, propagates the notion that the universities are still shaped by the epistemic tradition of the global North resulting in wider and louder calls to reform the university agenda and curriculum to suit and advance African epistemology. This is quite revealing considering that Africa has one of the universities widely touted as the world's first university, Timbuktu which was offering qualifications viewed to be at the same level as a PhD in the 15th century (Angu 2018; Khair 2003).

WHO agenda and funding

The WHO's core values of service orientation, integrity, being equitable, respect, collaboration, transparency, accountability, efficiency, inclusiveness and continuous improvement are derived from the United Nations (UN)'s core values of independence, impartiality, justice and universalism WHO 2019a). The organization is run on a budget funded by member countries, development partners and from voluntary contributions by well-wishers or interested parties. Contributions by member countries are calculated relative to the country's wealth and population of each of the 194 member states and 2 associate members. When facing critical challenges which require more funding, the WHO usually reaches out to well-wishers and development partners to bank-roll some of its activities. These include recent outbreaks of Ebola and the current COVID-19 pandemic. This extra funding provides support while accelerating activities such as research and development of vaccines for prevention and therapeutic drugs for treatment (WHO 2020b).

The ten major contributors to the WHO budget for 2019 were USA (15.18%), Bill & Mellinda Gates Foundation (12.12%), GAVI Alliance (8.18%), United Kingdom of Great Britain and Northern Ireland (7.91%), Germany (5.33%), UN Office for the Coordination of Humanitarian Affairs, UNOCHA (4.48%), Rotary International (3.32%), European Commission (3.05%), World Bank (3%) and Japan (2.59%). The major contributing African country was the DRC (1.28%), positioned 16th. However, the top ten beneficiaries of the fund are African countries and African organizations as follows: DRC, Nigeria, African Regional Office, Ethiopia, South Sudan, Uganda, Kenya, Angola and Mozambique. In the African region, the US$1.2B allocated was largely spend on programmes targeting among other things polio eradication (35.85%), vaccine preventable diseases (10.85%), establishing effective coordination and operations support (10.39%), early warning and health information management (6.04%) and fast track research for infectious hazards (2.75%). Little funding was dedicated to support reproductive, maternal, newborn, child and adolescent health (1.8%), malaria (1.55%), TB (1.39%), neglected tropical diseases (0.96%) and food safety (0%) (WHO 2019a). The picture emerging from these priorities as reflected in the expenditure is in sharp contrast to the reports that communicable (malaria, tuberculosis and HIV), maternal, nutritional and newborn diseases pose the greatest risk to African countries especially sub Saharan countries (World Bank 2013). African countries are also going through a demographic transition which still witnesses the dominance of communicable diseases but also experiencing an undeniable surge in non-communicable diseases.

Such disparities in resource allocation give rise to begging questions related to who prioritizes the funding areas and how much voice do the recipients of the funds have on fund utilization. The independence of the WHO in resource allocation and decision making is always brought in question if the recent dispute with the major funding partner (USA) is anything to go by. This is by no means an index case as a precedence already exists. Ructions have always existed between the UN and its multilateral institutions with member countries relating to voting rights in the different arms of the UN, sanctions, climate change and funding of multilateral institutions. Some of the disputes erupt within the multilateral institutions themselves and in more cases than one, countries aligning as regional or continental blocs to stand ground against perceived bullying by 'powerful' member states (International Crisis Group 2019).

The recent dispute between the USA and WHO which spilled into the public domain is hard to ignore and has become a reference point in questioning some of the functions of the WHO which are usually seen by liberals as noble (CNN 2020). After a long and protracted battle of wills emanating from who is to blame for the explosion of the COVID-19 pandemic of which the US was and still is a major casualty, the major funding partner of the WHO severed ties with the multilateral organization, cutting all funding. The USA laid the pandemic blame squarely at the footsteps of the WHO for its perceived catastrophic failure to arrest the imminent death of multitudes due to COVID-19, with the US being the worst affected in infections and deaths. While the WHO provided substantial evidence to support the claim that they acted within the limits of the scientific knowledge which existed at the time, they still lost their major funding partner, throwing into limbo all projects funded under the USA. The politicizing of funding of multilateral institutions impedes their faculties in making concise, eloquent, consensual and well-meaning decisions. This grossly infringes on their autonomy, bringing into doubt their independence and impartiality, threatening to or in actual fact making them irrelevant unless if they tow the political line of the former (CNN 2020).

The weaponising of funding is a direct assault on the multilateral organizations, which is akin to manipulation as the less privileged nations which rely on external funding to support essential health programmes retain little or no voice to publicly pronounce themselves on their standpoints. In the COVID-19 dispute between the WHO and USA which entangled the Director General, many African countries weighed in on their support for the beleaguered Director, but it ended on issuing sporadic statements, nothing more (BBC 2020b; BBC 2020c). The collective financial contribution of all African nations does not match that of the USA alone, with the same African countries being direct beneficiaries of the former's contributions to the WHO and other funding agencies. The funding of multilateral institutions and probable manipulation by powerful member states creates under currents of control and exercise of political power contrary to the ethos of good administration, independence and justice.

The WHO Health System Framework identifies six building blocks as being key in ensuring adequate delivery of healthcare. These are: service delivery, workforce, health information system, medical products, vaccines and technology, financing and leadership and governance (WHO 2010). Most of the African countries fall short even of the bare minimum expectations of adequate health coverage as evident from poor health infrastructure and none in some poor communities. African health systems suffer from neglect and underfunding, resulting in human capital flight to Western countries (WHO 2017). Low budgetary allocation, poor administration and coordination of healthcare systems especially in the public sector persist in Africa despite numerous undertakings and declarations signed by African heads of states at WHO and African Union (AU) forums, Ministerial conferences and seminars and at regional block level (WHO 2017). This is closely linked to the now growing trend of Africans, especially those of notable means seeking medical attention in healthcare systems even out of the continent in what is now commonly known as health tourism with the favourite destinations being USA, Europe, China and India and this business now generates several billions of dollars every year (Lunt et al. 2014).

There are hundreds of multinational companies operating in Africa with the majority extracting raw materials or sending waste from developed countries for disposition or recycling in Africa. However, it is generally accepted that these companies invest very little sometimes nothing back into the communities they are operating in. African leaders seem not to hold these companies to task largely due to poor governance or fail to find a voice as these companies operate under bilateral agreements signed with their countries of origin. These multinational companies should plough back into communities by providing healthcare funding. In some cases, these existing bilateral agreements are signed allowing multinational companies to conduct medical research in communities such as drug or vaccine clinical trials but with no investment in the communities affected (Oxfam International 2015).

Vaccination programmes and coverage

Vaccines have been credited with the decline in mortality rates around the world, preventing 2 to 3 million deaths every year with measles cases for example declining by 73% (WHO 2019c). Vaccine coverage around the world has remained high but WHO reported that in 2018, a sizeable number of infants (19.4 million) were not reachable and the majority of them (60%) lived in 10 countries, mostly in Africa. The Global Vaccine Action Plan (GVAP) whose mandate is to prevent deaths through equitable access to vaccines by 2020 reports that progress towards these targets is off-track. New resolutions urge continuous efforts to strengthen governance and leadership structures around national immunization programmes. More focus should be centred on improved monitoring and surveillance systems and advocacy to the value of vaccines (WHO 2019c).

Vaccine coverage in Africa was reported at 77% in 2014 although some countries had more than 90% coverage. The Ministerial Conference on Immunization in Africa (2016) reported several success stories in immunization which include interrupting polio transmission, immunization against meningitis and introduction of new vaccines for prevention of infectious diseases such as hepatitis B, haemophilus influenza, yellow fever and human papillomavirus. However, vaccination programmes are dogged by several challenges such as inequalities in immunization coverage with most of them witnessed in areas with lower education levels, lower incomes and higher poverty distribution in rural areas. These are compounded by weak health systems and lack of financial sustainability and poor surveillance (Immunization in Africa 2016).

Ironically, these areas hard hit by these challenges related to vaccine coverage of already existing vaccines are used for vaccine trials but ultimately becoming the least beneficiaries of the approved vaccines. Despite 10.85% of the WHO budget to Africa being spend on vaccination programmes, such gaps still exist, and African countries still face huge challenges with weak infrastructures and inequalities and poor communities are hardest hit. The assistance offered only provides vaccines as far as the funding can cover but does not adequately equip the nations to be self-sustaining, leaving the communities vulnerable to exploitation (WHO 2019a; WHO 2019b; WHO 2019c).

Vaccinology and COVID-19 vaccine fast-tracking

Vaccinology refers to the science of vaccines covering the basic science to the disease, infectivity of the microorganisms, how the body responds to the infection, modes of administration, production and monitoring and evaluating its effects in patients. Other important aspects of vaccinology include safety, legal and moral frameworks and financing of the production and eventual roll-out. Current vaccines prevent infections largely caused by bacteria and viruses although research is now focusing on developing some for the control of non-infectious diseases (Barrett 2016). The development of vaccines has resulted in the eradication of childhood diseases such as measles, diphtheria and polio in most parts of the world, with some scientists hailing this as the biggest invention of the 20th century. While the development of prophylactic vaccines to NCDs is a challenge, current research is focusing on therapeutic vaccines for them (Barrett 2016).

Improvements in science are dictating the rapid pace in developing vaccines with developers taking advantage of new knowledge in basic science and technology such as molecular biology, proteomics, transcriptomics and genomics to produce potent vaccines. However, these developments have resulted in the demand for more robust data from each of the developmental stages of the vaccine before they are approved to progress to the next phase let alone be tried or used in human beings to prove safety and efficacy, a prerequisite to licensing (Leclerc 2007).

There are fewer vaccines in the world than generally perceived by most people, with the WHO's Product Development for Vaccines Advisory Committee (PDVAC) listing only 26 of them as available and 24 being in the developmental pipeline (WHO 2019b). The research and development of additional vaccines is a very long and costly endeavour which pharmaceutical companies commit to and at the end of the day hoping to recoup their investment. The dengue vaccine was developed over a period of 24 years at an estimated cost of US$1.6 billion by Sanofi Pasteur (Lyon, France). In some cases, governments and Non-Governmental Organizations (NGOs) get involved in the process to offset some of the costs as was the case in the development of the Ebola vaccine in 2014-2015. While vaccine research and development faces these challenges, the implementation pathway is not spared either due to the sometimes impossible societal expectations. The consumers expect the vaccine to have absolute safety and efficacy, an impossible feat, while coming at no cost or very minimal if any. Furthermore, the consumer is only prepared to spend money when they feel their health is threatened, making cost recovery from investment by pharmaceutical companies an arduous task (Barret 2016; WHO 2019b).

On March 11, 2020 after 118,326 cases and 4,292 deaths due to COVID-19, the WHO declared it a pandemic and these figures were expected to increase rapidly due to the infectivity of the disease. The development of a safe and potent vaccine was identified as priority to prevent continued spreading of the virus and reduce the death rate. The speedy development of the vaccine has been hampered by the availability of very little information on the immunological response of patients. There is at present no human vaccine on the market and as of 23 June, 2020 there were 8 936 337 reported cases and 468 308 deaths, amounting to several hundred-fold increases. As the number of cases kept mounting and a vaccine remaining elusive, WHO launched a solidarity trial fund to find a potent vaccine for COVID-19. However, the development of such a vaccine requires the participation of a balanced population sample to make it global due to differences in circumstances in which it will be used and also the genetic disparities among different population, lest the vaccine be regional or localized (BBC 2020c; WHO 2020c). The development of the vaccine on the other hand is facing a new threat of misinformation, disinformation, a social media and mainstream media onslaught determined to mislead or feed fake news to the public creating what has been dubbed a plandemic and WHO is concerned on the impact this has on ongoing efforts to curb the disease. WHO has been partnered by member states in an effort to address this infodemic (BBC 2020c; WHO 2020c). Although there are divergent views as to which information is accurate, credible and which voice should be listened to in an era where there is no monopoly to information, the WHO carries the voice of member states and is viewed as the leader in fighting such pandemics.

Despite the huge cost of vaccine research and development, over 100 COVID-19 vaccines are being explored by different organizations of which 72% are being developed by private sector or industry developers including those who can be classified as small and inexperienced in large scale vaccine manufacture with most of the activity centralized in North America (46%) (Tung *et al.* 2020). What is intriguing about these vaccine candidates is the unprecedented pace with which they are getting approved for human clinical testing, bearing in mind the limited knowledge of the host immunological response and the surmountable basic science which has to be fully understood to develop a safe and potent vaccine (Tung *et al.* 2020).

It is generally acceptable that the effectiveness of a vaccine is lower than its efficacy as reported from clinical trials. However, WHO (2014) cautions that the safety of vaccines and the frequency and seriousness of untoward events are critical determinants to be considered before developing countries consider adopting a vaccine, especially newer vaccines being produced in the developed countries which are not presented with a long safety record. While the safety of vaccines is determined during clinical trials which are performed before licensing, this does not capture post marketing surveillance data which is a cardinal marker of the vaccine's long-term safety profile. Developing countries are encouraged to interrogate all data available and match it to the disease patterns in the country and other relevant demographic information before accepting a vaccine (WHO 2014).

Developing countries tend to fall short of these expectations and receive vaccines from development partners which do not match their disease profile and without adequate consideration of safety and efficacy of vaccine candidates or the vaccine itself. This is a disturbing trend especially with the now fast-tracked COVID-19 vaccines which are made in developed countries and proposed for trials in African countries, with little or no testing in the countries of origin (WHO 2014). This is despite the fact that the scientists may not have factored in the 'African factors' during the development process of the vaccine and also notwithstanding the fact that the high disease burden is in Europe and Asia, not Africa. The weak regulatory frameworks and monitoring processes in Africa for side effects even in those countries with safeguards at national level make the continent and its people a target for vaccine trials. This is even a travesty for vaccinology when some scientists appear to publicly agree in exploiting these weaknesses (BBC 2020c).

Huge advances in genomics, proteomics and transcriptomics have supported the fast development of vaccines (Barrett 2016). Urgent responses to epidemics through the development of vaccines has previously been used successfully with Ebola and Zika viruses. Producers have used existing technologies to scale up knowledge on emerging diseases. The regulatory issues are normally determined early in developmental stages because the final approval depends on it. The regulation is divided into, developmental, licensure and post licensure. The preclinical stage is done in the laboratory and either in vitro or in vivo techniques are used but the test is done on animals first (WHO 2014. The test on humans is done in three phases: In phase one the test is done on a small number of healthy adults (Lurie *et al.* 2020). And in phase two the major concern is on safety. In phase two a large number of persons is involved and information on the vaccine is also provided, this is to produce the desired effect. Phase three is crucial because, licensing is directly linked on how safe the vaccine is, for the purposes it was intended.

While vaccine development is usually a lengthy and costly process, quick development of a vaccine requires a new approach which deviates from traditional protocols as seen in Figure 1 below. Sometimes consecutive steps are taken concurrently resulting in scaling up of vaccine development without properly appreciating if the vaccine candidate is viable. While this is an option during pandemics, there is a growing call to stick to conventional protocols during the developmental stages. Safety concerns always remain a major issue especially when the vaccine is tested in communities with poor monitoring mechanisms and scanty background to the data generated during the developmental stages (Lurie *et al.* 2020).

The Ebola epidemic of 2013-2016 raised disturbing ethical, moral and regulatory flaws in vaccine trials in Africa. Although the WHO approves unlicensed treatment to be administered in the absence of a potent alternative, there were serious safety concerns with some of the vaccines which were availed to the Congolese government (Lurie *et al.* 2020). Some of the vaccines had questionable efficacy and despite misgivings from the government, they remained under pressure from developers, multilateral organisations and development partners to roll them out. The country also got flooded with unlicensed products and regulation and monitoring became an impossible task. Although the studies on vaccines did not use placebos as in randomized controlled trials, there was withholding of it to some individuals mimicking a placebo effect. That was a huge moral and ethical dilemma considering that the patients were infected with one of the most lethal pathogens known to mankind and eventually died (Lurie *et al.* 2020; Financial Times 2019). Figure one shows the procedure followed when developing vaccines.

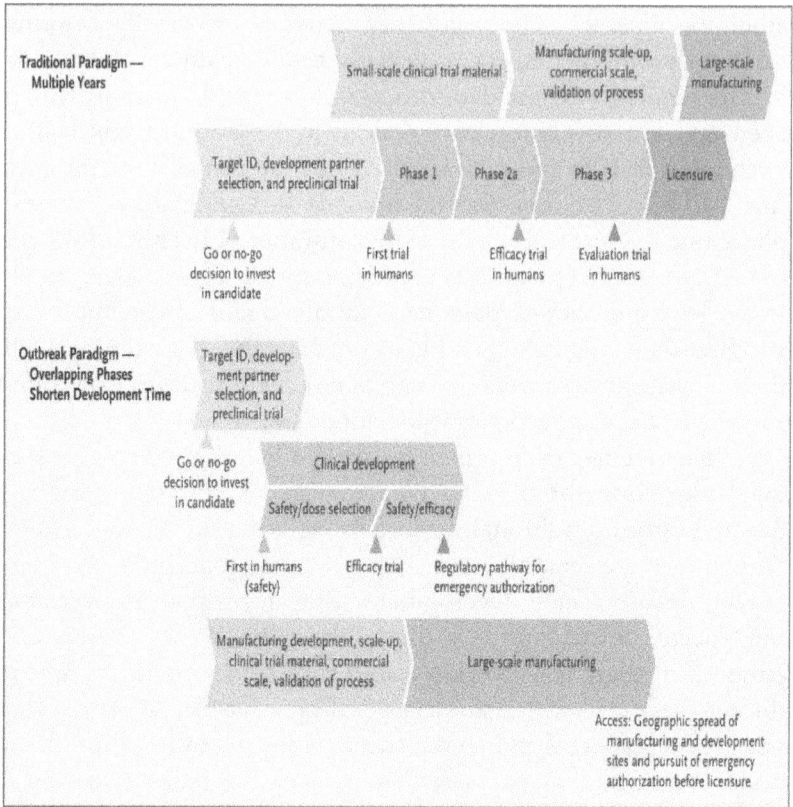

Figure 1: Traditional Vaccine Development and Development Using a Pandemic Paradigm
Adapted from:
https://www.nejm.org/doi/full/10.1056/NEJMp2005630

The acceleration of vaccines to new diseases such as COVID-19 has seen the heavy involvement of governments in funding research and development, eventually transferring the production and scaling up to private multinational companies who will eventually market and distribute (CNN 2020). The US government has been heavily involved in supporting vaccine developers to invent platforms that can be easily adapted to the emergence of new pathogens. However, trial of such vaccines largely ignores population dynamics with most of them being tried in low to medium income African countries (LMIC) or resource limited settings of LMIC where clinical and serologic studies are usually conducted post vaccine roll-out to identify missed populations (CNN 2020; BBC 2020c). This negates the very fundamental principle in vaccine development that vaccine development should be a global effort leading to a vaccine candidate that is globally balanced (Lurie *et al.* 2020).

There are over 100 COVID-19 vaccine candidates ready for clinical trials around the world and several African countries are already prepared to take part (WHO 2020d). Some of these vaccine candidates are being tried concurrently with developing countries to measure the efficacy at the same time in different populations. Although it is good for African countries to be involved in clinical trials, there is risk of severe adverse effects because they were made in developed countries where small scale trials may have been done with African countries only now exposed to large scale roll-out (University of Oxford 2020).

On 24 June 2020, South Africa announced that it was ready to take part in the first clinical trials of the COVID-19 vaccine, becoming the first country on the continent to do so. The country's new cases and deaths were rising unabated, with the hardest hit provinces being Western Cape, Gauteng and Eastern Cape in that order. Western Cape and Gauteng provinces have the highest GDP per capita amongst the 9 provinces of over $8000 per province while the Eastern Cape is the poorest Province in the country with a GDP per capita of less than $4000 (GeoCurrents 2011). The Eastern Cape, which borders the Western Cape, has one of the highest densities of poverty in the country and highest percentage of children under the poverty line while the Western Cape has the least on all accounts. Despite these glaring similarities in COVID-19 burden and disparities in economic outlook, the first vaccine is being conducted in the low-income areas of the country (Aljazeera 2020a). The presented scenario solidifies the long held conservative view that vaccine trials target the poor who bear the brunt of untoward effects and life-long sequel while provision of the effective product reaches them last, favouring the affluent communities. Poor communities have long been categorized as having the least vaccine covering under the expanded programme on immunization (EPI) compared to its counterparts (GeoCurrents 2011; Aljazeera 2020b).

Genetic and environmental factors are known to influence response to vaccines, and in this case there is scanty information on potential side effects to African populations before large scale trials (WHO 2019b). Post marketing and post-trial side effects need to be severely monitored but this is a daunting task in the African region due to poor health infrastructure and monitoring mechanisms in most countries, leaving populations at the mercy of long-term untoward effects which include death. The process has to consider scientific, ethical, and regulatory and safety requirements, but often it is defined through trial and error resulting in adverse events. These events are defined by genetic variations which strongly influence vaccine responsiveness with a number of them resulting in hospitalization, disability and death (WHO 2019b). While WHO has prioritized the fast tracking of COVID-19 vaccines for testing in humans under compressed timelines, the uptake has been low in vulnerable populations due safety concerns.

While emphasis is being put on developing, testing and upscaling vaccine products developed in the western countries, Africa has huge knowledge existing in communities which has been taped into for generations as part of primary healthcare. This knowledge could be explored, tested and up scaled to save the continent and the world at large, this is knowledge indigenous to Africa.

Indigenous Knowledge Systems

Indigenous Knowledge Systems (IKS) refer to knowledge that developed in particular settings without the influence of or before the advent of modern scientific knowledge. This information was used importantly for the survival of those communities in various sectors such as agriculture, engineering and health. These skills and philosophies which were developed from interaction with the environment ensured survival of communities in times of strife, whether famine or disease. With the advent of modern scientific knowledge most of these knowledge systems were relegated to the periphery with most societies opting to adopt modern science while others continued with the practice, in some cases combining both sets of knowledge (UNESCO 2019). Although indigenous knowledge systems are not given due recognition in their current form, cases of biopiracy in Africa have shown that modern scientific knowledge is derived from indigenous knowledge.

UNESCO is advancing the integration of indigenous knowledge holders and their knowledge into contemporary science fora in various critical factors such as climate change, sustainability and management of health systems. However, questions still prevail on the rights to knowledge and protection from biopiracy. One of the areas which has come into focus is the use of traditional medicine in the advancement of human health, a practice which has been in existence in many communities in Africa, China and Asia. Traditional medicine also referred to as alternative or complementary medicine is defined as the sum of knowledge, skills, and practices based on theories, beliefs and experiences indigenous to a culture which are used to maintain physical and mental health. With one third of the population lacking access to essential medicines around the world, these are used by 70-80% of the African population as a form of primary healthcare (WHO 2015).

WHO encourages African countries to promote and integrate traditional practices into the main health systems. Africa contributes about 25% of the world trade in biodiversity with Madagascar exhibiting 82% endemism, and has approximately 45 000 plant species some of which are used by indigenous people for the relief of various ailments from headaches and birth complications to treatment of viral and bacterial infections (Mahomoodally 2013). These plants, commonly referred to as medicinal plants have different components which contain chemical components which have been demonstrated in scientific experiments to be effective against microorganisms. These active chemical components have been used in modern times for the production of pharmaceuticals. Even before the advent of scientific knowledge proving the efficacy of these plants, they have been used in the prevention and treatment of cancer, urinary tract infections, sexually transmitted diseases, tuberculosis, malaria and a host of other ailments (Saki et al. 2015). What is interesting to note from scientific studies on medicinal plants is that some of them have been proved to be efficacious against microorganisms now classified as resistant to conventional drugs and the plants are being explored as viable alternative therapy (Mahomoodally 2013; Saki et al. 2015; Mukesi et al. 2019).

As much as 70% of Black South Africans and 40% of Americans have been known to use traditional medicine. For many years, traditional medicine was thought to be confined to rural areas as the nature of the practice was perceived to be suited for that environment (Makogbi 2013). However, the practice has moved to urban areas and there is now no difference in its use between rural and urban areas. In reality, sub Saharan Africa has witnessed a growing market of traditional medicine driven tourism with patients moving between Southern Africa and as far afield as West Africa. Some traditional healers have gone as far as building their own state of the art consulting rooms prompting pressure groups to raise the tempo in calling for the integration of traditional medicine into the mainstream health system (Makogbi 2013; USCSchaeffer 2017).

The integration of traditional medicine with Western inspired medicine is fraught with many challenges with both sides not trusting each other. Physicians think traditional healers are illiterate and seek to prove the efficacy of traditional medicine through rigorous empirical scientific methods (Mokogbi 2013). They view the practice as being based on abstract and subjective matter, lacking scientific objectivity, more so the grey areas are filled by reference to spirit mediums and at times witchcraft. Traditional healers on the other hand feel they are acknowledged within their sphere, do not trust western scientists whom they accuse of stealing their knowledge for personal gain and feel they are being judged on the wrong knowledge scale (Mokogbi 2013; Yuan *et al.* 2016).

The dilemma in comparing these two knowledge systems is that they share the same patients and in a variety of cases treat the same patient concurrently and unknowingly, potentially endangering the life of the patient from potential drug overdose or adverse drug interactions. Similarly, patients do not always reveal to one system that they are seeking the help of the other. Health practitioners in western medicine on the other hand provide a classic case of cognitive dissonance by working for the system and secretly seeking the service of traditional medicine, at times even clandestinely referring patients to perceived effective traditional healers. African governments have also not helped the situation as they have passively participated in the confusion by failing to certify and regulate traditional medicine which is indigenous, rather preferring to let the practice to be used as long as they do not seek recognition to the level of western medical practice (USCSchaeffer 2017).

The failure of public recognition of traditional medicine by many African governments while being shunned for western medicine despite widespread use in Africa, Asia and the Western countries means eventual breakthroughs from this knowledge system may not receive much recognition from around the world. The discovery of a potential cure for COVID-19 in the Republic of Madagascar is one of the current highlights but not an index case. An announcement by the government of Madagascar of the discovery of a COVID-19 remedy sparked widespread criticism, cynicism and outright outrage in some quarters of how irresponsible the announcement was perceived to be (BBC 2020b). This drew a sharp response from

African governments in support of the remedy, indicating that the whole world was seeking a cure and it could come from anywhere, Africa included. This move while applauded, smells of hypocrisy as many of the same African governments do not recognize traditional medicine in their own countries, do not promote or regulate it preferring to adopt a loudly passive approach (BBC 2020b).

The response by the western countries though not condoned by many is neither new nor wild. WHO encouraged the development of remedies to coronavirus from all parts of the world, but not surprisingly is working with a European company to prove the efficacy of the Madagascar medicinal plant (CGTN Africa 2020), leaving questions on the extent of knowledge in Africa and its researchers. Once again traditional healers will question the rationale of testing their knowledge in a different knowledge system which does not at the least acknowledge their intelligence.

Final thoughts

Western countries fund researches as part of research and development to advance the gathering of knowledge to build their economies, create wealth and jobs. They facilitate bilateral agreements with many countries especially in Africa to facilitate research and development with most of the funding coming in as foreign direct investment (Oxfam International 2015). Knowledge in the health sector is gathered through clinical trials, studying trends of diseases and health systems, optimizing the knowledge for local use and for export, with African countries being a lucrative market for Western medicinal products.

Studies have shown that adoption of human rights treaties, changes the behaviour of state parties, i.e. the adoption of CRC by member states may have reduced the infant mortality rates of children under 5 from 1 to 2 per 1000 live births. Countries should therefore strive towards the adoption of such international instruments (Reinbold 2019). In addition to the adherence to the international conventions, governments should not consider public safety as being superior to individual rights in all cases. They should first protect the individual autonomy (i.e. informed consent) than the common good of society (i.e., public health protection through obligatory vaccinations). There should also be a guarantee that the government or manufacturers take responsibility of any aftermaths as opposed to citizens being forced to take that responsibility after the coerced vaccination (Zagaja *et al.* 2018). As more testing is done in Africa, it is necessary to build capacity in both vaccine testing and vaccine development. This will decrease the cost of interventions and also create job opportunities in Africa. Progress is underway to set up such facilities in Tanzania, Kenya and Ghana (Idoko *et al.* 2013).

African leaders have a responsibility to guard against the abuse of human rights of their citizens. Human rights abuses are extensively defined in different International instruments. If African leaders fail to consent to the testing of COVID-19, they contravene a number of these international instruments that guarantee a right to life and proper healthcare. The instruments that grant such rights are the CCPR, UDHR, CRC and CPD. The same instruments also expect the leaders to guard against human rights abuses. In the same instruments, the citizens need to be treated with dignity and should not be subjected to any inhuman treatment that will dehumanize them in anyway. This includes being subjected to experiments and projects that are done without their informed consent. The views from Africa and African leaders, including the WHO representatives (Director General), is that Africa should not be looked at as a laboratory, and that the suggestion that Africa should be a testing ground for COVID-19 vaccine is demeaning, false and above all, racist (BBC 2020b). The African leaders have a responsibility to protect their population from such hideous conspiracies.

History is laced with cases of unethical practices in Africa during the acquisition of knowledge by foreign companies and researchers, with the continent being largely relegated to providing study subjects who bear the brunt of long-term side effects. This was the case at the turn of the 19th century and if the events of the current clinical trials on COVID-19 are anything to go by, the situation has largely remained the same. Current scientific development of the COVID-19 vaccine is done in the Western countries and Africa is only supplying candidates for clinical trials (BBC 2020c). While this is a good practice which ensures that the African population is taken into account, the practice does not ensure that the continent is wholly taken into account as knowledge, vaccine ownership and patents are still resident with the developers of vaccines eventually providing little capacity building for the continent. This continued status quo and unresolved political colonial issues fuel mistrust between Africa and the western countries as recently witnessed during the pre-trial phase of the COVID-19 vaccine.

Conclusion

The west is also not keen to quickly embrace inventions from Africa, opting to cast a suspicious look and at times outright rejection of African inventions. This view is not made easy by some African governments which do not promote their own knowledge systems in human health, preferring to watch them play second fiddle to western medicine despite those in government and health practitioners using traditional medicine themselves. The recent stance by African countries to throw their weight behind Madagascar while laudable, is a far cry from being a panacea to bridging the knowledge gap and exploitation of knowledge. While the majority of African countries are signatories to countless declarations and conventions on health, health systems on the continent have remained an eyesore facing continued underfunding, dilapidation, human resource flight and a perennial inability to support its own population. In the majority of cases, African health systems rely on funding from multilateral organizations such as WHO and other development partners to supplement their national budgets and be able to run crucial programmes thus remaining vulnerable to external influence. The propensity of African governments to underfund their health systems, ignore their rich knowledge systems and failure to grow them while providing their subjects as candidates for knowledge accumulation to western researchers is not only legendary, but rather unfortunate.

References

Aljazeera (2020a, May 14). 'Coronavirus vaccine should be 'free of charge for all'. Retrieved from https://www.aljazeera.com/news/2020/05/coronavirus-vaccine-free-charge-200514115146359.html?xif=.

Aljazeera (2020, June 12) 'Coronavirus pandemic exposes South Africa's 'brutal inequalities'. Retrieved from https://www.aljazeera.com/news/2020/06/coronavirus-pandemic-exposes-south-africa-brutal-inequality-200612161408571.html.

Amusan, L. (2016) 'Politics of biopiracy: An adventure into Hoodia/Xhoba patenting in Southern Africa', *African journal of traditional, complementary, and alternative medicines : AJTCAM, 14*(1), 103–109. https://doi.org/10.21010/ajtcam.v14i1.11.

Angu, P.E. (2018) 'Disrupting western epistemic hegemony in South African universities: Curriculum decolonization, social justice, and agency in post- apartheid South Africa', *International Journal of Learner Diversity and Identities, 25(1)*. doi: 10.18848/2327-0128/CGP/v25i01/9-22.

Barrett, A. (2016) 'Vaccinology in the twenty-first century', *npj Vaccines, 1*, 16009. Retrieved from https://doi.org/10.1038/npjvaccines.2016.9.

BBC (2020a, January 17) 'Fake drugs: How bad is Africa's counterfeit medicine problem?' Retrieved from https://www.bbc.com/news/world-africa-51122898.

BBC (2020b, May 12) 'Coronavirus: Madagascar President Rajoelina hits out at tonic 'detractors'. Retrieved from https://www.bbc.com/news/world-africa-52633630.

BBC (2020c, May 18) 'Coronavirus: Why Africans should take part in vaccine trials'. Retrieved from https://www.bbc.com/news/world-africa-52678741.

Bhatt A. (2010) 'Evolution of clinical research: a history before and beyond james lind', *Perspectives in clinical research, 1*(1), 6–10.

CGTN Africa (2020, May 15) 'Madagascar's COVID-19 drink undergoes testing in Germany'. Retrieved from https://africa.cgtn.com/2020/05/15/madagascars-covid-19-drink-undergoes-testing-in-germany/.

Ciolli A. (2008) 'Mandatory school vaccinations: the role of tort law', *The Yale journal of biology and medicine, 81*(3), 129–137.

CNN (2020, May 31) 'The real cost of Trump's WHO pullout', Retrieved from https://edition.cnn.com/2020/05/31/opinions/world-health-organization-trump-termination-naili/index.html.

Daily Nation (2018, April 5). 'Parents of paralysed children yet to get Sh40m payout'. Retrieved from https://www.nation.co.ke/kenya/counties/busia/parents-of-paralysed-children-yet-to-get-sh40m-payout-29458.

Financial Times (2019, August 26) 'Debate over vaccination strategies dogs Ebola efforts in Congo'. Retrieved from https://www.ft.com/content/02c671c0-b799-11e9-96bd-8e884d3ea203.

Gauri, V. (2011) 'The cost of complying with human rights treaties: The convention on the rights of the child and basic immunization', *Rev Int Organ 6*, 33–56. Retrieved from https://doi.org/10.1007/s11558-010-9100-7.

GeoCurrents (2011, May 17) 'Inequality Trends in South Africa'. Retrieved from http://www.geocurrents.info/economic-geography/inequality-trends-in-south-africa.

Idoko, O. T., Kochhar, S., Agbenyega, T. E., Ogutu, B., and Ota, M. O. (2013) 'Impact, challenges, and future projections of vaccine trials in Africa', *The American journal of tropical medicine and hygiene, 88*(3), 414–419. Retrieved from https://doi.org/10.4269/ajtmh.12-0576.

Immunization in Africa (2016) 'Ministerial Conference on immunization in Africa'. Retrieved from http://immunizationinafrica2016.org/immunization-in-africa.

International Crisis Group (2019, June 14) 'A tale of two councils: Strengthening AU-UN Cooperation'. Retrieved from https://www.crisisgroup.org/africa/279-tale-two-councils-strengthening-au-un-cooperation.

IOM UN Migration (2020, July 24) 'COVID-19 testing for truck drivers helps open trade in IOM-TMEA partnership'. Retrieved from https://www.iom.int/news/covid-19-testing-truck-drivers-helps-open-trade-iom-tmea-partnership.

Khair, Z. (2003) 'The world-class university of Sankore', *Timbuktu in MuslimHeritage.com*; 5 June 2003. Retrieved from http://www.muslimheritage.com/topics/default.cfm?ArticleID =371.

Leclerc, C. (2007) 'L'apport des nouvelles technologies en vaccinologie', [New technologies for vaccine development]. *Medecine sciences: M/S, 23*(4), 386–390. https://doi.org/10.1051/medsci/2007234386.

Lowes, S. and Montero, E. (2020) 'The legacy of colonial medicine in Central Africa'. Retrieved from https://scholar.harvard.edu/files/slowes/files/lowes_montero_colonialmedicine.pdf.

Lunt, N., Smith, R. D., Mannion, R., Green, S. T., Exworthy, M., Hanefeld, J., Horsfall, D., Machin, L., and King, H. (2014) 'Implications for the NHS of inward and outward medical tourism: a policy and economic analysis using literature review and mixed-methods approaches'. *NIHR Journals Library*.

Retrieved from
https://www.ncbi.nlm.nih.gov/books/NBK263147/.

Lurie, N., Saville, M., Hatchett, R. and Halton, J. (2020) 'Developing Covid-19 Vaccines at Pandemic Speed', *New England Journal of Medicine, 382*, 1969-1973 doi: 10.1056/NEJMp2005630.

Mahomoodally, F.M., (2013) 'Traditional Medicines in Africa: An Appraisal of Ten Potent African Medicinal Plants', *Evidence-based complementary and alternative medicine*. Retrieved from doi.org/10.1155/2013/617459.

Mhatre, S.L., Schryer-Roy, A. (2009) 'The fallacy of coverage: uncovering disparities to improve immunization rates through evidence. Results from the Canadian International Immunization Initiative Phase 2 - Operational Research Grants', *BMC Int Health Hum Rights*9, S1. Retrieved from https://doi.org/10.1186/1472-698X-9-S1-S1.

Mokgobi, M.G. (2013) 'Towards integration of traditional healing and western healing: Is this a remote possibility?' *African journal for physical health education, recreation, and dance, 2013*(Suppl 1), 47–57.

Mukesi, M., Iweriebor, B.C., Obi, L.C., Nwodo, U.U., Moyo, S.R. and Okoh, A.I. (2019) 'The activity of commercial antimicrobials, and essential oils and ethanolic extracts of Olea europaea on Streptococcus agalactiae isolated from pregnant women', *BMC Complementary and Alternative Medicine, 19(1)*:34. doi:10.1186/s12906-019-2445-4.

Obradovic, Z., Balta, S., Obradovic, A. and Mesic, S. (2014) 'The impact of war on vaccine preventable diseases', *Materia socio-medica, 26*(6), 382–384. Retrieved from https://doi.org/10.5455/msm.2014.26.382-384.

Oxfam International (2015, June 1) 'Multinational companies cheat Africa out of billions of dollars'. Retrieved from https://www.oxfam.org/en/press-releases/multinational-companies-cheat-africa-out-billions-dollars.

Reinbold, G.W. (2019) 'Effects of the convention on the rights of a child on child mortality and vaccination rates: a synthetic control analysis', *BMC international health and human rights 19(1)*, 24.

Riedel, S. (2005) 'Edward Jenner and the history of smallpox and vaccination', *Proceedings (Baylor University. Medical Center), 18*(1), 21–25. Retrieved from https://doi.org/10.1080/08998280.2005.11928028.

Saki, K., Shahsavari, S., Rafieian-Kopaei, M., Sepahvand, R. and Adineh, A. (2015) 'Identification of medicinal plants effective in infectious diseases in Urmia, northwest of Iran', *Asian Pacific Journal of Tropical Biomedicine*, 5, 858-864.

Shehata, S.M., ElMashad, N.M., and Hassan, A.M. (2017) 'Current Review of Medical Research in Developing Countries: A Case Study from Egypt, International Development', *IntechOpen*. doi: 10.5772/67282.

The East African (2020, May 20) 'Ghosts of (colonial) Vaccines past: Why East Africans shun clinical trials'. Retrieved from https://www.theeastafrican.co.ke/scienceandhealth/Why-East-Africans-shun-clinical-trials/3073694-5557296-rydn28z/index.html.

The New York Times (2007, July 31) 'Why Africa fears Western Medicine.. Retrieved from https://www.nytimes.com/2007/07/31/opinion/31washington.html.

Tiley, H. (2016) 'Medicine, Empires, and Ethics in Colonial Africa'. Retrieved from https://journalofethics.ama-assn.org/article/medicine-empires-and-ethics-colonial-africa/2016-07.

Tung, T., Zacharias, A., Arun, K., Raúl, G., Stig, T., and Stephen, M. (2020) 'The COVID-19 vaccine development landscape', *Nature Reviews Drug Discovery, 19*, 305-306. doi: 10.1038/d41573-020-00073-5.

UNESCO (2019) 'Indigenous Knowledge and Science Policy'. Retrieved from https://en.unesco.org/links-policy.

United Nations (2020, May 4) 'Investing in cultural diversity and intercultural dialogue'. Retrieved from https://www.un.org/en/events/culturaldiversityday/pdf/Investing_in_cultural_diversity.pdf.

University of Oxford (2020, June 28) 'Trial of Oxford COVID-19 vaccine starts in Brazil'. Retrieved from http://www.ox.ac.uk/news/2020-06-28-trial-oxford-covid-19-vaccine-starts-brazil.

USCSchaeffer (2017, July 11) 'The tension between traditional and western medicine'. Retrieved from https://healthpolicy.usc.edu/evidence-base/the-tension-between-traditional-and-western-medicine/.

WHO (2010) 'Monitoring the building blocks of health systems: A handbook of indicators and their measurement strategies'. Retrieved from https://www.who.int/healthinfo/systems/WHO_MBHSS_201 0_full_web.pdf.

WHO (2014, April) 'Principles and considerations for adding a vaccine to a national immunization programme: from decision to implementation and monitoring'. Retrieved June 23, 2020 from https://apps.who.int/iris/bitstream/handle/10665/111548/978 9241506892_eng.pdf?sequence=1.

WHO (2015) 'Traditional medicine, Regional Office for Africa'. Retrieved from https://www.afro.who.int/health-topics/traditional-medicine.

WHO (2017, September 1) 'Sixty-seventh session of the WHO Regional Committee for Africa'. Retrieved from https://www.afro.who.int/about-us/governance/sessions/sixty-seventh-session-who-regional-committee-africa.

WHO (2019a) 'Programme budget'. Retrieved from https://open.who.int/2018-19/contributors/contributor.

WHO (2019b, May 23) 'Vaccines and Diseases'. Retrieved from https://www.who.int/immunization/diseases/en/.

WHO (2019c, December 6) 'Immunization coverage'. Retrieved from https://www.who.int/news-room/fact-sheets/detail/immunization-coverage.

WHO (2020a) 'Immunization Agenda 2030: A Global Strategy to Leave No One Behind'. Retrieved from https://www.who.int/immunization/immunization_agenda_203 0/en/.

WHO (2020b, April 4) 'COVID-19 Solidarity Responses Fund for WHO'. Retrieved from https://covid19responsefund.org/en/.

WHO (2020c, June 23) 'Coronavirus Disease (COVID-19) Dashboard'. Retrieved from https://covid19.who.int/.

WHO (2020d, August 20) 'Draft landscape of COVID-19 candidate vaccines'. Retrieved from https://www.who.int/publications/m/item/draft-landscape-of-covid-19-candidate-vaccines.

World Bank (2007) 'Building Knowledge Economies: Advanced Strategies for Development', *WBI Development Studies*. Washington, DC: World Bank. Retrieved from https://openknowledge.worldbank.org/handle/10986/6853.

World Bank (2013, September 4) 'The Global Burden of Disease: Main Findings for sub Saharan Africa'. Retrieved from https://www.worldbank.org/en/region/afr/publication/global-burden-of-disease-findings-for-sub-saharan-africa.

Yuan, H., Ma, Q., Ye, L. and Piao, G. (2016) 'The Traditional Medicine and Modern Medicine from Natural Products', *Molecules (Basel, Switzerland)*, *21*(5), 559. Retrieved from https://doi.org/10.3390/molecules21050559.

Zagaja, A., Patryn, R., Pawlikowski, J. and Sak, J. (2018) 'Informed Consent in Obligatory Vaccinations?' *Medical science monitor: international medical journal of experimental and clinical research*, *24*, 8506–8509. Retrieved from https://doi.org/10.12659/MSM.910393.

Chapter Four

COVID-19 and Southern Africa Development Community (SADC): A Litmus Test for Regional Solidarity

Aaron Rwodzi

Introduction

The whole world at the time of writing, is facing a novel situation of the COVID-19 pandemic with limited remedial alternatives. For this reason, the World Health Organisation (WHO) declared the coronavirus disease (COVID-19) outbreak a pandemic on 11 March 2020. COVID-19 is the shortened version of 'corona virus disease' that originated in China in 2019. African countries were the last to experience the devastating effects of coronavirus on human lives, yet the continent is likely to face widespread economic fallout as business slows to a near halt due to governments' lockdown regulations that are meant to contain its spread. This chapter evaluates Southern Africa Development Community (SADC) countries' responses to the corona virus pandemic after many death cases were first recorded in the Chinese province of Wuhan in 2019. It argues that SADC member states took impulsive, individualistic and uncoordinated measures to deal with the deadly pandemic, with consequences for regional economic, social, political and military solidarity. This study serves as a litmus test for SADC's unity of purpose and can equally increase the capacity of states in southern Africa to adopt, in unison, effective and timely disaster response mechanisms in order to save human lives from devastating natural phenomena of a similar kind in future.

This chapter also has the novelty of exposing the challenges that the poor countries in SADC have in procuring testing equipment and providing accurate statistical figures of COVID-19 victims in their reportage. The argument is based on an analysis of border restrictions and porosity, deportations and their xenophobic tendencies especially coming from South African Black communities, *ad hoc* policy (in)consistencies by SADC governments in or out of line with WHO prescriptions and restrictions, in terms of preparedness;

coordination; preparation and monitoring; oversight; case investigation; prevention and control of infections; water , sanitation and hygiene (WASH); communication of threats and community participation, as well as advice to schools , workplaces and institutions (SADC Secretariat April 2020). The chapter also discusses the efficacy of sanctions especially on Zimbabwe in the COVID-19 era with a clear focus on covid(ised) political rivalries, the limited democratic space for dissenting voices in the pandemic era and the renewed conflict in Mozambique between Islamic insurgents and government troops against the backdrop of the pandemic. Because COVID-19 is a contemporary phenomenon, the methodological approach in this chapter is underpinned by a qualitative analysis of data collected through observation, focus group discussions, desk research including SADC Secretariat bulletins, webinars and Zoom meetings.

The term 'pandemic' usually refers to diseases that extend over large geographic spaces as highlighted by WHO's standard definition of pandemic. It refers to a situation in which a new and highly pathogenic viral subtype, one to which no one (or few) in the human population has immunological resistance and which is easily transmissible between humans, establishes a foothold in the human population, at which point it rapidly spreads worldwide (WHO 2011a). The word is commonly taken to refer to a widespread epidemic of contagious disease throughout the whole country or across continents at the same time (Honigsbaum 2009). Some of the key features of a pandemic are the wide geographical extension, rapid movement of pathogens, innovation, intensity, high attack rates and explosiveness, limited population immunity, infectiousness and contagiousness are its broad geographic extension (Gewald 2007). Therefore, a pandemic is categorized as trans-regional and global (Taubenberger & Morens 2009) and has the capacity to threaten all aspects of the economic and social fabric (Drake, Chalabi, & Coker 2012).

The most popular pandemic to have destabilized world economies was the influenza of 1918-1919 as Gewald (2007: 8) notes: "...the Spanish flu that circulated in 1918-19 was a direct killer. Victims suffered from acute cyanosis, a blue discoloration of the skin and mucous membranes. They vomited and coughed up blood, which also poured uncontrollably from their noses and, in the case of women, from their genitals. By comparative standards, what later became known as Spanish flu could have been more severe and infectious than COVID-19 because of its disrepute in terms of the number of lives it claimed globally: it caused about 50 million deaths worldwide (Taubenberger & Morens 2009; Mahmoud, et al. 2011; Phillips 2018: 2). In order to secure information regarding the best-known methods of combating influenza, prominent sanitarians are said to have begun with this advice: 'When you get back home, hunt up your wood-workers and cabinet makers and set them to make coffins. Then take your street labourers and set them to digging graves. If you do this, you will not have your dead accumulating faster than you can dispose of them' (Hobday & Cason 2009: 787).

In practical terms, the statement above was so important in the sense that it proffered immediacy to problem-solving especially once a pandemic hit society. This was so particularly when, in the United States of America (USA), many grave diggers were already suffering from the disease and so could not keep up with the demand for burials (Hobday & Cason 2009). To curb the spread of flu infections in the USA, the government banned public assembly, closed schools, isolated the infected and mandated the wearing of surgical masks (*Ibid.*). Hobday and Cason (2009) reflect on the open-air method as another strategy in England that was devised by the English physician, John Coakley Lettsom (1744-1815). Hobday and Cason (2009) further observe that the reasoning behind this strategy was that a combination of fresh air, sunlight, scrupulous standards of hygiene, and reusable face masks would substantially reduce deaths among some patients and infections among medical staff. Here, sick people were put outside in tents or specially designed open wards (Strange 1991), reminiscent of quarantine centres in the COVID-19 era, where they would either wait to recover or die helplessly. Children were the objects of experimentation in this open-air therapy (Strange 1991). What is of interest to the researcher is the fact that the British Prime Minister, Boris Johnson, proposed the same strategy when COVID-19 hit this islandic country in 2020 but was overwhelmed by those who felt otherwise. Interestingly, he became a corona virus victim himself who fortunately recuperated in hospital after having been hospitalized in the Intensive Care Unit (ICU) for some time.

John Oxford, a prominent researcher on the pandemic, noted that although there was agreement that the name 'Spanish Influenza' was unsuitable, the general conclusion is that the virus could have been designated (Oxford, et al. 1999: 1352). Estimates are that 50% of the South African population contracted Spanish flu in one month: it killed about 300 000 South Africans and this translated to 6% of the South African population especially working adults between 18 – 40 years (David Whitehouse, no date). For example, as put by Oxford *et al.* (1999), the De Beers Mining Company in South Africa resorted to mass company graves due to limited space. Whites blamed the spread of Spanish flu on Africans for which reason they called for a ban on Blacks from trains and inter-racial contact sports such as soccer, rugby among others to prevent transmission. In South Africa still, the epidemic led to "renewed 'sanitation syndrome' fears by white residents that infection was spread by black inhabitants," and gave further weight to calls for legally enforced racial segregation" (Worden 1994: 43). In outlining the development of segregationist legislation on colour or racial lines, and the Natives Urban Areas Act in particular, the great historian of South Africa, De Kiewiet (1941: 231) noted, "…the influenza epidemic horribly revealed the disease and misery which was bred and sheltered in windowless shacks and congested unsanitary backyards". Such racialized and derogatory speeches by colonial historians helped to heighten the African marginalization agenda by White supremacists in the pretext of flu control. Conversely, Africans believed the disease was a White plot to exterminate them and that European hospitals and vaccines had to be avoided at any cost (Whitehead, n.d.).

Spanish flu that wreaked havoc in the world during the course of World War 1 (WW1) became a major subject of scholarly attention even up to now. Phimister (1973: 143-148) describes how the Spanish influenza literally ended the productive life in the mining industry in Southern Rhodesia. Because of the severity of Spanish flu at a time production at mines had to continue to sustain the affected economy, priority was given to the well-being of the Black mining workforce. Management of Globe and Phoenix mine near the town of Que Que in Southern Rhodesia employed White nurses to take care of Black patients (van Onselen 1976: 58). Ranger cited in Simmons (2009: 32) also notes that in Southern Rhodesia the influenza epidemic led to a crisis of comprehension. This background of pandemics and epidemics that have inflicted a lot of human suffering through ages serves to inform our understanding of the COVID-19 pandemic which, however, caught the whole world off guard. It also helps us to critique the level of nation states' preventative innovativeness in this modern era of Science and to argue that no scientific breakthroughs are worth talking about as the same old traditional remediation methodologies have remained key to dealing with the COVID-19 pandemic.

Almost a hundred years after the Spanish flu pandemic, in 2020, the world witnessed the emergence of a new, viral, zoonotic pathogen (SARS-CoV2) causing an outbreak of coronavirus disease 2019 (COVID-19) (Rodriguez-Morales, et al. 2020). The WHO, on account of the high mortality and morbidity rates in China and then Spain, Italy and the United States of America (USA), was compelled to declare a Public Health Emergency of International Concern (PHEIC) (Rodríguez-Morales et al. 2020). In the early month of 2020, that is, from January to March, very few cases of COVID-19 infection were recorded in Egypt and Algeria first before all other African countries began to release data on corona virus victims to the public. The paucity of cases reported in Africa in the early stages of its detection on the continent is very likely the result of a lack of diagnostic resources (Gilbert, Pullano, Pinotti, et al. 2020). This spirit of denial commandeered by African leaders themselves allowed complacency to creep in. The President of Burundi, Pirre Nkurunziza, after having denied the existence of COVID-19, and having ignored WHO regulations regarding its mitigation and containment, succumbed to the same on 9 June 2020 (Burke 2020). It would appear that when reality dawned on African countries, when the myth that corona virus was a pandemic that targeted whites was strongly dispelled, and as more cases of infection particularly in South Africa increased, individual SADC countries reacted in predictable fashion by complying with WHO standards for its containment. In any case, there apparently was no regional blueprint for COVID-19 containment and mitigation beyond the old-age non-pharmaceutical intervention measures such as social distancing and quarantine. It was later during the year 2020 that SADC leaders began to contemplate a coordinated approach to COVID-19 mitigation, notwithstanding a broad array of challenges that were likely to affect the implementation of a new development paradigm since the disease was not likely to disappear early enough.

SADC regional response to COVID-19 pandemic

The policy initiatives adopted by policy makers around the world to handle the spread of COVID-19 can be categorized into five categories: public health initiatives; monetary measures; fiscal measures; travel and human control measures; and trade measures

(SADC Secretariat bulletin April 2020, No. 1: 6). This section is a synopsis of measures at a theoretical level by SADC countries in response to COVID-19 using the SADC Secretariat bulletins issued periodically during the pandemic era. Angola, Botswana, the Union of Comoros, the Democratic Republic of the Congo, Eswatini, Lesotho, Madagascar, Mozambique, Malawi, Mauritius, Namibia, Seychelles, South Africa, Zambia, Zimbabwe and the Independent Republic of Tanzania are the member states that constitute SADC. The measures are evaluated against what selected individual countries within SADC, such as South Africa, Zimbabwe, Lesotho and Zambia did and continue to do in order to minimise the impacts of COVID-19. The testing ability of COVID-19 remains limited on the African continent, including the SADC region, due to procurement challenges emanating from bankruptcy by governments, a handicap with a strong bearing on authenticity of the number of cases that countries are reporting. The outbreak of COVID-19 and its devastating effects on livelihoods seem to have exacerbated the situation of SADC countries, eroding community coping capacities and deepening food and nutrition insecurity of vulnerable households and individuals (SADC Secretariat bulletin No. 2: 2). The Secretariat also noted that with the lockout and stay-at - home steps, women who have been in abusive marriages, are now forced for a long time to be at home with their abusers, and that due to the disruption of public services and restricted access to contact infrastructure such as phones and helplines, the COVID-19 pandemic has made reporting of violations harder. (SADC Secretariat bulletin No. 2: 3). Adoption during the COVID-19 pandemic of the SADC Guidelines on Harmonization and Facilitation of Movement of Essential Goods and Services across Borders seemed problematic as the member states found it difficult and almost impossible to follow and aligning them with their national laws and procedures. In the framework of COVID-19, SADC and the United Nations Educational, Scientific and Cultural Organisation (UNESCO) established an Action Plan to ensure continuity of learning (SADC Secretariat bulletin No. 2: 3). The SADC Secretariat-Partnership with UNESCO focused making on distance learning for all learners at all levels possible (SADC Secretariat Bulletin No. 2: 4).

An initiative has also been announced by the Africa Centre for Disease Control (CDC) to scale up research known as "Partnership to Accelerate COVID-19 Testing." The aim of the initiative is to distribute one million test kits in four weeks and 10 million test kits in 24 weeks for Member States in the region of Africa (SADC Secretariat bulletin No. 3: 3). Many countries agreed to minimize disruption to household livelihoods and national economies, hence social security packages are extended to vulnerable communities adversely impacted by lockdowns and some lockdown restrictions are relaxed (SADC Secretariat bulletin, No. 3: 3). The same bulletin also provides an overview of progress on the implementation of COVID-19 decisions of the SADC Council, including efforts by Member States to conform to current legislation and regulations with the Regional Guidelines on the Harmonisation and Facilitation of Cross-Border Transport Operations across the Region (Ibid. SADC Secretariat bulletin, No. 3). The feedback was that case and cluster investigation and COVID-19 surveillance should be intensified by Member States. It was noted that as clusters get high, critical testing of suspicious instances continued in such instances, could be isolated, contacts quarantined, and chains of transmission broken (SADC Secretariat bulletin, No. 3: 3). Mass testing remains an essential component of the COVID-19 response and this, to be successful, is dependent largely on the financial capacities of individual member states within SADC to procure the equipment. It would appear that because of the fiscal constraints on most SADC member states, only South Africa embarked on mass testing, hence its highest number of COVID-19 victims not only in southern Africa, but also continentally and worldwide. Other countries that are severely handicapped did not start mass testing and this suggests that there was and still is no uniform implementation strategy in the SADC member states. Testing is one of the "effective ways of preventing diseases and saving lives by breaking the transmission chain through testing suspicious groups, according to the WHO" (SADC Secretariat bulletin, No. 3: 6). It was for this reason that the SADC Secretariat noted with serious concern that difficult decisions would have to be made to balance the criteria of reacting directly to COVID-19, whilst at the same time participating in strategic preparation and concerted action to ensure the delivery of critical health services, minimizing the risk of system collapse would need to make difficult decisions to balance the demands of responding directly to COVID-19, while simultaneously engaging in strategic planning and coordinated action to maintain essential health service delivery, mitigating the risk of system collapse (SADC Secretariat bulletin, No. 3).

The Eastern and Southern Africa Common Market (COMESA) established in 1994 and headquartered in Lusaka, Zambia, has 21 members. The East African Community (EAC) also appears to rival SADC whilst some members overlap as to be members of all the three regional economic groupings. SADC has had challenges in this regard as the three associations need to harmonize their approaches to regulation of transport during COVID-19 emergency (SADC Secretariat bulletin No. 4: 3). The Africa Centre for Disease Management and Prevention got from the Jack Ma Foundation and the Alibaba Foundation in Addis Ababa, Ethiopia, a third donation of medical equipment and supplies (SADC Secretariat bulletin, No. 4: 3). The Jack Ma Foundation in collaboration with Africa CDC held a special webinar on Tuesday 28 April 2020 entitled 'World MediXChange for Fighting COVID-19 (GMCC): China's Experience' (SADC Secretariat bulletin, No. 4). This was done in order to share expertise, experience and best practices for COVID-19 care by medical experts from Africa, China and other parts of the world. The Non-Tariff Barrierr 000-951, registered against Zambia's mandatory quarantine policy, remained unresolved for all incoming drivers and vehicles, including drivers carrying critical and perishable cargo (SADC Secretariat bulletin No. 4: 6) for a very long time and this testifies to lack of proper regional coordination by Member States. NTB 000-949 reported against Mozambique for the suspension of the issuance of visas to commercial truck drivers also remained unresolved and had a negative effect on Member States using the Beira port (SADC Secretariat bulletin, No. 4). In the Democratic Republic of the Congo (DRC), Lubumbashi and Kasumbablesa were put under lockdown on 28 and 29 April, respectively, after the first positive case was registered in the provincial capital (SADC Secretariat bulletin, No. 4). In terms of SADC guidelines and stated objectives on the harmonisation and facilitation of activities for cross-border transport, cross-border transportation across borders during the lockdown would not stop (SADC Secretariat bulletin No. 4:6). It was announced that cross-border transport drivers in Malawi went on strike demanding the supply of personal protective equipment (PPE) and the payment of COVID-19 risk allowance payments (SADC Secretariat bulletin No. 4). It was claimed that the striking drivers threatened to block foreign trucks from entering Malawi before their demands were met (SADC Secretariat bulletin, No. 4). As a result of the sudden drop in transport demand due to factories, mines and trade closures under lockdown measures, a number of transport companies are reported to be laying off staff and going into liquidation. The restructuring of the airline industry especially in the hardest hit South Africa, as a result of the COVID-19 pandemic, seems to be unavoidable.

Another SADC Secretariat Bulletin number 6 also presents the impact of COVID-19 on value chains, with emphasis on the fisheries and aquaculture value chain. On 22 May 2020, the meeting of Ministers responsible for Agriculture, Food Security and Fisheries and Aquaculture was held (SADC Secretariat bulletin No. 6: 2). In principle, the ministers decided on the continued implementation of the SADC Guidelines on the facilitation of cross-border transport with a focus on the adoption of harmonized test protocols, including the mutual acceptance of test results and the consensus on the validity of the test result duration (SADC Secretariat bulletin No. 6: 3). Cross-border transport is one of the vital services that must be preserved and supported throughout the COVID-19 cycle to ensure that vital supplies and goods are provided in a timely manner in Member States. The lockdowns associated with COVID-19 in the Member States and the related public health interventions have resulted in substantial delays in the movement of vehicles and consequently in the supply of critical supplies to the point of use. Good practice in cross border transportation was shown by Botswana and Zambia when they engaged in joint clearance collaboration at Kazungula on one hand and DRC and Zambia at Kasumbalesa on the other (SADC Secretariat bulletin, No. 6: 6). The Expanded Technical Committee on Health met in June 2020 to finalise the revised Regional Guidelines on Harmonisation and Facilitation of Cross Border Transport Operations across the region and the Regional Standard Operating Procedures (SOPs) for Management and Monitoring of Cross Border Road Transport at Designated Points of Entry and COVID-19 Checkpoints (SADC Secretariat bulletin No. 6). The Secretariat explored the possibility of tapping into global resources to assist member states in mitigating COVID-19's socio-economic consequences (SADC Secretariat bulletin No. 6: 6). The issue of tapping into global resources was problematic in the case of Zimbabwe in the sense that its relations with the western world were bad and the country's leaders including President Mnangagwa are still under US sanctions which have since 2002 made Zimbabwe not creditworthy and isolated. In any case, Zimbabwe's global resources here referred to COVID-19 related assistance from China and the fleet of buses from Belarus to be used to ferry commuters to work at subsidized transport fares.

For years to come, the SADC region has faced a dual public health and economic crisis with risks overwhelming healthcare systems, damaging livelihoods and scarring the economic prospects of the region. (SADC Secretariat bulletin No. 7: 5). COVID-19's economic effect is based on factors that are difficult to forecast. These include the evolution of the pandemic, the severity and effectiveness of containment measures, the degree of supply disruptions, the impact of drastic tightening in the conditions of the financial system, shifts in purchasing habits, behavioural adjustments (such as people avoiding crowded places like shopping malls and public transport), trust effects and volatile commodity prices (SADC Secretariat bulletin No. 7). As pointed out by the WHO Guidelines, the overlap of membership in the Common Market for East and Southern Africa (COMESA), the East African Community (EAC) and SADC continues to pose harmonization challenges to the COVID-19 guidelines. SADC, on behalf of the Tripartite Regional Economic Communities of COMESA, EAC and SADC and the delegation of the European Union to Botswana and SADC have signed addendum for additional services to the Tripartite Facilitation Program on Transport and Transit (TTTFP) for the development and implementation of the Corridor Trip Monitoring System (CTMS) in East and Southern African regional transport corridors (SADC Secretariat bulletin No. 7).

Ideas by SADC as presented in the periodic bulletins depended so much on a number of issues for them to be effective at a practical level. They were a nice display of ideas and quite sound, but circumstances on the ground compromised SADC's collective efforts to rise to the occasion and swiftly deal with the pandemic (Transparency International 2020). Common among SADC states were allegations of fraudulent behaviour by people in responsible positions to show transparency in procurement and disbursement of COVID-19 related funds and PPEs, the politicisation of the pandemic which characteristically eroded people's rights. Worst scenarios appeared in Zimbabwe, for example, where a quasi-military Zimbabwe African National Union Patriotic Front (ZANU-PF) government enjoyed unchallengeable solace in the realms of power in an environment obfuscated by the pandemic discourse.

Tourism and leisure, aviation and maritime, automotive, building and real estate, engineering, financial services, education and the oil industry are industries that have been severely impacted by COVID-19 policy initiatives (SADC Secretariat bulletin April 2020 No. 1: 6). Such policies and interventions include the cessation of non-essential economic operations, increased expenditure on health and social welfare networks, accommodative taxation interventions, economic stimulus packages, accommodative monetary policies and the development of emergency / solidarity funds (SADC Secretariat bulletin April 2020 No. 1: 5). As such, due to resource constraints and inadequacies in health systems in many of the Member States, the socioeconomic impacts of COVID-19 in SADC may be unparalleled (SADC Secretariat bulletin April 2020). A number of steps have been taken by SADC Member States, including preparedness and response mechanisms; awareness programs such as suspension of inbound and outbound flights, suspension of business and tourism travel, establishment of border and in-country test centres; social distancing and cancellation of meetings; adoption of self-isolation and compulsory quarantines for a minimum of fourteen.

In response to COVID-19, ten organised regional measures taken by SADC are: disaster risk management; suspension of regional face-to - face meetings and instead; use of digital technologies such as video conferences; webinars and skype calls before the situation is contained; re-establishment and extension of the technical committee to organize and track the implementation of the protocols (SADC Secretariat bulletin, April 2020: 3). In order to provide sustainable access and access to affordable and efficient critical medicines and health items, the SADC Pooled Procurement Services for pharmaceuticals and medical supplies are being introduced to supervise the adoption of guidelines on harmonization and facilitation of cross-border transport operations across the region during the COVID-19 period, to maintain partnership with the United Nation (SADC Secretariat bulletin April 2020: 3).

Socio-political and Economic Regional Security under COVID-19

Mass relocation of migrants especially from South Africa and Botswana into countries such as Zimbabwe and Mozambique have usually smacked of xenophobic tendencies The South African government constructed a 40-kilometre fence on its northern border with Zimbabwe at the onset of the pandemic to curb further immigrants, yet according to Rugunanan (2016) traversing borders merely perpetuates undocumented border crossings. The Scalabrini Centre for Democracy intimates that the South African government's heavy-handed efforts to deal with migrants, refugee reception offices that either closed or stopped receiving asylum seekers and refugees, the police that shut down immigrant-owned shops together took away the rights and dignity of asylum seekers (Rugunanan (2016). These measures implied that migrants could not renew their asylum permits and receive healthcare resulting in their bank accounts getting frozen. Migrants flowing from Botswana into Zimbabwe using the Plumtree route have found themselves being 'detained' at the Botswana-Plumtree testing camp. The author uses 'detained' to show the unwillingness of returnees to be quarantined or isolated for a period of three weeks when the urge to re-join with family members back home was so high. Statistical information as of 7 July 2020 states that over 10,800 migrants, including 5,982 men, 4,708 women and 196 children, have returned to Zimbabwe from neighbouring countries with the large majority of returnees, about 5,318, arriving through the points of entry of Beitbridge border post and 2,741 through Plumtree, Harare International airport recording 1,307 and Forbes Border Post, 646 (Zimbabwe Situation Report, 2020 July 10). Quite a number of returnees successfully evaded routes that would subject them to indiscriminate testing, isolation or quarantine. By 27 May 2020, a total of 118 returnees who were placed in isolation and quarantine centres countrywide sneaked out with the slightest opportunity and state authorities had to hunt them down with a view to bringing them back into the isolation camps with little success (The Herald, 2020: May 27). Given the phenomenal influx of returning migrants, the whole region's health security, amidst relentless medical shortages, was inevitably compromised. As for Zimbabwe, the situation of the returning migrants was compounded by the fact that the Beit-Bridge border post was used by all those returning from South Africa. Beit Bridge therefore became very convenient for testing for COVID-19 to the extent that health authorities could not cope with the large numbers. It can be argued that because of the congestion at the Beit Bridge border and the time taken for a returnee to be diagnosed, alternative routes to avoid the hassles were engineered, and as it later turned out, with The Zimbabwe National Army (ZNA), the Zimbabwe Republic Police (ZRP) and Municipal Police as accomplices who lined up their pockets with bribe money they solicited from returnees to allow them passage into Zimbabwe through illegal and makeshift entry points (Kubatana.net, 2020: May 25).

In line with the migrations that took place after the pandemic had spread to all South Africa's provinces, the Socialist Revolutionary Workers Party of South Africa argued against the steps that were likely to be taken to deal with the pandemic. It argued that COVID-19 worsens the crisis of capitalism with dramatic decline in economic activity resulting in increase in unemployment and the call by government officials for a "Put South Africans First" strategy to address the economic crisis (Socialist Revolutionary Workers Party, 2020: May 21). This opinion found expression in the Department of Labour's introduction of sector-specific job quotas to limit the number of migrants working in South Africa and the Minister of Finance, Tito Mboweni's argument for hiring more South Africans in a post lockdown economy (Socialist Revolutionary Workers Party, 2020: May 21). These pro-South African views somehow overlook the historical importance of migrant labour as fundamental in the creation of a colonially-driven capitalist economy. The COVID-19 pandemic aside, it must be remembered that African labour hired cheaply from Zimbabwe, Mozambique, Malawi, Namibia, Zambia and Angola among other countries in Sub-Saharan Africa generated wealth for the capitalists and helped to sustain a racist system that later translated into Apartheid based on ownership of wealth and power.

As the migrant phenomenon intensified across the porous borders, and as COVID-19 victims continued to be identified, there apparently appeared to be lack of accurate and responsible government reportage for various reasons that range from deliberate under-reportage to weak institutional testing capacity, is not only confined to the SADC region. Even when the Spanish flu decimated European populations between 1918 and 1919, governments are said to have falsified figures of flu casualties. Because of the scientific study and research carried out in Spain, the term "Spanish Flu" was wrongly identified, although the first appearance of the virus was made in the USA (Tsoucalas, Kousoulis & Sgantzos 2016). Europe was ravaged by the First World War in 1918, and Spain had all the time to deal with the disease and its effects as a neutral nation and claim the name. The most accurate scientific evidence for the disease came from Spain, giving the international community the false perception that Spain was the most affected country (Tsoucalas, Kousoulis & Sgantzos 2016).

In contrast with inaccurate reportage alluded to above, local health authorities in Japan during the COVID-19 pandemic are said to have been seriously monitoring the spread of COVID-19. These health authorities have been busy conducting contact tracing activities, active surveillance of severe acute respiratory diseases, and other epidemiological investigations because the country was adequately resourced to do so (Nishiura, Kobayashi, Yang, et al. 2020). One of the challenges in COVID-19 mitigation is the non-specific symptoms at early stages of COVID-19 compounded by the conspicuous absence of clear transmission links both of which are said to have defied conventional containment strategy by case isolation and contact quarantine (CCTV News 2020). This also suggests that at high socio-economic expense, China has adopted exceptional public health initiatives, moving rapidly and decisively to ensure early case detection, prompt laboratory testing, facility-based isolation of all cases, touch tracking, and quarantine because it has a functional health system (Wilder-Smith & Freedman 2020).

Mozambique represents a special test case of the region's ability and capability to act in unison if confronted by either internal or external threats to their avowed unity as SADC member states. The sudden upsurge of violence and renewed conflict masterminded by Islamic Insurgents in Carbo Delgado coincided with the COVID-19 pandemic. The cause of the instability in Cabo Delgado originates from the establishment of extractive industries in 2015, then the discovery of vast natural resources (rubies, gold, timber and natural gas) which saw the displacement of local populations through force and without regard for human rights (Perdigao 2020). The effect of COVID-19 in Mozambique is most worrying in the northern province of Cabo Delgado where in addition to being the province with the highest number of infections in that country, is where the population and government institutions are subjected to violent armed attacks by terrorists (Cossing & Mulhovo 2020). The province had already registered 58/80 cases as of May 2020 and the covid-19 virus is exposing the complexities of escalating violence and its roots in deep structural challenges (Perdigao 2020), the government's weak response notwithstanding. These Islamist militants have caused instability, weakening government's and humanitarian organisations' responses to COVID-19 in Cabo Delgado. The security of people in the province of Cabo Delgado is uncertain yet paramount, given the fact that they have not fully recovered from Cyclone Kenneth of 2019 (Perdigao 2020). As argued by Cossing and Mulhovo (2020), terrorist destabilisation manoeuvres have resulted in family dislodgments in affected groups of Mocimboa da Praira, Muidumbe, Macomia and Quissanga to safer areas of Nampula in Southern Cabo Delgado and northern Nampula. This has put pressure on, and exposed structural weaknesses in government as it battles to guarantee public basic services such as health assistance to the most vulnerable, particularly in areas of military instability to which displaced people are relocated. What all this means is that the arrival of displaced people from Cabo Delgado put strains in the provision of food supplies and in the control of COVID-19.

The coronavirus knows no boundaries and is also likely to spread even to places where people live in war zones, cannot easily lay their hand on clean water, and have no hope of securing hospital beds should they fall ill. Soderbaum (2010: 9) views SADC as a regional grouping that lays over-emphasis on sovereignty, territorial integrity and non-aggression, for which reason the bloc has been referred to as 'an old boys club'. This sounds like a lop-sided analysis of SADC countries because the question of territorial sovereignty is key to all nation states in the world. This is even more so with America and Britain. For example, at the bottom of Brexit, that is, Britain's exit from the European Union (EU) in 2019 are issues of sovereignty. This perhaps means that everyone in the world is an old boys' club as exemplified by the historical Anglo-Saxon relationship between Britain and America. Soderbaum's statement may simply have been meant to be derogatory to Africans. Territorial integrity is linked to individual integrity. People are fighting COVID-19 because they want personal or individual integrity which is connected to territorial integrity. Sovereignty is connected to autonomy in the sense that people and their governments the world over are fighting COVID-19 because they want human individual autonomy. Westerners are still interested in their colonial and imperial enterprise and do not want Africans to assert their sovereignty and autonomy because to do so would be to negate imperialism. This view directly contradicts Soderbaum's characterisation of SADC as an organisation that instead of guaranteeing peace and security for the citizenry of member states, guarantees the 'peace' and 'security' of regimes (Soderbaum (2010: 9). By extension, he perceives of SADC as providing for the material security and economic comfort of the elite in power and their cronies at the expense of the people.

The then SADC Chairperson, President Mnangagwa, in response to Islamist insurgency in the Mozambican province of Cabo

Delgado, declared that any attack by the Islamic Insurgents on a member state of SADC is an act of aggression against the entire southern African region as articulated in the SADC Declaration on Terrorism and the African Union Convention on Preventing and Combatting Terrorism (Ministry of Foreign Affairs, 2020: May 20). This resonated with the Pan-Africanist view of the former President of Mozambique, Samora Machel, that the liberation of Mozambique from Portuguese colonial oppression in 1975 was not appropriate unless it was combined with the complete liberation of Zimbabwe (Waterhouse, 2010: 11). Earlier, Kwame Nkrumah in Ghana had professed that the independence of Ghana in 1957 from British colonial rule, unless it was connected with the complete liberation of the entire continent of Africa, was meaningless (Rahman 2007). The declaration by President Mnangagwa was after allegations that Mnangagwa had sent the Zimbabwe National Army (ZNA) to assist Mozambique against these insurgents without the tacit approval of Parliament at home and SADC at regional level. In a very interesting comparative scenario, the USA and Britain attacked Saddam Hussein of Iraq on allegations of producing weapons of mass destruction (cite) without the approval of the United Nations Organisation (UNO). The USA and EU sanctions on Zimbabwe in 2002 were imposed without UN approval, yet the same logic become questionable when done by Africans. Mugabe, President Mnangagwa's predecessor, had in 1998 acted outside the precincts of SADC by using his position then as SADC's Chairperson to send the Zimbabwe National Army (ZNA) to the Democratic People's Republic of the Congo to militarily support Laurent Kabila without the tacit approval of SADC and worse still, without the authority of Parliament or Cabinet (Zimbabwe Human Rights NGO Forum, 1998: October 19). The DRC war did not fall into this category, except under Section 96 of the Zimbabwean Constitution, which provides that the President may declare war on a foreign state carrying out actions prejudicial to the security of Zimbabwe (Zimbabwe Human Rights NGO Forum, 1998: October 19).

The SADC Council of Ministers on 29 May through video conferencing that agreed to harmonise and synchronise border movements and to review the socio-economic impact of COVID-19 (ZBC TV 2020: May 29) came a little late as so much movement between borders had taken place already. For example, Zimbabwe's COVID-19 infection statistics rose sharply as a result of returnees from South Africa especially. Under these circumstances, by July

2020, infection statistics reported by the Ministry of Information led by Senator Monica Mutsvangwa shot for the first time shot up to three thousand one hundred and sixty-nine (Zimbabwe Human Rights NGO Forum, 2020: July 31). What remains unclear is whether the rise in the rate of COVID-19 infection was due to improved testing and the availability of testing equipment from China, the arrival of the winter season that makes more people prone to flu-like infections as to expose them to the virus or failure by governments to effectively regulate cross-border mobility. Arguably, this was an attempt by government to draw the attention of international sympathetic organisations for funding towards COVID-19 mitigation endeavours. The situation was worse in Zimbabwe on account of so many factors. One, the capacity or readiness of the government to deal swiftly and confidently with the pandemic was seriously in doubt due to sanctions. These had been renewed by the US Administration under Donald Trump when the Mnangagwa-led government assumed office under circumstances characteristic of a military coup (Harvard International Review 2018: 23). This impacted significantly and negatively on Zimbabwe's ability to implement preventative measures given the fact that the Zimbabwe government could not solicit funds towards COVID-19 from organisations like the European Union, the World Bank and the IMF, all of which were and are seemingly captured by the US as the biggest contributor of financial subscriptions that sustain them. Second, the government did not have money with which to contain the pandemic unless well-wishers across the globe chipped in with the requisite preventive resources. Thirdly, the chapter argues that the government was preoccupied with its own internal political stability originating from the disputed presidential elections of 2018 and had therefore to balance its scale between ensuring political stability on one hand and dealing with the COVID-19 pandemic in line with WHO's laid down rules and regulations on the other.

The presidential declaration of a curfew on 22 July ostensibly in a bid to curb COVID-19 transmission when victims' numbers soured into above two thousand was interpreted variously especially by the sceptics of the Zimbabwean government. The threat of demonstrations on social media throughout the country on 31 July 2020 and the arrest and detention of a popular journalist Hopewell Chin'ono for exposing Ministerial corruption (BBC News, 2020: July 22) followed by the dismissal of the Minister of Health and Child Care, Obadiah Moyo (Al Jazeera News, 2020: July 8), as well as the arrest of the leading activist behind the planned demonstrations were episodic developments of note in Zimbabwe. The fight against COVID-19 and political intrigue became two sides of the same coin and therefore quite difficult to separate.

When the pandemic began to impose socio-political, economic and cultural impacts within the region, SADC states devised domestic policies of an *ad hoc* nature (Dafuleya 2020: 252). In Plumtree 278 deportees from Botswana were taken to Plumtree high school in ZUPCO buses and some trucks to join other 400 deportees from Botswana. In Bubi, the councillor was seen distributing rice to ZANU-PF supporters only upon production of a party card to people who were queuing for social welfare food aid (Zimbabwe Human Rights NGO Forum 2020). South Africa and Botswana began turning inward and giving priority to their own citizens in terms of employment. Returnees to Zimbabwe from Botswana and South Africa started causing serious strains on Zimbabwe's resources (Zimbabwe Human Rights NGO Forum 2020). Price distortions in Zimbabwe's struggling economy worsened the plight of the ordinary workers as rent-seeking tendencies and profiteering proliferated especially from the elite. The poor in Zimbabwe increasingly became more vulnerable to economic vicissitudes as UNDP Zimbabwe (2020) noted that the poor and vulnerable, small and informal businesses and small-scale agricultural producers would be badly affected. Given the choice between contracting COVID-19 infection and staying free from it by 'staying at home', the ordinary people in Zimbabwe usually expressed their preference to the former, arguing that the economic meltdown in the country and in the cities was a push factor that increased mobility for the sake of survival.

Testing for COVID-19 was not well received in some parts of the world and by individuals and organisations. Three examples suffice here. The British Prime Minister, as alluded earlier in this chapter, preferred 'no treatment' to the activation of the human immune system therapeutically. The Moldovan Church in Moldova despised COVID-19 vaccines allegedly being developed from human body parts especially from aborted foetuses (Wadman 2020). Emmanuel Makandiwa of the United Family International Church (UFIC) denounced COVID-19 vaccines being developed in laboratories as a western ploy to exterminate the African race altogether (https: technomag.co.zw 5: April 2020). This perspective reigned supreme in the theology of the Moldovan Church which denounces COVID-19 vaccine, if ever it is discovered by scientists, as an anti-Christian plot (Balkan Insight, 2020: May 20). Conspiracy theories cannot be proven using the historical scientific method because their validity depends on evidence. Authors on posthumanism and the remote controlling of human beings, among them Wilson (2017) and Martin (2015), have added their voices to the COVID-19 vaccine initiatives being undertaken in Europe and America. On the basis of the views of proponents of posthumanism, the conservative or reactionary section of some churches in the world, the main church in Moldova included, claim that a vaccine against COVID-19 could allow Microsoft or other entities to take remote control of human beings. The Orthodox Church in Moldova calls it a satanic plan to microchip people, or introduce other foreign devices into the human body (Balkan Insight, 2020: May 20). The Orthodox church calls it 'the global anti-Christian system and claims it wants to introduce microchips through the 5G technology' (Balkan Insight, 2020: May 20). Deleuze (1991:76) in (Bryden, 2001) being very critical of religion argues that religion is nothing but fanciful, illegitimate and extensive use of rules of association.

The above conviction informs the scholars and thinkers behind what is happening, and these are actually stating what they want to do, and that they are Antichrists. They are also stating that they want to turn human beings into bodies without organs. The motif about bodies without organs is also found in Deleuze and Guattari (1988) and what is happening now has already been written on in scholarly literature. The global elites seem to be driving humanity towards posthumanism and so do not want anyone to be clever enough to know what they are actually aiming at. Anyone who is clever is dismissively described as a conspiracy theorist. The church's conviction was such that the Prime Minister of Moldova, Ion Chicu, had to lift the restrictions on gatherings in churches earlier than 30 June 2020, or he would be struck off the prayer list. The church affirmed "…otherwise we will take the canonical and moral right to exclude you from remembrance in the church's prayers" (Balkan Insight, 2020: May 20).

The alleged negative effects of 5G have intensively been promoted during the COVID-19 pandemic by conservative circles in Europe and USA as well as Russian media affiliated to the Kremlin (Ibid.). This presupposes that those that support the 5G are progressives and those that are conservative are retrogressive. The argument is that the vaccine introduces nanoparticles into the body, and these are feared to react to the waves transmitted by 5G technology and allow the system to control humans remotely (Balkan Insight, 2020: 20 May). The church together with many scholars and NGOs claim that Microsoft boss Bill Gates owns a company called ID2020 for biometric identification and is primarily responsible for creating microchipping technology in order to gain control of people through funding the development of a COVID-19 vaccine (The New Humanitarianism, 2020: April 15). Allegations are that Bill Gates supports mandatory vaccination and the implantation of microchips or 'quantum dot tattoos' into COVID-19 patients (The New Humanitarianism, 2020: April 15). In Zimbabwe, the leader of United Family International Church (UFIC), Emmanuel Makandiwa challenged coronavirus 5G testing as a conspiracy, arguing that the pandemic is being spread via 5G and spectrum (Toneo toneo, 2020: April 5). Makandiwa also questioned why it was going to start with Africa when the continent was the least affected at that time and reasoned that western countries want to immunize Africa by introducing the same dosage to try and create mutation through enforced vaccination (Toneo toneo, 2020: April 5). He further argued: "This is an opportunity for them to install whatever it is in your bodies [and] if they try it to me and my children [and by extension, his congregants], they will have to arrest me and jail me for disobeying their rules, we are not fool, we are in this world but not of this world (Toneo toneo, 2020: April 5). Though Makandiwa openly the idea of subjecting people to indiscriminate COVID-19 testing mandatory, he indeed represented the ideas of many people and churches in Zimbabwe at tha.t time (Toneo toneo, 2020: April 5).

The Zimbabwe COVID-19 Taskforce chaired by Vice President Kembo Mohadi, established eight Inter-Ministerial sub-committees with the mandate to streamline delivery of its monitoring the situation and managing the response to the pandemic (The Herald, 2020: April 7). The first corona case in Zimbabwe was recorded on 21 March and immediately the President Emmerson Mnangagwa declared a three weeks' national lockdown on 30 March. The Taskforce became the Zimbabwe COVID-19 'Theftforce' as allegations of lack of transparency in tender procedures emerged. These were circulated first on social media before Namibia and South Africa's Economic Freedom Party (EFP) expressed shock as briefcase companies were preferred over genuinely established companies in the distribution of PPEs throughout the country. The Taskforce was mandated to mobilise both domestic and international material and financial resources and was expected to meet daily, reporting on actions being implemented in line with the President's clarion call to all Zimbabweans and all corporates as well as other collaborating partners to stand together and respond to the call for national unity under the trying times (*The Herald*, 2020: April 7). The Taskforce would visit all the country's ten provinces and meet with the Ministers of State and Heads of Government Departments for regular updates on the COVID-19 situation. Under these circumstances, Vice President Mohadi gave assurances to the nation that the government was prepared and ready to deal with the pandemic, but was quick to warn people that there were not sufficient medical facilities as well as testing and mobilization resources (*The Herald*, 2020: April 7) in the event of a full-scale COVID-19 attack.

In Zimbabwe, COVID-19 bred challenges of exclusion in the education system as children from less affluent families were the only ones who could afford e-learning (Catholic Church News, April-June 2020: 1). Children from disadvantaged families in rural schools could not access the internet, neither did they have smart cell phones like their urban counterparts. Therefore, WHO guideline emphasizing the indispensability of Personal Protective Equipment (PPE) were to be complied with. These ranged from medical gowns, sanitizers to face masks. The old adage 'cleanliness is next to godliness' stressed the need for personal hygiene as a fundamental non-pharmaceutical mitigation and preventive strategy against the spread of COVID-19. The Zimbabwe government through the Ministry of Higher and Tertiary Education challenged tertiary institutions to be innovative and where necessary, capacitated them financially and materially to locally produce, rather than import, PPEs. Even after the first phase of Zimbabwean lockdown, the President stated that the country was yet to meet WHO conditions for lifting the lockdown which also warned countries throughout the world against lifting restrictions when infections were on the increase. When Zimbabwean COVID-19 victims' statistics remained so low in the first three months of the pandemic, it was almost certain that the pandemic would spread so rapidly in Zimbabwe and that it was a matter of time before this happened. Such a conclusion was not far-fetched because historically the health institutions in Zimbabwe were poorly resourced even before the pandemic. The author argues that the decades-old sanctions that the US Administration renewed against the Zimbabwe government and its connected elite exacerbated perennial shortages in the health sector. It is to these sanctions that I now turn.

The efficacy of sanctions in the COVID-19 era: the case of Zimbabwe

Sanctions in whatever form destroy a nation's capacity to deal decisively with pandemic situations. The extension of the Zimbabwe Democracy and Economic Recovery Act (ZIDERA) in 2018 by the Donald Trump Administration came when the Second Republic under President Emmerson Mnangagwa assumed office (Rwodzi 2019: 197). The Second Republic under President Mnangagwa inherited from President Mugabe's First Republic the legacy of economic underperformance after the imposition of Economic Structural Adjustment Programmes (ESAP) by the International Monetary Fund (IMF) and World Bank (WB). It can be argued that both ESAP and sanctions on Zimbabwe ravaged the economy in Zimbabwe. This economic ruin continued unabated even when the Ministry of Finance was under an internationally acclaimed Professor of Finance, Mthuli Ncube. Zimbabwe, therefore, found itself in an invidious situation once WHO made a proclamation that the whole world was under threat from COVID-19 pandemic and that nation states had to adhere to its guidelines to curb transmission because it was bankrupt and relied on transitory notes called 'bond money' only usable in Zimbabwe as legal tender.

This chapter argues that sanctions are incompatible with COVID-19 mitigation measures and their continuation is not only a blatant violation of people's rights to medication and life, but also aggravate the plight of the poor in a country already reeling under such economic restrictions for close to twenty years since the introduction of United States and European Union sanctions on Zimbabwe in 2002. It is not so surprising that during the COVID-19 pandemic era in Zimbabwe, the Taskforce was exclusively partisan in its composition, with Ministers and key personnel from the administrative side being drawn into the fray to denounce the USA and its associates. One interesting case is that of the Minister of Defence and War Veterans, Oppah Muchinguri Kashiri in which she castigated western countries over unilateral sanctions on Zimbabwe and overtly expressed the myth that corona virus was engulfing white people as nature's logical response to unwarranted sanctions on Zimbabwe. She was quoted as saying: "Coronavirus is the work of God punishing countries who imposed sanctions on us" [Zimbabweans] (Associated Press: 16 March 2020). On the other hand, so worrying has been the high levels of secretive procurement of COVID-19 control equipment as the Minister of Health and Child Care saw the pandemic era as an opportunity to make money ostensibly out of financial greed. The former Minister of Health and Child Care, Obadiah Moyo's case, in which he was implicated in a PPE procurement scandal, could be one case among many such cases of corruption by the political elite to benefit out of the pandemic. The Minister was charged following his arrest on allegations of corruption in relation to a US$60m deal to procure coronavirus (COVID-19) test kits and medical equipment (Economic Intelligence Unit: 13 July 2020). The prosecutors claim that two companies— Drax International and Drax Consult were illegally awarded contracts by the Ministry of Health without a competitive tender process and with highly inflated prices for equipment.

In Lesotho and South Africa, there were allegations of PPE procurement misconduct by the responsible authorities, with serious detrimental effects on COVID-19 victims who needed them (SABC News, 2020: August 5). The same sentiment was raised by the South African President Cyril Ramaphosa in his address to the nation on 15 August when he lambasted those people who had chosen to benefit from the pandemic and threatened to have them punished for their insincerity and abuse of office (SABC News, 2020: August 5).

Sanctions, despite all diplomatic attempts by the Minister of Foreign Affairs, Retired Lieutenant Sibusiso Moyo, for re-engagement with the west, ideologically cemented the Zimbabwe government's 'Look east policy' especially with China and Belarus as a response to these western imposed sanctions (Ojakorotu & Kamidza 2018). Chinese sanitisation and testing equipment poured into the country for distribution to all corners of Zimbabwe. Technical teams of Chinese COVID-19 treatment experts visited Zimbabwe and Cuban doctors visited South Africa to offer 'free' assistance to Zimbabwean and South African nurses and doctors respectively in state medical institutions. COVID-19 Task Team of Ministers. Zimbabwe's preparedness for the pandemic; reportage and transparency.

Covid(ized) political rivalries and democratic space in the pandemic era

This chapter argues that political rivalries during the COVID-19 pandemic in Zimbabwe were in favour of the governing party ZANU-PF. First of all, the ZANU-PF government disguised itself as a COVID-19 Task Force chaired by the Second Vice President Kembo Mohadi with Oppah Muchinguri, the Minister of Defence and War Veterans as his vice. Both of them are war veterans. Evidence to support this claim resides in the approaches taken to educate the populace about the pandemic. In Zimbabwe the Ministry of Information and Publicity under Senator Monica Mutsvangwa was used to spew party propaganda on the Zimbabwe Broadcasting Corporation (ZBC) television prime time under the pretext of informing the public about government advances in the fight against the pandemic. There was mass production of face masks with one side showing President Mnangagwa's face and the other clearly labelled ZANU-PF. According to the Ministry of Health and of Child Care records of COVID-19 related assistance from China (Ministry of Health ZW, 2020: March 24), Zimbabwe received 20 000 lab diagnostic test kits, 100 000 medical face masks and 10 000 PPEs from the 'philanthropic' Chinese Jack Ma Foundation with very strong links with the CCP since 2014. In this case, the appeal to Chinese philanthropy ought to be examined against what Mishra (2020) refers to as Chinese 'Donation Diplomacy' with first African recipient countries such as South Africa, Zimbabwe, Ethiopia, Nigeria, Cameron and Algeria. It must be noted that these were 'donated' to Zimbabwe and not to ZANU-PF as a party, but the mere fact that the face masks were inscribed with the picture of the President of Zimbabwe on one side and the party logo on the other testify to the importance attached to party politics between ZANU-PF and the Chinese Communist Party (CCP) that has ruled China since 1949. Even when the pandemic was still at an elementary stage in Africa, China was quick to embark on the distribution of 'philanthropic donations' of PPEs. medical supplies and gears (Ministry of Health ZW, 2020: March 24). Most Airlines on the African continent were facing liquidation challenges during the covid-19 COVID-19 pandemic and Ethiopian Airline was the only principal Airline to transport consignments to all beneficiaries (Ministry of Health ZW, 2020: March 24). Face masks put on by party supporters and mourners at the burial of a national war hero, Absalom Sikhosana, were clearly inscribed ZANU-PF on one side and COVID-19 on the other. It means these masks were distributed at political rallies where only ZANU-PF supporters attended *en masse* contrary to WHO standing rules and regulations that stipulated gatherings not exceeding fifty people.

An equally significant observation in this debate is the fact that China, through a company known as ChinaBrand International Commercial, provided relief assistance to Mai Auxillia Mnangagwa's Organisation, Angel of Hope Foundation (Rupapa 2019), not through the Ministry of Health and Child Welfare. It can therefore be interpreted to mean assistance for the ruling ZANU-PF party using the President's wife as part of the political groundwork for Mnangagwa to firmly position himself as the party's presidential candidate ahead of the 2003 elections. However, the donation could be part of China's rapprochement with African governments in a renewed ideological struggle with the USA because China's First Lady, Professor Peng Liyuan handed over the COVID-19 anti-epidemic supplies to the Organisation of African First Ladies for Development (OAFLAD) to which Auxillia Mnangagwa is its Vice President (ZBC News, 2020: July 7). This development smacks of interference in the affairs of the states by China capitalizing on the countries' First Ladies who are in government by default of merely being the presidents' wives. It was anticipated that all COVID-19 foreign assistance ought to come through state institutions, in this case, the Ministry of Health and Child Care. During food distribution, beneficiaries were provided with party masks and the distribution centres had the President's photograph hung for everybody to see. These became political rallies punctuated by party sloganeering and condemnation of the opposition that was alleged to have invited sanctions against the Second Republic (The Herald, 2020: April 1). In countries like Zimbabwe and Mozambique for example, the poor have no choice in circumstances of poverty and hopelessness. They choose the ruling party that is distributing food and other necessities as opposed to the opposition that promises things in the future. This preceding point also can also be used as reason for Europe and America to impose sanction on Zimbabwe – so that they would not have choice but to support these former imperial powers.

Another example of covid(ised) political campaigns in Zimbabwe was the arrest of MDC Alliance trio of Harare East Member of Parliament Joanna Mamombe together with female activists Netsai Marova and Cecilia Chimiri. They were accused of demonstrating and flouting COVID-19 regulations after the presidential declaration of a ban on mass gatherings of people exceeding fifty at any given point (BBC News, 2020: June 11). Zimbabwe's MDC abductees arrested for lying about torture. They allege that state agents abducted them from the police, beat them sexually assaulted them and compelled them to drink each other's urine (Ibid.). The three were denied bail on 15 June, the same date the President declared a national day of fasting and prayer (Daily News, 2020: June 16). In the context of these demonstrations, Minister Sibusiso Moyo, in indirect reference to the MDC Alliance president Nelson Chamisa, used the analogy of a son who wants to burn the whole house so that he becomes a father, and he regarded him as an enemy of the state. These developments, it can be argued, exhibited the extent to which the state was prepared to limit the democratic space for its citizens under cover of the COVID-19 pandemic. The arrest of journalist Hopewell Chi'nono and opposition leader of the 31 July Movement, Jacob Ngarivhume are two cases in point. The state alleges that they belong to that camp of evil wishers (Western Embassies) (Press Release, 2020: July 25). The arrest of these two individuals, from the point of view of the state, had nothing to do with their anticorruption stance as with their ploy to violently destabilize the country and unconstitutionally seize power, the West being complicit in this regime change agenda (Press Release, 2020: July 25). It can also further be noted that the trial of the three MDC-A members could be a case of justice denied on grounds of gender, and can equally be used to expose the patriarchal system still operative in the country.

Another outspoken politician of the opposition National Patriotic Front (NPF) party, Jealousy Mawarire, from on his tweet raised issues in relation to the rising cases of COVID-19 infection in Zimbabwe (Mawarire 2020). He lamented that the President did not have a Minister of Health and Child Care, that there was no Health Ministry Permanent Secretary, that all referral hospitals had no medical directors, that Natpharm, the central medical stores, had no directors and that hospitals had no doctors and nurses due to industrial action (Mawarire 2020). He, in this light, critiqued the government's readiness to deal with the devastating pandemic and equated this with a leader who goes to war without an army commander, without field marshals, without a fighting force and still believe people would take him seriously (Mawarire, 2020). This analogue personifies COVID-19 as a monster to be fought and defeated, yet individuals, rural villages, districts, provinces and the government in Zimbabwe, apart from being resourced to deal with the pandemic, had to grapple with issues of enforcing COVID-19 compliance. The sad state of affairs in Zimbabwean hospitals was the industrial action by doctors and nurses that continued unabated as to stifle successful interventions for infected people requiring healthcare. COVID-19, given the rapid spread of infections in the month of July 2020 in Zimbabwe and South Africa, did not only require people to stay at home, but also needed a robust and holistic medical response to combat it.

One of the most outstanding government critics and a member of the opposition MDC-A, David Coltart, lamented about why Cyril Ramaphosa, the South African President and Chairman of the African Union (AU), could remain mute about the wholesale destruction of basic human rights with reference to the arrest of Chi'nono and Ngarivhume. He averred: "I wonder what part of the new lockdown policy is motivated by genuine medical concerns and what part is motivated by fear and a desire by a paranoid, fearful regime desperate to prevent citizens from protesting against corruption" (Coltart 2020). This came after the President had announced stage four of the lockdown measures in view of the increase in the number of reported COVID-19 positive cases in the country that coincided with the 31 July 2020 anticipated demonstrations at national level (Coltart 2020). Coltart further intimated: "The brazenly partisan acts of many magistrates and judges in Zimbabwe have brought our entire justice system into disrepute" (Coltart 2020).

Conclusion

Like elsewhere in the world, the COVID-19 pandemic in the SADC region has had so many ramifications in the socioeconomic and political, governmental, religious, cultural and even ideological dimensions of member states. This chapter has demonstrated that despite the willingness of the member states to collaborate by pooling their resources together towards the elimination of the pandemic in their midst, most, if not all, member states are financially and materially handicapped to deal with the pandemic without WHO and other forms of humanitarian and expert medical assistance. The disparities in levels of health systems in SADC and the continuing decline of health institutions due to states' incapacity to hold their own have rendered effective cooperation against the lethal virus a pipe dream as individual countries devise their own coping and mitigation strategies.

The argument that the pandemic does not move: people do, saw inter-governmental efforts to curb mass movements of people from one state to another. This approach could not produce the desired results because, for example, xenophobic tendencies exhibited by many South African Blacks victimized Zimbabweans and other migrants into relocating *en mass* to their countries of origin. In the process the pandemic could not be contained but rather spread swiftly across the porous borders especially given the fact that governments were under the circumstances obligated to accept their citizens back home. In consequence, this development put pressure on already weakened health institutions and systems in poverty-ridden states within SADC. The high mobility that characterized the region in terms of cross border movements either by individuals migrating to their countries or by truck drivers made containment of the pandemic untenable and infection high.

Politically, COVID-19 and attempts to mitigate its spreading from one person to another by SADC governments resulted in proactive and *ad hoc* measures. Most of these measures, unfortunately circumscribed human rights, political openness and constructive criticism. This chapter has singled out the behaviour of the Zimbabwean government's manoeuvres, through the courts and security services, to appear to vindicate people's rights to life by deploying force and jerrymandering tactics to achieve and restore its waning glory as a party government. At the time of writing this chapter, pressure on the Zimbabwean government from the AU Chairman, President Ramaphosa, Human Rights Groups, civic society both internal and external, the Zimbabwe Council of Bishops Conference (ZCBC) among others is mounting to compel it to respect human rights and stop arbitrary arrests and torture of MDC-A opposition members, journalists and all and sundry. It can be concluded that politically SADC has not performed to expectation during the COVID-19 era and ruling parties in the region have usually recoiled into their brotherhood of the liberation era even in the face of overt recalcitrance by a member state. This brotherhood also manifests itself in the EU and USA in sanctioning Zimbabwe as SADC continues to pressurise for their unconditional removal so that Zimbabwe can participate in the regional block as an equal partner.

The sanctions imposed on Zimbabwe impact negatively on the regime's efforts to fight the pandemic and save lives, thereby thwarting SADC's resolve to act in unison under trying times of the coronavirus pandemic. The author has argued that sanctions are incompatible with regional efforts to pursue WHO protocols on containment of the pandemic and instead only help to harden the target. Despite all the good and noble intentions by SADC to uniformly adopt measures to curb the virus and resuscitate economies that have been on halt for close to six months since March 2020, there is lack of political commitment by the elite in power to discharge their duties as honestly as they can, resulting in corruption being sanitized by those in key leadership positions. Lastly, the chapter recommends that SADC government leaders take a more determined stance to institutionalise regional, if not democratic governance under difficult times, stamp out cronyism and clandestine deals, walk the talk and above all, restore its legacy as a truly regional organisation that acts in all fairness in dealing with challenges at the level of a pandemic such as COVID-19.

References

AJPH, (1918) 'Weapons against influenza', *American Journal of Public Health*, Public Health No. 8 (10), 787-788.

Al Jazeera News, (8 July 2020) "Zimbabwe Health Minister Obadiah Moyo sacked amid graft scandal", Retrieved from https ;//www.aljazeera.com news.

Balkan Insight, (2020, May 20) 'Moldovan Church Denounces COVID Vaccine as Anti-Christ Plot'.

BBC News, (22 July 2020) 'Hopewell Chin'ono: Whistle-blowing Zimbabwean journalist arrested'.

Bryden, M. (Ed.). (2001) 'Deleuze and Religion', 1st Edition, London: Routledge.

Burke, J. (Africa Correspondent) (2020, June 9) 'Burundi President dies of illness suspected to be coronavirus', *The Guardian*, Retrieved from https://www.theguardian.com.

Catholic Church News, (2020, April-June) 'COVID-19 Breeds Challenges of exclusion in Education'.

CCTV News, (2020, *Feb 17)* 'Ministry of Education: national elementary and middle school network cloud platform opens for free use today'. Retrieved from http://www.chinanews.com/sh/2020/02-17/9094648.shtm.

Coltart, D. (2020, July 24) 'Tweet, Zimbabwe Pay Back Our Money, Law Society of Zimbabwe'.

Cossing, O. and Mulhovo, H. (2020) 'ACCORD: The impact of the insurgency in Cabo Delgado on Mozambique's response to covid-19'. Retrieved from https://www.accord.org.za.

Dafuleya, G. (2020) 'Social and Emergency Assistance Ex-Ante and During Covid-19 in the

SADC Region, The International Journal of Community and Social Development', 2(2), 251–268. Retrieved from https://doi.org/10.1177/251660260936028.

Daily News, (2020, June 16) 'The National Day of Prayer.... President Emmerson Mnangagwa'.

De Kiewiet, C. W. (1941) *A History of South Africa: Social and Economic*, Oxford: London.

Deleuze, G. and Félix, G. (1988) *A Thousand Plateaus: Capitalism and Schizophrenia*. Translated by Brian Massumi. London: Athlone Press.

Drake, T. L., Chalabi, Z. and Coker, R. (2012) 'Cost-effectiveness analysis of pandemic influenza preparedness: what's missing?' *Bull World Health Organ*, 90(12), 940-941. doi: 10.2471/BLT.12.109025.

Economic Intelligence Unit, (2020, July 13). London: United Kingdom.

Gewald, J. B. (2007) 'Spanish Influenza in Africa: Some comments regarding source material and future research', *African Studies Centre Leiden*, The Netherlands, Working Paper 77.

Gilbert, M., Pullano, G., Pinotti, F. et al. (2020) 'Preparedness and vulnerability of African countries against importations of COVID-19: a modelling study', *Lancet*, 20 (2020), 30411-30416.

Harvard International Review (2018) 'Emmerson Mnangagwa: The Unlikely Saviour'.

Herald Reporter, (2020, May 27) '118 escape from isolation centre', *The Herald*.

Hobday, R. A. and Cason, J. W. (2009) 'The open-air treatment of Pandemic Influenza', *American Journal of Medical Health 99*, Supplement 2.

Honigsbaum, M. (2009) 'Historical keyword Pandemic'. *The Lancet*, 373. Impact of covid-19 pandemic on SADC economy, Vol. 1, April 2020.

Toneo toneo (2020, April 5) 'Makandiwa challenges 5G Corona Virus Conspiracy-TechnoMag'. Retrieved from https://technomag.co.zw.

Kubatana.net, (2020, May 25) 'Corruption reversing the gains made against the covid-19 pandemic in Zimbabwe'.

Mahmoud, H., Cengiz, A., Behrouz, G. and Ghiti, K. (2011) 'H1N1 virus and sport, risks of transmission and methods of prevention', *Journal of Infectious Diseases and Immunity,* Vol. 3(7):117-123. Retrieved from http://www.academicjournals.org/JIDI.

Martin, G. A. (2015) 'For the Love of Robots: Posthumanism in Latin American Science Fiction Between 1960-1999', *Theses and Dissertations--Hispanic Studies. 21.* Retrieved from https://uknowledge.uky.edu/hisp_etds/21.

Mawarire, J. (2020, July 25) *Community Radio Harare, corahfm ·* Broadcasting and Media Production Company. Retrieved from www.facebook.com/corahfm.

Ministry of Foreign Affairs, (2020, May 20) 'SADC Declaration on Terrorism and the African Union Convention on Preventing and Combatting Terrorism'.

Mishra, A. (2020, April 13) 'Covid-19: China's donation diplomacy towards Africa turns into a public relation disaster'. Retrieved from www.orfonline.org.

Mnangagwa, E. (2020, May 20) 'An attack on one is an attack on all-Mnangagwa', Ministry of Foreign Affairs, Communique of the Extraordinary Organ Troika plus Republic of Mozambique Summit of Heads of State and Government-Harare.

Mutsvangwa, M. (2020, July 25. 'Press release', Minister of Information, Publicity and Broadcasting Services.

Nishiura, H., Kobayashi, T., Yang, Y., Hayashi, K., Miyama, T., Kinoshita, R. et al (2020) 'The rate of under ascertainment of novel coronavirus (2019-nCoV) infection: estimation using Japanese passengers' data on evacuation flights'. *J Clin Med,* 9.

Oxford, J. S. et al. (1999) 'Who's that lady? In', *Nature Medicine,* Vol. 5, No. 12.

Perdigao, N. P. (2020) 'Responding to covid-19 in an area of increasingly violent insurgency and inadequate government support', African Leadership Centre, Kings College: London.

Phillips, H. (ed.) (2018) 'In a Time of Plague: Memories of the 'Spanish' Flu Epidemic of 1918 in South Africa', *Cape Town: Van Riebeeck Society, 2nd series. No. 50.*

Phimister, I. R. (1973) 'The 'Spanish' Influenza Pandemic of 1918 and its Impact on the Southern Rhodesian Mining Industry', in *The Central African Journal of Medicine,* Vol.19, No. 7, 143 – 148.

Rahman, A. A. (2007) *The Regime Change of Kwame Nkrumah Epic Heroism in Africa and the Diaspora,* Palgrave Macmillan: New York.

Ranger, T. (1988) 'The influenza epidemic in Southern Rhodesia: a crisis of comprehension', 172 – 188 in Arnold, D. (ed). *Imperial Medicine and Indigenous societies,* Glasgow.

Rodriguez-Morales A.J., Bonilla-Aldana, D.K., Balbin-Ramon, G.J., Paniz-Mondolfi, A., Rabaan, A., Sah, R. et al. (2020) History is repeating itself, a probable zoonotic spill over as a cause of an epidemic: the case of 2019 novel Coronavirus. *Infez Med*, 28:3–5.

Rodríguez-Morales, A.J., MacGregor, K., Kanagarajah, S., Patel, D. and Schlagenhauf, P. (2020) 'Going global – travel and the 2019 novel coronavirus'. *Trav Med Infect Dis*.101578.

Rugunanan, P. (2016) 'Migrant Communities, Identity and belonging: Exploring the views of South Asian Migrants in Fordsburg, South Africa', unpublished DLitt et Phil thesis, University of Johannesburg.

Rwodzi, A. (2019) 'Democracy, Governance and Legitimacy in Zimbabwe since the November 2017 Military Coup', *Cadernos de Estudos Africanos*, Vol. 38, pp. 193-213. Retrieved from http://journals.openedition.org/cea/4559; DOI: https://doi.org/10.4000/cea.4559

SABS News, (2020, August 15) 'SADC response to covid-19: Report on the covid-19 pandemic in the SADC Region', Bulletin No. 3.

SADC Secretariat. (2020) 'SADC regional response to covid-19 pandemic: an analysis of the regional situation and impact', Bulletin No. 2.

SADC Secretariat. (2020) 'SADC regional response to covid-19 pandemic: Report on the covid-19 pandemic in the SADC Region', Bulletin No. 4.

SADC Secretariat. (2020) 'Response by SADC to covid-19 pandemic: Report on the covid-19 pandemic in the SADC Region, Aquaculture Value Chain', Bulletin No. 6.

SADC Secretariat. (2020) 'SADC Regional Response Report', Bulletin No. 7.

Simmons, D. (2009) 'Religion and Medicine at the Crossroads: A Re-Examination of the Southern Rhodesian Influenza Epidemic of 1918', *Journal of Southern African Studies*, 35:1, 29-44, DOI: 10.1080/03057070802685536.

Soderbaum, F. (2010) 'With a Little Help from My Friends: How Regional Organisations in Africa Sustain Clientilism, Corruption and Discrimination', School of Global Studies, University of Gothenburg.

Strange, F. G. (1991) 'The history of the Royal Sea Bathing Hospital Margate 1791-1991', Rainham: Meresborough Books.

Taubenberger, J. K., and Morens, D. M. (2009) 'Pandemic influenza - including a risk assessment of H5N1', *Revue Scientifique Et Technique-Office International Des Epizooties*, 28(1), 187-202.

Rupapa, T. (2019 December 4) 'First Lady Charms Chinese Investors', *The Herald*.

The New Humanitarianism, (2020, April 15) 'How a tech NGO got sucked into a COVID-19 conspiracy theory'. Retrieved from https://www.thenewhumanitarianism.org.

The Socialist Revolutionary Workers Party. (2020, May 21) Press statement, 'Xenophobia is a class project! People before profits'.

Transparency International (2020, May 13) 'Corruption risks in Southern Africa's response to the Coronavirus'. Retrieved from https://www.transparency.org/en/news/corruption-risks-in-africas-response-to-the-coronavirus#.

Tsoucalas, G., Kousoulis, A. and Sgantzos, M. (2016) 'The 1918 Spanish Flu Pandemic, the Origins of the H1N1-virus Strain, a Glance in History'. *European Journal of Clinical and Biomedical Sciences*. Vol. 2, No. 4, pp. 23-28. doi: 10.11648/j.ejcbs.20160204.11.

UNDP Zimbabwe, (2020, June 11) 'Covid-19 could prove "disastrous" for Zimbabwe', UNDP study finds.

van Onselen, C. (1976) *Chibaro: African Mine Labour in Southern Rhodesia 1900 –1933,* London, 1976, 58.

Wadman, M. (n.d.) 'COVID-19 Vaccines that use human fetal cells draw fire: Abortion opponents urge, United States and Canada to avoid "ethically-tainted" cell lines', *Science,* Vol. 368 (6496), 1170-1171, DOI: 10.1126/science.368.6496.1170.

Waterhouse, R. (2010) *Mozambique: Rising from the ashes*, An Oxfam country profile https://oxfamlibrary.openrepository.co.

World Health Organisation. (2011a) 'The classical definition of a pandemic is not elusive', *Bull World Health Organ*, 89(7): 540-541. doi: 10.2471/blt.11.088815.

Wilder-Smith, A. and Freedman, D.O. (2020) 'Isolation, quarantine, social distancing and community containment: pivotal role for old-style public health measures in the novel coronavirus (2019-nCoV) outbreak'. *J Travel Med* 2020; 27: taaa020.

Wilson, R. (2017) 'Avenues of Concern in the Rise of Enhancement Technology: Is a Transhumanist and Posthumanist Future Really

Better?' *Religious Studies Review*, Vol. 43, No. 2. Retrieved from
https://doi.org/10.1111/rsr.12898

Worden, N. (1994) *The Making of Modern South Africa: Conquest,
Segregation and Apartheid,* Oxford: London.

ZBC News, (2020, July 7) 'China supports African First Ladies fight
against the covid-19 Pandemic'. Retrieved from
www.zbcnews.co.zw.

ZBC Television, (2020, May 29).

Zimbabwe Human Rights NGO Forum, (1998, October 19)
'Military Action by Zimbabwe in the DRC', Press Release.

Zimbabwe Human Rights NGO Forum, (2020, April 17)
'Zimbabwe Covid-19 lockdown monitoring report'. Retrieved
from kubatana.net.

Zimbabwe Human Rights NGO Forum, (2020, July 31) 'Zimbabwe
COVID-19 Lockdown Monitoring Report – day 122'. Retrieved
from kubatana.net.

Zimbabwe Situation Report, (2020, July 10) Office for the
Coordination of Humanitarian Affairs (OCHA). Retrieved from
https://reports.unocha.org/en/country/zimbabwe/.

Chapter Five

Inclusive Contextual Approach in the Fight Against the COVID-19 Pandemic: A Case for *Ubuntu* and the Zimbabwe Constitution

Edmore Dube

Introduction

This research rejects postulations from some quarters that propose a two-pronged approach to the fight against COVID-19; with the elderly and the infirm (chronically ill) on one side and the relatively young and the youth with no pre-conditions for coronavirus, on the other. The contention here is on the approach to the fight against COVID-19, a viral disease caused by coronavirus, whose fatalities have been recorded mainly among the elderly and the infirm, especially those suffering from cardiovascular disease, chronic respiratory disease and cancer (Segell 2020: 4). The suffix '19'stands for 2019, the year the disease came to light in the Chinese city of Wuhan, with its actual source shroud in mystery. Three contentious theories about its origins are discussed in the next segment. Based on the peculiar trends of fatalities, some advocates of human rights saw it prudent to limit lockdowns to the elderly and the infirm, which UNAIDS (2020) rejected citing possibilities of stigimatisation and sub-cultures that would fight against rolling back the epidemic. UNAIDS precedents for this argument are discussed below, relating to how UNAIDS struggled to contain HIV and AIDS wherever there was no united effort. Of course, while taking cue from UNIAIDS, where its arguments fit into our proposed unitary scheme, with Africans as authors of their destiny, we remain vigilant that as a world body and a Western front, its hands are not always clean. Afrocentric scholars have meticulously documented how the United Nations and its ancillary bodies have acted as vanguards for the western nations in their endeavour to pillage African tangible and intangible heritages, in addition to making then guinea-pigs in nonconsensual clinical trials (Nhemachena, Warikandwa & Mpofu 2020). Though the World Health Organisation (WHO) rejects the allegation, it has often been accused of colluding with international pharmaceutical companies in bio-pirating of African medicines and making Africans guinea-pigs (WHO Report 72 2020: 1). This chapter stresses the necessity to respect indigenous knowledge (IK) in "both national legislation and international law, the principle that any acquisition, publication, scientific use, or commercial application of IK must be in accordance with the Customary Laws of the peoples concerned, as determined by them" (Marie and Henderson 2000: 10). Pirates should not be allowed to exclude the owners of the knowledge from its market value. Pertinent to the importance of the elders upheld by this chapter, is the fact that "in Zimbabwean traditional medicine, therapeutic herbs are considered supernatural" (Abbot 2014: 6). Moreover, the elders are the ones who grant access to traditional medical knowledge "through ceremonies where knowledge is revealed as a gift" from the supernatural (Abbot 2014: 6). The same elders, as the traditional ritual masters, have the capacity to find traditional medicine for COVID-19 in cooperation with the whole community.

The other obvious reason for rejecting a two-pronged approach in the current research is that it infringes on the elderly and the infirm's rights to life, community care and belonging, once they are separated from the rest of the community. Instead, this research recommends an inclusive contextual approach as the best model in the fight against COVID-19 in the African context. An inclusive contextual approach finds it meritable for the local community to fight any threat including epidemics as an organic whole, utilizing indigenous knowledge systems (IKS) reputable in the local context. The argument is premised on historical precedents and *unhu/ubuntu* (humanism, human essence, humanness) philosophy as practiced by the Karanga of southern Zimbabwe and their fellow Bantu of sub-Saharan Africa (Nhemachena, Warikandwa & Mpofu 2020: 2). The fight against HIV and AIDS presents the most pertinent historical precedent, signalling the dangers of associating a condition with particular sectors, which breeds sub-cultures that work against the elimination of the condition. The elderly have in many cases risen to the occasion through astute adjudication based on IKS, with respect to eradication of epidemics and cleansing of the affected communities. If they are given their rightful place in a united search for the COVID-19 cure, it is highly likely that they will pick upon the most relevant herb, leading to the survival of the whole community. As will become apparent, reference to the whole community (inclusivity) here refers to those indigenes working towards the common good, and not the witches, sorcerers and those inventing weapons of mass destruction. In reality, African wellbeing often involved proscriptions against such anti-life individuals, who were often forced to relocate to allow the return of tranquillity to the affected communities (Humbe 2018: 278-281). The common good advanced by *unhu/ubuntu* locates merit in old age, and puts the patients in the hands of the entire community of kinsmen with good will. This research is motivated by the need to interrogate how local communities united by *unhu/ubuntu* can utilize their IKS to come up with health solutions to the current epidemic. This is position in undergirded by the conviction that even where they have to utilize international, regional, and national knowledge, they have to make use of subsidiarity. This means that anything that is received has to be adapted to the local context, run by elders through IKS. Subsidiarity negates the idea of top-bottom dictations, but locates merit in the abilities of those on the ground to know and select what is best for them. This means any constitution or law that negates subsidiarity, is against the people and must be resisted. As will become apparent, the constitution of Zimbabwe respects the rights of the elderly and the sick, including their rights to life, rights to care by their communities and rights to full participation in those communities (Constitution of Zimbabwe 2013). These constitutional rights of the elderly and the infirm are discussed in the second segment of this chapter.

The chapter opens with an attempt to put the pandemic into perspective, in terms of its origins and the way forward proposed by the United Nations bodies, including testing, contact-tracing, quarantine of those with the coronavirus and their contacts, and outright lockdowns. After that the chapter moves on to evaluate the constitutional and legal guarantees for the at-risk groups (the elderly and the infirm). From there it interrogates the interrelationship between the individual and society, with special reference to the Karanga cultural and religious contexts. The argument is reinforced by the Bantu philosophy of *unhu/ubuntu* (humanness), which defines the individual in terms of the community, without which one loses identity (Ramose 1999). It follows that the community is defined through individuals and the individuals, through the society. This means society must find solutions to problems besetting any of its well-meaning components, in an inclusive manner, for all are identified corporately. Society should only proscribe those that exclude themselves through inhuman activities falling outside

113

unhu/ubuntu, including witchcraft, sorcery and manufacture of weapons of mass destruction (Humbe 2018: 278-281). It follows that all the well-meaning elderly and the infirm must be allowed to do their part in finding solutions to the current epidemic, in cooperation with their communities as guaranteed, first by *unhu/ubuntu* and secondly by the constitution of Zimbabwe. Working with the elderly brings a window of hope since history shows that they have been able to deal with past epidemics, including spiritual disorders following such traumatizing wars as the Zimbabwe liberations struggle, Rwandan genocide and the Ugandan massacres (Fontein 2009; Sosnov 2008: 125). The government of Zimbabwe, in applying a constitution which seeks to protect the elderly and the infirm, just as their health counterparts, follows *unhu/ubuntu* in charting a united approach. In that regard the current lockdown put in place by the government affects everyone member of society, calling upon each member to help resolve the problem in their best way. That COVID-19 fatalities target mainly the aged and the infirm does not call for tempering with the socio-moral cohesion that cements intra-community relations in both good and trying times. This means the community must approach the COVID-19 pandemic with the view of the common good for all its members; the elders, infirm, the young and the strong, that is, without age or condition bias. In shepherding their communities to transcend the current hurdles caused by COVID-19, the elders should remain steadfast, well aware that "it is not necessary for Africans to transition from power and authority associated with it" (Nhemachena, Warikandwa & Mpofu 2020: 14). Instead, they should use that power and authority to better the health of their communities in line with *unhu/ubuntu.*

Putting the pandemic into perspective

The origins of the coronavirus contagion are still shroud in mystery. One theory suggests that COVID-19 emanated from consumption of seafood from a wet market contaminated with the virus; but the first case of COVID-19 had no contact with seafood (Ignatius 2020). WHO supports this theory of food contamination, noting that the Wuhan market was either the source, or amplifier of the virus (CNBC 8 May 2020). The Chinese authorities closed the market back in January 2020 and prohibited trade in game meat, though it is not clear whether live animals, vendors or shoppers brought the virus (CNBC 8 May 2020: para.2). Mike Pompeo, the US secretary of State, backs a second theory on laboratory leakages, alleging that there is "a significant amount of evidence" though inconclusive (CNBC 8 May 2020). The theory maintains that Chinese scientists collected bat viruses with the express intention for disease control, but poor security "in high risk biohazardous laboratories" resulted in leakages of the virus into humans (Ignatius 2020). Although a publication by Chinese scholars in support of the second theory was subsequently pulled down from the website for alleged lack of concrete evidence, the actual reason could be connected to attempts at public relations (Ignatius 2020). Though that theory may be yet another theory, the research facilities dealing with disease control are actually within the area of the first case. If we take the second theory of the alleged natural bat virus, Wuhan, the location of the first case, may well be the location where the bat virus changed hosts from bats to humans resulting in the contagious strain, which has sent the world into panic mode. But it is not too late to come to grips with what actually transpired; for at the beginning of this decade it took one year to identify camels as the source of the Middle East Respiratory Syndrome (MERS), which broke out in Saudi Arabia in 2012 (Chithood 2020).

There is yet another more contentious theory associated with the culling of dependents (elderly and the infirm) to give room to transhumanism. Transhumanism is a term introduced by Julian Huxley in 1957 denoting "an international movement that states that adding technological implants and inserting DNA will improve the human being" (Salinas 2018: 381). In that case, the selective nature of COVID-19 could be an illicit human experiment, directed towards classes seen as burdens by the elite Euro-Americans; classes specified as victims of the modern warfare for the 2020s by the NASA document (NASA 2013). If we buy the theory, then we may postulate that with the success of the current selective experiment, the elite may move on to the technological implants that will make humanity automatons at the service of the rich western elites. By removing the old and the infirm, the new oligarchy intends to replace them with manufactured slaves who are "stronger, faster, more athletic and more intelligent human beings" (Salinas 2018: 381). Thus, "prestigious institutions like the United Nations, US and European universities, and governments are adopting the transhumanism as a part of their government plans" (Salinas 2018: 382). They do this by "developing technologies for editing and deleting genes," and many scholars are worried COVID-19 could be the harbinger of the new game of power versus complete emasculation through machines (Nhemachena, Warikandwa & Mpofu 2020: 12; Salinas 2018: 381). That probably explains why those privileged to have hindsight (USA and China) counter-accuse each other of manufacturing the disease in a laboratory (Ignatius 2020). Moreover, Hartmann (2014) has proposed the Malthusian Anticipatory Regime for Africa (MARA), which links contraceptives to the larger motive of population culling in Africa, under the guise of land reclamations through depopulation. He accused non-governmental organizations from the West, of deliberately contributing to the population reduction of Africans in order to create a niche for the West. The same is said of African wars, in which the West often sides with a friendly faction. All these arguments help frame COVID-19 as a pre-planned scheme to satisfy the egos of the Euro-American millionaire elites. More frightening assertions from this school of thought come from Kaufmann (2020), who warns that COVOD-19 vaccines may be used to genetically modify people's genes. He warns the world to distance itself from such vaccines, particularly because such vaccines may not be based on tangible experiments based on coronavirus isolated from the COVID-19 patients, as in the tradition when making vaccines.

Whatever the precise origins of COVID-19; the world woke up to a threatening epidemic early 2020, sending scholars scrambling for explanations, with the three theories above being among the leading contentions. It was particularly intriguing why China had kept the epidemic to herself for quite some time (Ignatius 2020). Meanwhile the pace at which it was spreading forced the WHO director general, Tedros Adhanom Ghebreyesus, to declare it a world pandemic on March 11, 2020 (The WHO v Coronavirus 2020). He directed nations and communities to identify those infected, track their associates and isolate both groups for quarantine, in order to arrest the fast spread of the virus. Such procedures were insufficient to contain the pace of the pandemic, whose fatalities were generally limited to the elderly and those with predispositions for COVID-19 (across age groups). WHO emphasized the institution of non-discriminatory lockdowns across nations and communities, though the young and the healthy majority populations generally survived the condition. It was WHO's submission that "public health and social measures to slow or stop the spread of COVID-19 must be implemented with the full engagement of all members of society" (WHO Report 72 2020: 1). This statement bolstered its non-discriminatory position. The pertinent question is, Was WHO sensitive to the individual rights of the majority who would otherwise survive the scourge without participating in lockdowns? UNAIDS, which has weighed in on the pandemic, answers the question in the affirmative. Experience has taught the world institution in its four decades war against HIV and AIDS that wherever labelling occurred with contextual encouragement, the pandemic was difficult to control. Where there was no competing substitute to the virtues of "kindness, solidarity and an ethic of care" in the fight against the HIV and AIDS epidemic, the situation was reasonably under control (UNAIDS, 2020: 4). UNAIDS had a mammoth task disconnecting the problem of HIV and AIDS from the Semitic religious concepts of sin (Kagimu et. al. 2012: 287). This is because religion, just as the broader culture, impacts the human understanding of disease and how humanity must react to it (Benn 2002). The infected persons often refused to come in the open for fear of being condemned as sinners, where religious segregation and stigmatization were strong (Bocci 2013). In the meantime, they continued to share unsafe sex with their unsuspecting partners, which propelled the epidemic in place of arresting it. By the time the infected could no longer contain the infection as a secret, it was often too late for meaningful interventions to take effect, and they passed on, leaving a trail of associated infections. Condom use was anesthetized by Abrahamic religious groups as harbinger to sin, in the same grade with homosexuality (Ndzovu 2017: 122; Genrich & Brathwaite 2005: 121), which put a lot of lives into danger, which positive support and empathy could easily avoid. UNAIDS strongly recommends these lessons of the past as better weapons against the COVID-19 menace.

The current research supports a united front against COVID-19, and rejects arguments about individual rights taking precedence in the face of the harrowing pandemic (Friedman 2020: para.2). The research is inspired by the common good as the only way that can take us through the pandemic, if lessons from HIV and AIDS are to be fully utilized, as forewarned by UNAIDS. Though the HIV and AIDS epidemic affected more those in the active sexual groups (below forty years of age), the elderly did not shy away, but weighed in with kindness, solidarity and care. In the Zimbabwean context where children's homes are largely cultural taboos, the children of the sufferers and those of the deceased would have followed their parents to the graves had the elderly not played the roles of kind nurses, in line with *unhu/ubuntu* philosophy hinged on solidarity (Chuwa 2014: 48). This time the epidemic is largely that of HIV and

AIDS in reverse. The Karanga people of Zimbabwe, a branch of the Shona people on whose morality this argument is largely based, have a wise saying of reciprocity: *Chindiro chinopfumba kunobva chimwe* (literally, the plate goes where the other one comes from) (Hamutyinei & Plangger 1987: No. 209). *Unhu/ubuntu* stresses reciprocity, maintaining that one turn deserves another, as motivation for fairness, justice and unity (Chuwa 2014: 48). The question is, if experience is the best master, will the young and the healthy shy away from returning a good turn? If they do, what moral lesson is this for the future? If the healthy, and especially the young, were to opt out of the lockdowns leaving the elderly and the infirm to the care of the 'winds,' the Karanga would pronounce the most scathing statement of regret and disgust: *Ukarera imbwa nomukaka mangwana inofuma yokuruma* (literally, if you bring up the dog with milk, tomorrow it will bite you) (Hamutyinei & Plangger 1987: Nos. 26;1665). This clearly presents a moral dilemma for the Karanga as will be argued subsequently, but first we turn to constitutional matters. The current provisions for respecting the roles of the elderly and the infirm as respectable members of their communities, in the current home-grown constitution of Zimbabwe, 2013, were tailor-made to graft international rights protocols on indigenous cultural heritages. Of the fourteen culture groups acknowledged by the constitution, the Shona are the largest in comparison to the other thirteen combined (Doke 2005). Below we deal mainly with those sections of the constitution that advance the rights of the elderly and the infirm within their cultural and national contexts.

Constitutional inclusivity and the *unhu/ubuntu* model of non-segregation

The Constitution of Zimbabwe categorically states that "every person has the right to life" (Constitution 2013: Section 48[1]). In cases of health emergencies, no person may be denied medical treatment at any health facility in the country; and the government has to do all in its power to prevent the "spread of disease" (Constitution 2013: Section 29[2, 3]). It further stipulates that all agencies of government must "secure respect, support and protection for the elderly persons and enable them to participate in the life of their communities" (Constitution 2013: Section 21[1]). The elderly and the infirm, like all other citizens, possess an inherent dignity, and have a commensurate "right to have that dignity respected and protected" (Constitution 2013: Section 51). Section 53 of the same constitution entitled "freedom from torture or cruel, inhuman or degrading treatment or punishment," obliges the State to ensure that "no person may be subjected to physical or psychological torture or to cruel, inhuman or degrading treatment or punishment." All persons are equal before the law and are entitled to fair treatment and protection irrespective of nationality or age (Constitution 2013: Section 56 [1, 3]). The infirm are covered under Section 76 (Right to health care), paragraph 2, which states that "every person living with a chronic illness has the right to have access to basic health care services for the illness." Specific to the elderly is Section 82 (Rights of the elderly), which states that the elderly have the "right (a) to receive reasonable care and assistance from their families and the State; (b) to receive health care and medical assistance from the State." The rights of all citizens may be limited for the common good in such instances where such restrictions guarantee "interests of defence, public safety…public health…" (Constitution 2013: Section 86 [2b]). The performance of activities that affect rights of the people must be done in line with international rights protocols, as specified in the conventions and agreements signed by the state (Constitution 2013: Section 34).

Kinship bonds are strengthened by the constitution, which obliges families to grant the weak and the elderly "reasonable care and assistance." The cultural aspects that cement the community bonds through blood and customary relations are strongly guaranteed. Cognizant of the key role played by language in soldering community bonds, the constitution recognizes fourteen local languages as official, in addition to English and sign languages (Constitution 2013: Section 6). The elderly are considered the custodians of these local languages, presented as identity markers. These languages are locally called *ndimi dzaamai,* which literally translates as 'mother tongues.' The cultural focus intensifies institutional support for the promotion and preservation of "cultural values and practices which enhance the dignity, well-being and equality of Zimbabweans," "protects Zimbabwe's heritage," "and ensures due respect for the dignity of traditional institutions" (Constitution 2013: Section 16 [1, 2, 3]). Traditional institutions, which are largely in the hands of the elderly, are recognized in line with the performance of "cultural, customary and traditional functions" (Constitution 2013: Section 280 [1, 2]). The recognitions of customary law and traditional functions enhance the position of the elderly in society because they are the custodians of customary law and its various levels of operation, from family to chieftainship. Customary practices, including medicinal systems, are recognized as valid and worth of preservation by the state (Constitution 2013: Section 33). Legislation recognizes the Zimbabwe National Traditional Healers Association (ZINATHA), as a local association with an indigenous approach to the well-being of the indigenous peoples.

All these constitutional provisions, and the attendant legislative acts and statutory instruments, leave no provisions for ditching the elderly and the infirm to go it alone in the struggle against COVID-19. The constitution allows the partial withdrawal of individual rights in the interests of the state emergencies, including health emergencies. This is exactly what has happened with the current all-encompassing lockdown regimes. The UNAIDS (2020) notes that there has been some querying whether forcing everyone to comply with lockdown conditions meant to serve the infirm and the elderly, was not an infringement of other people's rights. The Zimbabwe constitutional position is that it is indeed an infringement, but a necessary one. The constitution, which is meant to guarantee the security of all citizens, does not segregate in its approach, because that would set a bad moral precedent for the future. Just as the elderly have taken the younger groups through their health perils with full commitment and responsibility, so should the younger generations reciprocate, because as will become apparent, an indigenous community bereft of the elderly is faced with an insurmountable crisis. Below we discuss the place of the elderly and the infirm in the Shona culture, for which the Karanga are part; with liberal references to specific cases of similar gravity among fellow Africans of Bantu origins. We continue to pose a moral question in line with the unitary approach to lockdowns, in the true spirit of reciprocity, cultural functions of the elderly and the Bantu philosophy of *unhu/ubuntu*, summarized as *tiritose/sisonke* (we are together as one inseparable organic whole).

The elderly and the inclusive contextual cultural paradigm

Karanga cultural etiquette, like in many Bantu contexts, is in the hands of the elderly, the kingpins of socio-cultural cohesion. They are the all-encompassing legal 'sanitizers' of the land and its people. True, culture is dynamic and not static. Lugard, the former British imperial think-tank, categorically states that;

the impact of European civilization on tropical races has indeed a tendency to undermine that respect for authority which is the basis of social order. The authority of the head, whether of the tribe, the village, or the family, is decreased, and parental discipline is weakened (Lugard 1965: 426).

Lugard correctly observes effects of cultural diffusion that obtain where two systems exist side by side for a long time, though this does not lead to a deliberate exclusive model in dealing with community disasters (Lewis 1980: 60-64). Cultural diffusion among the Karanga has not resulted in the decimation of the local culture, nor has it eventuated the exposure of the elderly to complete redundancy, as intended by the Westerners seeking to decimate African culture by plundering its tangible and intangible heritage (Mawere, Sagiya & Mubaya 2012: 23). Posselt and Carl Mauch, were among the pioneers of those Westerners, who despite acknowledging an awesome religion among the Karanga, sought to dismember it so as to take control (Hubbard 2009: 110; Fontein 2006). That was the whole essence behind ascribing foreign origins to the Great Zimbabwe Monuments, claiming that the Karanga as *tabula rasa* could not fathom such a grandiose structure (Carroll 1988: 236). The idea was to dismember the African polity, which they only partially succeeded in doing, because the young who opted for jobs in urban areas, the hub of westernization and cultural diffusion, still kept rural homes (Muzondidya 2007: 334). The old consolidated their cultural hold in the absence of the young, with the result that the status quo somehow continues to hold on to this day, despite several returnees from cities. The cities were augmented by Christian villages like Gokomere, Chishawasha and Mogenster, which literally removed the young from their parents so that they could substitute priests for their fathers (Zvobgo 1996). This too was not a success story, with the result that the elders continued to hold their own.

The control of the elderly particularly continues to be felt in the areas of traditional justice and spiritual leadership. They are the undisputable ritual masters. The government ensures that each communal area has the requisite traditional leadership: village head, headman and chief. Particular customary matters are put in the hands of these traditional leaders to be adjudicated in their *dare* courts (Masitera 2018: 114-118). The important customary matters in the hands of traditional authority include those relating to land. The traditional leadership possesses the powers to allocate housing and arable land in the communal lands (Mupfuvi 2014: 30). Land is particularly a powerful asset required by all age groups, and from time to time there are land disputes. These are also settled by traditional leadership, which has powers to reinforce land boundaries as well as cleanse the same land when desecrated by abominable acts, including murder. Their powerful mediatory functions in the cleansing of those who have committed murder have continued to flag the elderly as an enduring community asset. Murder cases cover proven and unproven cases, which is why after just wars, such as liberation wars, all the indigenous belligerents have to be cleansed through traditional rituals in order to bring closure to the past conflicts. Such ceremonies were ubiquitous at the end of Zimbabwe's liberation war in 1980. Cleansing ceremonies continued into the 1990s during re-burial of victims of the war, and construction of memorial sites for those massacred in Chimoio and Freedom Camp in Mozambique and Zambia respectively (Fontein 2009).

Such mediatory and propitiation functions are not limited to Zimbabwe. The Setswana of Botswana have the *kgotla* court, where the elderly, well-resourced in indigenous knowledge systems, sit to adjudicate cases in justice (Togarasei 2012: 233; Schapera 1992). After the 1994 Rwandan genocide in which an estimated 800 000 Tutsi and moderate Hutu perished, suspects were brought before four international and national formal courts. It is regrettable to note that;

> none of these courts has been able to resolve the enormous problems related to adjudicating genocide suspects. In 2001, the government created *gacaca*, a fifth system for prosecuting genocidaires, to solve the problems it saw in the other courts. Gacaca is highly lauded by the government and many outside observers as the solution to Rwanda's genocide (Sosnov 2008: 125).

Unlike the approaches in the other four courts;

> the *gacaca* trials also served to promote reconciliation by providing a means for victims to learn the truth about the death of their family members and relatives. They also gave perpetrators the opportunity to confess their crimes, show remorse and ask for forgiveness in front of their community (Outreach Programme on the Rwanda Genocide and the United Nations 2014: 2).

The whole process was therapeutic, with the result that it secured a closure which has left Rwanda as a shining beacon of reconciliation in today's world. In addition, many researches have been concluded with regards massacres in Northern Uganda. The same can also be said about the programme of memorialization and transitional justice in Northern Uganda; a process that could not be completed without involvement of traditional justice systems of reparations and cleansing. The elderly were required to utilize their memories and customary knowledge to cleanse the land for the inhabitants and re-draw community boundaries where necessary (Uganda Human Rights Commission 2011: x, 59, 87; Ovonji-odida 2016: 25-30). Formal courts could not ritualize the process in order to achieve both psychological and spiritual healings. This is why Nhemachena, Warikandwa and Mpofu state categorically: "Africans must go back to their *Ubuntu* driven societies which placed emphasis on restitution, reparations, restoration, and the best interests of the African people and not the well-connected selfish elites" (2020: 17). In the above cases, it was only the elders, acting as the village priests or ritual masters, who had the honour to put such problems to rest. This is because they are the oral ritual repositories, which is why it is said that when an elderly person dies, the 'library burns' and the whole community has been dismembered. The Karanga say that 'where an elderly person has passed on, the home is full of rubbish.' The statement describes the confusion that descends onto such homesteads, once the peace makers pass on. It means that the *dare* is bereft of knowledge, justice and unitary care. If the deceased is a paramount chief the Karanga announce such a death by simply saying, 'the mountain has fallen.' The elderly chiefs are seen as symbols of stability as firm as massive mountains. Naturally, if the mountain tumbles away the unexpected movement creates feelings of awe among observers. The feelings of the community are unimaginable if this has been caused by the neglect and exposure to disease by those around the elderly torch bearer of the community.

One taboo relates to permanent translocation of the elderly; especially sending them to old people's homes, which would fall into the cogs of the Western agenda for dismembering the African polity (Nhemachena, Warikandwa & Mpofu 2020). This opens up homes to invasion by all sorts of evils, including unending disputes, fights, and failures to ritually cleanse the land and its people whenever that becomes necessary. The foregoing has shown that three nationalist governments in African (Uganda, Rwanda and Zimbabwe) had to enlist the services of the elderly to do what the modern professional courts and other government institutions had failed to do. Such

123

elders were accessed from their domiciles in the communal lands where they were respectable experts of their communities. Sending the elderly to old people's homes is like selling one's war armour and going for war (Achebe 1958). In our present case it would be like selling all your masks and sanitizers and flying into the storm of COVID-19. It is a mammoth task to translocate the *mudzi mukuru* (generally rendered ancestor but literally meaning taproot) from the normal domicile to an exotic home, such as a home for the aged. This poses a moral problem, because the *mudzi mukuru* is culturally entitled to the care of his or her offspring, and never to be cast into the hands of strangers (Constitution 2013: Section 82).

It is difficult to see how the elderly and the infirm as a sector can be quarantined without bringing them into some kind care-giving homes, where they are catered for by some paid strangers. It is beyond the scope of the current research to go deep into the dangers of bringing the elderly and the infirm into institutions, as currently reported from those countries with numerous such institutions. The nagging question remains that of praxis in the current context. The question concerns the applicability of leaving them home and moving out for work in the morning and coming back home in the evening to provide the necessary care. Some members of the two groups actually need assistance through their toilet. How will that be performed by one who has been through the storm of COVID-19, unperturbed? If the contagion should be found to have carelessly moved from the one assisting them, then such a person is taken as directly responsible for their deaths. The Karanga are wont to say, *Asundindidzira danda rakavora ndiye ariwisa* (literally, one who has pushed over a rotten log is responsible for felling it [euthanasia]). The moral implications of this statement are deep, to the extent that in the worst scenario the accused may be forced to relocate, either by the traditional court or out of bad conscience (Humbe 2018: 278-281). It is farfetched to discuss social distancing within an ordinary Karanga home in this short chapter. In that regard we respect and praise the government for pronouncing a suitable all-encompassing lockdown premised on *unhu/ubuntu* principles of unity and loving care (van Niekerk 2013: 111).

This section has clarified the importance of the elderly among the Karanga and similar communities. Considering their roles in strengthening kinship ties and restoring sanity to life-rending situations, it would be difficult to abandon them to the COVID-19 scourge. If the Karanga and their fellow Bantu communities were to do that, the results would be worse than accompanying them through the dark hours of the lockdowns. It is beyond the scope of this research to give details of *kutanda botso*, a painful degrading ritual performed by those Karanga who allow their mothers to die in grief (Makaudze & Shoko 2015: 261-275; Shoko 2007: 42, 60; Mwandayi 2011: 222). It suffices to say that the ritual is meant to lull the avenging sprit of the mother who has nursed her grief to death. If *kutanda botso* is read in light of the individual rights leading mothers to die harbouring grudges of neglect, then a united fight against COVID-19 is the only option covering the common good, as presented by the communitarian *unhu/ubuntu* (Chuwa 2014: 48). In a Karanga context, even the infirm cannot be abandoned as will be demonstrated below.

The Karanga well-being in light of COVID-19

Among the indigenous Karanga of southern Zimbabwe, life must be lived to the full. Though death is the natural end of life, which must come when it must, it is not expected early. Steps are taken to ensure longevity by eliminating the menace of death symbolically presented in dark colours (Bourdillon 1990: 336). If someone has been sick for quite some time and does not seem to respond to treatment, two things often happen. The first of these is called *bembera,* a carnival but serious announcement, which is authorized by the village elders, when all villagers are believed to be home (Shoko 2007: 47). A powerful announcer speaks from an elevated place at dusk or dawn, calling upon any villager with knowledge about the sickness of a member whose name is withheld. Sometimes villagers get together and those with knowledge take advantage of the anonymity paused by the crowd, to secretly cure the sick. The idea here is that the sick belongs to the whole community and everyone must have something positive to do with the wellness of that person. The second option is *kusengudza,* which literally means carrying someone away (Mwandayi 2011). This method involves temporarily removing the sick from the normal place of domicile to a quarantine place, expected to have more favourable conditions. This is done just in case the sick could be reacting to environmental conditions of home. These two methods often work successfully as a complementary duo. This is sometimes true even with those who have been returned for home-based care by modern hospitals. Cure or care for the sick is applied with no discrimination to age or sex.

The aged actually have the advantage of the extended relations which often pour in resources for their well-being. In the traditional context people who lived to very mature ages had their backs smeared with cow dung to ease pain (Mwandayi 2011: 204). To date the aged still exude a much more keenly felt centripetal force of family care, as they are seen as close to ancestors and are indeed called *midzimu* (ancestors). That alone is a moral of astronomical dimensions, which entitles them to delicate care due to the ancestors, deemed the originators of morality and guardians of the land (Schoffeleers 1979).

The aura associated with ancestorship means that those who manage to reach such mature ages are not to be pitted but to be revered for representing the epitome of societal wisdom (Eyre 2001: 77). This wisdom is to be protected by taking care of the elderly and tapping such wisdom gradually as future knowledge reservoirs-in-making. This is made easier by the communitarian nature of Karanga life. The same communitarian practice has been noted by John Mbiti on the continental scale. Mbiti has summarised the African life as "notoriously religious," and based on the identity principle, "I am because we are; and since we are, therefore I am" (Mbiti 1969: 1). This means that the young and the firm, who are not in direct fatality danger of COVID-19, find their being in the infirm and elderly members of the same society. The vice versa is also true for the infirm and the elderly who are also defined in terms of the young and the firm (Ramose 1999). They have no plausible source of identity apart from the community to which they all belong. This kind of morality means that one should sacrifice to save society and not the vice versa. It follows, therefore, that in the case of COVID-19, it is immoral to save oneself by sacrificing the elderly and the infirm; rather society must fight together to the bitter end. All this is well reposed in the Bantu *unhu/ubuntu* philosophy to which the Karanga subscribe. Though scholars are not unanimous whether its source is religious or sociological, they are agreed that its basic rendering would be, 'injure one, injure all' (Wiredu 1998: 35). There is no place for survival of the fittest as presented by Thomas Hobbes, and elaborated by several philosophers and theologians (Peterson 1998: 5).

This pro-life-togetherness brought about by *unhu/ubuntu* has united the Karanga against witchcraft despite the Witchcraft Suppression Act of 1899. The witches are anti-life which is why the Shona resort to protective charms to save life (Humbe 2018: 269-282). Magesa, a Tanzanian Catholic cleric and theologian is straight to the point: "Witchcraft is *the* enemy of life" (1997: 186). The issue of whether witchcraft is a reality or just the figment of the mind is something that has been debated between Africans and Westerners, including the colonized and their colonizers, for a long time. The colonial enterprise used the legislature to enforce western perspectives on witchcraft by criminalizing witchcraft accusations, as well as personal affirmations of the same (Rhodesia Government 1899). To date Non-Government Organizations (NGOs), are continuing with the fight to frustrate efforts to arrest the problem in the name of human rights (Ashforth 2015: 2; UNICEF 2010). That debate is not central to the current research, whose focus is simply on the African non-discriminatory approach to health and well-being. This research concentrates on the praxis without getting deeper into the bitter discourse that Sibanda confines to Afrocentric approaches only (2018: 298-300).

During the peak of the HIV and AIDS scourge the burden of looking after the sick and their offspring fell on the elderly members of society as intimated above. To date, many orphans are still in the hands of the aged, struggling to feed and to get them through education (Chitando 2007: 111; Bird & Martin 2008). What happens if the elderly are abandoned to face the COVID-19 pandemic alone? What happens to the young children under their care, in a country where children's homes are a distant option, mainly for the abandoned children whose parents are not even known? It is indeed the time for the society to hold together and say, 'thank you' to the aged for a job well done. This is only possible through the *unhu/ubuntu* reciprocation, which entitles them to protection by the larger family in their time of need, through acts of love. This means the government is right in declaring non-discriminatory lockdowns. The kinship ties are more capable of taking us through than any other approaches based on individual rights, where these do not conform to the common good as envisaged by the Bantu philosophy of *unhu/ubuntu*. In essence, the elders, the *unhu/ubuntu* torch-bearers, must be in the driving seat to see the indigenes through the current epidemic, and any external knowledge must be toned down to the local context.

Conclusion

This chapter justifies inclusive lockdowns infused by *unhu/ubuntu*, demonstrating the agency of African societies. The justification for restricting the whole society to protect a few (the elderly and those with preconditions for COVID-19), has been located in history and the local indigenous context. Judging from history, UNAIDS stresses the need for unity of purpose, as this removes stigmatization, which may prevent marginalized groups from receiving the much-needed care. Sub-cultures develop among the segregated sectors, creating pretenders who hide their true identities to avoid stigmatization. Pretence is counter-productive, since it defeats the whole purpose of rolling back epidemics. Associating a condition with particular groups of people has a tendency of endangering them by creating xenophobic spirit among the population, which has tendencies of cutting resources to such people. The isolation of the labelled groups exacerbates the problem by putting them in worse off situations, and making it difficult to defeat the problem, as stigma has to be dealt with first. This delays the whole process of rolling back the epidemic.

Subsidiarity, that is, utilizing local expertise at the expense of the top-down dictations, has been seen as a key component in dealing with epidemics within specific communities. The current research has opted for the inclusive lockdown paradigm, which respects cultural values of local communities. The *unhu/ubuntu* philosophy, operational among the Karanga and their Bantu counterparts, does not give room for segregation on account of age or health condition. Every person in the community is defined through others, making the community key to everyone's identity. Segregating the old among the Karanga is particularly difficult, because the elderly are the knowledge reservoirs in charge of communal justice and ritual cleansing. Failure to protect them puts the community in danger in times of instability, because the formal courts fall short of psychological and spiritual healings. A disrespectful community also opens itself to female avenging spirits called *botso*, and epidemic lockdowns must avoid such dissentious approaches, especially among the Shona of Zimbabwe where anyone endangering any lives is taken as a common enemy. The name given to such a person is 'witch', a term that calls for resistance against that person, accused of planting infirmity in the community. In the worse scenario the witch must relocate to leave people to their ways; which is believed to be therapeutic to the sick.

The curing of the sick belongs to the whole society, at the invitation of the *bembera* announcer. For the COVID-19 lockdowns to be effective they must not disrupt respected unitary local perceptions and procedures. Stress on subsidiarity within the *unhu/ubuntu* paradigm captures the common good more succinctly than any other approach, because the *unhu/ubuntu* philosophy takes the whole community as a supportive organic whole. In light of these insights, this research recommends whole communities to accompany the elderly and the infirm through COVID-19 lockdowns, utilizing local structures to facilitate searches for local therapies to the current COVID-19 epidemic. Based on their past competencies, and with the support of the whole community, the elders should be able to shepherd the community past the current hurdles besetting our health.

References

Abbott, R. (2014) *Documenting Medical Traditional Knowledge*. World Intellectual Property Organization. Retrieved from www.wipo.medical_tk.

Achebe, C. (1958) *Things Fall Apart*. London, England: Heinemann.

Ashforth, A. (2015) 'Witchcraft, justice, and human rights in Africa: Cases from Malawi', *African Studies Review, 5*, 5-38. doi: 10.1017/asr.2015.2.

Benn, C. (2002) 'The influence of the cultural and religious frameworks on the future course of the HIV/AIDS pandemic', *Journal of Theology for South Africa, 113,* 3-18.

Bird, K. & Martin, P. (2008) 'Vulnerability, poverty and coping in Zimbabwe', *United Nations University research paper, 41,* 1-32.

Bocci, D. (2013) 'The cultural and religious debates on HIV and AIDS in the Muslim world'. Retrieved from https://muftah.org/the-cultural-and-religious-debates-surrounding-hiv-aids-in-the-muslim-world/#.Xr_PmunRYSw.

Bourdillon, M. F.C. (1990) *Religion and society: A text for Africa*. Gweru, ZW: Mambo Press.

Carroll, S. T. (1988) 'Solomonic legend: The Muslims and the Great Zimbabwe', *The International Journal of African Historical Studies* 21(2), 223-247.

Chitando, E. (ed.) (2007) *Theology in the HIV and AIDS era series: Module 5: Africa Indigenous Religions in the HIV and AIDS contexts.* Geneva, Switzerland: World Council of Churches. Chitwood, K. (2020) 'Hajj Cancellation Wouldn't be the First- Plague, War, and Politics Disrupted Pilgrimages long Before Coronavirus'. *The Conversation*. Retrieved from *https://theconversation.com/hajj-*

cancellation-due-to-coronavirus-is-not-the-first-time-plague-has-disrupted-this-muslim-pilgrimage-13590.

Chuwa, I. T. (2014) *African indigenous ethics in global bioethics.* Harrisburg, Pennsylvania: Springer.

CNBC. (8 May 2020) 'Wuhan market had role in virus outbreak, but more research needed, WHO says'. *Health and Science.* Retrieved from https://www.cnbc.com/2020/05/08/who-wuhan-market-had-role-in-coronavirus-outbreak-moreresearch-needed.html.

Doke, C. (2005) *The Unification of the Shona Dialects* (2nd ed.). Harare, ZW: Allex Project.

Eyre, B. (2001) *Playing with fire: Fear and self-censorship in Zimbabwean music.* Copenhagen, Denmark: Freemuse.

Fontein, J. (2006) 'Silence, destruction and closure at Great Zimbabwe: Local narratives of desecration and alienation', *Journal of Southern African Studies,* 32 (4), 771-794.

Fontein, J. (2009) 'The politics of the dead: Living heritage, bones and commemoration in Zimbabwe'. Retrieved from http://www.theasa.org/publications/asonline.htm.

Friedman, H. (2020) 'South African Court Upholds COVID-19 Ban over Objections of Mosque and Imams', *Religion Clause.* May 5. Retrieved from http://religionclause.blogspot.com/2020/05/south-African-court-upholds-covid-19.html?m=1.

Genrich G. L. and Brathwaite B. A. (2005) 'Response of the religious groups to HIV/AIDS as a sexually transmitted infection in Trinidad', *BMC Public Health, 5,* 5-121. doi: 10.1186/1471-2458-5-121.

Government of Zimbabwe. *Constitution of Zimbabwe Amendment (No.20) Act of 2013,* Harare, ZW: Fidelity Printers and Refiners.

Hamutyinei, M. A. and Plangger, A. B. (1987) *Tsumo-Shumo: Shona Proverbial Lore and Wisdom.* Gweru, ZW: Mambo Press.

Hartmann, B. (2014) 'Converging on disaster: Climate security and Malthusian anticipatory regime for Africa', *Rethinking Climate Change, Conflict and Security,* 19 (4), 757-783. *doi:* 10.1080/14650045.2013.847433.

Hubbard, P. (2009) 'The Zimbabwe birds: Interpretation and symbolism', *Honeyguide.* 55(2), 109-116.

Humbe, B. P. (2018) '*Divisi* witchcraft in contemporary Zimbabwe: Contest between two legal systems as incubation of social tension among the Shona people'. In M. C. Green, T. J. Gunn &

130

M. Hill (eds.). *Religion, Law and Security in Africa* (pp.278-281). Stellenbosch, ZA: African Sun MeDia.

Ignatius, D. (Reporter). (2020, April 2) 'How did Covid-19 begin? Its Initial Origin Story is Shaky', *Washington Post.* Retrieved from www.washingtonpost.com.

Kagimu, M., Guwatudde, D., Rwabukwali, C., Kaye, S., Walakira, Y. and Ainomugisha, D. (2012) 'Religiosity for HIV prevention in Uganda: A case study among Muslim youth in Wakiso District', *African Health Science, 12(3),* (282-290). PMCID: PMC3557679.

Kaufman, A. (2020). 'They want to genetically modify us with the COVID-19 vaccine'. Retrieved from https://www.bitchute.com/video/KAuubVytZT05/.

Lewis, I. M. (ed.) (1980) *Islam in tropical Africa.* London, England: Indiana University Press.

Lugard, F. D. (1965) *The dual mandate in tropical Africa.* London, England: Frank Cass.

Makaudze, G. and Shoko P. H. (2015) 'The reconceptualization of Shona and Venda taboos: Towards an Afrocentric discourse', *The Journal of pan-African Studies, 8(2),* 261-275.

Magesa, L. (1997) *African religion: The moral traditions of abundant life.* New York, NW: Maryknoll.

Marie, B. & Henderson, J. Y. (2000) *Protecting indigenous knowledge and heritage: A Global challenge.* Saskatoon: Purich Publishing Ltd.

Masitera, E. (2018) '*Ubuntu* Justice and the power to transform the modern Zimbabwean rehabilitation justice system'. In E. Mastera and F. Sibanda (eds.). *Power in Contemporary Zimbabwe* (pp.109-120). London, England: Routledge.

Mawere, M. Sagiya, M. E. and Mubaya, T. R. (2012) 'Convergence of diverse religions at Zimbabwe heritage sites: The Case of Great Zimbabwe National Monument', *International Research Journal of Arts and Social Sciences,* 1(2), 22-31.

Mbiti, J. S. (1969) *African Religion and Philosophy.* London, England: SPCK

Mupfuvi, B. M. (2014) 'Land to the people: Peasants and nationalism in the development of land ownership structure in Zimbabwe from pre-colonialism to the unilateral declaration of independence (UDI) period'. Unpublished PhD Thesis, University of Salford, Manchester, England.

Muzondidya, J. (2007) '*Jambanja*: Ideological Ambiguities in the Politics of Land and Resource Ownership in Zimbabwe', *Journal of Southern African Studies, 33(2),* 325-341.

Mwandayi, C. (2011) *Death and After-life Rituals in the eyes of the Shona Dialogue with Shona Customs in the Quest for Authentic Inculturation.* Bamberg, Germany: University of Bamberg Press.

NASA (2013) 'NASA war document vs Humanity found on NASA site make viral now'. Retrieved from https://www.youtube.com/watch?v=dF87VBOsCPM.

Ndzovu, H. J. (2017) 'Muslim and Christian contestation over the entrenchment of the *kadhi* courts in the constitution of Kenya: Challenging the principle of a secular state'. In M. C. Green, R. I. J. Hackett, L. Hansen. and F. Venter (eds.). *Religious Pluralism, Heritage and Social Development in Africa* (pp.121-136), Stellenbosch, ZA: African Sun MeDia.

Nhemachena , A., Warikandwa T. V. and Mpofu, N. (2020) 'Worse Than "Bushmen" and Transhumance? Transitology and the Resilient Cannibalization of African Heritages', *Journal of Black Studies*, 00(0), 1–21. doi.10.1177/0021934720917572.

Outreach Program on the Rwanda Genocide and the United Nations. (2014) 'The Justice and Reconciliation Process in Rwanda'. *United Nations 2.* Retrieved from www.un.org/preventgenocide/rwanda.

Ovonji-odida, P. K. (2016) *Landscapes of Memory: A Study of Memorialization in Northern Uganda.* Unpublished MPhil. Dissertation, Dalhousie University, Halifax, Nova Scotia.

Peterson, M. L. (1998) *God and evil: An introduction to the issues.* Denver, Colorado: Westview Press.

Ramose, M. B. (1999) *African philosophy through ubuntu.* Harare, ZW: Mond Press.

Rhodesia Government. (1899). *Witchcraft Suppression Act* 1899.

Salinas, D. F. (2018) 'Transhumanism: the big fraud-towards digital slavery', *International Physical Medicine and Rehabilitation Journal*, 3(5), 381–392. doi: 10.15406/ipmrj.2018.03.00131.

Schapera, I. (1992) *Married Life in an African Tribe.* London, England: Faber.

Schoffeleers, J. M. (ed.). (1979) *Guardians of the land: Essays on central African territorial cults.* Gweru, ZW: Mambo Press.

Segell, G. (2020) 'How Tangible are Contacts between Africa and Islam: COVID-19 aka Coronavirus', *Research on Islam and Muslims in Africa (RIMA).* Retrieved from https://www.researchgate.net/publication/340050350.

Shoko, T. (2007) *Karanga indigenous Religion in Zimbabwe: Health and Well- Being.* London, England: Ashgate.

Sibanda, F. (2018) 'The legality of witchcraft allegations in colonial and postcolonial Zimbabwe'. In M. C. Green, T. J. Gunn and M. Hill (eds.). *Religion, Law and Security in Africa* (298-300). Stellenbosch, ZA: African Sun MeDia.

Sosnov, M. (2008) 'The adjudication of genocide: *Gacaca* and the road to reconciliation in Rwanda', *Denver Journal of International Law and Policy*, 36(2), 125-153.

'The WHO v Coronavirus: Why it can't handle the pandemic'. Retrieved from https://theguardian.com/news

Togarasei, L. (2012) 'Paul and masculinity: Implications for HIV and AIDS responses among African Christians'. In E. Chitando and S. Chirongoma, (eds.). *Redemptive Masculinities: Men, HIV, and Religion*, 229-248, Geneva, Switzerland: WCC Publications.

Uganda Human Rights Commission and United Nations Human Rights Office of the High Commissioner. (2011) 'The dust has not yet settled: Victims' views on the right to remedy and reparation: A report from the greater north of Uganda'. Retrieved from http://uganda.ohchr.org UNAIDS. (2020) 'Rights in the time of COVID-19: Lessons from HIV for an effective, community-led response'. Retrieved from https://www.unaids.org.

UNICEF. (2010) 'Children accused of witchcraft: An anthropological study of contemporary practices in Africa', *Dakar: UNICEF WCARO*. Retrieved from https://www.wcaro_children-accused-of-witchcraft-in-africa.

Van Niekerk, J. (2013) 'Ubuntu and moral values'. Unpublished PhD Thesis, University of Witwatersrand.

WHO. (2020) 'Coronavirus disease 2019 (COVID-19) Situation Report – 72'. Retrieved from https://reliefweb.int/report/world/coronavirus-disease-2019-covid-19-situation-report-72-1-april-2020. Wiredu, K. (1998) 'Toward decolonizing African philosophy and religion', *African Studies Quarterly, 1(4)*, 17-46.

Zvobgo, R. J. (1996) *Transforming Education: The Zimbabwean Experiences*. Bulawayo: Belmont.

Retrieved from http://www.etcgroup.org/en/issues/bio-piracy.

Chapter Six

Implications of the Fourth Industrial Revolution and COVID-19 on African Education Systems: A Case Study of Namibia

Rumbidzai E. Makamani, Susan Shamaoma-Katowa & *Ndinaani Mwashita*

Introduction

The Fourth Industrial Revolution (4IR) can be understood as a new industrial era characterised by technologies such as Artificial Intelligence (AI), machine learning and Internet of Things (IoT) which all blur boundaries between physical, digital and biological spheres (Xu, David, & Kim 2018). The technologies of the 4IR are expected to reshape governments, education and healthcare among other aspects of life. 4IR will lead to the loss of jobs and benefit the advanced economies in manufacturing (Naudé 2017). Information of the digital tools of the 4IR has been spread and people's expectations about their benefits is so high. Only a small population of enlightened people have taken an extra mile to dig deeper into how these technologies are going to deprive humans of their autonomy to be individuals. As the world was bracing with challenges posed by digital technology, Covid-19 pandemic broke out causing disruptions in many aspects of life such as education, tourism and sporting activities (United Nations 2020). More than 160 countries immediately closed schools leaving many children and youths out of school (World Bank 2020). COVID-19 outbreak has fast tracked the magnitude at which digital technology is used in most if not all institutes of learning (World Economic Forum 2020). Similarly, the Namibian education system could not smoothly roll on to the new mode of learning as a result of computer illiteracy of the educators and unavailability of the digital devices. The situation in Namibia mirrors the reality across the African continent.

Development of world industrial revolutions

The steam engine was developed in the late 18th century (Xu et al. 2018). Xu et al 2018) argue that it had great effects in Europe mainly in Britain and that it improved transport network especially canal and railway network. The first industrial revolution ushered in a new era for Europe (Kayembe & Nel 2019).

The second industrial revolution (2IR) was propelled by Faraday and Maxwell who unified magnetic force to generate electricity (Coey & Ni Mhíocháin 2016). The 2IR stretches between 1870 and 1914. It is a period which was characterised by various innovations directed towards improving living standards. However, it should be noted that the expansion of industries in European countries left out Africans in the peripheries (World Economic Forum 2015). It rather was a source of exploitation (Rodney 1973), as Europeans rushed to Africa without the intentions of treating Africans as equal partners in development.

The second half of the twentieth century experienced the third revolution which was characterised by information technology. Roberts (2015) noted that the third industrial revolution saw a lot of development of technology in manufacturing, distribution and energy. The first quarter of the twenty-first century should be a transitional period in the history of human development from the 3IR to the 4IR. Schwab (2016) mentions that 4IR involves artificial intelligence and machine learning which also include autonomous vehicles, advanced biotechnology, robotics, the Internet of Things and block chains. Schwab (2016) acknowledges that there is already evidence of 4IR use in things such as self-driving cars and drones. In Western countries progress has been noted in 4IR and increase in computing power is noted in many sectors such as Medicine and Engineering.

An overview of the impact of 4IR in Africa

Schwab (2016: 1) views 4IR as "the advent of cyber-physical systems involving entirely new capabilities for people and machines by combining technologies from the digital, physical and biological worlds." As elsewhere in the world, African education systems have been trying to maintain the pace of emerging technologies on the human development that build on the technological advancements of the 3IR. Nevertheless, Gillwald (2019) asserts that countries that are still developing are not yet ready for the full implementation of the 4IR. This entails that the advanced technology can be accessed and dominated by foreign companies and personnel. Consequently, some technological revolutions of the 4IR have immensely tended to benefit agents of digital capitalism who own and control technologies, influencing everyone to resort to digital world (Schwab 2016).

Naudé (2017) alluded that most African politicians, policy makers and educators have adapted 4IR as a fashionable phrase in their speeches without a deeper insight of its positive and negative impact. He further argues that many teachers are still wrestling to comprehend technologies of 3IR which could serve as a foundation to prepare learners for the 4IR. The prevailing situation therefore exacerbates the existing gap and deepens inequalities especially for the majority of the rural population. Mhlanga and Moloi (2020) explained that 4IR is more applicable to some urban communities than rural communities as rural areas are mostly deprived of modern technology.

Naudé (2017) highlighted that African entrepreneurs will not be able to produce some robots in Africa noting that producers of robots are currently in Germany, Japan and the USA. This shows that African industries will have to import robots and adapt to them as the suppliers would require. It is observable that countries that manufacture and export robots will have a competitive advantage in manufacturing. Africa will not have control over imported 4IR tools invented outside the continent with different social economic conditions. Schwab (2016) supports the above by stating that those who benefit from 4IR are the ones who provide, innovate and invest, thus African systems remain at the receiving end. In a similar vein, Nhemachena, Hlabangane and Kaundjua (2020), further view 4IR as ushering an era of digital slavery. Consequently, they stressed the need to decolonise Africans by re-centring Africans as owners or masters of African material resources and of indigenous knowledge including indigenous Science, technology and Engineering. This entails that 4IR is not likely to benefit Africa as much as it would to the Western world due to different levels of technological development between the global North and South. In this regard, there is a possibility that 4IR will deepen inequalities in most African countries, including Namibia with respect to accessing knowledge and skills required in the digital world.

The outbreak of COVID -19

In December 2019 the world became aware of the first report of the outbreak of COVID-19 from Wuhan, China (Kumar, Malviya and Sharma 2020). It could have been transmitted by the humans who were contaminated by the animal meat from pigs, birds, cats, mice, snakes and dogs from the meat market (Kumar, Malviya and Sharma 2020). Sansa (2020: 1) explains that "COVID-19 caused by severe acute respiratory syndrome Coronavirus 2 (SARS-COV-2) …". It is transmitted through small droplets produced by coughing, sneezing, talking and by touching contaminated surface followed by touching one's face, eyes, mouth and nose (Sansa 2020). The outbreak of COVID-19 was declared as an International Public Health Emergency (WHO 2020). Namibia announced its first two COVID-19 confirmed cases in March 2020 (Nyaungwe & Roelf 2020). This marked the onset of disruptions to all sectors country wide including the education system and the community at large.

The mystery behind the origin of COVID-19

Van Beusekom (2020) noted that some politicians blame China for the pandemic by accusing the rich people to have intentionally transmitted COVID-19 with the intention of creating a market for of vaccines. Furthermore, Cohen (2020) explains that a theory promoted by United States (US) President, Donald Trump and allies, claim that COVID-19 was developed at Wuhan Institute of Virology (WIV) lab where it leaked and caused international havoc. However, such claims have not been substantiated to date; therefore, Shi, in collaboration with other Chinese Scientists refuted the above (Cohen 2020). Professor Kristian Andersen, a microbiologist with his team in California observed that COVID-19 was not created but started naturally (Beaumont 2020).

Most African sectors including the education systems perceive the coming of COVID-19 as a catalyst for the use of the emerging 4IR tools. Mahaye (2020) explains that COVID-19 uplifts the prevailing system of education as it facilitates fullness of golden opportunities and provides insights for creativity. A recent study in South Africa by Mhlanga and Moloi (2020) indicates that COVID -19 has greatly influenced the use of various 4IR tools in the education sector. Similarly, like other African countries, Namibia has attempted to reach to the majority of the learners using various techniques during the lockdown period which started in March 2020.

The Impact of COVID-19 on the African education systems

The coming of the COVID-19 pandemic has heavily disturbed the African education systems among other sectors across the globe. Lockdown measures were put in place to avoid the spread of the corona virus. In March 2020, President Hage Geingob of Namibia announced a state of emergency which included the premature closure of institutions of learning from pre-primary to tertiary education. As of April 2020, the World Bank (2020) reported that many learners in the world have been affected by pre-mature closures of schools and higher institutions of learning (United Nations 2020). Millions of learners in Africa have been affected by the COVID-19 pandemic, leaving Namibia with about 745 566 learners being denied of face to face learning (UNESCO 2020).

The Namibian education system response to COVID-19 pandemic

COVID-19 pandemic has prompted the education systems to realise the need for other learning platforms for children to continue with learning activities outside the classroom walls (Nyariki 2020). As a way of ensuring on the continuity of learning, the Southern Africa Development Community (SADC) Secretariat and UNESCO signed a Joint Statement and Action Plan under the banner, "#LearningNeverStops" (UNESCO 2020). The development entails looking for every possible way to conduct virtual lessons to mitigate the impact of sudden closures of schools. Using our experience as practicing teachers, we note that the impact of COVID-19 has drastically changed the role of the educators in the classroom to shift to emerging technologies for online teaching even without or with less digital literacy.

According to the SADC report (2020), UNESCO took part in supporting countries by ensuring that learning continues after the sudden closure of schools by mobilizing resources and implementing innovative pedagogies to provide continuity of education through distance and blended teaching and learning. In Namibia, the Ministry of Education, Arts and Culture (MoEAC) in collaboration with various stakeholders, has been actively involved in ensuring that learning continues during the COVID-19 lockdown period. The MoEAC Executive Director, in the circular issue highlighted that Namibia as a member of the African Union (AU) and that it is obliged to adhere to the AU Education Sector Response plan to COVID -19 pandemic by ensuring the following: ensuring continuity of learning be it on-line and off-line, document good practices in the e-learning and monitor learning engagement thereby share information with the African Union Commission (AUC) to facilitate intercountry learning and upscaling of good practice (Ministry of Education, Arts and Culture 2020 Circular). Furthermore, the roadmap suggests the need to revise the plan for the reopening of schools and tertiary institutions and to consider the missed learning time.

The above demonstrate MoEAC's Preparedness and Response Plan (PRP) for COVID-19 (2020) to ensure there is continuity of learning during lockdown. Therefore, at the national level e-learning platforms were established. For example, "My Zone Online Learning," for pre-primary to grade 7 learners was accompanied by the print materials that could be used by learners with and without access to internet facilities. The MoEAC partnered with Namibia Media Holding and United Nations International Children's Emergency Fund (UNICEF) to print booklets which were distributed to all the schools. Furthermore, some booklets were printed and issued in national newspapers to maximize accessibility. Parents were tasked to collect these booklets from schools with the instruction that they would return such materials to respective schools upon completion within the allocated time. Other platforms included Namibian Broadcasting Corporation and radio streaming of lessons on Namibian Broadcasting Corporation.

Additionally, the minister of MoEAC, Honourable Anna Nghipondoka, through the regional directorate of education called for teachers to make use of other available platforms such as google classrooms, google hangout meet and YouTube where applicable in all schools. To ensure inclusive continuity of learning by all learners, teachers also engaged in making booklets and handing out such to all learners through their parents including those without access to internet facilities.

Furthermore, the MoEAC partnered with Namibia College of Open Learning (NAMCOL) to make materials and video lessons which were accessed by grades 8 to 10 learners online. The examination classes of grade 11 and 12 returned to school for face to face learning as they were divided into smaller groups to adhere to the WHO COVID-19 pandemic regulations of social distancing. Similarly, higher institution of learning such the University of Namibia partnered with the Namibian Telecommunication Company (TELECOM) to offer free data to the students to access online study materials and video conferencing. However, those without internet access had to go for face to face lectures during lockdown relaxation period to catch up with the rest.

Effects of 4IR and COVID-19 on African education system

Although the MoEAC has tirelessly engaged in measures to ensure that there is continuity of learning, the existing challenges and negative impact of COVID-19 in the education system cannot be overlooked. Potterton (2020) argues that the long school-closing shock leads to learning loss, increased school dropouts, deepening inequality, and that the economic shock could exacerbate the damage and harm households. This is due to the fact that similar impact was observed in the previous pandemics in the African countries affected by Ebola. According to Malala Fund (2020), enrolment rates for girls reduced during Ebola epidemic in Sierra Leone, Guinea and Liberia due to teenage pregnancies and child labour as a result of upsurge in poverty and domestic violence when children are not in school. The reopening of schools was difficult as fear dominated the thinking patterns of parents and those in authority. The country did not want to risk the learners not completing their studies and thus e-learning and other non-face to face approaches of teaching had to continue. There is a possibility that the long school closing shock could be similarly experienced in Namibia, as schools have been closed for more than five months.

Our experience has exposed us to the reality that learners of primary school age who experience reading problems and whose learning is dependent on the teachers' guidance, faced learning barriers during lockdown period. Consequently, learners with learning difficulties were excluded from effective learning activities including those from the disadvantaged and marginalized communities who have no access to Information and Communication Technology (ITC) tools. As Ziyu (2020) stresses that the majority of learners in Sub-Saharan Africa do not have access to computers and internet at home. According to the survey carried out by the MoEAC (2020), learning platforms will be accessed by only

2% of learners in Namibia during the national lockdown. Electricity and internet connectivity are other stumbling blocks for learners to continue with online learning. The scenario has caused many learners to be left behind as they could not benefit from the available online platforms. Such situations will force the Namibia's education system to stretch and embrace the 4IR tools.

Staying a long time away from school is likely to result in some learners especially those with learning difficulties to forget what was learnt from their current grade and before lockdown period. Saavedra (2020) holds this view when he highlights that the learners who were struggling with the basics at foundation level might become worse and have been suddenly deprived of their right to education. It implies that learning gaps could widen in some cases causing teaching and learning to be more complex during the adjusted 2020 school calendar and post COVID-19 period. Teaching might be more challenging because learners in the same grade might be at different levels that would have been created by their social backgrounds. It is highly likely that those who had opportunities to access the learning materials and had assistance at home may outshine those who lacked materials and support from the family.

Caryalho and Hares (2020) postulate that COVID–19 school closure could exacerbate existing inequities due to the fact that it would be difficult for learners from poor background to have the opportunity to access distance learning. It follows logic that online and print materials distributed to the parents are a one-size-fits all approach. The pedagogical methods used could not accommodate learners who learn differently. Although the online video clips lessons from MoEAC included the Sign Language interpretation to narrow exclusion, a concern still remains on inclusive education pedagogies for learners with learning difficulties and those who learn through braille print. After the government's relaxation of lockdown regulations, President Hage Geingob announced the re-opening of grade 11 and 12 with an exception of the high-risk areas which experienced rising numbers of new COVID-19 cases. It meant that face to face teaching and learning activities from the higher risk region continued to be hampered. Thus, it can be deduced that COVID-19 has largely contributed to the increase of inequality in the Namibian education system. Potterton (2020) relates the existing inequalities + to meaningfully adapt to 4IR.

Implications of 41R on the Namibian education system

It is imperative that educators are enlightened on the new methods and approaches that are relevant to understand the new world order. The Namibian government can fund researchers on how to be innovators of 4IR and not just consumers. If a country becomes innovative then gradually it will become independent and master of its own education system. In the same vein, Naudé (2017) added the need for Africa in general to invest more on Technical and Science, Technology, Engineering and Mathematics (STEM) skills. The education system should therefore shift its lens to improve STEM so as to help learners acquire technological skills and improve their critical thinking and collaborative skills compatible to the digital job industry (Morr 2019).

The uplifting of the education system was echoed again by Pather (2020) who argues on the need for academics to be furnished with new methods and approaches to teaching. Resources and funding are needed to transform education so that it can meet the needs of the 4IR. It should be noted that the present curriculum in schools was mainly crafted by the colonial masters who had their own objectives. Africans were trained to become workers in the European structures and to continue with it means Africans will not benefit from the 4IR. The curriculum must focus on the exploration of resources for the benefit of the African population.

The 4IR technology has to invest in agriculture so as to improve food security. The subjects taught in schools have to be integrated so that learners develop dignity of labour to utilise the technology physically. Morr (2019) cited John Dewey, a Philosopher and Educator, advocating that, "if we teach today's students as we taught yesterday's, we rob them of tomorrow." This implies that learners should not be taught to memorise facts but should be engaged to construct what they have learnt. Learning should be appropriate for the current and future demands of the 4IR relevant to the African community.

Lessons to learn from the 4IR and COVID -19 pandemic in Namibian education system

Like in other African countries, there are numerous lessons to be learnt from both the 4IR and COVID -19 pandemic in the Namibian education system. Both the 4IR and COVID-19 pandemic have placed a heavy burden on the education system to respond to the demand of digital transformation. Although the education ministry is one of the government's priorities in terms of budget allocations which received N$14.2 billion for 2020/2021 (The Minister of Finance, Iipumbu Shiimi 2020), there are numerous emerging needs especially those arising from the impact of COVID-19. There is a continued need to upgrade infrastructure and other resources to meet challenges posed by digital colonisation and COVID–19 prevention and management in schools. Given the current scenario of the overcrowded classrooms, implementation of new technologies and physical distancing is likely to be too costly for the government. For example, an average class of 45 learners would not contain an arrangement of 1m by 1.5 m apart. In some areas there would be need for additional teachers and classrooms when all the learners are back to school. Besides, utilization of emerging 4IR gargets in classrooms during COVID-19 means the end of sharing resources such as textbook gadgets and computers to prevent the spread of the virus. This implies that individual ITC tools to facilitate teaching and learning are crucial.

There is need for the digital capacity building for the educators to acquire new technologies and teaching methods that are applicable in the 4IR. This will serve as a transition to the digital industry for future generations. A massive integration of ICTs is crucial to ensure learning continues with meaningful outcomes that will enable the future generation to be productive. Classroom teaching should shift to online whereby learners should be taught to realise the importance of constructing their own knowledge in a participatory manner while teachers serve as facilitators (Wikramanayake 2005). Internet in the 4IR has become a necessity and not a luxury, hence the importance of a wider connectivity in rural schools is crucial.

It is time to restructure the curriculum and assess what is suitable in preparing learners for their future. This is critical because the curriculum, in general, should be 4IR based to match to social and political aspects due to the advances of technology and future disruptive pandemics (Penprase 2018). Hence, the use of 4IR technologies can be instrumental in preparing the education system for future pandemics or other unforeseen factors and digital industry.

Conclusion

It is well documented that the world has gone through three industrial revolutions that have shaped human lifestyles. The chapter explored the implications of the developments and the readiness of African countries in embracing the looming 4IR particularly in the education sector. As the world moves towards the new industrial era, Africans have to participate in the global village and become innovative and empower themselves to become masters of their economies. It should be noted that the 4IR technologies are tools that need to benefit people globally. Education is the tool that must be used to destroy barriers that might prevent Africans from accessing their wealth and achieving sustainable economic development. It is therefore imperative to structure the African education system in line with digital industry demands that cater for African standards. The Education system in Africa has been instantly altered in many ways due to the outbreak of the COVID-19 pandemic exposing the shortcomings and inequalities within the system. The Namibian education system in particular was also ambushed by the COVID-19 pandemic, hence, most rural schools were mainly unable to migrate to the new modes of learning. Nevertheless, both 4IR and COVID-19 have shown the education fraternity that learning has to embrace the new technologies. For Africa, technology is the new norm in the type of education that needs be provided to learners to enable them to fit and survive in a technology-saturated environment.

References

Beaumont, P. (2020) 'Where did covid-19 come from? What we know about its origin'. Retrieved from https://www.theguardian.com/world/2020/may/01.

Carvalho, S. and Hares, S. (2020) 'More from Our Database on School Closures: New Education

Policies May Be Increasing Educational Inequality'. Retrieved from https://www.cgdev.org/blog/more-our-database-school-closures-new-education-Policies-may-be-increasing-educational.

Cohen, J. (2020a) 'Trump 'owes us an apology.' Chinese scientist at the centre of COVID-19 origin theories speaks out'. Retrieved from https://www.sciencemag.org/.

Cohen, J. (2020b) 'Wuhan coronavirus hunter Shi Zhengli speaks out', *Science*, 369(6503),487-488. DOI:10.1126/science. 369.6503.487.

Coey, J. M. D. and Ni Mhíocháin, T. R. (2016) 'History of Magnetism'. In *Reference Module in Materials Science and Materials Engineering*. Retrieved from https://doi.org/10.1016/b978-0-12-803581-8.01110-3.

Gillwald, A. (2019) 'South Africa is caught in the global hype of the fourth industrial revolution', *The Conversation*. Retrieved from https://theconversation.com/south-africa-is-caught-in-the-global-hype-of-the-fourth-industrial-revolution-121189.

Kayembe, C. and Nel, D. (2019) 'Challenges and opportunities for public administration in the Fourth Industrial Revolution', *African Journal of Public Affairs*. 11(3), 79-93.

Kumar, D., Malviya, R. and Sharma, P. (2020) 'Corona virus: A review of Covid -19 history and origin', *EJMO, 4(1), 8-25*. *doi*:1014744/gmo.2020.

Mahaye, M. E. (2020) 'The Impact of COVID-19 Pandemic on South African Education: Navigating Forward the Pedagogy of Blended Learning'. Retrieved from http://www.researchgate.net/publications/340899662.

Malala Fund. (2020) 'Malala Fund releases report on girls' education and COVID-19'. Retrieved from https://www.Malala.Org/.

Mhlanga, D. and Moloi, T. (2020) 'COVID-19 and the digital transformation of education: What we are learning in South Africa'. University of Johannesburg, South Africa. Educ, Sci.2020.10.180 Retrieved from: https://www.researchgate.net/publication/340604511_COVID-19_. doi.org/10.3390/educsci 10070180.

Ministry of Education, Arts and Culture. (2020) 'Circular: Form ed.3 2020. Guidelines for education staff to ensure continued learning and preparedness for face to face tuition post covid-19 national lockdown'. Retrieved from https://www.moe.gov.na/files/downloads/ee6_Guidelines.for.%20Education.%20Staff.pdf.

Morr, B. (2019, May) '8 things every school must do to prepare for the 4IR'. Retrieved from https://www.forbes.com/sites/bernardmarr/2019/05/22/8-things-every-school-must-do-to-prepare-for-the-4th-industrial-revolution/#10cf51a3670c.

Naudé, W. (2017) 'Entrepreneurship, Education and the Fourth Industrial Revolution in Africa', Maastricht University: The Netherlands. *IZA Discussion Paper No. 10855*. Retrieved from http://ftp.iza.org/dp10855.pdf.

Nhemachena, A., Hlabangane, N. and Kaundjua, M. (2020) 'Relationality or hospitality in Twenty first century research. Big data, internet of things, and resilience of coloniality on Africa', *Modern Africa: Politics, History and Society*, 8(1), 105-139. doi: https://doi.org/10.26806/modafr.v8i1.278.

Nyariki, L. (2020, June 23) 'Africa supports reading and learning during the COVID-19 pandemic', *Global partnership for education*. Retrieved from https//www.globalpartnership.org.

Nyaungwe, N. and Roelf, W. (2020) 'U.S News. Namibia Reports First Two Cases of Coronavirus, Imposes Travel Ban'. Retrieved from https://www.usnews.com/news/world/articles/2020-03-14/namibia-reports-first-two-cases-of-coronavirus.

Pather, S. (2020, April 9) 'COVID-19 and higher education. Today and tomorrow. Impact analysis, policy responses and recommendation'. Retrieved from http://www.iesalc.unesco.org/en/wp-content/uploads/2020/04/COVID-19-EN-090420-2.pdf.

Penprase, B. E. (2018) 'The fourth industrial revolution and higher education', *Higher Education in the Era of the Fourth Industrial Revolution*. Retrieved from https://doi.org/10.1007/978-981-13-0194-0_9.

Potterton, M. (2020) 'World bank on COVID-19's effect on education is disappointing'. Retrieved from https://mg.co.za.

Roberts, B. H. (2015) 'The Third Industrial Revolution: Implications for Planning Regions and Cities'. Retrieved from https://www.researchgate.net/publication/278671121._

Rodney, W. (1973) *How Europe Underdeveloped Africa*. Retrieved from http://abahlali.org/files/3295358-walter-rodney.pdf.

Saavedra, J. (2020, March 30) 'Educational challenges and opportunities of the Coronavirus (COVID19) pandemic', *World Bank Blogs*. Retrieved from https://blogs.worldbank.org/education/educationalchallenges-and-opportunities-covid-19-pandemic.

Sansa, N.A. (2020) 'Analysis of the impact of the covid-19 to the petrol prices in china', *Diverse Journal of multidisciplinary research*, 2 (2), 33-37.

Schwab, K. (2016) 'How Can We Embrace the Opportunities of the Fourth Industrial Revolution?' *World Economic Forum*. Retrieved from https://www.weforum.org/agenda/2016/01/how-can-we-embrace-the-opportunities-of-the-fourth-industrial-revolution/.

The Southern Africa Development Community. (2020, April 14) 'Towards a common future'. Retrieved from https://www.sadc.int/news-events/news/sadc-and-unesco - sign-agreement-ensure-learning-never stops.

United Nations. (2020) 'Policy Brief: Education during COVID-19 and beyond'. Retrieved from https://www.un.org/development/desa/dspd/wp-content/uploads/sites/22/2020/08/sg_policy_brief_covid-19_and_education_august_2020.pdf.

United Nations Educational Scientific and Cultural Organization. (2020) 'COVID-19 Educational Disruption and Response'. Retrieved from Unesco.Org. https://en.unesco.org/news/covid-19-educational-disruption-and-response.

United Nations. (2020) 'The impact of Covid -19 on sport, physical activity and well-being and its effects on social development', *Department of Economic and Social Affairs, Covid-19 Response. Police brief No 73*. Retrieved from https://www.un.org/development/desa/dpad/wp-content/uploads/sites/45/publication/PB_73.

Van Beusekom, M. (2020) 'Scientists: Exactly zero' evidence covid-19 came from a lab'. Retrieved from https://www.cidrap.umn.edu/news-perspective/2020/05/scientists-exactly-zero-evidence-covid-19-came-lab.

WHO (2020a) 'Novel Coronavirus (2019-nCoV) Situation Report-9'. Retrieved from https://www.weforum.org/agenda/2016/01/how-can-we-embrace-the-opportunities-of-the-fourth-industrial-revolution/.

WHO. (2020b) 'World Bank Education and Covid-19'. Retrieved from http:www.worldmank.org/en/data/interactive/202/03.24/world-bank-education-and-covid-19

World Economic Forum. (2015) 'How Africa's colonial history affects its development'. Retrieved from https://www.weforum.org/agenda/2015/07/how-africas-colonial-history-affects-its-development/.

World Economic Forum. (2020) 'The Covid-19 pandemic has changed education forever: This is how'. Retrieved from https://www.weforum.org/agenda/2020/04/coronavirus-education-global-covid19-online-digital-learning/.

Wikramanayake, G. N. (2005) 'Impact of Digital Technology on Education', 24th National Information Technology Conference. University of Colombo School of Computing, Sri Lanka. Retrieved from https://www.researchgate.net/publication/216361364_Impact_of_Digital_Technology_on_Education.

Xu, M., David, J. M. and Kim, S. H. (2018) 'The fourth industrial revolution: Opportunities and challenges', *International Journal of Financial Research*, 9(2). Retrieved from https://doi.org/10.5430/ijfr.v9n2p90.

Ziyu, Z. (2020, April 26) 'Distance learning during COVID-19 worsens educational inequality'. Retrieved, from: https://news.cgtn.com.

Chapter Seven

Shona Culture and a New World Order: Fissures, Strategies and Mitigation in COVID 19 Era

Enna Sukutai Gudhlanga & Angeline Mavis Madongonda

Introduction

The coronavirus (COVID-19) which was first identified in Wuhan, China, towards the end of 2019 has greatly affected how communities live and relate to one another. The origins of the virus are still not properly known. However, China claims that it came from animals while others believe that it was manufactured in a Chinese laboratory in Wuhan. It is also apparent that some powerful institutions, governments and individuals have propounded different versions for the origins of the virus to serve their specific interests. Most parts of the world have, nevertheless, agreed and witnessed that the coronavirus is not only highly infectious, but fatal resulting with the World Health Organisation (WHO) declaring it a pandemic on 11 March 2020. As of 2 September 2020, there were more than 25 776 601 confirmed cases of COVID-19 and more than 857 448 deaths have been reported from more than 210 countries globally (European Centre for Disease Control and Prevention 2020). The pandemic is also accountable for the socio-politico and economic disruption of lives of millions across the world. In order to combat this pandemic and its spiral effects, countries have come up with various mitigation strategies which emphasise on general hygiene, use of sanitisers, physical distancing and national lockdowns among others. Some of these strategies, rather than alleviate the situation, have further adversely affected people's livelihoods and cultures. This chapter intends to investigate how Zimbabwean culture has been affected by such strategies imposed by the Zimbabwean government in an effort to combat the spread of COVID-19. It endeavours to demonstrate the fissures in African culture which were/are a direct result of the new world order ushered in by COVID-19. The research is largely qualitative in nature and a sample of 12 purposively selected community elders in Harare's Central

Business District (CBD) were interviewed. It is hoped that the cultural fissures brought about by COVID-19 are recognised and put under the spotlight for the benefit of Zimbabwe's wellbeing. The chapter also hopes to recommend some mitigation strategies which would reduce drastically the destruction of Zimbabwean culture. The study is informed by *Ubuntu/Unhu* philosophy which implies being properly socialised in indigenous African culture.

The coronavirus has been characterised by a trail of devastating destruction across the world. Loss of human life has occurred in magnitudes unprecedented than ever before. Economies have crumpled leading to loss of employment, general misery and suffering across developed countries. With such effects witnessed in developed countries, speculation was rife that developing countries and particularly countries in Africa were likely to fare badly. Surprisingly the effects of coronavirus have taken a different twist from what was predicted to happen. This chapter offers the different ways the Zimbabwean socio-economic and cultural landscapes have been affected. It demonstrates how Zimbabweans have used their own strategies to survive the onslaught of the pandemic. In other words, the effects of the pandemic have been contextualised to get the real experiences of Zimbabwean people against a pandemic ravaging the whole globe. However, the chapter also endeavours to demonstrate how the used strategies have created some fissures in African culture.

Contextualising COVID-19 in Zimbabwe

Zimbabwe has had its own fair share of myths around COVID-19. Zimbabweans were made to believe through the media that only White people, those with underlying conditions and those with history of travel outside the country were more vulnerable to the virus (Ross 2020). Little did Zimbabweans realise that there would be possible local transmissions. This instilled among the people of Zimbabwe some false comfort and immunity to the virus. This false comfort relates very well to the false immunity towards HIV that people had when they thought that HIV and AIDS was a disease of homosexuals and those in heterosexual relationships were safe (Gudhlanga & Chirimuuta 2012). This false sense of immunity resulted in very high HIV and AIDS related deaths in Zimbabwe in the period 1996-2004 (Gudhlanga & Chirimuuta 2012).

With respect to COVID-19 pandemic, another sad development in Zimbabwe was delayed response by the government to acknowledge the problem and take appropriate action. Those in leadership rarely addressed the subject in speeches and when they finally did it was with sad consequences. Of note was the remark from Zimbabwe's defence minister, Honourable Oppah Muchinguri Kashiri, who while addressing party stalwarts at a rally in Chinhoyi, a city situated about 110km north west of Harare on Saturday 14 March 2020, seemed to celebrate the spread of the virus through Europe and the United States. In her own words Muchinguri-Kashiri said, "God is punishing them now and they are now indoors while their economy is screaming like what they did to ours by imposing sanctions on us" (Fedschun 2020: n.p). Muchinguri-Kashiri also aimed her criticism against Donald Trump the President of the United States and further said in the local Shona language, "(Donald) Trump should know that he is not God. They must face the consequences of coronavirus so that they also feel the pain" (Fedschun 2020: n.p). Such remarks coming from a senior government official would continue to give false comfort to ordinary people. Muchinguri's remarks were however not taken lightly by opposition parties who described them as "reckless, morbid and inhuman" (Okello 2020: n.p). Renowned government critic and Law lecturer at the University of Kent in the United Kingdom, Alex Magaisa, tweeted: "How does she face her Chinese counterparts, where the pandemic began when she makes such insulting and insensitive statements?" (Okello 2020: n.p).

Without mentioning Muchinguri-Kashiri's name and her reckless comments, the Head of State President Emmerson Mnangangwa was prompted into making a statement on coronavirus on national television on Monday 16 March 2020. He said, "His government empathises with affected people around the globe…Pandemics of this kind have a scientific explanation and know no boundary, and like any other natural phenomenon cannot be blamed on anyone" (Fedschun. 2020: n.p). He had to counteract Muchinguri-Kashiri's remarks and reminded the world that what the defence minister had said was not the official statement from government on the coronavirus. This reaction of the government of Zimbabwe was seen as public relations stance bent on mending diplomatic relations that had been tattered through Muchinguri-Kashiri's remarks. Soon after making that statement, President Mnangagwa declared the coronavirus pandemic a national disaster to allow the government to mobilise resources to defend against it. Of note, the country's premium showcase, the Zimbabwe International Trade Fair was cancelled. Furthermore, the 40th independence celebrations which were set for the 18th of April were also cancelled in a bid to channel resources towards fighting COVID-19 in anticipation of whenever it reached the country's borders.

Zimbabwe soon announced its first COVID-19 case of a 38-year-old man from the resort town of Victoria Falls who had travelled from the United Kingdom through South Africa (Cassim, 2020: n.p). The country's second confirmed case was Zororo Makamba who had travelled to the United States on 29 February and returned into the country on 9 March 2020. Makamba became the country's first confirmed COVID-19 death. He succumbed to the virus on 22 March and was buried within 24 hours, on the 23rd of March 2020 at the family farm in Mazowe in line with WHO guidelines that all people who died due to COVID-19 infection should be buried within 24 hours (Chipunza & Marunya 2020: n.p). COVID-19 had finally come to Zimbabwe but still some people still believed that those who had contracted the virus had done so because they had travelled abroad or had some underlying conditions. The fact that local transmission could also occur was totally uncomprehended. From the perspectives of this study this is another myth which helped to fuel the spread of the pandemic among the Zimbabwean populace.

As a follow-up on the declaration, the President set up an 11-member Coronavirus Taskforce which was chaired by the then minister of Health and Child Care, Minister Obadiah Moyo, who has since been replaced by Vice President Constantino Chiwenga. The taskforce was mandated with coordinating the efforts to fight the coronavirus. "The taskforce was supposed to monitor the situation and manage the response to the COVID-19 outbreak and identify any gaps for corrective action" (Ndoro 2020: n.p). It comprised of various government ministers who were supposed to monitor the situation and advise the Head of State on the way forward. Ironically, Defence minister, Oppah Muchinguri, who said that coronavirus was God's punishment for the west was also a member of the taskforce (Ndoro 2020: n.p). The president of Zimbabwe further declared the first 21-days of "total" lockdown on 27 March 2020 effective from 30 March 2020. This "total" lockdown meant curtailing movement within the country, shutting most shops and suspending flights in and out of Zimbabwe (Africa Research Bulletin 2020). Only essential services staff had authorisation to move and these comprised of health, military, police, security guards and a limited number of government personnel who worked hand-in-hand with the ministries to provide the much-needed service to prevent and manage the virus. The few essential shops and pharmaceuticals operated from 9am to 3pm. Those without authorisation were not allowed to freely move, these could only move within a 6km radius when going to seek medical services or replenish food supplies. Movement was severely restricted with the police and the military mounting checkpoints on all major routes leading into the central business districts of major towns and cities to enforce compliance.

Police patrols both on foot and horseback in some urban areas and shopping centres in residential areas would announce, "We do not want to see people here on the streets. We do not want to see people who have no business in town just loitering... Everyone to their homes" (Africa Research Bulletin 2020: n.p.). The lockdown also saw the banning of private commuter omnibuses, popularly known in Zimbabwe as *kombis*. The Zimbabwe United Passenger Company (ZUPCO) buses were the official mode of public transport. Public gatherings including weddings, funerals and church services were suspended and limited to only 50 people per gathering as well as observing the WHO guidelines. Intercity travel was also banned. The lockdown was initially extended by another 2 weeks, and at the end of that extension it was further extended indefinitely although with some relaxation in some sectors. It is against this background that one can understand the cultural fissures that have emanated in Zimbabwe as result of combatting coronavirus.

Statement of the problem

The current mitigatory strategies imposed by the Government of Zimbabwe to prevent the spread of the dreaded COVID-19 pandemic have however created some fissures in African culture. They have threatened socio-cultural norms and values that are pivotal to African societies and are now facing severe risk of disappearing into oblivion. The chapter therefore seeks to demonstrate the various measures imposed by the Government of Zimbabwe to curb the spread of the COVID-19 pandemic. It examines how the mitigatory strategies have further adversely affected people's livelihoods and culture among the Shona people of Zimbabwe as well as highlight some strategies that can help curb the spread of the virus at the same time upholding the African cultural values and heritage.

Methodology

The study adopted a qualitative methodology design which made it possible to appreciate the effects on the mitigatory strategies imposed by the Government of Zimbabwe on Shona culture. Purposive and snowball sampling methods were used in identifying the research informants who would clarify on the issue of the fissures in African culture which were/are a direct result of the new world order ushered in by COVID-19 and how these are best understood by certain groups of people, namely the mature and elderly ones. Therefore, these two types of sampling methods enabled the researchers to get the right people who could easily assist the researchers. The study sample was determined by data saturation, while purposive sampling was used to select participants that were regarded as data rich sources (Creswell 2014). Data was collected through in-depth open-ended interviews with 12 elderly people in Harare CBD. Despite assurances of anonymity and privacy, one of the informants later confessed that they were not quite sure what the researchers wanted to do with the information and did not want to be found on the wrong side of the law by discussing how the government strategies were fast putting cultural values into oblivion.

Theoretical framework

This study is informed by the *Ubuntu/Unhu* theoretical framework which is premised on "humanity through recognising the humanity of others" (Samkange & Samkange 1980) and creating a communal atmosphere that emphasises "kinship among and between the indigenous people of Africa" (Ramose 1991: 271). Among the Shona people of Zimbabwe being human means having *hunhu/ubuntu* and culture which implies being properly socialised into the cultural dictates of the Shona people (Furusa 2006: 20). According to Gelfand (1973: 104) *hunhu* refers to "an appreciation of values that are more than the material or useful" to personhood. It is imperative to ground the study in Afro-centred theoretical underpinnings that emanate from African culture and history. Such theories have Africa as the centre and therefore recognise Africans (in this case the Shona people of Zimbabwe) in their bid to combat the COVID-19 pandemic to try and prevent the spread of the epidemic and its ravaging effects and the same time preserve the Shona cultural values which are at the core of the African people's existence. Inasmuch there is a need to tackle the epidemic which has befallen the nation, the mitigatory strategies should not disregard *Ubuntu/unhu* which undergirds African people's lives in general and the Shona people in particular. Furthermore, *Ubuntu* is pertinent to this study which hopes to proffer mitigatory strategies that hope to uphold African culture. The African philosophy of *Ubuntu* which "connotes humanness, a pervasive spirit of caring, and community harmony and hospitality, respect and responsiveness, that individuals and groups display for one another" is very relevant to this study (Mangaliso 2001). *Ubuntu* philosophy is taken from the belief that one neighbour's misfortune is empathised and shared. Thus, for adherents of the *Ubuntu* philosophy, the first reaction was working as a team while anything that worked against them was considered inhuman and unAfrican. It is hoped that within this framework African nations and Zimbabwe in particular would find ways of curbing the spread of the coronavirus and the same time uphold their African culture.

Current strategies used to combat COVID-19 in Zimbabwe and the resultant fissures in Shona culture

As already alluded to in the previous section, Zimbabwe has embraced a number of mitigatory strategies which include physical distancing, total lockdown, wearing of face masks, production of COVID-19 test results before one can be admitted into hospital, isolation of COVID-19 patients without having their loved ones visit them in hospital, quarantining of exposed people, use of hand sanitisers and handwashing using running water and soap. However, some of these mitigatory strategies have created fissures in the Shona people's culture. The fissures in African culture as a result of COVID-19 mitigatory strategies have been observed by UNESCO (2020: 6) where they opine that:

> social norms, ethics and human rights are under threat…One of the unintended consequences of the imposition of strict measures by African governments in the wake of the pandemic is the threat they pose to the very fabric of African societies…socio-cultural norms and values that are at the centre of African societies now face severe risk of disappearing into oblivion.

This amply demonstrates that some of the mitigatory strategies have either created fissures in African culture or threaten total oblivion of these African cultural values, the very ethos upon which the African people's life revolves around. According to p'Bitek (1986) writing within the Ugandan context, cultural values are a people's philosophy as lived and celebrated in their society. These cultural values inform and govern a people's various institutions. Once these are banned, or tempered with it really creates some fissures and total oblivion of cultural values and practices at the core of existence of any specific cultural group.

One of the major strategies that Zimbabwe has embraced is what has been termed social distancing in most circles (Muherjee & Dias 2020; Ladan 2020; Manshur & Husni 2020; Lee 2020; Koor, Cook, Park, Sun, Sun & Lim 2020). Social distancing is a public health strategy which attempts to prevent or slow the spread of a highly infectious pathogen such as coronavirus (Lee, 2020; n.p.). However, in this chapter we use the term physical distancing instead of social distancing. This is because there is a difference between social distancing and physical distancing. Inasmuch as people are physically distant through geographical location, the closeness of social relations is still emphasised although it is being exercised through technology rather than through actual physical closeness. For instance, husbands and wives/parents and children continue to be socially close even though they may be physically distant, for instance one is in the United Kingdom and the other is in Africa. This chapter therefore uses the term physical distancing and not social distancing to refer to the public health strategy of physically separating people as a way of slowing down the spread of the epidemic. The government of Zimbabwe has enforced physical distancing through the national lockdown. Schools have been closed, churches services suspended and also socio-cultural functions like weddings suspended and funerals restricted to only about 50 people. Furthermore, COVID-19 death burial is supposed to be conducted within 24 hours. This is normally before even very close relatives and friends arrive. This has resulted in even very close relatives fail to attend a loved one's burial.

Since the intercity travel is banned, and general movement restricted it has been a mammoth task for one to travel to other cities or rural areas to pay their last respects to loved ones. In Zimbabwe during lockdown if one wants to travel for a funeral in another city or in the rural areas they normally have to get an authorisation letter from the police with the copy of a burial order which is normally send through WhatsApp. One respondent stated that:

When my brother passed away in Gokwe, I had to go and explain myself to the police in order for them to give me a letter of travel. On the first day I did not get the letter from Makoni Police Station but was advised to go the Central Police Station at Charge Office [in the city centre 32 km away]. Getting to charge office was a mammoth task for me during the first very strict 21 days of the lockdown. I went back home without the authorisation letter. Upon conferring with my neighbour, she advised me to go and pay the police 5USD as bribe in order for them to write the letter for me. I did not have that kind of money. I had to borrow from my neighbour who gave me. I then went back to the police station and was given the authorisation letter. Armed with that letter it was still difficult to get to Gokwe since public transport was banned. I got to Gokwe soon after the burial of my brother. Also, all the way the private cars that I hitch hiked still charged in United States dollars. I was so devastated. Apart from being bankrupt, I could not perform the traditional rites of burying my brother. Furthermore, my siblings based in rural areas could not properly understand why I could miss such a critical family occasion since they did not quite understood about the national lockdowns since it was business as usual in the village.

This demonstrates that apart from failing to perform the cultural rites of laying to rest her brother, the respondent also had some problems which threatened family unity by failing to participate in such critical family functions.

Furthermore, the payment of a bribe to the police to get an authorisation letter also threatened communal cohesion which is typical of the African culture. Instead of the respective officer who assisted the respondent to empathise with someone who had lost a sibling and greatly assist them without being bribed as happens in African cosmology, the respective officer found an opportunity to cash in from a very desperate person. It was further revealed that the private cars that the respondent hitch hiked to Gokwe never empathised with the respondent but continued to fleece her from the borrowed money she was using. The cultural ethos of *Ubuntu* is thus being threatened by these new developments. Instead of everyone empathising with the person who had lost a loved one they all found opportunities to charge exorbitant prices for services in USD where almost everyone in Zimbabwe earns the Zimbabwe Local currency which has an official exchange rate of 1USD: ZWD86 and 1USD: ZWD100 at the black-market rate.

The ban on public gatherings and reducing the number of people attending a funeral to only 50 also greatly affected the cultural ethos of the African people. In African culture people have been socialised to attend funerals and assist one another in such sombre occasions. With the ban most family members and even neighbours failed to pay their last respects to friends and loved ones. The ban on intercity travel and the need to bury those who had died of COVID-19 infection within 24 hours has also made it very difficult for people to be buried in their rural homes as is per tradition. Even the night vigils and body viewing of COVID-19 corpses have been banned. One respondent whose daughter passed away in New Zealand could not have the body flown back to Zimbabwe for burial. Neither could they send family members to go and witness the burial in New Zealand as a result of the ban on international travel due to COVID-19. Her daughter had succumbed to breast cancer and the family observing the lockdown restrictions only met briefly at her house in Greendale (Harare) and watched the burial online. Only her two granddaughters aged 26 and 23 based in New Zealand managed to attend their mother's funeral. The deceased's siblings and other relatives could not perform the final funeral rites as is per custom in African culture. The family could not even travel to New Zealand to be with their daughter during her sickness and final days on earth. The respondent further said that she has no closure to her daughter's death since participating in the final rites such as night vigils saying eulogies about the deceased and finally physically witnessing the burial place helps in creating some form of closure. She lamented that apart from decimating the population, COVID-19 has also shaken the core of the African cultural values and ethos.

The fissures in African culture are not happening in Zimbabwe alone but even in South Africa. Luhanya and de-Greef (2020: n.p.) have noted a similar occasion where one could not be buried in their ancestral home. They state that:

> In ordinary times, there would be no question where Zinzile Mweli would be buried: alongside his ancestors in the village where he was born but now he will have to buried here in Khayelitsha so far away from his ancestral home. Even his relatives cannot travel due to restrictions put on interprovincial

travel. Attendance at funerals is capped at 50 and overnight vigils and body viewing are banned.

Thus, the fissures in African culture are also affecting many African societies. The ban on public gathering has also affected weddings. In African culture marriage is solemnised by the payment of *lobola* to the bride's family. This is a grand occasion where relatives from both the groom and the bride's families meet to witness such an event. Most families postponed such events and some brides ended up eloping, going to live with their man-friends without the consent of both families. Even the church wedding which is normally attended by all the relatives was also banned. Thus, the Shona people could no longer witness such joyful occasions which resulted in new families being formed through marriage.

The ban on public gatherings have shaken the fundamental values of African culture. UNSECO (2020: n.p.) has also observed this and asserts that:

> The ban on public gatherings, for instance, in response to the pandemic has had consequent impact on family and community life, increased possibility of fracturing relationships and undermining trust between states and their citizens with long term implications for cohesion and social harmony.

This amply demonstrates that some of the mitigatory strategies have shaken the fundamental principles of African culture which thrives on social cohesions which demonstrated through the banned public gatherings such as weddings and funerals.

The fissures have also been observed in the health sector. In Shona culture when one falls sick she is looked after by family members or even the community might step in to assist where possible. With the advent of hospitals sick people are now admitted and treated in hospitals with relatives and friends being allowed to come and see the sick person on prescribed visiting times three times a day depending with the type of hospital. The aspect of isolating COVID-19 patients has also put a ban on hospital visits. Relatives and friends cannot freely visit their loved ones in hospital. Even those who have tested positive and advised to isolate at home cannot freely interact with family members. Furthermore, if one had to be admitted in hospital they have to produce a COVID-19 test result first and cannot be easily admitted into hospital upon arrival. The Shona culture of quickly taking care of the sick and giving the necessary help and medication upon arrival has been shaken through COVID-19 mitigatory strategies. Additionally, nurses and doctors are being shunned in public transport. Commuters using the ZUPCO buses do not want to sit next to medical personnel on the bus. One respondent stated that he "would not want to sit next to COVID-19 people, these nurses, doctors and ambulance personnel are the transmitters of COVID-19 and I do not want to sit next to them on the bus for they will pass on the virus to me." The concept of communal cohesion has been shaken to the core, people now label some professions as high-risk groups and transmitters of the deadly virus and try to avoid them as much as possible on buses, in the shops or any public place. These are easily identifiable through their uniforms thereby fuelling stigma. One lady standing in a ZUPCO bus queue stated that; "It is better for these COVID-19 transmitters to have their own bus rather than to be packed together with us on the same bus." Commuters would prefer what they now term 'staff' to board first on their own and they encourage them to stand in their own queue. The 'staff' are the uniformed forces and the health personnel. Thus, people no longer feel secure to sit next to such people on the bus and try to create some physical distancing as much as they can. Looking down upon other people is unAfrican and the segregation and refusing to sit next to others is unAfrican. It shakes the very core values of *Ubuntu*.

The extended 'total' lockdown has also taken away the African family's ability to fend for themselves. The lockdowns have resulted in disruption of livelihoods. Most Shona families live from hand to mouth and the declaration of national lockdown left most families in very dire situations in which they could not fend for themselves especially those in the informal sector and do not get paid if they do not go to work. Most families do not have maize meal, the staple food, to feed their families since the past two years have been characterised by drought in Zimbabwe. This implies that locking down people giving them a very short space of time left many families without any food. One respondent stated that before coronavirus kills him, he would have died of hunger. This has been supported by Muronzi (2020) who argues that many families in Zimbabwe were taken unawares by the lockdown. The majority of the people live from hand to mouth and were found queuing for the scarce mealie-meal just before the commencement of the total lockdown. Such biosecurity measures deprived the ordinary citizen of the ability to fend for their families. Household heads could no longer put food on the table. Failure to fend for the family is unAfrican. The new measure stripped the families of the ability to look after themselves.

The preceding section has highlighted some of the mitigatory strategies that have brought some fissures to the coherent African culture. We propose that it would make a lot of sense to promote mitigatory strategies that do not force African cultural values into oblivion. The succeeding section tries to proffer strategies that are in tandem with African culture.

Possible mitigation strategies in tandem with Shona culture

Inasmuch as the promulgated biosecurity measures set by the government in a bid to slow the spread to COVID-19, these have also been seen to have a negative on African culture as highlighted in the previous section. This therefore implies that there is need to come up with prevention strategies to combat the spread of COVID-19 and as well as uphold the African people's cultural values and ethos. Even the WHO has noted the same and have recommended that there should be "safe and dignified burials or risk 'free burials with dignity'" (Tayerne, Kra, Akindes, Laborde-balan, Sow & Egyrot 2020: n.p.). By dignity in this context WHO meant respecting the family's cultural and religious practices and safe meant employing the biosecurity guidelines. The biosecurity guidelines were not supposed to be done at the expense of a people's culture. It is therefore important to come up with prevention strategies that do not create fissures in African cultural practices.

The first possible strategy would be to rope in traditional leaders such as chiefs in the intervention strategy. At the moment it is only the government which is giving directives to the community raising awareness about the deadly effects of COVID-19. The general populace normally does not take top down initiatives but if these were coming from their traditional leaders they would at least listen to their community leaders and it would be easier to implement the various strategies like physical distancing and wearing of masks. Hashmi, Iqbal, Haque and Saleem (2020: 19) has also noted the importance of engaging community leaders in warding off epidemics and states that:

> There is need to engage religious and traditional leaders of
> the respective societies and communities, and their influence on

their followers can greatly benefit the efforts against COVID-19. The same influence can be used to raise awareness and change the attitudes and practices of community dwellers as community members listen to their religious and traditional leaders, healthcare organisations should take religious leaders on board while handling and managing COVID-19.

Engaging community leaders respected by society would greatly assist in preventing the spread of the epidemic. Currently there is no one to enforce physical distancing in rural areas, and even the wearing of face masks and use of hand sanitisers. One of the respondents stated that the wearing of face masks was an urban thing. He had recently travelled to his rural home and there was nothing like COVID-19, the people in his rural home were still conducting business as usual. If community leaders had been involved in raising awareness they were going to be in a better position to be listened to by the community as compared to top-down approaches that come from very high offices. The use of traditional leaders in combating epidemics has also been observed by Miller and Rubin (2011) in the context of HIV and AIDS.

Furthermore, the restriction of funeral gatherings to only 50 could be left open, such that all those who need to bid farewell to their loved ones could do so but keeping the physical distance of about 1-2 metres from each other. Moreover, the awareness messages about COVID-19 are mainly broadcast in English, nothing much is being done to send the messages in indigenous languages. If everybody understood how coronavirus is transmitted and its devastating effects they would observe the physical distance even in very large gatherings like funerals and weddings. Instead of banning the large gatherings it was necessary to raise awareness through traditional leaders and using indigenous languages that are intelligible to the general populace. Once everybody is aware what COVID-19 is all about, it would be easier to implement the biosecurity measures among large crowds without creating any fissure or resulting in the extinction of certain cultural practices.

Additionally, there is need to adopt a Training-of-Trainers model in training community leaders who live with people in the community about the dangers of COVID-19 and how best it can be prevented from causing further havoc in our societies. The Training-of-Trainer model ensures sustainability because of its potential for up-skilling the workforce rapidly and economically (Momina & Pinder 2018).

The community members who would have been trained would in-turn train other members on coronavirus.

Also, funeral wakes and body viewing of COVID-19 corpses could still be done provided sealed caskets with a glass cover on the face section are used. The sealed caskets would make it possible to be in the same room with dead body without getting any infection through inhalation of whatever gases that might be coming from the corpse. The glass showing the dead person's face would make it possible for people to still view the body of their loved one during the funeral service without putting themselves at risk. Singing in groups observing biosecurity measures such as wearing of face masks and observing physical distancing could still be performed. This, therefore, means that the funeral wakes which normally gives the Shona people the opportunity to sing and dance throughout the night could still be performed but observing biosecurity measures. The singing and dancing would be punctuated by eulogies that are said in honour of the deceased relative. Funeral wakes give the mourners and the family the opportunity to appropriately bid farewell to their loved one and come to terms with what would have happened. Thus, both biosecurity measures would be observed, and traditional practices still performed to the satisfaction of the mourners. Commenting on COVID-19, Maluleke (2020: n.p.) also highlighted the need to observe cultural values when he stated that:

> In times of plagues and epidemics, we need more than the WHO types of containment strategies designed to give scientists enough time to search for a vaccine. We need all our psychological, cultural and spiritual resources as a people. We have to summon them all if we hope to win the long war which has only just begun against coronavirus.

This amply demonstrates that focusing on biosecurity measures without considering their implications on cultural practices will not make the world win the war against COVID-19. Instead there is need to harness even the cultural beliefs and practices in a bid to win the war against COVID-19 there needs to be a comprehensive strategy and not piece meal efforts.

It is also imperative to look into the African traditional past on how they handled such epidemics like respiratory infections. In African culture such respiratory infections could easily be controlled through the use of inhalation of certain herbs that were boiled in water. One would be covered under a blanket and inhale the steam which would greatly give relief to such pain. Most of the respondents stated that they still practice this inhalation of steamed traditional herbs and these have greatly given them a lot of relief. They also stated that through steaming they did not have the usual problems of flu infections this winter. Most of the respondents use public transport to go to work but at the end of each day they would steam themselves to ward off whatever infection that might have affected them. Madagascar has tapped from traditional medicine but sadly this has been rejected by WHO. In future such knowledge from African countries should be given a chance. Thus, it is very important to tap from the traditional practices and see how the traditional communities responded to such threats in the past.

Conclusion

The chapter has discussed the history of COVID-19, contextualised it in Zimbabwe, and demonstrated how some of the beliefs that evolved in a bid to understand the origins of the coronavirus have not assisted in understanding the pandemic, but rather have created confusion and resistance in the fight and mitigation against the pandemic. Biomedical strategies used to combat COVID-19 have also created some fissures in African culture, threatening African traditional beliefs and practices. The chapter has also demonstrated that in order to win the war against COVID-19, there is need to contextualise traditional African beliefs and practices rather head for a collision course that results in culture conflict and hence adverse effects on the people. If *Ubuntu/ Unhu* is used in the fight against COVID-19 it would go a long way in combatting current fissures that seem to be widening with the use of bio-security measures that disregard cultural practices and values. With statistics in Africa proving to the world that it has its own unique ways of combatting the virus, it can be deduced that Africa has lessons that could save the world from the devastation it is facing. The chapter thus amply advocates for the understanding for comprehensive indigenous strategies against COVID-19 that take into consideration the environment that influences the behaviour of a people not top-down prescriptive approaches.

References

Africa Research Bulletin. (2020) 'Zimbabwe coronavirus Lockdown'. *Africa Research Bulletin: Political, Social and Cultural Series,* 57(3). Retrieved from https://doi.org/10.1111/j.1467-825X.2020.09393.x.

Cassim, J. (2020) 'Zimbabwe reports first COVID-19 case'. Retrieved from https://www.aa.com.tr/en/africa/zimbabwe-reports-first-covid-19-case/1773705#:~:text=Zimbabwe%20announced%20Friday%20the%20country's,said%20Health%20Minister%20Obadiah%20Moyo.

Chipunza, P. and Marunya, K. (2020) 'Zim records first coronavirus death'. *The Herald,* 24 March. Retrieved from https://www.herald.co.zw/zim-records-first-coronavirus-death/.

Creswell, J. W. (2014) *Research design: Qualitative, Quantitative and Mixed Methods Approaches,* 4th edn, Thousand Oakes: SAGE Publications.

European Centre for Disease Prevention and Control. (2020) 'COVID-19 situation update worldwide as of 2 September 2020'. Retrieved from http:www.ecdc.europa.eu/en/geographicaldistribution-2019-ncov.

Fedschun, T. (2020) 'Coronavirus is Punishment for sanctions, 'US must also feel the pain' Zimbabwe official says'. *Fox News.* Retrieved from https://www.foxnews.com/world/coronavirus-us-zimbabwe-sanction-pain-viral-outbreak.

Furusa, M. (2006) 'The muse of history and politics of gender representation in Zimbabwean women's literature', in Z Mguni, M Furusa & R Magosvongwe (eds.), *African womanhood in Zimbabwean literature: new critical perspectives on women's Literature in African languages,* College Press Publishers (Pvt) Ltd, Harare, 1-23.

Gelfand, M. (1973) *The genuine Shona: survival values of an African culture,* Gwelo: Mambo Press.

Gudhlanga, E.S. & Chirimuuta, C. (2012) 'Advocacy as a tool of community development: Zimbabwe women writers breaking the silence on HIV and AIDS in the anthology', *Totanga Patsva (We Start Afresh). IMBIZO International Journal of African Literary and Comparative Studies,* 3(12), 59-75.

Hashmi, F.K., Iqbal, Q., Haque, N. & Saleem, H. (2020) 'Religious cliché and stigma: A brief response to overlooked barriers in Covid', *Journal of Religion and Health*.
Doi:org/10/10/1007/510943-020-01063-y.

Koor, J.R., Cook, A.R, Park, M., Sun, Y., Sun, H. and Lim, J.T. (2020) 'Interventions to mitigate early spread of SARS COV-2 in Singapore: A modelling study', *The Lancet Infectious Diseases*.
doi:10.1016/51473-3099(20)30162-6.

Jaja, F.I., Anyanwa, M.U. and Jaja, C.I. (2020) 'Social distancing: How religion, culture and burial ceremony undermine the effect to curb COVID-19 in South Africa', *Emerging Microbes and Infections*, 9(1), 1077-1079.
DOI:10.1080/22221751.2020.1769501.

Ladan, S.I. (2020) 'Response to the spread of coronavirus by Katsina State Government, Nigeria', *African Journal of Biology and Medical Research*, 3(2), 126-139.

Lee, B.Y. (2020) 'What is social distancing? Here are 10 ways to keep the coronavirus away'. Retrieved from https://www.forbes.com/sites/bruce/lee/2020/03/14/with-covid-19-coronavirus-here-are-10-ways-to-social-distance-yourself/#60932765602.

Luhanga, P. and de Greef, K. (2020) 'In South Africa burial traditions upended by coronavirus'. *New York Times*. Retrieved from https://www.nytimes.com/2020/07/10/world/africa/coronavirus-capetwon-south-africa-html.

Mangaliso, M. P. (2001) 'Building Competitive advantage from Ubuntu: Management lessons from South Africa', *Academy of Management Perspectives*, 15(3). Retrieved from https://doi.org/10.5465/ame.2001.5229453.

Manshur, M.F. and Husni, H. (2020) 'COVID-19 and anti-globalisation issues: A critical perspective', *Journal of Critical Reviews*, 3(14), 209-213.

Maluleke, T. (2020) 'The social and cultural implications of COVID-19', *News24*. Retrieved from https:///www.news24.com/news24/columnist/guestcololumn/opinion-the-social-and-cultural-implications-of-covid-19.

Miller, A.N. and Rubin, D.L. (2011) *Health communication and faith communities*. Sudbury: Hampton Press.

Momina, M and Pinter, S. (2018) 'A conceptual framework for training of trainers (TOT) interventions in global health', *Globalisation and Health*, 14(1), 1-16.

Muronzi, C. (2020) 'We'll die of hunger first before': despair as Zimbabwe lockdown begins'. Retrieved from https://www.aljazeera.com.news/2020/03/die-hunger-despair-zimbabwe-lockdowmn-begins-200330054919081.html.

Ndoro, T.E. (2020) 'Mnangagwa Sets Up COVID-19 Taskforce To Deal With Coronavirus Pandemic', *iHarare*. Retrieved from https://iharare.com/mnangagwa-sets-up-covid-19-taskforce-to-deal-with-coronavirus-pandemic/.

Okello, C. (2020) 'Zimbabwe's President Emmerson Mnangagwa has tried to defuse controversy sparked by comments from his defence minister claiming the coronavirus was God's punishment on the west', *RFI*. Retrieved from https://www.rfi.fr/en/africa/20200318-zimbabwe-mnangagwa-calm-coronavirus-from-god-controversy-revenge-west-defence-minister-muchinguri-covid-19.

P'Bitek, O. (1986) *Artist the ruler: Essays on art, culture and values*. Nairobi: Heinemann.

Ramose, M.B. (2002) *Philosophy from Africa: a text with reading*. Oxford: Oxford University Press.

Ross, J. (2020) 'Coronavirus outbreak revives dangers of race myths and pseudoscience: Most fictional claims about black immunity to the coronavirus are connected to the long history of contradictory but uniformly racist ideas'. Retrieved from www.nbcnews.com.

Samkange, S. and Samkange, T. M. (1980) *Hunhuism or ubuntuism: a Zimbabwe indegenous political philosophy*. Salisbury: Graham Publishing.

Tayerne, B., Kra, F., Akindes, F., Laborde-balan, G., Sow, K. and Egyrot, M. (2020) 'Funeral rites and COVID-19: What must be done to respect tradition and keep people safe', Trans'd from French by Heathwood, A. *Conversation FR*. France: Institute de Recherché pour le Development (IRD).

United Nations Educational Scientific and Cultural Organisation. (2020) 'Socio-economic and cultural impacts of COVID-19 on Africa, UNESCO responses: Executive summary'. Retrieved from https://en.unesco.org/sites/default/files/stand_alone_executive_summary_fin_pdf.

Chapter Eight

Dark Humour and its Implications: A Semiotic Reading of Comic Clips on the COVID-19 Pandemic on Shona Culture

Angeline Mavis Madongonda & Enna Sukutai Gudhlanga

Introduction

As the old adage goes, there is a thin line that divides crying and laughing, and indeed laughter has been called the best medicine in times of distress. At the same time, humour sometimes conceals grave messages. Humour has played the role of articulating people's responses to situations and crises - as ways of coping, registering their fears and hopes. This chapter was prompted by the growth of comic clips on the coronavirus (COVID-19) pandemic in Zimbabwe. Faced with the serious consequences of the COVID-19 pandemic, humorous clips have been met with mixed feelings with many condemning the dark humour as unfeeling in the face of numerous deaths around the globe; a phenomenon frowned upon by *hunhu/ubuntu*. Regarding the responses to the virus, Zimbabweans have found themselves facing numerous socio-economic hardships that the country is experiencing. Coupled with rampant unemployment, most families rely on hand to mouth informal survival strategies. As a result, the affected communities have roundly condemned the total lockdown that was meant to mitigate the effects of the virus. Within the context where the ambivalence of poverty and comic clips on the virus abounds, this chapter explores the nature of the comic clips on the COVID-19 pandemic, the possibly hidden messages behind their creation as well as the effects they have on the populace. A selection of conveniently selected texts and visual social media messages (mainly from WhatsApp) is used for analysis. The chapter is structuralist in approach and uses text and semiotic analyses as the tools of navigating around the selected clips. It was revealed that more serious messages are hidden from beneath the humour and laughter that they are meant to generate in a bid to point at ways of resolving Zimbabwean societal challenges during the

COVID-19 period. The chapter is also informed by theories of humour.

This chapter therefore focuses on some of the cultural responses by Zimbabweans to the COVID-19 pandemic. While the use of humour during times of distress has been criticised as unethical, this chapter demonstrates how humour can be viewed as one of the survival strategies in combatting the virus. A significant number of scholars are agreed that laughter is the best medicine and indeed the use of humour in times of distress has assisted those facing the anxiety associated with the enforced lockdowns, compliance as well as preventative measures- the new normal -as spelt out by Vinkateswaran (2020). Since Zimbabweans in general do not have the luxury of choice in terms of entertainment, comic clips via social media, particularly WhatsApp, have provided Zimbabweans with the entertainment in the face of a ravaging pandemic. This chapter therefore examines the nature of the comic clips, how they have affected the people and the lessons that they impart with respect to the treatment and reaction to the coronavirus. The sample of comic clips utilised in this research were conveniently selected and analysed using text and semiotic analyses.

Background to the study

As the old adage goes, laughter is the best medicine. In this way, laughter is taken to have healing effect to individuals and whole societies suffering any form of malaise. Chiduku (2020: n.p) cites an American Laura Ingalls Wilder who asserted that, "a good laugh overcomes more difficulties and dissipates more dark clouds than any other one thing." The coronavirus, however, is no laughing matter hence such humour associated with suffering, where the world is engulfed in mourning and deep sadness might sound misplaced. It is, therefore, important to contextualise the laughter within the Zimbabwe situation is insensitive to the tragedy surrounding numerous countries in the world. It is for this reason that this kind of humour is viewed as dark owing to the subject of the banter, which may be considered taboo. For reasons mentioned earlier, the humour in Zimbabwe has provided some comic relief from the daily challenges that most Zimbabweans have had to grapple with during the time of the pandemic.

This chapter will not harp on the situation the world over which has resulted in the enforcement of lockdowns in order to contain the virus. Rather, it dwells on the lockdown in Zimbabwe and how people have come to grapple with an unprecedented experience such as forced stay at home, loss of various forms of livelihood, and observance the World Health Organisation (WHO) guidelines to prevent the spread of the virus. This has obviously negatively affected and disrupted the lifestyles people had gotten used to, factors that this chapter seeks to address as people adopt intervention strategies in order to cope with pandemic. Martarelli and Wolff (2020) outline some of the restrictions (apart from being confined at home) such as physical distancing, suspension of most social and economic activities, prolonged isolation and self-quarantine leading to loss of freedom, loss of routines, psychological challenges such as anxiety, fear and the all-encompassing word - boredom. Compliance to some of the COVID-19 routines is also regarded as another form of challenge as people are forced to embrace such new practices as washing hands and wearing masks, routines that are enforced rather than voluntary. The new habits, according to Venkateswaran (2020), may be irritating on the part of those exercising them. Being shielded from the pandemic and keeping indoors has not resolved the challenge of the pandemic in its totality as newer challenges are emerging. Martirrelli and Wolffe (2020) go on to demonstrate how such challenges have materialised into subversive behaviour such as gambling and violence. Domestic and gender-based violence have been reported as some of the ills that have emerged during lockdown periods across the world. This calls for interventions that involve change of behaviour, as Martirelli and Wolffe (2020) put it. The boredom "triggers pro-social interactions" (Martirelli and Wolffe (2020: 2) that include some form of creativity so as to cope. While some turn to ready comedy on TV and other forms of entertainment, others create their own jokes to entertain themselves. In Zimbabwe the only television station does not give much in terms of entertainment, hence social media has offered a cheaper alternative to comic relief than would subscription-based television channels. Cheurfa (2020) has also observed the same amongst many Algerians during the 2020 month of Ramadan under lockdown noting that they turned to television for entertainment even though comic shows, particularly of a political nature, are banned in that country. What is clear is the need for entertainment to divert people from the depression, fear and anxiety associated with the COVID-19 pandemic.

The coronavirus has been presented in various media messages some of which have created confusion rather than clarity. COVID-19 comes with a combination of fear, anxiety and grief, fear of catching the virus, anxiety over safety and how to deal with it as well as fear of death (Salari, Hosseinian-Far, Jalali, Vaisi-Raygani, Rasoulpoor, Mohammadi, Shabnam Rasoulpoor & Khaledi-Paveh 2020). Coupled with this fear are some messages and unsubstantiated myths that claimed that the coronavirus was a white man's disease, and that it does not affect countries that experience hot weather among others (Ross 2020). Some influential individuals have had their stake on the effects of the coronavirus on the African continent. Gates (2020: n.p), wife to Microsoft mogul Bill Gates is on record as having said, "Africa will have dead bodies on the streets" all of which exacerbated the fears. This has resulted in heightened fear and anxiety particularly among Zimbabweans whose healthcare system is currently undergoing serious challenges and is overburdened (UNDP Zimbabwe 2020). Medical personnel have engaged in strikes prior to the inception of the coronavirus and thus without a functional health system, speculation was high that Zimbabweans were going to be some of the worst affected on the continent.

Among the Shona people of Zimbabwe, the saying *Kurerutsa ndima* – making light of a heavy burden means even at a funeral, people are supposed to laugh to do away with the draining effects of grief associated with the loss of a loved one. It is the role of the *sahwiras* (close family friends) and *vazukurus* (nephews) to enact the humorous episodes in the deceased's life. It is therefore not abnormal for people to share lighter moments, laughter and dance at funerals. However, when it comes to the pandemic, the fear of the unknown and the uncertainty surrounding the carnage it has left behind in numerous developed countries, has led many to frown at any kind of humour associated with the COVID-19. In Zimbabwe today, the majority of the population is grappling with a myriad of challenges most of which are stemming from the flagging economy. Many Zimbabweans live on informal enterprises and most families survive from hand to mouth. The coronavirus has thus brought with it more unprecedented challenges than was before and amongst Zimbabweans, laughter is one of the survival strategies. However, this idea of laughing when there are serious challenges has been frowned upon by many who feel that it is unAfrican and goes against the spirit of *Ubuntu* which dictates empathising with one's neighbour. Comedians have therefore been subject to criticism during such periods. Mukurunge (cited in Chiduku 2020) confirms this when he says, "Matters of life and death such as coronavirus might lead humour to be interpreted as insensitive unless it is just harmless banter. Most people do not take them too seriously…." Apart from humour being regarded as taboo in times of a pandemic, not many people, realise the serious messages that are enshrined in comic banter (Chiduku 2020). Furthermore, people acknowledge the therapeutic nature of laughter but fail to realise the socio-economic or even cultural flaws that comic banter wishes to address. In this chapter, laughter and humour are almost used interchangeably since laughter and even a smile are expression of humour (Antonovici 2015).

This chapter uses semiotic and textual analyses visual images comprising text, still pictures and moving images. The analyses are based on two video clips, two images and three text messages which were conveniently selected from personal communication through WhatsApp messages. It should be underlined that the writers do not claim or have any rights to the media in question. Reference is made to other clips in passing but the chapter dwells at length on the ones mentioned above. Textual and semiotic analyses give room to interpret messages in a multitude of ways –connotatively and denotatively. While textual analysis (McKee 2003) is used to dissect text messages, semiotic analysis has been used for both still and moving messages. Semiotic analysis (de Sassaure, Pierce cited in Yakin & Totu 2014) allows for the polysemic reading of any given messages. Signs that are generated in media messages are meant to drive home certain messages whether overtly of covertly. The analysis is presented in themes drawn from the several messages under study. It should also be noted that this chapter underscores positive effects that humour engenders for both the creators and consumers of the comic clips as well the dark side of humour.

Theories of humour

As has been highlighted before, emotions play a major role in the way people react and they also influence one's reasoning and ultimately one's behaviour (Venkateswaran 2020). As a result, scholars and theorists of humour have come up with reasons why humour is so important and critical. There are quite a number of theories of humour and the most renowned being relief theory, the superiority and the incongruity theories. However, in this chapter we use two theories of incongruity and relief. Relief theory is the most popular owing to its justification of the need to have humour to alleviate negative emotions. Freud (cited in Morreall 2020) is credited with giving the biology side of laughter when he says laughter releases tensions and nervousness, an explanation that is best described by Morreall (2020: n.p) who avers that relief theory is "an hydraulic explanation in which laughter does in the nervous system what a pressure-relief valve does in a steam boiler." In the context of COVID-19, the anxiety, fear and grief associated with illness and loss creates room for relief theory whose offering is laughter as a coping mechanism (Antonovici 2020). In this chapter however, we argue that in the Zimbabwean cultural context, humour is usually removed when there is illness and eventually death. In other words, people do not joke about the death or its cause. The scrutiny of social media messages on coronavirus that the researchers have come across also underline this fact- there were no messages that joked on actual illness and death. This is in line with the spirit of *Ubuntu* where Zimbabwean people tend to empathise with fellow humans.

Incongruity theory posits that laughter arises out of unfulfilled expectations and according to Kant and Schopenhauer (cited in Morreall 2020), when expectations are dashed, when what one expects and what is presented are at odds. The greater the distance between one's expectations and the result the funnier the joke. This theory draws its strength from the role humour plays "as a response to .... ambiguity, logical impossibility, irrelevance, and inappropriateness" (Kant & Schopenhauer, cited in Morreall 2020). Humour thus thrives on these elements of incongruity, which attempt to offer reason in unreasonableness. Among Zimbabweans, the delivery of a functional health system has been cause for banter amongst comedians. One Zimbabwean comedian has joked that the coronavirus would take long to get to Zimbabwe (even give up coming to Zimbabwe) owing to the long winding queues even at the border, queues for mealie meal and the bumpy potholed roads. From the foregoing, it is evident that Zimbabweans have their own fears regarding combatting the coronavirus, hence failures in other sectors have implied failure to deal with the pandemic.

Scholars also agree to the correlation between laughter and pain. When one is in pain or anxious as highlighted before, there is a tendency to look for relief. Humour is one such relief agent and results in reduction of stress levels. According to Antonovici (2015: 419), "Humour is the highest manifestation of the defence mechanisms being able to involve energy of the pleasant affect about to trigger and transform by ease into pleasure….." Mental health challenges therefore are eased with laughter replete with serious awareness messages. Arning (2020: n.p) adds that:

> humour was already becoming an antidote to what has become a 'new normal' of uncertainty across the sphere: …. Laughter increases happiness and dissolves stress. This is a key reason for the pervasiveness of humorous content: it is a drug that we increasingly cannot do without.

However, it should be noted that the effects of laughter, in spite of offering relief to recipients of such messages, are transient and the relief short-lived. It is for this reason that this chapter analyses messages with the hope of unearthing the serious side of the situation at hand- in this case the COVID-19 pandemic.

Contextualising the COVID-19 lockdown in Zimbabwe

As has been mentioned, the threat of the coronavirus has brought with it another kind of fear, not fear of the virus itself but fear of dying from hunger. The lockdown restrictions meant that there is no economic activity, particularly on the informal market. While the lockdown of the country was meant to mitigate the effects of the pandemic, and was meant to be met with rejoicing, for the majority of Zimbabweans this was met with trepidation particularly with those in the informal sector whose survival is based on hand to mouth daily survival. Those in the formal sector, particularly in the essential services have had to grapple with a myriad of challenges including cash and transport woes. Therefore, instead of keeping the Zimbabweans safe and having a sense of security, the lockdown and other restrictions have left them more vulnerable as people have to queue for almost all necessities. People queue for water, mealie meal, buses to name just a few and because such resources are too few and stretched over a large number, it means they are a struggle to acquire. Mcworth-Young, Chingono, Mavodza, McHugh, Tembo and Dziva-Chikwari (2020: 4) say this of the situation, "Zimbabwe, like many countries in sub-Saharan Africa, has an under-resourced healthcare system, high levels of unemployment, densely populated urban areas, and shortages of basic commodities, including water and food." Consequently, in such queues physical distancing and caution are ignored as the practice of observing distance creates opportunities for queue jumpers and ultimately degenerates into chaos. So, to curtail this, queues are closely observed with people packed together creating a rich environment for viral infections.

The period under review is from the first day of total lockdown, 30 March 2020 to the present day partially open economy. It can be concluded that the environment does not offer a lucrative safe haven to the occupants of locked down or restricted homesteads, instead, starvation would be lurking in the shadows. Many have also complained that the curfews are shortening the working days even when the lockdown has been eased. Mcworth-Young, et al (2020: 9) adds that, "Limited access to water and mealie meal (which makes the staple food sadza) shortages have been ongoing challenges in Zimbabwe which limited individuals' options of staying indoors and maintaining social distancing." Satirical banter over COVID-19 has thus been closely linked to this socio-politico and economic system. One is bound to lose the essence of some of the COVID-19 jokes should they fail to contextualise the Zimbabwe situation and the pandemic. The intricate connections between restricted movement, poverty and starvation are almost inextricable. Comedians have had a field day demonstrating the failure to understand the pandemic and its implications on the livelihoods of the populace.

With such a context in mind, where nothing appears to be working and against the serious threat of a ravaging pandemic, makes Zimbabwe a hub for distress for many. The fear that the ordinary Zimbabwean has to face on a daily basis is multifaceted. It is thus not surprising that Zimbabweans enjoy humour, both as creators and consumers. Some of the clips under consideration capture both these roles where the comedians themselves by creating humorous clips find an outlet for their own pent up emotions.

Redefining social media messages and the paradox of COVID-19

Social media messages have become a force to reckon with. In Zimbabwe where the media landscape is limited for the ordinary man on the street, social media has become the answer to accessing as well as participation in social discourses. As a result, social media has been replete with both serious and less serious messages. Concerning the COVID-19 pandemic, social media has also played an innumerable role in spreading messages faster than formal media with the terms 'viral' or 'trending' capturing the rate and speed at which messages are spread globally. Depoux, Martin, Karafillakis, Preet, Wilder-Smith and Larson (2020) agree with this by highlighting the speed at which social media messages travel. In this chapter, humorous clips shared over social media are used to disseminate messages that can reach those in distress, offering a reprieve to the distressing news associated with formal news whose obsession with statistics is depressing.

However, understanding the dynamics of humorous social media messages is thus of importance. Humour has tended to be effective when shared and associated with human contact amongst groups in interpersonal communication. Stand-up comedy has of late been gathering place where people gather just to share the feel-good ambience of laughter. Goleman, Boyatzis and McKee (2013: 10) articulate this succinctly when they say;

> Hearing laughter, we automatically smile or laugh too, creating a spontaneous chain reaction that sweeps through a group. Glee spreads so readily because our brains...[are] designed specifically for detecting smiles and laughter that make us laugh in response.

It is incontrovertible then that the warm experience of humour that engulfs any group creates a special relationship, a bond, between the people in the group. Goleman et al. (2013) state that it is the contagious nature of smiles that makes others smile in return. Laughter, they argue offers a "unique trustworthy sign of friendliness." However, Goleman et al. (2013) distinguish between a smile and laughter where unlike laughter, a smile can be feigned while the former is involuntary. In a public theatre this can be evidenced in the spontaneous uproarious laughter from the gallery.

However, social media is fast revolutionising the way people view humour. While stand-up comedy has brought together unknown groups of gatherings with a common goal of sharing a good time in a physical setting, social media appears to do the opposite. It would appear as if the humour that is shared on social media lacks the human warmth as what is underlined in the cold separateness and detached individual use of media messages. Individuals who share the media messages are separated by distance and time. The physical distancing, quarantining and isolation that have been brought about by COVID-19 have not helped matters either, with distance between

179

individuals being widened further, many would agree that nothing beats sharing a humorous clip with a colleague at work even when it is on WhatsApp. Nevertheless, with the lockdowns and attendant restrictions, this has widened the interaction gaps. In terms of distance, Goleman et al. (2013) conversely make an interesting observation, that laughter represents shortest distance between two people. This means, despite the physical separation, there is the covert camaraderie that is shared by social media users as they interact and share humorous clips. The overt camaraderie is best understood by users who belong to the same WhatsApp group. Reactions to messages are captured by icons represented by respective *emojis* and indexed onomatopoeic "kikikikiki" symbolising the shared sniggering experienced from one end of the message to another. In other words, people warm up to those who share humorous clips with them. This is experienced whether one is in natural physical group setting of using social media space. This is aptly captured in the following statement:

> Of all the emotional signals, smiles are the most contagious; they have an almost irresistible power to make others smile in return. Smiles may be so potent because of the beneficial role they played in evolution: smiles and laughter scientists speculate, evolved as a non-verbal way to cement alliances, and signify that an individual is relaxed and friendly rather than guarded or hostile (Goleman, Boyatzis & McKee 2013: 10).

In a similar vein, Wasserman (2020) talks of humour building a community. This means in spite of the physical distance instigated by the COVID-19 pandemic, people from varied backgrounds are drawn together when they share humorous messages.

While social media has availed alternative media voices to the average person, it has not been without its own challenges. Despite the much-needed comic relief in an adverse environment, scholars have also highlighted some of the negative effects of social media messages which include misinformation or 'infordemic' (Wasserman 2020; Venkateswaran 2020). On the harmful side, this 'infordemic' captures the perils associated with misinformation on social media. Instant messaging means encoders and distributors of the messages sometimes do not have the mandate to edit and reflect on the effects of the message particularly messages to do with more serious issues such as health. Content from social media has also fuelled anxiety, fear, discrimination/stigma, unproven remedies and the phrase social media almost always collocates with 'fake news.' In a study Mcworth-Young et al. (2020) pointed out how rumours, myths and facts doing round on social media often shape media messages and responses coming from them. The United Nations Development Programme Zimbabwe (UNDP -Zimbabwe) (2020) has underlined this in a twit that misinformation can result in people being left uninformed, unprotected and vulnerable. The twit encourages consumers of social media massages to "choose content verified by reliable sources." Depoux, et al. (2020) call for a fight against social media 'trolls' who cause confusion over serious issues of the pandemic.

In spite of the aforementioned, it cannot be denied that the laughter of social messages is also fleeting, providing momentary relief before one returns to gloomy reality at hand. Nevertheless, this does not distract one from the fact that social media platforms have gained traction through instant messaging platforms (Venkateswaran 2020). Chiduku (2020: n.p) contends that "We should not underestimate the power of social media. Social media platforms have the power of simplifying complex issues by making fun out of them." The reader is given the leeway on how best to utilise the message the way he/she sees fit. Small doses of pleasure do go a long way in providing relief in the largely gloomy atmosphere of the COVID-19 pandemic.

Presentation of media messages

In the following section are two video clips and other media messages in the form of text and still images. These are described and then analysed. Note that the display of still pictures has been limited, as the text, accompanying them has been found representative of the humour exuded in the message. It should be noted that the text that accompanies the still pictures augments the hilarious nature of some of the media messages.

Video skits

Owing to the nature of video skits that are moving pictures, the writers give brief descriptions of what the videos are all about. Since both skits are presented in the Shona language, translations are also offered.

Presentation of video 1

The caption 'The phrase running water is now confusing the non-English speaking' (sic) gives a guide to the content in the following video:

Video 1: (Screenshot of video)

In the video clip a journalist interviews two young men on what 'running water' is.

One says, *Tinongonzwa muma*TV *asi isu kuno* running water *kunoku hatisati tamboiwona tinotonzwa muma*TV *kuti ndiyo inodzivirira* coronavirus *saka kunoku hatitasi tamboiona* (We hear about it on TV but here we have not seen it. We have heard that it helps prevent coronavirus, but we have never seen it).

On further probing *"Saka munoreva here kuti kunoku munhararunda yenyu hapana mvura inobuda muma*tap *zvachose?"* (Do you mean to say in this whole area you do not have water coming from the tap at all?), the young man answers, *Aiwa mvura inobuda chero ma*shower *togara tichigeza isu. Asi iyiyi yavanoti* running water *iyi ndoyatisati taona. Titori nechikumbiro kuti vatotiigirawo kunoku* (Ahh that!! Water is in abundance here, we are always taking our shower from the tap. But this, which they call 'running water', we have not seen it. We actually have a request (to the authorities) to bring us that water here).

Video 2

In the video Bitz, a well-known comedian, shoots a video of himself and his double (Baba Emy) in a clip named *"Kwarentini yaakupengesa"* (Quarantine drives one mad). He narrates how bad things were out there where everyone is talking about quarantine. He

182

tells his double that: *Ini ndaifunga kuti kwarentine inachisi* (I thought quarantine was a variety of a naartjie). He says he misses doing comic skits but then for one to do it successfully one needs a partner just like other comedians in Zimbabwe such as Maggie and Gonyeti, Mai Titi and Baba Titi, Mai Rwizi and baba Rwizi among others. He however in his litany of comedians includes Chidhumo and Masendeke the infamous criminals *Mabhinya* (thugs). He chides himself for speaking to himself like a mad man (*Kutaura ndega kunge ndopenga*). Coincidentally, upon his reference to *mabhinya*, his double touches his unkempt beard and Bitz contemptuously tells his alterego to go and have a haircut (*Enda unogerwa iwee*). The following is a shot of Bizt's double from the video:

Video 2: *Kwarentine yaakupengesa* (Quarantine drives you mad) can be viewed on https://www.youtube.com/watch?v=vasF9LfCUiU

Text and still image messages

Text 1: An individual upon feeling the heat in the soaring prices of basic commodities lamented "*MaOk mahwani. Dai vachititora futi temperature pakubuda munhu wese aitonzi ane Corona haaa unobuda uchinzwa dzungu pamwe nekutsva*" (Going into Ok supermarket is really daunting! If they took our temperature upon exiting the store, everyone would be diagnosed with coronavirus. When you leave you would be feeling hot and dizzy."

Text 2: This is in the form of a letter

Dear Money

The social distance does not concern you pliz (sic) come closer.

Text 3: The text reads *Mari dzerent dzanetsa* guys....*Vamwe takatoisa ma*landlord *pama*profile picture (Nowadays it is difficult to find rent money guys...Some of us have resorted to putting the landlord's picture in the WhatsApp profile picture).

Image 1: The caption reads 'Online Learning.' This text accompanies a picture in which a young man is seen reading two sheets of paper that are hung on a washing line.

Image 2: This captures the image of a popular Nigerian comedian in a brooding mood and the following caption reading:

> My landlord served me a quick notice that it is either I pay rent or pack out of his house even with this Lockdown. I have just sent his contact details that he has symptoms of coronavirus and has refused to self-isolate. We shall see who will leave the house first. I hate nonsense.

Analysis of the social media messages

The humour that this chapter is focusing on is the humour of and about the coronavirus. Laughter in general lifts any depressive situation but in this case jokes and clips have been coined around the name of the pandemic, how it is spread, preventive measures and its effects. Most of the clips encapsulate satirical humour; this is best presented through the use of irony. As with all satirical messages, the clips have more serious issues that need correction (Adejuwoni & Alimi 2011). The following sections are analyses of the various media messages that have been categorised into themes.

Lack of adequate information

This, by far, is the section that is oversubscribed in terms of the media messages that are under scrutiny and the butt of many coronavirus jokes. Most of the social media messages have pointed to the lack of information during the restrictive period under review. This section refers to the period when people were inundated with messages from both formal and informal media channels thereby creating confusion over the understanding of COVID-19. As a result, authorities were not in a position to confidently talk about the pandemic as it had not fully gathered ground on African soil. People relied on what formal news sources stated but mostly relied on hearsay and social media. One of the myths that was rife on the grapevine was that COVID-19 does not affect black people (Moyo 2020; Ross 2020). This consequently created in people a potentially false sense of comfort and security. One of the respondents in a study conducted by Mcworth-Young et al. (2020) captures this succinctly when he says "I still feel like people have so many questions, they want answers in lay man's language. Like how [the coronavirus is] spread? What is it exactly? How can we stop it?"

Video 1 above bears testimony to this. Viewers of this skit are most likely to be taken aback and laugh about the young people's ignorance of what running water is but claim to use tap water for showering every day! It is clear that one of the key components regarding prevention of the virus- washing hands with running water- is severely misunderstood. From the surrounding areas in the video, it is clear that this is an urban setting and the young people well established urbanites. One would expect them to be well versed with the phrase running water as this is the common source of water in urban areas. However, the reverse is true. The clip tells the sad story of the under-informed Zimbabwean populace about how to manage the virus. The skit reveals this confusion in people whose awareness of the pandemic is limited. This goes on to indicate hypotheses surrounding possible sources of messages on the virus: that communication on the virus has largely been done using English language, or people have accessed details of COVID-19 through foreign media channels in the English language and a lack of information in the indigenous languages in Zimbabwe. As a result, there is miscommunication between what the young people in the clip understand and the real issues on the ground.

The background in the skit denotes an urban high-density area and the individuals in the skit are all young people. One would expect young people in the video to be knowledgeable with the nature of the pandemic and how to manage it. The dark humour in this video is the failure to understand what is presumed to be simple knowledge. The young people fail to realise that they possess the key component at their disposal- running water. Their main challenge being the lack of explanation and translation of what the phrase 'running water' means. This could best be explained in an ironic way; tap water is a rare resource in most high-density suburbs and the comedian appears to take a jibe at the authorities over the people's lack of knowledge of running water as it is hardly there!

Another shocking reality is underlined in their lack of knowledge regarding their vulnerability in the face of the pandemic. The iconic mask that the journalist is wearing is a clear indication of the prevalence of the coronavirus. Conversely, his interviewees wear no masks. The journalist's outstretched hand presents one with the indexical meaning of physical distancing that the young men he is interviewing are failing to observe. It reflects the casual approach characterizing how many Zimbabweans view the coronavirus owing to ignorance. The pandemic has been mystified to the extent that people do not grasp even what is considered basic safety measures such as washing hands and physical distancing. Only a selected few such as the journalist appear privileged with that information and practice. The suspense on what they could have been washing their hands with is both hilarious and striking. It can safely be concluded that this skit satirically chides those in positions of authority for not availing critical awareness information to citizens of the country. It takes humour to criticise the system, which has not sensitised its citizens enough on what the coronavirus is and how to prevent it. Such lack of information is also underlined in other comic strips elsewhere where the syntactic and semantic ramifications of the name of the virus are bantered. In one such clip an old man refers to COVID-19 as COVID-91, coronavirus as 'conoravirus' while the sanitiser is referred to as '*usanditarise*' the closest indigenous Shona word but whose meaning is both nonsensical and far removed from the virus at hand (*usanditarise* means do not look at me). Without the correct nomenclature, it becomes obvious that knowledge is severely limited.

Another seemingly harmless image (Image 1) is that of a young man (probably old enough to be in university) reading off sheets of paper hung on a wash line. This image points at the futility of online learning without the recipients of such learning having a clue what it is. It is a reflection of a society that purports to be part of the global village complete with assumptions that everyone knows what online learning is all about. The image of the young man however, points at society replete with ignorance, a society without the means to successfully launch online learning programmes. It indicates a society that does not possess the basics to counteract the effects of the coronavirus on the education system. Most students in Zimbabwe were grounded due to this technicality.

The bottom line is lack of adequate information in dealing with the virus. By the time Zimbabwe locked down, it had not made significant inroads in spreading awareness of the COVID-19 pandemic. Information that readily found its way to the ordinary person on the street largely bordered on hearsay and speculation with the Ministry of Health and Childcare being accused of not doing much in terms of spreading awareness on the pandemic.

Socio-economic effects of the coronavirus: Lack and want during the pandemic

It is clear that the stagnation that pervaded the country had larger implications to the working ordinary Zimbabweans, most of whom are informally employed. A significant number of general clips have been doing the rounds on social media. An example is the image of an old lady in a pensive mood who declares that she is not adding 2020 to her age because she did not use it. This is rather ironic. At her age she should be retired but still laments time wasted through idleness, a reflection of a ruthless economy where even old women have to scrounge for a living. Another clip resonates well with this one where an interviewee justifies the inactivity in the year 2020 by stating that he spent most of his time washing hands.

Text 1 in the previous paragraphs both connotatively and denotatively refers to the multifaceted effects of the COVID-19 pandemic. According to the persona in the clip, what heats up one's body temperature is not a symptom of infection from the virus but the rising cost of living. In other words, this is a reflection of the socio-economic status of most Zimbabweans. Most are extremely poor (Bhoroma 2019) and live below the Poverty Datum Line to the effect that the ever-rising cost of living is always met with shock. The "Dear Money" clip takes on the epistolary form and puns with the idea of the phrase 'physical distance.' The personified money appears to exercise physical distance away from a potentially COVID-19 infected human being. The appeal by the human being for closeness is a clear demonstration of the abject poverty that has rendered people helpless in the face of the pandemic. The physical distance that the letter writer is talking about underlines the clear lack of money, which haunts most of the households. What is disturbing is the worsening of this poverty as the economy is further depressed by the COVID-19 restrictions as predicted by UNDP (2020).

The ripple effects of poverty and survival move closer to the hard-hitting realities of life such as failure to pay for one's shelter. Text 3 reveals a tenant who wishes to put his landlord's picture in his WhatsApp profile picture. Not only is this both hilarious but at the same time sad. Connotatively one if bound to laugh without giving serious thought to it but at the same time it demands some introspection over the motive behind this message. While WhatsApp profile picture in one's phone is deemed private space, normally reserved for the close and loved ones, the prospect of inserting the landlord's picture is meant to hoodwink him into believing that he is significant in the tenant's life. The tenant's cunning and manipulative nature reveals his hidden objective of evading any questioning over delayed or non-payment of rentals. The ultimate goal is hoping to curry favour with the landlord. The fact that this joke is told to other parties not the landlord himself points at the mischief behind it and at the same time demonstrates desperation. The tenant is a marooned being with nowhere to run.

The second clip on rentals in image 1 where a young man looks smug and collected but what appears to be going on in his mind (as captured in the accompanying caption) is some serious scheming whose effects are going to be detrimental to his landlord's freedom. The young man's dilemma: he knows he does not have money to pay for rent but at the same time does not have anywhere to go. His solution involves getting rid of the landlord on the grounds that he is displaying symptoms of the virus and should therefore be reported to the authorities. The result is a forced quarantine for the landlord but how long this survival strategy by the tenant will last is left to the imagination of the reader. What is witnessed is a picture of likely reversal of positions of power between the young man and the property owner and readers are given the leeway to imagine how the landlord would react. Even more hilarious is the image of the young man, quite unperturbed by his scheme nor the anger it might induce in the property owner should he be taken for forced quarantine or isolation. The sub-narrative of survival is almost overrun by humour that the clip engenders. Readers usually detach the gloomy effects of the pandemic and focus on the less grievous effects thereby missing out the serious sub-plot that plays out. The serious message however is worth exploring.

Effects of lockdowns: Isolation and loss of social routine

It is incontestable that the coronavirus and resultant lockdowns have had negative effects on the freedoms of the general populace. The skit by Bitz in Video 2 above serves to demonstrate such effects not just to the ordinary Zimbabwean but on the artist and those in the entertainment industry. Bitz takes comfort in creating a double for himself as he embarks on a monologue on the effects of the lockdown. The humorous skit starts off with what he has heard people sharing about quarantining without necessarily understanding the meaning. He thinks quarantine is a variety of a naartjie (fruit from the citrus family). What is hilarious and ironic is his failure to understand the meaning of quarantine yet as a white person English is supposed to be his first language. The fact that he presents the skit in indigenous Shona language is a clear demonstration that it does not target the white community nor does it represent their interests but those of the majority of Zimbabweans. What is also hilarious are the dramatic twists and turns in his monologues reflecting the culture conflict he experiences. While he tries hard to represent the Shona, the part on not understanding 'quarantine' which he takes for variety of a citrus fruit does not fit the cultural semiotic codes of the Shona people. In Shona culture there are no varieties of naartjies among the Shona – one naartjie represents all the varieties of naartjies there are!

The dilemma of being an entertainer is highlighted, when Bitz laments missing his partner Gujuru "*akavharirwa kumba kwake*' (he is shut up in his house) clearly articulates the enforced restrictions on movement. For him entertainment needs teamwork and he mentions a few examples of comedians and deliberately throwing in the mix the notorious criminals, Chidhumo and Masendeke. His double quickly corrects him- the duo does not belong to the mix of entertainers as they are popularly referred to as *mabhinya* (thugs). Inadvertently, Bizt touches his unkempt beard as if to imply that he appears like one (*bhinya*- thug) which resonates well with the end of the clip where he chides his alter ego to go and have a haircut ("*Enda unogerwa iwee*"). Sadly, hilarious is the lonely figure who in reality is speaking to himself. He clearly admits that he has resorted to talking to himself like a mad man. Marston and Morgan (2020) have demonstrated the unpleasant feeling associated with social disconnectedness that could lead to serious depression and how social media platforms and technology can provide adults with opportunities to stay socially connected. The humour in this skit is a reflection of the sad reality of a people who are isolated and locked up in their homes. For Bitz, his creativity helps him out of this quagmire and reaching out to his fan base through social media.

His T-shirt runs a sub-script that is also clearly telling its own story of the effects of the pandemic. On the front it written '*Nhasi handidi doro*' (Today I do not want beer) but at the back indicating (*Aaaa! Kutamba zvangu.*) (Ahh! I did not really mean that). The normal well kempt Bitz has his name inscribed on his T-shirt. This individual is missing his old self and the usual routine preoccupations of entertaining and drinking but denied access to both. The skit is clever way of coping with the lockdown, a story of survival. Semiotic analysis works best with binary oppositions. When one uses this method of analysis the more hilarious the comic clip is. The image of the normal clean, well-groomed Bitz is seated on that settee playing games while his alter ego is the antithesis- unkempt, old wrinkly T-shirt and a figure whose double even detests to be associated with. The comedian has been far removed from his usual trade and is reduced to being entertained by electronic games on TV, thus missing out on socio-economic activities that he is used to. The clip, thus, gives us a picture of an individual who steps out of himself to observe the unfolding negative effects of the pandemic on his person. What he discovers is a conflicted individual who is at odds with himself. His appearance, career as a comedian and general confidence take a knock from the effects of the pandemic. In other words, the scenario is driving him crazy! The name of the skit captures this succinctly: "*Kwarentine yaakupengesa*" (Quarantine drives one mad!). A human being needs to work and relax! What is encouraging for the artist is his ability to invoke his creative side, be able to present solo performance and still achieve the same effect even in the absence of his partner Gujuru.

Beyond the laughter: Implications of comic media messages

We have seen how social media messages on face value capture in a comic way the experiences of Zimbabwean people, how they react to them and at the same time how the comic messages offer reprieve from the many challenges that are associated with the coronavirus. This is in line with relief theory explanation that postulates that laughter does not go beyond the relief in tense circumstances. Indeed, the tension and anxiety brought on by COVID-19 provided the much-needed reprieve and in this way, laughter became the medicine. While the chapter has largely dwelt on the entertaining side of the comic messages under study, it has also been revealed that comic media creators have their own agendas often hidden beneath the laughter of the surface meaning. Messages that are more serious are directed at both the consumers of the messages in general but in particular people in positions of power to rectify some of the serious challenges that require serious reflection to unravel. In other words, readers should take time to go through comic messages knowing that there is a more serious side to them that are covered by the mirth and laughter. This is in tandem with the incongruity theory of humour that targets anomalies in situations and attempt to expose them. The satire that has been utilized in the analyses worked best uncovers the serious socio-economic incongruities that Zimbabweans were facing which needed addressing.

Decoders of messages should be able to unpack the serious messages so that hey benefit fully from, not just the laughter, but irony surrounding the satire, the symbols that unravel them. The same applies to people in positions of authority. Since all comic messages respond to unfolding developments, authorities need not underestimate them but take them seriously and address the issues that are being raised. Depoux *et al.* (2020) agree with this and encourage health authorities to harness social media messages in combatting the pandemic. They state,

> Analyses of discussions on social media with regards to the epidemic situation geographically (geocoded tweets/messages) and over time (timestamped tweets/messages) can result in real-time maps. Such real time maps could then be used as a source of information on where to intervene with key communication campaigns (n.p).

From the analyses done above, it is prudent that awareness programmes be unrolled in indigenous language so that all citizens have access to information as well as provide such utilities as running water a basic requirement for the prevention of infection. There is also needed to take into consideration the majority of the population who have been pushed to desperation through COVID-19 induced restrictions. The majority of families in Zimbabwe were being pushed to desperation and the situation was likely to degenerate had the total lockdown persisted.

Conclusion

This chapter has dwelt on humour in the era of a global pandemic. While the pandemic and its effects are harmful, people take time to share lighter moments. However, the chapter has established that humour during dark times is critical but emphasises that the laughter should not be fleeting and short-lived. A deeper reflection on the messages offers some solutions to the challenges that are bantered about. A semiotic analysis of the messages gave room for the scrutiny of both what is present and that which is absent, the abundance and the lack; binary oppositions that are meant to unpack hidden meanings in seemingly just jocular messages. However, it takes a trained eye to unearth many of the media messages that may be communicated overtly or covertly by those messages. It becomes the privilege of the semioticians to delve into the messages enshrined in visual messages. The same needs to be done by consumers of humorous messages when they take time to reflect on the messages and possibly offer solutions to challenges hidden within such messages.

References

Adejuwoni, A. and Alimi, S. (2011) 'Cartoons as Illustration: Political Process in Nigeria', *The Journal of Pan African Studies,* 4(3), 57-76. Retrieved from http://www.jpanafrican.com/docs/vol4no3.

Antonovici, L. (2015) 'A Theory of humour', in L. Boldea (ed.) *Discourse as a form of Multiculturalism and Communication: Literature and Communication,* Arhipelag XXI Press, Tîrgu Mureș, 417-430.

Arning, C. (2020) 'The risks and rewards of humour in COVID-19'. Retrieved from https://www.warc.com/newsandopinion/opinion/the-risks-and-rewards-of-humour-in-COVID-19/3640 .

Bhoroma, V. (2019) 'Zimbabweans now living in extreme poverty as economy implodes', *The Zimbabwe Independent.* Retrieved from https://www.theindependent.co.zw/2019/09/13/zimbabweans-now-living-in-extreme-poverty-as-economy-implodes/.

Bidzy Films. (2020, May 6) *Kwarentine yaakupengesa* [Video], You Tube. https://www.youtube.com/watch?v=vasF9LfCUiU.

Chiduku, C. (2020) 'Zimbos drown lockdown sorrows in humour'. https://www.newsday.co.zw/2020/05/zimbos-drown-lockdown-sorrows-in-humour/.

Comic Pastor. (2020, March 9) 'Corona Virus in Zimbabwe', [Video] You Tube. https://www.youtube.com/watch?v=Viq1vKWesZ0.

Depoux, A., Martin, S., Karafillakis, E., Preet, R., Wilder-Smith, A. and Larson, H. (2020) 'The pandemic of social media panic travels faster than the COVID-19 outbreak', *Travel Med*, 27(3). Retrieved from https://pubmed.ncbi.nlm.nih.gov/32125413/.

Gates, M. (n.d.) 'Africa will have dead bodies on the streets'. Retrieved from https://www.youtube.com/watch?v=MPFXsJokaHM.

Goleman, D., Boyatzis, R. and McKee (2013) *A Primal Leadership: Unleashing the Property of Emotional Intelligence.* Harvard Business Review Press, Boston.

Internet Encyclopeadia of Philosophy. *Humour.* Retrieved from https://iep.utm.edu/humor/.

Cheurfa, H. (2020) 'Controversial Humour in Algerian TV: Ramadan Comedies and the Limits of Laughter'. Retrieved from https://www.academia.edu/43072059/Controversial_Humour_i n_Algerian_TV_RamadanComedies_and_the_Limits_of_Laught er.

McKee, A. (2003) *Textual Analysis: A Beginner's Guide.* London: Sage Publications.

Mackworth-Young, CRS., Chingono R., Mavodza C., McHugh, G., Tembo, M, Dziva-Chikwari C, et al. (2020) 'Here, we cannot practice what is preached': early qualitative learning from community perspectives on Zimbabwe's response to COVID-19', *Bull World Health Organ.* doi: http://dx.doi.org/10.2471/BLT.20.260224 Retrieved from https://www.who.int/bulletin/online_first/20-260224.pdf?ua=1.

Martarelli, C. and Wolff, W. (2020) 'Too bored to bother? Boredom as a potential threat to the efficacy of pandemic containment measures', *Humanities and Social Sciences Communication* 7, 28. Retrieved form https://doi.org/10.1057/s41599-020-0512-6.

Marston, H. R. and Morgan, D. J. (2020) 'Technology & Social Media during COVID-19 Pandemic', *International Psychogeriatric Association* (IPA Bulletin). Retrieved from https://www.ipa-online.org/publications/ipa-bulletin/featured-articles/covid-19-bulletin-articles/technology-social-media-during-covid19.

Morreall, J. (2020) 'Philosophy of Humour', *Stanford Encyclopedia of Philosophy* Retrieved from https://plato.stanford.edu/entries/humor/#RelThe.

Moyo, J. (2020) 'Myths on COVID-19 pandemic spread across Zimbabwe: Myths derailing fight against disease in Zimbabwe'. Retrieved from https://www.aa.com.tr/en/africa/myths-on-covid-19-pandemic-spread-across-zimbabwe/1925786.

Ross, J. (2020) 'Coronavirus outbreak revives dangers of race myths and pseudoscience: Most fictional claims about black immunity to the coronavirus are connected to the long history of contradictory but uniformly racist ideas'. Retrieved from www.nbcnews.com.

Salari, N., Hosseinian-Far, A., Jalali, R., Vaisi-Raygani, A., Rasoulpoor, S., Mohammadi, M., Rasoulpoor, S. and Khaledi-Paveh, B. (2020) 'Prevalence of stress, anxiety, depression among the general population during the COVID-19 pandemic: A systematic review and meta-analysis', *Globalization and Health*, 16 (57), 1-11. Retrieved from https://doi.org/10.1186/s12992-020-00589-w.

United Nations Development Programme Zimbabwe. (2020) 'Policy brief: A preliminary assessment of the socioeconomic impact of coronavirus (COVID-19) on Zimbabwe'. Retrieved from http://www.undp.org>home>coronavirus.

Vinkarteswaran, T. V. (2020) 'Tale of two videos: Frame and narrative structure analysis of two COVID-19 communication social media messages', *Journal of Scientific Temper Vol 8(1&2)*, Jan-June, pp. 18-37.

Wasserman, H. (2020) 'Laughter in the time of a pandemic: Why South Africans are joking about coronavirus', *The Conversation*. Retrieved from https://theconversation.com/laughter-in-the-time-of-a-pandemic-why-south-africans-are-joking-about-coronavirus-133528.

Yakin, H.S.M. and Totu, A. (2014) 'The Semiotic Perspectives of Peirce and Saussure: A Brief Comparative Study', *Procedia - Social and Behavioral Sciences*, 155, 4 – 8.

Chapter Nine

Fourth Industrial Revolution and COVID-19: An Agenda for African Languages

Rewai Makamani

Introduction

Even though riddled with innuendos of inequalities, exploitation and underdevelopment of Africans by western powers (Rodney 1973; Moyo 2009), it is evident that the first three industrial revolutions contributed to rapid growth in industrial mechanized production, electricity-powered technological developments and processing of goods, services and products, internet streamlined rapid production processes and communication technologies (Hornberger & Vaish 2009; Prisecaru 2016; Ayentimi & Burgess 2019). During these historical epochs, African languages maintained a threatened but critical role as conveyances of culture, belief systems, African Knowledge Systems (IKS), unity, entertainment, resistance against the vicissitudes of white "monopoly capital" (Wiegratz 2019: 357) and exploitation of black people (Ani 2016; Ndlovu-Gatsheni 2020), the spirit of Ubuntu/African humanism with a vivid presence in education, economic, health and political sectors thus shaping human conditions of people on the continent (Fnnegan 1988; Igboanusi 2008; Hays 2009; Hornberger & Vaish 2009; Okombo & Muna 2017). In the three industrial revolutions, African languages were an important economic sector with a critical foothold in education, economic and health delivery systems (Osborn 2006, Okombo & Muna 2017) in Africa and beyond. This study presents an aspirational overview of the projected role that African languages need to play in the Fourth Industrial Revolution (4IR) in all spheres of life particularly in combating diseases such as COVID-19 and other threats to human existence. Using an Afrocentric and decoloniality-informed-"Discourse Historical Approach" (Wodak & Reisigl, in Wodak & Meyer 2010: 87) as an epistemological barometer, the study conceives African Languages as aptly endowed to inform Africa's response to the Fourth Industrial revolution and opportunities and challenges it poses. The chapter views African Languages as harbingers of African resilience, identity, consciousness, psychological fitness of purpose, beingness and wellbeing of African people which have been at the heart of African struggles, civilization and quest for existence since time immemorial (Finnegan 1988, Pongweni 1982; Ouane & Glanz 2005; Adegbite 2004; Osborn 2006; Childs 2008). As Africa and the rest of the third world are marshalled into the Fourth Industrial revolution, it is perceived in the chapter that, being custodians of African Knowledge Systems (IKS), African languages are mandated to play a pivotal role in circumventing the perceived threat to consciously or unconsciously annihilate Africans by merchants of "digital capitalism" (Birgit 2019: 1). The chapter is motivated by historical resilience of Africans who have used their languages to wade off mental, social and physical tribulations through strategic harnessing of IKS as espoused in these tried and tested repositories of knowledge and Africans' quest for survival though the mechanism of African Languages.

Contextualising the nexus between Fourth Industrial Revolution and the COVID-19 pandemic

It is now known that the world presents a terrain of heavily contested ideas and human activities particularly between the global North and South. Sadly, in such contestations the global North always emerges as the 'victor' with the global South the victim. With respect to African states, the foregoing is a historical inevitability since: "Even though you push back colonization as a physical process (the physical Empire), colonialism as a power structure continues as a metaphysical process and as an epistemic project, because it invades the mental universe of people, destabilising them from what they used to know, into knowing what is brought in by colonialism, and it then commits "crimes" such as epistemicides where you kill and displace pre-existing knowledges, linguicides (killing and displacing the languages of people and imposing your own) and *culturecides* (where you kill or replace the cultures of a people) (Ndlovu-Gatsheni in Omanga: January 2020: 2). From a Marxist vantage point, the world curves itself as blanketed by a superstructure that rests upon a base, an economic base. Therefore, just like its predecessors, the Fourth Industrial Revolution is perceivable as manifesting a superstructure (idea) and economic base (reality) whose representations are evident in the social, educational, economic, health and political systems of countries on the globe. However, the foregoing representation of the world is silent on how racism has been unpacked as having an influence on how the modern world is being re-engineered. As revealed by Ani (2016: 4), "While Marx offers a systematic analysis and critique of capitalism, he does not deal with either the European world view or racism/white supremacy. To do so would be especially difficult for Marx since he was himself, afflicted by that pathology." At stake is the need to re-examine 4IR, revealing its merchants and their perceived ideological underpinnings thus being able to intellectually link COVID-19 as a product of such human endeavours. This is important particularly as one rethinks the role that African languages can play in decentring industrialization, technological inventions, scientific modelling of events and their attendant benefits. The above is critical as the study views the Fourth Industrial Revolution as a reality and the new norm; African countries have no choice but to float or sink, in other words, shape up or ship out. Scholars (Prisecaru 2016; Wim 2017; Xing & Marwala 2017; Balkaram 2019) have argued that, Africa faces a real risk of being left behind and potentially being relegated to the dustbin of the proverbial history. As put by Birgit, (2019: 8), "For some emerging markets such as Brazil, India, Indonesia, Malaysia, Mexico, Thailand and Turkey the World Bank identifies some evidence for 'smart production' processes. But for most of the developing countries which are constrained by scarcity of trained technicians and engineers and by infrastructure issues such as a reliable electricity support, the Word Bank offers a quite dark future scenario." Africa faces multiple challenges to effectively respond and, or, position herself to maximally benefit from the opportunities embedded in the 4IR. From this perspective, and as has been alluded to earlier, the 4IR poses real danger in Africa: linguistic genocide, epistemicides, linguicides, cultural imperialism, healthcare catastrophes and potentially physical annihilation of many African languages (Ouane & Glanz 2005; Childs 2008; Stroud 2010; Mufwene 2017) and African people. Sharing a critical perspective to explicate why Africa finds herself in this desperate situation is Adegbite (2004: 13) who contends that, "…the lack of development of African nations can be mainly linked to the lack of recognition of African languages and cultures." The majority of Africans live in rural areas where African languages need to be supported to deliver Health, Education, Agriculture and attendant socio-economic practices and order. Even in urban centres the myth of modernity needs to be debunked to meaningfully account for the livelihoods of people in informal economic sectors who normally dwell in informal settlements and shacks and are associated with underdevelopment and poverty (Moyo 2010; Mchombu & Mchombu 2014; Uwizeyimana 2017; Tjirera 2018). Such people are also associated with low literacy levels and use indigenous languages to communicate orally for survival (Finnegan 1988; Alexander 2007; Hays 2009; Hornberger & Vaish 2009). The prevalence of low literacy levels in some rural and urban communities in Africa calls for rethinking about perceived deliverables of the Fourth Industrial Revolution and to position Africans to wrestle real and imagined catastrophic dilemmas that the era ushers. There is definitely the digital divide which remains an impediment for real development in Africa (Osborn 2006; Birgit 2019). Thus:

> At the end of 2018, a little bit more than half of the global population was using the internet - more than 80 percent of the population in developed countries, but already 45.3 percent of those living in developing countries. Even though the strongest growth of all regions was reported in Africa, still not more than a quarter of its population is using the internet and the proportion of households with access to a computer is still very low. But what is even more problematic: in all developing countries the overall fixed-broadband penetration and especially subscriptions at higher speeds remains very low (ITU, 2017 in Birgit 2019: 4).

The above is testimony to the fact that Africa is not at the same pedestal with Europe; it has never been and must never ever be. This is so because Africa can leverage her own full potential through independence from, and not interdependence with Europe. Africa needs rethinking, in order to chart her own developmental trajectories using her own resources, including linguistic resources with an umbilical cord rooted in the continent. This needs to be the case as African languages are easily accessible by both urban and rural populations in Africa. Reliance on exotic languages as de facto languages for operationalizing activities in government, education, health, trade and commerce has not yielded desired results on the continent (Ouane & Glanz 2005; Osborn 2006; Alexander 2007; Hays 2009; Hornberger & Vaish 2009). Certainly, Africa cannot chart through the unknown waters of 4IR, Covid-19 and other pandemics in an environment where foreign languages take precedents over

African languages; it will spell disaster for the continent: health disaster; economic disaster; educational disaster; technological disaster; and, political disaster including disaster of governance. Thus, "as language is gateway to other economic, cultural and social resources, control over linguistic resources is indirectly also control over economic and social advancement in general. Employing languages that the people themselves master will facilitate the transference of technology and know-how to those who need them most. Using local languages also enhances democracy" (Stroud 2010: 17).

Methodology

In this chapter, I take an Afrocentric-decolonial outlook, a deliberate measure to prop perceptions on the study's renditions regarding the human conditions of African people during 4IR. Also informing the conceptual framework of the study is the Discourse Historical Approach employed to "demystify" and transcend hegemonic traits of discourse of Fourth Industrial Revolution thus showcasing how African Languages need to shape up to mitigate vicissitudes of 41R including rapid unemployment and disease outbreaks thus positioning Africans and Africa to embrace opportunities embedded in the 4IR. The Afro-centred decoloniality perspective is adopted specifically to de-centre 4IR through "Afro-futuristic imagineering" and "disidentification" (Ogunyakin 2018) language politics and discourse. It advocates that the inevitable repositioning of African Languages implies the positioning of African people and humanity in general to equitably benefit from the deliverables of 4IR and to overcome threats posed to humanity in general such as physical, psychological, spiritual, social and econo-political dangers faced by Africans in particular .

To put the chapter's orientation into perspective, I draw lessons from success stories involving shrewd Language Policy and Planning issues in South Africa, Zimbabwe and Tanzania. Such case studies demonstrate how vested interest in African Languages has potential to arm Africans with a survival means and to give them a competitive urge during the Fourth Industrial Revolution. The three nations have been purposively selected as a befitting sample foregrounding the study. From a Language Policy and Planning perspective, and in the view of this study, the three countries are an adequate representation of the potential inherent in African languages to offset negative effects of 4IR and the COVID-19 pandemic on the continent, hence their selection.

Insights from related literature

Literature attests that African challenges during 4IR will be compounded by inherent problems in Africa such as nepotism, corruption, regionalism, ethnicity, tribalism, civil strife which threaten stability and social cohesion and governance practices:

> Development and investment scholars including international and local policy think-tanks across Africa have recognised the significant natural resource endowment and human capital opportunities as drivers of development... yet many emerging and less developed economies in Sub-Saharan Africa are generally characterised by over reliance on rain-fed Agriculture and primary production,... limited and poor public infrastructure, low investment in education, mass unemployment, low application of Science, technology and innovation, weaknesses in institutional structures and mismanagement and wide-spread corruption (IMF in Ayentimi & Burgess 2019: 243).

In this chapter I argue that, as custodians of peoples' culture, sense of belonging, consciousness, identity, history, epistemology, religious and political orientations and philosophies, African languages can play a pivotal role in stabilizing human conditions in Africa during 4IR. African Languages are critical in developmental imperatives on the continent because, in addition to facilitation of communication and understanding of issues by the majority of the African population, they mould Africans with character and fortitude that is less susceptible to corruption as African cultures lay emphasis on collectivism, strict adherence to codes of practice and life styles that celebrate social cohesion, oneness, respect for one another and social ethos. Ubuntu values enshrined in African languages create African people with positive personality traits; those who will consciously define their existence in terms of other people, the community at large; you thus do not harm that which you treasure through antisocial behaviour patterns like mis-governance, and corruption (Mbiti 1990). In this regard effort to position Africa for the 4IR cannot be divorced from socio-historical conditions that explain the Africa we have today. The reality is:

> Frantz Fanon warned us that colonialists are not satisfied by mere physical domination, but they go on to destroy the colonized's history, making the colonizer's history, the colonized's, with the consequence of making the latter lose confidence in one's language, one's names, one's cultures, one's histories…if you remove colonialism physically without removing it epistemically, it will not disappear (Ndlovu-Gatsheni in Omanga, January 2020: 2).

The brainwashing effect of coloniality is echoed by Ani (2016) who regards it as a system of "white supremacy." She avers: "…the academy, knowing it as a product of the European world view, and the values and behaviours promulgated by white culture. The academy assumes the "rhetorical ethic" … "Never say what you are really thinking"… "Hypocrisy is the norm"… "Always hide your true agenda" (Ani, 2016: 3).

It should be borne in mind that coloniality is a global system that transcends geographical locations and historical epochs. Historically, it has created a perpetual master-servant relationship between dark coloured people and those with a white pigmentation. It is a racist system which seeks to relentlessly devour black people by relegating them to the dustbins of history whereby they wallow in abject poverty, disease, unimagined psychological pain and, or, even become extinct. It is an orchestrated system of displacing and dispossessing others. It is a merciless system that has taken various sheds as dictated by socio-historical conditions and geographical locations. Thus, scholars have variously identified it as coloniality, imperialism and white supremacist system. Regarding coloniality, Nhemachena *et al.* (2020: 1) observe: " While the devolution of heritages among Africans would require peace, order, hierarchies, and structures, the imperial system has consistently subjected Africa to disorder, coups, insurgencies, rebellions, covert and overt wars, divisive ideologies, spying, and surveillance operations wherein rebels were supported and sponsored." There is consensus among scholars that the system does not self-exterminate; it needs human agents of like minds, like effort, fortitude and resources to push it back. There is need to go "toe-to-toe" against it (Ani 2016: 3). It needs to be fought from all fronts, because it ravages people from multi-layered and multi-pronged vantage points. Such a response would restore black mental health: "Black mental health" is "patterns of thought, logic, speech, action, and emotional response in all areas of people activity that simultaneously reflect self and group respect and respect for harmony in the universe" (Cress-Welsing in Ani 2016: 3). One such front is the restoration to glory, of African languages through strategically deploying them to confront challenges borne of 4IR and its debilitating offshoots like the COVID-19 pandemic.

African languages as the lifeblood of Africans

African people's livelihoods including human activities ranging from "war, hunting and work" which is a typical characterization of lifestyle of African societies in pastoral settings, to human conditions of rural, semi-literate and literate but economically disadvantaged communities (Finnegan 1988: 206) revolve around their languages. However, there is a problematic group of 'elites' and 'privileged' classes on the continent who, even though they do not entirely depend on African languages for communication, sense of belonging, and all the other well documented advantages of African languages (Finnegan 1988; Ouane & Glanz 2005), tends to resort to African languages for sentimental and religious reasons (Mbiti 1990). The reality though is that all aspects of life including education: Mathematics and Science education; Economics, Religion, Philosophy, Agriculture, Politics and Law, were (and should continue to be) regulated by African languages both for developmental, growth (Osborn 2006; Alexander 2007) and sanity reasons. Arguing in this line Makamani (1991: 3) asserts, "Before the advent of whites, aspects of life such as sharing, marriage, greed, hospitality, birth, burial, aid, sovereignty, good neighbourhood (values), industry, politics and respect were regulated by orature especially proverbs." Thus, the Shona proverbs: *Kuwanda huuya kunotorambwa nemuroyi*; (It's a blessing to be many/to multiply/to procreate; only a witch is opposed to this phenomenon); and, *Chara chimwe hachitswanyi inda/Gunwe rimwe haritswanyi inda* (One swallow does not make a summer) celebrate oneness/the other or being together with others in the community thus encouraging population growth and not population curbing or control. So, arguments in favour of population control, for example, have no place in Africa; they are alien and anti-Africa. Ani (2016: 6) asserts:

There are 30,000 species of edible plants on earth at this time. Less than 100 are being cultivated. The yurugu (white) collective controls the cash food market. They create scarcity for profit. (Global, monopolistic capitalism). About 90 percent of what the world eats comes from only 20 species of grains and vegetables. This group cultivates the foods that they choose, that suit their taste, and that make them money. ... So, the claim of "inadequate food supply" due to inordinate population growth is a "big white lie," a cover for the extermination of what the white racist capitalists, call "useless eaters."

It follows therefore that the rhetoric of food shortages that is sometimes peddled to justify population curbing has no place in Africa. It is unjustified; it is un-African and anti-Africa. In this regard, African languages enable Africans to address their own challenges using IKS while at the same time they interface with the global community on equal terms just like Japanese, Chinese, Malaysians, Americans, Portuguese, Koreans and Russians do. The so called, international languages such as English, Spanish, Portuguese, French and so on will then be used to fill in gaps in global multilingual and multicultural contexts to facilitate communication and other needs while other languages including African languages are assisted to catch-up. This is critical for language issues are important for development and for mental health (Ani 2016; Hornberger & Vaish 2009; Mufwene 2017). This means if one's language is marginalized for one reason or the other, it has an effect of peripheralizing, inferiorization and brainwashing such people usually to serve global capitalist interests. As the world seeks solutions to negative effects of 4IR and COVID-19, Africa needs to step-up her game to defend the interests of Africans. Scholars have increasingly established linkages between developments on planet earth to calculated human activity associated with the quest for power, domination, control and exploitation (Moyo 2009; Wiegratz 2019). Africans, in particular, have been called upon to have critical minds and to be alert as Ani (2016: 7) avers:

The 2016 eugenicists claim to "love humanity," especially Afrikan/Black people and other "underdeveloped" first world people. Their weapons of choice are: vaccines (2.3 million women and girls in Kenya sterilized through tetanus vaccines); GMOs (controlling the food supply); HAARP (High Frequency Active Auroral Research Program) using the environment (weather) to create unnatural disasters (for more information, go to geoengineeringwatch.org); chemicals polluting water; and forced vaccinations in Afrika. All of these are forms of race-based genocide. The Rockefellers have always been eugenicists; the World Health Organization is a vehicle for Afrikan extermination; The Centres for Disease Control helps to spread disease among Black people and promotes unnecessary and harmful vaccinations. In the 1950s and 60s only three vaccinations were recommended for children; now there are 60-70!

The above presents the world as involved in covert and overt war whereby black people are targeted for a well-orchestrated population curbing. In this regard, Africa needs to deploy IKS enshrined in African languages to protect citizens. Ani (2016: 8) further alerts:

> The work of the Bill and Melinda Gates Foundation is to stop the expansion of the world's non-white population. According to Melinda Gates, she "loves" the people whose destruction she finances, and when asked what she considered the greatest gift to humankind in recent times, she quickly answered, "Vaccines." The Gates couple believes in "population control." What population? Who controls? Ted Turner says that the total population of the world should ideally be 250-300 million, a fraction of what it is now. The present population is approximately 7 billion, 280 million. Do the math. Who are the "extraneous" people? Who decides? Who does the killing? One guess. Ted Turner says that the world would be better off if almost 7 billion people no longer existed!

The foregoing makes it imperative for Africa to utilize her knowledge systems embedded in African languages to confront challenges posed on the continent by 4IR and diseases such as the COVID-19 pandemic. Therefore, from the perspective of this chapter, Africa is confronted by multifaceted challenges. On one hand are inherent ideological challenges borne of existing contestation of African knowledge systems by the West which history presents as having persistently resented alternative knowledge systems and ways of knowing from Africa. The menu of resistance features inherent ontological contestations whereby African ways of being have always been subjected to unfair and unjustifiable scrutiny by Western scholars, anthropologists and people (Finnegan 1988).

Equally questioned and habitually dismissed as irrelevant have been African axiological systems, where African values were either dismissed as irrelevant and backward (Finnegan 1988). African cosmology has also been a victim of a similar bashing, bastardisation and dismissal (Finnegan 1988; Ndlovu-Gatsheni 2020). The cumulative effect of this onslaught has been to deface African people's sense of pride, ways of healing, Agricultural practices, education system, ways of socialization and to cause psychological trauma, stress, lack of confidence and even premature deaths among Africans. Apparently, the world is awash with information about transhumanists who seek to redesign people by inserting dangerous technological implants (nanobots) which can erode memory of victims who ultimately become perpetual slaves of industrialists and merchants of digital capitalism (Flores 2018). Such anti-people ideologies and activities need to be resisted through the invocation of indigenous knowledge systems as espoused in African languages. With regards to COVID-19, for instance, African theories that explicate the origin of COVID-19 and its possible cure have been dismissed as 'conspiracy theories', in a manner reminiscent of historical denialism by the Western world that anything from Africa manifests backwardness and savagery. On the other hand, is well known manoeuvring by the Western world through multi-pronged strategies including perceived deliberate manufacturing of diseases for the purposes of domination, economic and political control of the world as is dictated by digital capitalist philosophy and practices (Ani 2016; Birgit 2019). This chapter, therefore, conceives African languages as a necessary front for resistance that African people can use as a bastion to ward-off the anti-Africa digital capitalism and its attendant dangers as presented by pro-West 4IR and diseases such as the COVID-19 pandemic. African languages invest potential for Africans to approach the modern world holistically. African languages present Africans with the advantage of using memory to design solutions to current and future challenges.

For example, it has been showcased that proverbs foster communal values in society which is very critical in combating negative effects of 4IR and diseases such as COVID-19. Like other genres of orature, proverbs also encourage society to work together in harmony in times of plenty and trouble or hardships. They encourage good neighbourly behaviour and order in society. Proverbs like *Mweni haapedzi dura* (Giving food to a stranger does not make one poor) encourage hospitality and activities associated with charity work in society. In Africa, genres of oral literature are performed in "funerals, weddings, celebrations of victory, soothing a baby, accompanying work" (Finnegan 1988: 12). Oral literature is also used by governments for "propaganda or as a source in education (Finnegan 1988: 46). African languages were thus used in all aspects of life including Mining, Healthcare provision and governance. Finnegan chronicles how a wide range of orature genres such as "panegyric poetry, -poetry that lay stress on the significance of personal achievement in war or hunting" (Finnegan 1988: 111); elegiac poetry –"performed at funeral or memorial rites by non-professionals (often women) rather than state officials are associated with oral literature" (Finnegan 1988: 147). So, African languages are utilized in all aspects of life of the African people.

To side-line African languages will be deleterious and tantamount to sideswiping the Africans themselves, thus delinking people from global, social and econo-political developmental imperatives. The Chapter seeks to proffer introspections on pathways through which African languages can be repositioned to thrust Africans into the global economic lifeline. As Africa faces the Fourth Industrial Revolution, it should be borne in mind that in Africa, English remains "a minority language" (Obondo 2007: 41). It remains the former colonial master's language with no relevance to local cultures and philosophies. It will be a miscalculation to let English determine how Africa will respond to linguistic and communication challenges presented by 4IR to African people. It will equally be disastrous for Africa to sit on her laurels and wait for English – informed and inspired solutions to COVID-19 and other threats posed to people by calamities of digital capitalism, and, or slavery (Flores 2018). In this chapter I re-examine the Fourth Industrial Revolution in terms of its impact on the world particularly the African continent.

Scholars present the 4IR as ushering both possibilities and impossibilities to human life causing unimagined disruptions to the world order with human-things interaction; with skilled labour force becoming jobless in proportions matched by none in the history of civilization; with the rise of cognitive capitalism; digital capitalism and algorithmic capitalism; pandemics; a new world order of Cobots characterised by a watershed in robotization and accelerated technological unemployment and global disruption of knowledge systems (Peters and Jandrić 2019; Prisecaru 2016) and, in this chapter I add, educational, health and economic systems. Since in the 4IR African countries face a "double breasted dilemma" (Ayentimi &

Burgess 2019: 442) of job losses and skills deficit (Ayentini & Burgess 2019), it follows logic that the call for decolonizing 4IR by repositioning African Languages becomes synonymous with the call for the very survival of Africans during the 4IR. It is evident that in the 4IR the livelihoods and wellbeing of Africans remain threatened from multiple ends.

Perceived as the "post work" era due to unprecedented unemployment levels, 4IR calls for a new set of skills among job seekers which are, "critical thinking, people management, negotiation, cognitive flexibility as well as knowledge production and management" (Prisecaru 2016: 51). This means there will be a mismatch between existing jobs and skilled workers with 50% of current jobs expected to have disappeared in 50 years (Marwala et al. 2006 in Prisecaru 2016). The period is manifest with intelligent robots that are powered by artificial intelligence. Prisecaru (2016: 52) further avers:

> Fast changes in physical (e.g., intelligent robots, autonomous drones, driverless cars, 3D printing, and smart sensors); digital (e.g., the internet of things, services, data and even people); and, biological (e.g., synthetic, biology, individual genetic make-up, and bio-printing); technologies, and generally in the way we work, we learn, and we live, make it a force of economic competitiveness and social development.

The period will culminate in unprecedented changes in geopolitical, social and economic and perhaps political changes worldwide (Prisecaru 2016, Ayentimi & Burgess 2019). It is a period full of positive and negative aspects characterizing human history hence the need to re-think the role African languages should play during this historical epoch. As alluded to earlier, in this study, I take an Afrocentric decolonial outlook, a deliberate measure that is meant to prop perceptions on the study's renditions regarding the human conditions of African people during 4IR. Obondo (2007) warns about the danger of perpetuating linguicism whereby dominant languages are chosen at the expense of indigenous languages thereby leaving out the masses from developmental initiatives. Arguing a case for inclusive multilingual and multicultural language policies in Africa, Obondo (2007) contends that linguicism, is propelled by the erroneous thinking that some languages are better than others.

The efficacy of African languages-informed responses

"The COVID-19 pandemic has created both a medical crisis and an economic crisis. ... we face challenges just as big as those in the Spanish Flu Pandemic and the Great Depression – all at once" (Susskind & Vines, August 2020: 1). Therefore, there is need to think in and outside the box; there can never be a one solution-fits-all. This means all knowledge systems of the world need to be harnessed is search for solutions to challenges posed by 4IR and COVID-19. History has it that past solutions have not yielded the best results for Africa as they were not home grown mainly due to lack of meaningful involvement of Africans themselves through peripheralizing of African languages, cultures and knowledge systems (Osborn 2006; Igboanusi 2008; Hornberger & Vaish 2009; Wiegratz 2019). A quick perusal of information of the World Health Organizations' Website is worrisome as, once again, Africa is not designated as an active contributor to resources on the coronavirus disease. Instead, and as expected, the Website makes reference to sources such as, BMJ's Coronavirus (Covid-19) Hub, University of Cambridge, Centre of Disease Control and Prevention; Chinese Medical Association, Cochrane; Elsevier; European Centre for Disease Preventions and Control, Oxford Press and research centres from the Western world. From an Africa-centred perspective, the foregoing connotes a problem. For, Africa is only mentioned through research articles either as a case study or as a burden of the world: "...there is growing evidence that the health impacts of COVID-19 are particularly harmful for black, African and minority ethnic (BAME) communities (Susskind & Vines, August 2020: 5). This is corroborated by Dandara, *et al.* (2020: 2) who aver:

> The economic difficulties experienced by most African countries such as Zimbabwe meant that what most governments could do was to impose lockdowns and quarantine, with minimal or no contact tracing due to lack of resources and inadequate critical governance.... With a lack of investment in health infrastructure and research and development, most African countries could not source the much-needed ventilators and PPEs because the usual sources of these supplies in the global village, the industrialized countries, are busy stocking for their own unmet needs.

This shows that people who have been ravaged by the history of oppression, humiliation and subjugation face a real threat as targets of COVID-19 and negative effects of 4IR. To repel the onslaught, and, from the perspective of this chapter, Africa needs to be propelled by decoloniality: "a necessary liberation struggle aimed at freeing the world from global coloniality (transhistorical expansion of colonial domination and the perpetuation of its effects in contemporary times) (Ndlovu-Gatsheni in Omanga: January 2020: 1).The need for a different approach can never come at a better time than the current. This is so because Africa no longer has excuses for not championing her own cause.

Alexander (2000) recommends the adoption of additive multiligualism as the case in South Africa where the official language is used in complementary relationship with national languages. In this regard language planning and policy implementation activities in South Africa are encouraging. For example, the formation of Pan South African Language Board (Pan SALB) was a very positive development. The Pan SALB website presents it as a board with a serious mandate. Its briefing is as follows:

> The Pan SALB was established in order to promote and create conditions for the development of official languages, the Khoe and San languages, and sign language,; and to promote and ensure respect for all languages commonly used by communities in South Africa, including German, Greek, Gujarati, Hindi, Portuguese, Tamil, Telegu and Urdu, and Arabic, Hebrew, Sanskrit, and other languages used for religious purposes in South Africa (Raborife 2016: 1).

The use of African Languages will enable South Africans to succeed in the fight against COVID-19 and the negative effects of 4IR as the above languages will enable communication with all South Africans.

However, there seem to be challenges presented by some Pan SALB board members. For example, a news24 report indicates that Minister Mthethwa dissolved the Pan South African Language Board due to inefficiency and non-compliance with established code of conduct (Raborife 2016: 1).

Apart from Pan SLAB involvement in championing the agenda for African languages in South Africa, universities such as UNISA, the University of Cape Town, Rhodes University and other universities are leading the African Languages Association of Southern Africa (ALASA) which holds annual conferences and publishes the South African Journal of African Languages (SAJAL). In addition, the Linguistic Society of Southern Africa and the South African Folklore Society are additional examples of efforts by academics and relevant stakeholders to support African languages. Such associations are important in positioning African Languages to meet 4IR, COVID-19 pandemic and related challenges. The region has also witnessed a number of Webinars held by universities and other researchers in response to the COVID-19 pandemic. An example is the Webinar Series held in August 2020 between the North West University of South Africa and the Namibia University of Science and Technology. The Webinar series enabled academics to share research outputs that could inform a regional response to the pandemic. Similarly, in July 2020, the National Research Foundation of South Africa engaged a group of experts to review and select suitable project proposals on Scientific Communication of, and general response to, COVID-19 in Africa by African scholars and researchers. The aim of the sponsorship was to capacitate African communities with an informed response to the pandemic. As a member of the reviewing panel, I observed that most of the projects were aimed at invoking indigenous Knowledge Systems to fight the COVID-19 pandemic. Projects emphasized the need to utilise existing structures to reach out to vulnerable groups such as orphans, women, the youths and children including the girl child. Project proposals also pointed to the need to use African languages and to use radio stations that use various African languages which has an essential decolonising effect much as it is emancipatory and refreshing. However, lack of funding is still an impediment as more funding would ensure more equitable sharing of outcomes of such activities and research outcomes with wider communities on the continent using languages they understand.

In Zimbabwe, the African Languages Research Institute (ALRI) has published a number of dictionaries such as *Duramanzwi Guru reChishona* (Extended Monolingual Shona Dictionary) and *Duramanzi reUrapi neUtano* (A Dictionary of Medical Terms). The latter makes it possible, for instance, to communicate COVID-19 response message to Shona speakers in Zimbabwe. As has been alluded to earlier, such messages can be churned out through newspapers such as *Kwayedza*, Zimbabwe Broadcasting Corporation's Radio Zimbabwe and *Nehanda* radio among others. However, ALRI has been hampered by lack of funding. Its activities have slowed down. It should be understood that the Zimbabwe constitution accords 16 languages an official language status namely, "ChiNambya, ChiKalanga, ChiVenda (XiVenda), ChiShangani (Tsonga), Sign Language, ChiTonga, ChiChewa, ChiBarwe, English, Sotho, Koisan/Tshawo, Tswana, Xhosa, ChiNdau, Shona and Ndebele" (Mazuruse, 2016, p.80). However, despite this constitutional provision, there has been no indication of the "commitment of the Zimbabwe government in promoting linguistic pluralism given its failure to implement the previous provisions of the 1987 Education Act on languages to be taught and used in schools" (Mazuruse 2016: 80). Sadly, elsewhere in Africa government commitment to African languages have largely been found wanting (Ouane & Glanz 2005; Stroud 2010; Mufwene 2017). To navigate around the numerous challenges, it faces including those borne of the Forth Industrial Revolution and COVID-19, Africa needs to tap into local solutions and capability. This is the case as, in general, "the pandemic offers a silver lining for Africa: the prospects to integrate omic research with long-standing expertise in herbal medicine in Africa, thus accelerating advances toward novel molecular therapeutic targets for COVID-19 and precision herbal medicine worldwide" (Dandara, Dzobo & Chrikure 2020: 3). In this regard, Africa appears to be missing immense opportunities.

From the perspective of the study, the case of Kiswahili mainly demonstrates the role that African languages could play in the 4IR and other attendant challenges. Even though there has been contestations to Kachru's Three Circles of World Englishes Model (Pung 2009; Mair 2016) due to activities associated with "sociolinguistics of globalization" (Blommaert 2010 in Mair 2016), in the study, Kachru's model has been adapted to reflect on the potential for growth for the African languages and their use to promote national development under the current circumstances. Being more proactive will enable Africans to turn the curve and transform the perceived 4IR and COVID-19 doom into development and life-saving opportunities through the use of African languages. For example, in Tanzania and Kenya, Kiswahili has immensely contributed to national development (Okombo & Muna 2017). The figure below showcases the spread of Kiswahili. With modern alternative avenues of spreading language such as social media platforms and through music, it is possible that the number of

Kiswahili speakers has increased beyond the figures shown in figure 1.

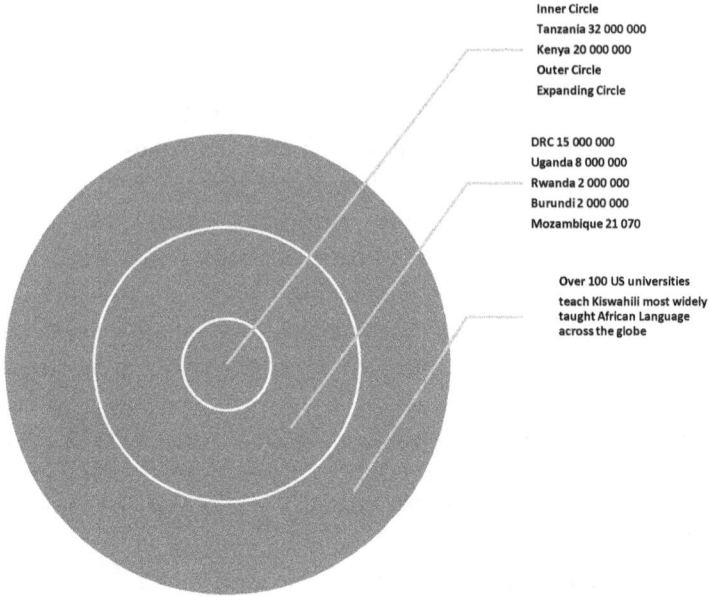

Figure 1: Adapted from Kachru's Three Circles of World Englishes (Pung 2009: 8)

The table presents the role played by Kiswahili in and beyond the inner circle. The above demonstrates that the Swahili language can be used as a model African language which needs to be utilised in combating challenges posed by 4IR and COVID-19 pandemic. Swahili language's use on various media platforms means it is ready to be used in response to challenges of the 21st century to meet the needs of many African people in Africa and beyond. Table 1 further showcases the achievements realised in the implementation of Kiswahili since 1967.

Table 1: Landmark achievements in the implementation of Kiswahili since 1967

Source: Information obtained from Okombo & Muna, 2017 and mazon.com/institute of Kiswahili-

Activity	Description
Teaching levels in the Inner Circle	Taught from creche to university
	Taught as a subject up to PhD level
Research and Development Institutes	Institutes of Kiswahili Research (Tanzania e.g University of Dares Salaam
	Institute of Kiswahili and Foreign Languages in Zanzibar
	Research Institute of Swahili Studies of Eastern Africa (National Museum in Kenya)
Research and Development Organisations	Baraza la Kiswahili Zanzibar (BAKIZA)
	Baraza la Kiswahili Tanzania (BAKITA)
	Chama cha Kiswahili Taifa (CHAKITA)
Publications (literature)	Poetry, plays, short stories and novels
Publications (Dictionaries)	Kiswahili dictionaries (e.g, English-Swahili Dictionary (Kamusi Ya Kingereza-Kiswahili; Standard Swahili-Swahili Dictionary
Publications (Journals)	Kiswahili: Journal of the Institute of Swahili Research; MULIKA; KISWAHILI; KIOO CHA LUGHA
Radio Broadcasting Services in Africa	Kenya Broadcasting Station; Radio Citizen; Radio Muisha; Radio Jambo; Redio Tanzania; Sauti ya Zanzibar
Musicians who sing in Kiswahili	**Tanzania:** Mbarak Mwinshehe, Mwaruka of Morogoro Jazz, Salum Abdalla of Cuban Marimba Jazz; **Kenya:** Daudi Kabuka, David Aminga, Paul Mwachupa
Newspapers	Taifa Leo in Kenya Mwanauchi in Tanzania
Kiswahili in Universities Abroad	**United States of America** Harvard, Yale, Cornell, Ohio, Illinois Urbana-Champaign, Michigan State University, Florida at Gainesville, St Lawrence, Stanford, Texas at Austin, Wisconsin at Madison

Research-Dictionaries

In addition to its use in Africa, Kiswahili is also taught in more than a dozen countries in Europe and Asia including Britain,

Germany, Russia, Belgium, France, Switzerland, Norway, China, Japan, Sweden, South Korea and Finland (Okombo & Muna 2017: 63). World Radio and Television broadcasting stations that use Kiswahili include BBC Radio, BBC Television, Voice of America, Voice of Cairo (Egypt), Deustsche Welle (Germany), Radio Moscow International, Radio South Africa and Channel Africa in South Africa (Okombo and Muna 2017). This demonstrates that Kiswahili's use in tertiary education will continue in the Fourth Industrial Revolution. Its use in computers and the internet suggests that the status of Kiswahili as lingua franca will meet with minimum disruptions during the 4IR. This positions Kiswahili as a model African language that can be emulated by African people as they grow and promote their languages to meet 21st century and future needs and challenges.

Discussion

African languages are like shadows to African people; they follow us wherever we go. African people collectively have a duty to perpetuate survival of their languages in a multilingual context where exotic languages can be used to fill in communication gaps and nothing more. African languages remain fortresses of epistemic, ontological, axiological and epistemological realities that African people face in life. Maintenance, cultivation and standardization of African languages remain the responsibility of African people as through such efforts Africans remain relevant and in meaningful existence. African people, need to tap on local languages to tackle vicissitudes of 4IR and to remain competitive on the global sphere. African languages are sacrosanct for they are both socially constitutive and constituted. They can play a pivotal role in socio-economic development in Africa and beyond. It is through African languages that home-grown solutions to challenges of the Fourth Industrial Revolution are digested, and opportunities transformed into developmental milestones. With regards to challenges of 4IR such as job losses, fear, anxiety and depression African languages inculcate Ubuntu values that foster social cohesion, humility, love for one another, generosity and social support that are crucial in ensuring that society faces such challenges in unison. African languages also enable African people to identify alternative ways of healing the pandemic using protocols that were used by past generations to overcome similar challenges. For example, *kunata* (steaming) has been used as a cure for disease with flu like symptoms in many parts of Africa. To this end, the medicine in Madagascar needs to be supported rather than to be quickly dismissed at the whim of the World Health Organisation (WHO) which tends to be a mouthpiece of the West because of funding.

As the world continues to be heavily contested for space, economic growth and domination, African people need to relentlessly seek home grown solutions through a well-planned and sustained use of indigenous languages. African languages are embedded with solutions to medical, mining, educational, scientific, social and legal challenges that Africans face on a daily basis. They remain a unifying factor between urban and rural populations on the continent and thus can be used as a rallying points in search for a unified approach to life challenges and opportunities. African languages are the vehicle for true and homegrown decolonization ethos that Africa needs to embrace in order to develop like other people elsewhere in the world. It is through African languages that Africans can meaningfully benefit from the post-independence era and to be able to gain dignified coexistence with other nations in the global community. Failure to embrace African languages will perpetually relegate African people to the periphery of socio-economic, historical and political developments in the world, and thus facing real danger of perpetual slavery and even annihilation. This must never be the option for Africa. African people can use their best judgement to rank and deploy their languages to address social, economic, governance, religious, healthcare needs and challenges that confront the continent now and in future. Languages like Kiswahili needs to be deployed more strategically on the continent without disenfranchising and peripheralizing other African languages. African people have knowledge and the technical know how to make this happen for the benefit of Africa.

Conclusion

This chapter has been informed by a three-tier theoretical perspective, namely, the Afrocentric, decoloniality and discourse historical perspectives to flesh out challenges presented by the 4IR and the COVID-19 pandemic to African people and to advise how African languages need to be deployed to ward-off vicissitudes of digital capitalism in Africa. The theories in use made it possible for the chapter to unravel the discourse on the 4IR and the COVID-19 pandemic within a historical context and reality whereby it was possible to reveal power structures and ideological underpinnings of both the 4IR and COVID-19 pandemic. The seamless deployment of the theories has made it possible to navigate through the real and perceived effects of 4IR and the COVID-19 pandemic on African people and how they can use their local languages to resist negative effects of digital capitalism as the harbinger of 4IR and diseases such as the COVID-19 pandemic. The holistic deployment of theoretical perspectives also enabled the chapter to harness relevant literature to expose ideological underpinnings of any existential challenge including 4IR and its offshoots such as the COVID-19 pandemic. The chapter's main rendition is that African languages need to be utilised to provide local solutions to challenges of the 21st century which are products of human activities and well-orchestrated manoeuvrings as dictated by social, economic and political interests of dominant digital capitalist forces. African people can mobilise local languages to cushion citizens against job losses, fear, anxiety, psychological trauma, and physical harm experienced as a result of 4IR and the COVID-19 pandemic.

Recommendation

African governments, universities, governmental and non-governmental organisations in Africa and like-minded people elsewhere should relentlessly cultivate and promote African Languages in the manner and seriousness with which Kiswahili has experienced since 1967 in order for African countries to maximally benefit from opportunities presented by the 41R as well as to overcome its challenges including diseases such as the COVID-19 pandemic.

References

Adegbite, W. (2004) 'Bilingualism and biculturalism and the utilization of African languages for the development of African nations', In Oyelele, L. (2004). (Ed.). *Language and Discourse in Society,* Ibadan: Hope Publications, 13-31. (ir.oauife.edu.ng/bistream/handle).

Alexander, N. (2007) *The role of African Universities in the intellectualization of African languages.* African Academy of Languages (ACALAN).

Ani, M. (2016) 'A praise song for Dr. Frances Cress Welsing, our race champion', *Atlanta Black Star*. Retrieved from info@atlantablackstar.com.

Ayentimi, D.T. and Burgess, J. (2019) 'Is the Fourth Industrial Revolution relevant for sub-Saharan Africa?' *Technology Analysis and Strategic Management*, 31 (6), 641-652.

Balkaran, S. (n.d.) 'The fourth industrial Revolution its impact on the South African public sector'. Retrieved from https://www.academia.edu/22826511/

Birgit, M. (2019) 'The '4th wave of industrial revolution'– a promise blind to social consequences, power and ecological impact in the era of 'digital capitalism'', *Memo Euro Group, Discussion Paper No. 01/2019.*

Childs, G.T. (2008) 'Language endangerment in West Africa: Its victims and causes', Applied Linguistics Faculty Publications and Presentations, Portland State University. Retrieved from https://pdxscholar.library.pdx.edu/ling_fac.

Chimhundu, H. (2001) *Duramanzwi Guru reChiShona*. Harare: College Press.

Dandara, C., Dzobo, K. and Chirikure, S. (2020) 'COVID-19 pandemic and Africa: From the situation in Zimbabwe to a case for precision Herbal Medicine', *OMICS: A Journal of Integrative Biology*, (Ahead of Print Commentary), Retrieved from https://www.liebertpub.com/doi/10.1089/OMI.2020.0099.

Errington, J. (2019) 'Getting language rights: The rhetorics of language endangerment and loss', *Language, Politics and Practices*, 105(4), 723-732.

Flores, D.S. (2018) 'Transhumanism: the big fraud-towards digital slavery', *International Physical Medicine & Rehabilitation Journal*, 3(5), 381-392. Retrieved from https://www.33rdsquare.com/2017/07/nick-bostrom-explains-how-advent-of.html.

Finnegan, R. (1988) *Oral Literature in Africa*. Oxford: Oxford University Press.

Hays, J. (2009) 'Steps forward and new challenges: Indigenous communities and mother-tongue education in southern Africa', *International Journal of Bilingual Education and Bilingualism*, 12(4), 410-413.

Hornbeerger, N. and Vaish, V. (2009) 'Multilingual language policy and school linguistic practice: Globalisation and English language teaching in India, Singapore and South Africa', *Compare,* 39(3), May 2009, 305-320.

Igboausi, H. (2008) 'Mother tongue based bilingual education in Nigeria', *International Journal of Bilingual Education and Bilingualism,* 11(6), 721-734.

Obondo, M.A. (2007) 'Tensions between English Language and mother-tongue teaching in post-colonial Africa', *International Handbook of English Language,* Rinkeby Institute of Multilingual Research; Sweden, 37-47.

Okombo, P.L. and Muna, E. (2017) 'The international status of Kinswahili: The parameters of Braj Kachru's Model of world Englishes', *Africology: The Journal of Pan African Studies,* 10(7), September 2017, 55-67.

Ouane, A. and Glanz, C. (2005) 'Mother tongue literacy in sub-saharan Africa', *Education for all Global Minority Report 2006. Literacy for Life.* UNESCO Institute for Education (UIE).

Mair, C. (2016) 'Beyond and between the three circles: World Englishes research in the age of globalisation', 17-36. In Seoane E. and Suarez-Gomez, C. (Eds.) (2016) *World Englishes: New Theoretical and Methodological Considerations,* Benjamins.

Makamani, R. (1992) 'Change of Expression and Constancy of Meaning: A Critical Survey of Shona Proverbial Expressions'. Unpublished M.A. Dissertation, University of Zimbabwe.

Mazuruse, M. (2016) 'Interrogating paradoxes in the multilingual provisions of the new 2013 Zimbabwean Constitution'. Retrieved from www.repository.unam.edu.na.

Mbiti, J.S. (1990) *African Religions and Philosophy.* Oxford: Heinemann.

Mchombu, K.J. and Mchombu, C.M. (2014) 'The role of information and knowledge in poverty eradication in Africa: A case study of Namibia'. In *IFLA 2014 LYON.* Retrieved from http://library.ifla.org/996/1/189-mchombu-en.pdf.

Moyo, D. (2009) *Dead Aid: Why Aid is not Working and How there is Another Way for Africa.* New York: Penguin.

Mpofu, N. (2004) *Duramanzwi reUrapi neUtano.* Gweru: Mambo Press.

Mufwene, S.S. (2017) 'Language Endangerment: What have Pride and Prestige got to do with it', *Language,* 93(4), e224-e233. Retrieved from https://www.researchgate.net/publication/322044267.

Nhemachena, A.N., Warikandwa, T.V. and Mpofu, N. (2020) 'Worse than "Bushmen" and Transhumance? Transitology and the resilient cannibalization of African heritages', *Journal of Black Studies*, 1-21.

Obondo, M.A. (2007) 'Tensions between English and mother-tongue teaching in post-colonial Africa', 37-47, *International Handbook of English Language Teaching*, Rinkeby Institute of Multilingual Research, Sweden.

Ogunyankin, G.A. (March, 2018) 'A "scented declaration of progress": Globalisation, afropolitan imagineering and familiar orientations', *Antipode*, 50(4). Retrieved from https://doi.org/10.1111/anti.12392.

Omanga, D. (January 2020) 'Decolonization, Decoloniality, and the Future of African Studies: A conversation with Dr. Sabelo Ndlovu-Gatsheni. African Peacebuilding Network and Next Generation Social Sciences'. Retrieved from https://items.ssrc.org/from-our-programs/decolonization-decoloniality-and-the-future-of-african-studies-a-conversation-with-dr-sabelo-ndlovu-gatsheni/.

Osborn, D.Z. (2006) 'African languages and Information and Communication Technologies (ICTs): Literacy, access and the future', *Selected Proceedings of the 35th Annual Conference on African Linguistics, Somerville, M.A.: Cascadilla Proceedings Project*. Retrieved from http://www.lingref.com/cpp/acal/35/paper1299.pdf.

Peters, M.A. and Jandrić, P. (June, 2019) 'Education and technological unemployment in the Fourth Industrial Revolution', *The Oxford Handbook of Higher Education Systems and University Management*. Retrieved from DOI: 10.1093/oxfordhb/9780198822905.013.27.

Pongweni, A.C. (1982) *Songs that Won the Liberation War*. Harare: College Press.

Prisecaru, P. (2016) 'Challenges of the Fourth Industrial Revolution', *Knowledge Horizons-Economics,* 8 (1), 57-62.

Pung, C.S. (2009) 'Beyond the three circles: A new model for world Englishes'. Unpublished M.A. Dissertation, National University of Singapore.

Reisigl, M., & Wodak, R. (2009) 'The discourse historical approach', (DHA), 81-121. In R. Wodak and M. Meyer (Eds.). *Methods of Critical Discourse Analysis* (2nd revised edition). London: Sage.

Rodney, W. (1973) *How Europe Underdeveloped Africa*. Dar-Es-Salaam: London and Tanzanian Publishing House.

Raborife, M. (January, 2016) (Reporter). 'Mthethwa dissolves Pan South Africa language Board'. Retrieved from https://www.news24.com/news24/southafrica/news/

Stroud, C. (2010) 'Postmodernist perspectives on local languages: African mother-tongue education in times of globalisation', *International Journal of Bilingual Education and Bilingualism*, 6(1), 17-36.

Susskind, D. and Vines, D. (August, 2020) 'The Economics of the COVID-19 pandemic: An assessment. Oxford Review of Economic Policy'. Retrieved from https://doi.org/10:1093/oxrep/graa036.

Tjirera, E. (2018) 'Providing basic public service remains a challenge for Namibia's Government', *AFRO Barometer*, No. 29.

Uwizeyimana, J.B. and Samuel, K. (2017) 'Social Connectedness and Poverty Eradication: A South African Perspective', *Global Challenges Working Paper Series*, No. 2, May 2017.

Wiegratz, J. (2019) 'They are all in it together: The social production of fraud in capitalist Africa', *Review of African Political Economy*, 357-358.

Wim, N. (2017) 'Entrepreneurship, education and the Fourth Industrial Revolution in Africa', IZA Discussion Papers, No. 10855, Institute of Labour Economics (IZA), Bonn. Retrieved from http://hdl.handle.net/10419/170839.

Xing, B. and Marwala, T. (Third Quarter, 2017) 'Implications of the Fourth Industrial Age on Higher Education', *The Thinker*, (73). Retrieved from https://ssrn.com/abstract=3225331.

Chapter Ten

The Healing Practitioner has Retreated Back to the Trenches: Healing and Spirituality During COVID-19

Peter Masvotore

Introduction

The history of humanity has always been characterized by pandemics. In the Old Testament, we learn that the deliverance of the Israelites from Egypt was possible after a series of pandemics and disasters that rocked Egypt (Exodus 7:20-10:13). While the term 'pandemic' is modern and was never used in the Scriptures, Hebrew and Greek words for pestilence and plagues are recorded at least 127 times in the Bible (Rosenberg 2020). Gusha (2020) argues that since 165AD-2015, pandemics have been killing people with the worst death caused by the Plague of Justinian (Byzantine Empire) around 541 - 542 CE that claimed ten percent of the world's population, followed by HIV and AIDS, a global pandemic that claimed over thirty five million people, third was the America Plague of the sixteenth century that claimed ninety percent of the indigenous population (Gusha 2020). From the arguments raised by Rosenberg (2020) and Gusha (2020), COVID-19 is one of the pandemics that humanity has experienced leading to the closure of the chapels, mosques, sanctuaries, shrines and temples across the world that fundamentally changed the way of being church, from being a centre of healing to a platform of contamination and infection.

The Coronavirus Disease 2019 (COVID-19) is a global pandemic that has decimated religious life of many systems, cultures, institutions, individuals and communities. As a result, churches, place of worship and sanctuaries from corner to corner globally are shut down. Many people are unable to gather because of the indispensable but upsetting social distancing rules that have forced the populace to remain indoors religious people included. Answers to the COVID-19 pandemic have basically altered the way of being church that may have consequences on ecclesia beyond the deadly disease. The church further urges its members to stay at home as a preventative way to bring to an end the increase of COVID-19. It can be observed that the ecclesiological healing centres disengaged from being an assembly of believers, who gather together for fellowship meals, sacraments, liturgical services and to receive both physical and spiritual healing to become possible infectious places of contamination due to COVID-19. Using a desk research method, this chapter explores the theological dilemma the church found itself in and figures out the relevance of the practitioner and the church's healing modes in the wake of COVID-19. Responses were gathered from both print and electronic media. The chapter concluded by arguing that, the definition of the church, has to be redefined to family sanctuaries (Black 2019) and not limited to structures such as temples, cathedrals, mosques etc that are used as places of worship. Key terms like healing and COVID-19 are defined in order to put them into the context of this chapter.

Definition of key terms

Research conducted on the definition and meaning of healing shows that the term has been used in a general sense, but the understanding of the word remains perplexing and inaccurate (Glaister 2001: 63). Healing as a word is derived from the old-English expression *haelen*, denoting "wholeness" and frequently means the practice of moving towards a required completeness or accomplishment of unity (Kritek 1997). For Levin (2008: 302) healing therefore becomes an involvement, an end result, and a procedure, and at times, all three facets. It also expresses an aptitude or control, vigour, and flushing out of pain, problem, or sin (Astin 2000: 903). The concept of healing is applicable in an array of disciplines that includes medicine, nursing, psychology, public health, education, religion, and spirituality. Healing happens in numerous magnitude that include physical, mental, emotional, spiritual, familial, social, communal, and environmental. It also originates from inside the human being and from outside sources for example human being healers and supernatural being or materials such as herbs and medicines. According to Cowling (2005: 32) perceptions on curing come from healthcare experts, the sick patients, clerics, energy consultants, religious healers, those close to death, individuals living with pain and other chronic disease, the abused and neglected, and many who have been subjected to hardship such as break up, miscarriage, or bereavement of a child.

222

The World Council of Churches (WCC), Christian Medical Commission (CMC), in union with World Health Organisation (WHO) met to design principles of the Community-Based Health Care System based on issues of healthiness, medicinal and entirety. At the end of the meeting and also responding to the prelude to the tripartite Constitution of WHO, CMC and WCC the following definition of health was agreed in 1988: "Health is a dynamic state of well-being of the individual and society, of physical, mental, spiritual, economic, political, and social well-being of being in harmony with each other, with the material environment and with God" (Commission on World Mission and Evangelism (CWME 2005).

This approved definition by the WCC became the source of reference for the ecumenical understanding of health. Consequently, WHO sequentially revised as well as developed its meaning of health to define it as "a state of complete physical, mental and social well-being and not merely the absence of disease or infirmity" (WHO 1997). It can be deduced that there are positive elements that were incorporated in the definition of healing. Firstly, health is not only envisaged as exclusively the situation of a person, to a certain extent community reasons that control human being health are embraced. Secondly, the welfare of the person is perceived in consideration to the manner in which the social order is formed. Thirdly, the fraternal cohorts made this clear by exclusively dealing with diverse aspects namely: body, soul, spirit, economy, politics and society. In this chapter the working definition of healing takes an ecumenical understanding where issues of health are not only limited to the nonexistence of illness but embraces various categories of body, spirit, economy, politics and society as factors influencing individual fitness.

It is worth to note that the ecumenical definition has also dealt with the contestations between science and religion. In other words, the definition has shown that there is binary between the two because science itself is a religion or a belief. Without delving much in the arguments on correlation involving science and religion because of space this chapter however notes that there has been suggested ways put forward that explain aspects of relating science and religion. Scholars such as Barbour (1988), Russel (2002), Murphy (1985), Stenmark (2010), Sanda *et al.* (2017) and others wrote extensively about this relational aspect of science and religion. According to Murphy (1985: 16) "theology could be a transformer not only of culture in general but even of science in particular." Be that as it may scholars have generally agreed that;

> while science and religion are indeed distinct ways of knowing, however in the real world they cannot easily be separated. "Contact" allows for interaction, dialogue and mutual impact, it prohibits both combining and separating, insists on keeping differences, but at the same time develops mutual (interdisciplinary) relations between science and religion (Sanda et al. 2017: 6).

From this contestation debate among scholars the interdisciplinary and trans-disciplinary are suggested approaches to explain the connection among science and religion.

An additional term that needs to be understood is COVID-19. It is prudent at this point to draw the readers to an understanding of this vicious virus code named Covid-19. WHO publicized that COVID-19 is the authorized name of the pandemic (WHO 2019). WHO chief Tedros Adhanom Ghebreyesus further elucidated that,

> *CO* stands for *corona*
> *VI* stands for *virus*
> *D* stands for *disease*,
> While *19* is for when the outbreak was first identified on 31 December 2019 (WHO 2019).

The name had been preferred to circumvent a direct mention to a particular geographical locality (e.g. China), mammal species or crowd of citizens, in line with global advices for naming meant to prevent stigmatisation (Taylor-Coleman 2020). According to WHO (2019) Covid-19, is a transmittable sickness originated by Severe Acute Respiratory Syndrome Coronavirus (SARS-CoV-2). This type of illness was first well-known in December 2019 in Wuhan, the capital city of China that is located in Hubei region. This pandemic has since spread internationally without exception (Hui *et al.* 2020; WHO 2019). Additionally;

> The known Common symptoms include fever, cough and shortness of breath. Other symptoms may include fatigue, muscle pain, diarrhoea, sore throat, loss of smell and abdominal pain. These and other symptoms may appear two to fourteen

days after exposure based on the incubation period of MERS-COV viruses (Centre for Disease Control and Prevention (CDC 2020a; WHO 2019).

The virus is mostly passed on through close contact and via minute drops formed when individuals contaminated cough, sneeze or converse (CDC 2020b; WHO 2019). These tiny droplets might as well be created at some point in breathing; nevertheless, they quickly drop to the floor or surfaces of objects. Individuals could as well be infected through touching an infected area and subsequently touch their face. Owing to the quick scattering of this bug the suggested process to avoid contagion incorporate regular hand washing, upholding social distance of between one metre fifty centimetres (1,5m) and two metres from other people (particularly from those with symptoms), cover coughs and sneezes by a tissue or else inside elbow, and keep unclean hands afar from the face (WHO 2020). The wearing of masks became compulsory for all people in some countries while others were flexible but to those who suspect they have the virus and their caregivers it was strict (CDC 2020c; Feng *et al.* 2020). Presently, both scientists and researchers have no readily available vaccine or precise antiviral cure for COVID-19. Temporal measures involve management of warning signs, caring, seclusion and untried methods. Consequently, this has led many governments to call for lockdown for a period of days as a preventative way of the spread of the pandemic which has seen churches closing doors. Having discussed the two concepts of healing and COVID-19 as key terms in this chapter it is now prudent to look at the methodological considerations employed in this chapter.

Methodological considerations

The chapter has used a qualitative research methodology of reviewing existing data through a desk research analysis method. According to Creswell (2009) a desk study is collecting data without fieldwork. It can be further defined as secondary analysis which means, "an analysis of an existing data which presents interpretations, conclusions or knowledge additional to, or different from, those presented in the first report on the inquiry as a whole and its main result" (Hakim 1982: 1).

Contextually this chapter has used the term desk research in a wider spectrum to embrace all information gathered without the involvement of a field survey. The use of this method will employ gathering data from libraries and the internet. Additionally, desk study analysis is examination of information that was assembled by somebody else intended for a different main purpose (Masvotore & Tsara 2019). The use of existing information presents a feasible alternative for researchers who could have inadequate resources and time for field work. Desk study analysis is a pragmatic method that utilizes similar fundamental research ideology as studies using primary data and has rules to be pursued just as any research method. In as much as secondary data scrutiny is further defined as a logical research method, however, not many frameworks are obtainable to direct researchers as they carry out desk research data analysis (Andrews et al. 2012; Smith et al. 2011).

The desk research methodology has been selected in this chapter because of lockdown due to COVID-19. The most important merit linked with desk research is the cost efficacy and expediency it is endowed with (Dale et al. 1988). In view of the fact that someone has previously gathered the data, it follows that the researcher will save financial resources to the collection of data. It therefore give equal opportunity to all researchers including the beginners and builds competence for experiential research (Hakim 1982). Furthermore, it is quicker to conduct desktop research as one skips other time-consuming research steps such as measurement development and data collection thereby enabling the researcher to easily answer time-sensitive policy related questions (Doolan & Froelicher 2009; Magee et al. 2006).

In this chapter the researcher conducted this research through accessing sources from the internet, news articles, published books, articles and journals because of the lockdown as indicated elsewhere. In a bid to fill in these gaps the study made use of published materials from World Health Organisation (WHO) on COVID-19 and information from published sources for a cautious deep in thought assessment and decisive appraisal of the data as a mitigating measure to avoid most limitations of desk research methodology (Boslaugh 2007; Dale et al. 1988; Kiecolt & Nathan 1985).

The background of faith healing

The practice of faith healing in the analysis, management and cure of an excess of health concerns is ancient and dates back into the distant past in many countries (Kale 1995: 1183). More significantly the modern epoch has witnessed a rising operation prototype of faith therapeutic services for health-giving reasons predominantly in the sub-Saharan African region (Kar 2008: 721; Levin 2009: 77). Faith healers are more often than not perceived Christians who go to either Mainline or African indigenous churches, or traditionalists who mostly cure using prayer, touch patients when laying hands, administer holy oil and water over and above medicinal herbs for traditionalists (Peprah, et al. 2018; Igwe 2020). Spiritual and faith healers consider that their curative authority is derived from supernatural being through euphoric positions and trance-contact with the Holy Spirit and/or ancestral spirit. In Zimbabwe the rising use of faith healing packages can partially be accredited to the growing alertness during advertisement made over the radio and television. According to Masiiwa, Moyo, and Mujuru (2018) the political insecurity and the occurrence of fatal ailments such as HIV and AIDS in the sub-Saharan African region have contributed to a sharp increase in the utilization of traditional medication and faith-based healing. They further state that, Zimbabwe's unstable economy as well forces the demand for such healing services. Faith-based healing is repeatedly an inexpensive option to clinical health care. This also shows a long-lasting practice among Zimbabwe's healers: They rely on customer transfers, print media and radio to advertise and broaden their message of faith cure.

In administering treatment to patients, faith healers examine healthiness and sickness via the incorporation of mind, body and spirit mainly in the context of family and community. This means that the healers call for direct conduct with their patients hence the establishment of healing centres and to a certain extent one on one with the prophet. This move towards faith healing goes further than the WHO's characterization of health as "a state of complete physical, mental and social wellbeing and not merely absent of disease or infirmity" (Abdool-Karim, Ziqubu-Page & Arendse 1994: 7). Remarkably, a considerable number of sick patients run after the cure of prophetic healing because these services are frequently and voluntarily accessible and cheaper to would-be clients (Masiiwa, Moyo & Mujuru 2018). On the other hand, some types of cure such as bio-western medicine, sick people regularly move longer distances and endure long waiting period to get the necessary health care (Kar 2008: 720).

While faith curing remedies are generally reasonably priced, the choices to make use of such remedies are stimulated through hope, accessibility plus ease of use, suggestions from significant other and belief into the mystical causation of sickness (Chadda et al. 2001: 71). Nevertheless, an inquiry into the success of faith healing by means of scientific examination is contentious whereas there is inadequate proof of healing success of faith curing modalities such as prayer (Astin, Harkness, & Ernst 2000: 903). The above notion is what Foucault (1977: 166) describe as politics of health, where medical fraternity is infiltrated and draws its support from structures of power to downplay other forms of healing that are not scientifically proven. Further to that

> There is also the development of a medical market in the form of private clienteles, the extension of a network of personnel offering qualified medical attention, the growth of individual and family demand for health care, the emergence of a clinical medicine strongly centred on individual examination, diagnosis and therapy, the explicitly moral and scientific (Foucault 1977: 167).

Universal bodies such as WHO are seen to control the operations and sidelining the faith healers whom they see as dump, but surprisingly people flock to them in numbers. From an analytical point of view one can deduce that there is an issue of contested truth where there is imposition of Western knowledge and rules about evidence that is scientific.

This leads me to the Foucault's idea of the care of the identity where scientific practitioners are unconvinced of customary medicinal approaches centred on sciences of the personality, the psy-sciences, as Rose (1989) explained them, as well as their allied qualified specialists. Furthermore,

> A joint journey led by the sufferer, where the self and other accept the account of suffering and the challenge of finding a way out of social isolation. Both the doctor and patient are seen as equals. In this case the idea of healing or care is rooted in a relation of mutual equality rather than of expert authority, and it is grounded upon willingness to share and accept the narrative of the other (Randal & Munro 2010: 1497).

Be that as it may, it is apparent that a major fraction of sick people go for faith healing as a first preference in diverse cultures as well as believing in its efficacy (Puckree 2002: 247). Patients in sub Saharan

Africa, Zimbabwe in particular hunt for the cure of faith healers for every type of diseases including societal and psychosomatic matters. On the other hand, Masiiwa, Moyo, and Mujuru (2018) state that some prophets focus in handling particular health challenges and in case of emergency they advise patients to seek formal health care facilities for treatment.

Critically the question being asked today is: has the pandemic of the COVID-19 created the ending of faith healing traditions in the globe, particularly in Africa and Zimbabwe to be specific? This question has become necessary among scholars because a few days, weeks, months and years ago traditional and Christian faith healing declarations have been widespread. These claims included curing persons who suffers from different kinds of sickness, the sightless, lame or those with HIV and AIDS. Shockingly, subsequent to COVID-19 catastrophe, practitioners and organizations that allege to have power over faith healing have retreated back to the trenches. Even though some practitioners such as a Nigerian faith healer (Kungleo) said that he want to go to China to tear down the disease. According to Kungleo in a video that went viral he declared that,

> The critics, who are questioning God's power and ability to heal coronavirus, should bring patients of said disease for healing as proof that God is still the greatest Physician. This follows after the prophet vowed to go to China and destroy Coronavirus personally using prophetic means (Kingleo 2020: n.p.).

Nevertheless, from the time when the disease was recognized in Nigeria, no one has heard from this seer of God including other highly praised faith practitioners in Zimbabwe and across Africa. Furthermore, they have been so silent and have declined to make any further claim to heal any infected human being. The questions to ask are why? What has gone wrong? Be it for the reason that faith therapeutic is not effective anymore? Or else that faith healing is not applicable to coronavirus? As already indicated elsewhere in this chapter these and other questions can be answered by viewing the silence of faith healers not as a surprise but as issues embedded in politics of knowledge as demonstrated by Foucault (1977). The same developments where religious organisations were silenced giving priority to scientific medicine that took place during the nineteenth century are repeating. This is substantiated by Foucault when he indicated that;

The progressive emplacement of what was to become the great medical edifice of the nineteenth century, cannot be divorced from the concurrent organisation of a politics of health, the consideration of disease as a political and economic problem for social collectivises which they must seek to resolve as a matter of overall policy (1977: 166) .

He further observes that,

Medicine, as a general technique of health even more than as a service to the sick or an art of cures, assumes an increasingly important place in the administrative system and the machinery of power, a role which is constantly widened and strengthened throughout since the beginning of COVID-19. The doctor wins a footing within the different instances of social power (Foucault 1977: 176).

The practitioner and modes of healing

During this advent of lockdown, the assertions of Dag Heward-Mills can be revisited and authenticated where he claims that,

Many people have received the anointing through listening to tapes and reading books, but they do not understand what has happened to them. Many of those who have received the anointing through this channel cannot teach it because they do not fully understand it. I believe that it is my duty to teach this simple and real method of catching the most essential ingredient in ministry which is the anointing (Heward-Mills 2000: 2).

This implies that together the manufacturers and end users of these media materials, they hold a definite sacramental significance in which material possessions are conduits for ontological graces. This progression has in the previous two decades been assisted extremely by the movement's all-embracing commandeering of contemporary mass media technologies (Asamoah- Gyadu 2005). COVID-19 has further authenticates that imagery of broadcasted neo-Christianity are consequently intended to mirror victory and validate the idea by clerics, that they are sources or intermediaries of an extraordinary power that radiate as healing and 'the anointing'. Television, WhatsApp messages, audios code named e-Conferencing platform and face book increases visibility and importance. Through this fourth industrial technology the leaders of churches enjoy great admiration not just around the country, but also beyond. Televised Charismatic Christianity in Africa is personalised because the practitioners are the sole presenters of the religious programmes in question. Their audio and video-cassette tapes also circulate among local Christians and migrant communities in other countries. This allows them to get to wider viewers with their preaching of instantaneous answers to life's unbearable predicaments. The flamboyant pictures of the clergy who host a range of activities and the individual achievement stories used to embellish their preaching, are all calculated to underscore the 'workability of faith' (Gifford 2004: 33).

Being one and the same with the functional supremacy of the Spirit, healing and anointing has by tradition been connected with the spoken word and touch or the laying on of hands (Asamoh-Gyadu 2005). In support of the above Sanneh reiterates that,

> As his reputation for holiness grew, so too did a superstitious reverence for his person: people sought physical contact with him in order to receive healing or protection from danger. The water in which he washed was collected and dispensed as containing magical properties. His words were received as charged with spiritual force (Sanneh 1983: 182).

The important words in the course of mediating the supernatural here are healing and anointing, which are equally comprehended in this stream of religious conviction as the power of God or divinity in action and strongly present in the office of the practitioner. Anointing has immense touching plea when it comes to African religious sensibility since the native religious milieu itself is one in which authority decides the viability of religion.

The introduction of new technology into the contemporary African led Churches is believed that, anointing can now be practised via texts and tapes that contains the inspired word of the pastor particularly in times of disaster. These expressions, like the words of Meyer (2006), are understood to be filled with a divine power that can make things happen. Thus, to catch the anointing, as Dag Heward-Mills has titled one of his books,

> one has to read his books and listen to his tapes because many people are limited to be in close association with [great] men of

God. It is only possible through the medium of books and tapes (Heward-Mills, 2000: 4).

The ban on spiritual gatherings and maintenance of social distancing has worsened the situation hence churches were left with no choice serve to adopt the technological way. This is a sacred exercise that individuals and devout congregants in the church have to acclimatize and take seriously and religiously. What we have in these advancements are not simple texts and tapes but charmed latest media that intercede mystical power for healing and deliverance. Morgan argues that,

> Although language is a symbolic form that is generally shared, it should not be understood as an isolated or autonomous operator in the construction of reality. Language and vision, word and image, text and picture, are in fact deeply enmeshed and collaborate powerfully in assembling our sense of the real (Morgan 1998: 9).

The spread of the pandemic of COVID-19 world over, Africa in particular has seen the conglomerate character of present-day church being proactive and inventive through appropriations of contemporary media technologies. In the process Morgan further reiterate that,

> African sacramental worldviews have found a place to feel at home in the hearts and lives of people going through challenges of the pandemic as they attempt to find their way within the maze of COVID-19 and its numerous challenges. Belief occurs through the medium, which is the locus of religious sensations. The new Church in African we have encountered in this period of COVID-19 has taken the uses of the media to another level as both for healing and deliverance and pastoral initiatives during lockdown (Morgan 1998: 9).

COVID-19 has been seen as an opportunity for technological advancement in different aspects of human life. However, this technological development has promoted in one way or the other the trans-humanism ideology which according to the World Trans-humanism Association (WTA) is a thinking that support for making use of technological advancement for the reason of overcoming

232

biological precincts and to change human circumstance (Salinas 2018: 381-392). Salinas further states that,

> The transhumanists state that adding technological implants and inserting DNA in human beings will improve their condition; man would leave biological evolution and would begin an evolution based on technology, the post-human species would be born. The essence of transhumanism is applying the so-called four emerging technologies that include the nanotechnology, the biotechnology, the information technologies and knowledge sciences in the human being. The transhumanists do not only seek to improve health, to eliminate the disabilities or to cure the diseases but also to produce stronger, faster, more athletic and more intelligent human beings with technology. For the transhumanists the time has come for human beings to take control of their own evolution, this evolution based on the technology will open the doors to create a new species descending from the homo sapiens. The human beings will be replaced progressively by "trans-humans" (H+) or "post-humans" (H++) who will live 500 years (Salinas 2018: 381).

Gonzalez (2010) also hold the same views regarding transhumanism and its negative impact on society.

This foregoing is one among many negative impacts of technological promotion even though from the general view technology seems to be a welcome move especially during lockdown because of COVID-19. Some of these promotions are done undercover and they are worth unearthing for the society to choose their destiny wisely. A closer analysis of transhumanism shows that,

> The fact of hiding the adverse effects of technological implants by the transhumanists , the non-use of the transhumanists of the brain implants that they promote, the billionaire promotion and financing of transhumanism by the economic powers and the transnational of technology and the illicit human experimentation that is suspected be the real secret method of these transhumanists projects reveals that the transhumanism is a swindle, in order to lead humanity towards the digital slavery and towards a fascist society where an elite will enslave digitally the rest of citizens with technological implants (Salinas 2018: 391).

A theological consideration to the pandemic

From this chapter one can deduce that there are two types of practitioners since the advent of COVID-19. First there are those who are taking heed of the government's call for lockdown and social distancing (Tazira, 2020; Tapfumaneyi 2020). Second there are those who are to a great extent rash and irresponsible, tempting God and ignoring all that might thwart death and the pandemic. They disregard the utilization of medicines; they do not stay away from places and individuals infected with the coronavirus, they also experiment and desire to demonstrate how self-regulating they are (Wilson, 2020). It is however interesting at this point to mention that although there is a general belief that medicines come from God, there are however some medicines, including some vaccines, that are not acceptable to some churches because they are produced out of human foetuses (Gomez- Tatay 2020). Should human beings eat or cannibalise other human beings? Other vaccines are made out of viruses that are then injected into human beings. According to Wadman (2020) higher-ranking Catholic leaders from United States and Canada, together with some antiabortion groups, are raising moral protests to up-coming COVID-19 vaccine aspirants that are made by means of cells derived from human foetuses. In retaliation to vaccines obtained from foetuses Wadman further states that;

> It is critically important that Americans have access to a vaccine that is produced ethically: no American should be forced to choose between being vaccinated against this potentially deadly virus and violating his or her conscience," members of the U.S. Conference of Catholic Bishops and 20 other religious, medical, and political organizations that oppose abortion wrote to Stephen Hahn, commissioner of the U.S. Food and Drug Administration (FDA), in April 2020 (Wadman 2020).

The information that some vaccines are manufactured in cells obtained from aborted foetuses hoists numerous ethical problems about material involvement with an immoral act, to be exact abortion. This ought to be examined, not only to provide scientists answers on the way to carry out research in this field, but besides patients themselves, who might be faced with the predicament of having to decide between their wellbeing (or that of their children) and their ethical integrity. Following this ethical dilemma Gomez-

Tatay (2020) raised a number of questions which are valid today when faced with the use of these vaccines;

> Is it immoral or hypocritical to benefit from something that is condemned as an evil? Or, on the other hand, since the abortions have already been performed and there is no going back, is it not right to take advantage of the good that can be derived from these abortions? In that case, though, would it be promoting the use of aborted foetuses for research? And what happens if the abortion has not been induced but has occurred spontaneously, i.e. a miscarriage? Is it licit for the parents to donate its body to science? In this case, would the moral implications of the use of the derivatives be lessened (Gomez-Tatay 2020: n. p)?

However, those who protect these contentious vaccines argue that, given that the abortions were procedures unconnected in time, agency, and use from vaccine manufacturing, their use would be morally adequate (Zimmerman 2004).

Furthermore, those who take the second position say that,

> It is God's punishment; if he wants to protect them he can do so without medicines or our carefulness. This is not trusting God but tempting him. God has created medicines and provided us with intelligence to guard and take good care of the body so that we can live in good health. If one makes no use of intelligence or medicine when he could do so without detriment to his neighbour, such a person injures his body and must beware lest he become a suicide in God's eyes (Luther 1999: 129).

Martin Luther further demonstrated that,

> By the same reasoning a person might forego eating and drinking, clothing and shelter, and boldly proclaim his faith that if God wanted to preserve him from starvation and cold, he could do so without food and clothing. Actually, that would be suicide. It is even more shameful for a person to pay no heed to his own body and to fail to protect it against the plague the best he is able, and then to infect and poison others who might have remained alive if he had taken care of his body as he should have. He is thus responsible before God for his neighbour's death and

is a murderer many times over. Indeed, such people behave as though a house was burning in the city and nobody was trying to put the fire out. Instead they give leeway to the flames so that the whole city is consumed, saying that if God so willed, he could save the city without water to quench the fire. No, my dear friends, that is no good (Luther 1999:129).

The question whether Christians should flee the Coronavirus or not, is provided by Martin Luther as a guide to Christians facing epidemics, is his strict rule not in favour of suicide and self-damage. We got our bodies as a gift from God therefore it has to be protected. In his essay "we must not tempt God Luther said "humanity should not cause danger to others through acts of neglect or irresponsibility (Stone 2020). An analysis of Luther's essay gives confidence to Christians to religiously follow quarantine regulations and take preventative measures to prevent spreading of the virus. Accordingly, the first sacrifice that the church should do is to participate aggressively on sanitation awareness process and observe social distancing. This category of care for people is a powerful strength. When good sanitary procedures are done they seize to be concerning saving our individual skin and begin to be in relation to loving our fellow citizen, and becomes not just lifesaving but soul reviving. The whole ethic behind closing doors of the church is derived from the inspiration of individual sacrifice to mind for others and proposed instruments to minimize infection, presumes the survival of society in which everyone is a stakeholder. Though we may forgo handshaking or embracing, and maintain social distance, listen or watch services in our homes we still commune in spirit.

In his letter Luther encourages practitioners:

> Use medicine; take potions which can help you; fumigate house, shun persons and places wherever your neighbour does not need your presence or has recovered, and act like a man who wants to help put out the burning city. What else is the epidemic but a fire which instead of consuming wood and straw devours life and body? You ought to think this way: "Very well, by God's decree the enemy has sent us poison and deadly offal. Therefore, I shall ask God mercifully to protect us. Then I shall fumigate, help purify the air, administer medicine, and take it. I shall avoid places and persons where my presence is not needed in order not to become contaminated and thus perchance infect and pollute others, and so cause their death as a result of my

negligence. If God should wish to take me, he will surely find me, and I have done what he has expected of me and so I am not responsible for either my own death or the death of others. If my neighbour needs me, however, I shall not avoid place or person but will go freely, as stated above. See, this is such a God-fearing faith (Luther 1999: 129).

Notwithstanding challenges brought by this COVID-19 there are also opportunities created by this pandemic in the whole world. Coronavirus has managed to bring together people to be each other's keeper despite economic strength, political affiliations and religious attachments. Unity of purpose has been created where all stakeholders are coming together in-spite of all these differences to seek for solutions together. In Zimbabwe political parties, religious groups have all come together to speak with one voice. COVID-19 has come as a wake-up call like what Jakes (2020) said when he was giving an update of Coronavirus to his church. For him the virus has made churches to revert back to its biblical foundations where the church is not defined as an assembly of people at a building rather it makes houses as sanctuaries of God. This was also supported by Maponga (2020) who is a cultural activist pastor, for him coronavirus has come to legitimise true Christianity and shame fake enterprising prophetic healing and deliverances that had taken centre stage instead of Christian ethic of love and care. For him the Bible taught hygiene standards of washing of hands and feet as one enter the place of worship and as you come out. There is also the ritual of burning incenses which signify the fumigation to get rid of viruses and bacteria. The working through E-platforms has come as a way to re-direct members that their faith should not be focused on a building but should be in their hearts.

Major findings and conclusion

The question of the relevance of the practitioner and the church's healing modes in the wake of COVID-19 is central to this research. The chapter has managed to discuss COVID-19 in the context of churches being closed thereby forcing practitioners to retreat back to the trenches without performing healing and deliverance in sanctuaries. It has been observed that scientific medicine has been authenticated and supported through structural powers hence the politics of health in play that has caused the faith healers to retreat in

237

obedience to the government as instructed by Paul in Romans 13:1—7. Instead practitioners had to adapt quickly to the fourth industrial revolution where technology had to be the only means to spread the gospel through the use of media. The chapter also demonstrated that in taking heed of the government's call for social distancing and lockdown the church did not falter but it was guided by Luther's call never to tempt God by endangering others rather people must act out of a love ethic. The chapter raised ethical issues in the production of vaccines using human foetuses and concluded that it is veiled cannibalism into which everyone is being recruited using vile means. It is inhuman when animal lives are deemed sacred at the expense of unborn human foetuses/lives. It is also through the advent of COVID-19 that the shenanigans of the prophetic, healing and deliverance activities that had taken the centre stage in the past were exposed. As much as the chapter articulates the negative impact of the pandemic to the church it also brings to the fore some positive aspects such as unity of purpose among citizens and members of faith as well as redirecting Christians to the fact that they should not focus their faith on practitioners, buildings rather they should put focus to God and their faith should be in their hearts. From these findings it can be concluded that churches are individuals at different places and not as people gathered together at a cathedral, mosque or church building.

References

Abdool-Karim, S. S., Ziqubu-Page, T. T. and Arendse, R. (1994) 'Bridging the gap: Project report for the South African Medical Research Council', *South African Medical Journal*, 84,1–14.

Andrews, L., Higgins, A., Andrews, M. W. and Lalor J. G. (2012) 'Classic grounded theory to analyse secondary data: Reality and reflections', *The Grounded Theory Review*,11(1), 12 - 26.

Asamoah-Gyadu, J. K. (2005) 'Anointing through the screen: Neo-Pentecostalism and Televised Christianity'. Retrieved from https://www.researchgate.net>2502.

Astin, J. A., Harkness, E. and Ernst, E. (2000) 'The efficacy of "distance healing": A systematic review of randomized trials', *Ann Intern Med*, 132(11),903-910.

Barbour, I. (1988) 'Ways of relating science and theology'. In: Robert J. Russel., William R. Stoeger and George V. Coyne (eds.). *Physics, philosophy and theology. A common quest for understanding.* Vatican City: LEV and University of Notre Dame Press.

Black, B. (2019) 'The family sanctuary'. Retrieved from https://www.dynastus.com>family.

Boslaugh, S. (2007) *Secondary analysis for public health: A practical guide.* New York, NY: Cambridge. doi: https://doi.org/10.1017/CBO9780511618802.

CDC. (2020a) 'Symptoms of coronavirus', *Centres for Disease Control and Prevention.* Retrieved from https://www.cdc.gov/coronavirus/2019-ncov/symptoms-testing/symptoms.html.
(2020b) 'How COVID-19 spreads', *Centres for Disease Control and Prevention.* Retrieved from https://www.cdc.gov/coronavirus/2019-ncov/prevent-getting-sick/how-covid-spreads.html.
(2020c) 'What to do if you are sick', *Centres for Disease Control and Prevention.* Retrieved from https://www.cdc.gov/coronavirus/2019-ncov/if-you-are-sick/steps-when-sick.html.

Chadda, R. K., Agarwal, V., Singh, M. C. and Raheja, D. (2001) 'Help seeking behaviour of psychiatric patients before seeking care at a mental hospital', *International Journal of Social Psychology,* (47), p. 71–78.

Cowling, R. W.(2005) 'Healing through reflection and action: Narrative from unitary appreciative praxis', *International Journal of Human Caring,* 9(2).

Creswell, J.W. (2009) *Research design: Qualitative, quantitative, and mixed methods Approaches,* 3rd Edition, Thousand Oaks, CA: Sage.

Dale, A., Arbor, S. and Procter, M. (1988) *Doing secondary analysis.* London., UK: Unwin Hyman.

Doolan, D.M. and Froelicher E. S. (2009) 'Using an existing data set to answer new research questions: A methodological review', *Research and Theory for Nursing Practice: An International Journal,* 23(3), 203 - 215. Retrieved fromhttps://doi.org/10.1891/1541-6577.23.3.203.

Feng, S., Shen, C., Xia, N., Song, W., Fan, M. and Cowling, B. J. (2020) 'Rational use of face masks in the COVID-19 pandemic', *The Lancet Respiratory Medicine.* doi:10.1016/S2213-2600(20)30134-X.

Foucault, M. (1977) *Power/Knowledge selected interviews and other writings 1972-1977*. New York: Pantheon Book.

Gifford, P. (2004) *Ghana's new Christianity: Pentecostalism in a globalizing African economy*. Bloomington and Indianapolis: Indiana University Press.

Glaister, J. A. (2001) 'Healing: Analysis of the concept' *International Journal Nurse Practice*,7, p. 63-68.

Gomez-Tatay, L. (2020) 'Is it true that there are vaccines produced using aborted foetuses?' *Bioethics Observatory Institute of life Sciences*. Retrieved from https://boiethics.georgetown.edu>is.

Gonzalez, F. (2010) 'Transhumanismo (humanity +): la ideología que nos viene', *Pax et Emerita*. 6 (6) pp. 205–228.

Gusha, I.S. (2020) 'Covid -19 and the politics of identity. Unpublished paper presented to the Zimbabwe Council of Churches E-leaning Platform'. 16 May.

Hakim, C. (1982) *Secondary analysis in social research: A guide to data sources and method examples*. London, UK: George Allen & Unwin.

Heward-Mills, D. (2000) *Catch the anointing*. Accra: Lighthouse Chapel International.

Hui, D.S., Azhar, E., Madani, T. A., Ntoumi, F., Kock, R., … Dar, O. (2020) 'The continuing 2019-nCoV epidemic threat of novel coronavirus to global health: The latest 2019 novel coronavirus outbreak in Wuhan, China', *International Journal of Infectious Diseases,* 91, p.264-266. doi:10.1016/j.ijid.2020.01.009. PMID 31953166.

Igwe, L. (2020) 'Covid-19 and end of faith healing?' *News Ghana*. Retrieved from https://newsghana.com.gh/covid-19-andend-of-faith-healing/.

Jakes, T. D. (2020) 'An update on the coronavirus', *TD Jakes Ministries*. Retrieved from https://www.tdjakes.org/coronavirus/.

Kale, R. (1995) 'Traditional healers in South Africa: A parallel health care system', *Biomedical Journal*, 310, p. 1182–1185.Retrieved from https://bmcpublichealth.biomedcentral.com/track/pdf/10.1186/s 12889-018-6277-9.

Kar, N. (2008) 'Resort to faith-healing practices in the pathway to care for mental illness: A study on psychiatric inpatients in Orissa', *Mental Health, Rel & Cult*, (11), p. 720–40.

Kiecolt, K.J. and Nathan, L. E. (1985) 'Secondary analysis of survey data', *University Paper Series on Quantitative Applications in the Social Sciences*, 53. Retrieved from https://doi.org/10.4135/9781412985796.

Kingleo, D. E. (2020) 'Major Prophet challenge critics to bring coronavirus patients for Healing', *YouTube channel Possibility TV*. Retrieved from https://iharare.com>local.

Kritek, P. B. (1997) *Reflections on healing: A central nursing construct.* New York, NY: NLN Press.

Levin, J. (2008) 'Scientists and healers: Towards collaborative research partnerships', *Explore*, 4(5), 302-310.
(2009) 'How faith heals: A theoretical model', *Explore*, (NY), (5), 77–96.

Luther, M. (1999) 'Whether one may flee from a deadly plague. In Luther's works'. In, J. van Pelikan, H. C. Oswald and T. Helmut (eds.) *Devotional Writings II*, 43, Philadelphia: Fortress Press. Retrieved from https://www.christianitytoday.com>.

Maponga, J. (2020) 'Life happens: How the virus has affected', *SAfm*. Retrieved from https://iono.fm>.

Masiiwa, G., Moyo, F. and Mujuru, L. (2018) 'Zimbabwe's ban of faith healing broadcasts gets mixed reviews'. Retrieved from https://globalpressjournal.com/africa/zimbabwe/zimbabwes-ban-faith-healing-broadcasts-gets-mixed-reviews/.

Masvotore, P. and Tsara, L. (2019) 'South Africa's road to democracy could have suffered a still birth had it not been for the unseen role played by women: Interfacing with the undercover operations of women', *Alternation Interdisciplinary Journal.* doi: 1029086/2519-5476/2019/sp26a5.

Meyer, B. (2006) *Religious sensations: Why media, aesthetics and power matter in the study of contemporary religion*, Amsterdam: Vrije Universiteit.

Morgan, D. (1998) *Visual piety: A history and theory of popular religious images*, Berkeley/Los Angeles/London: University of California Press.

Murphy, N. (1985) 'A Niebuhrian typology for the relation of theology to science', *Pacific Theological Review*. 18, pp. 16–23.

Peprah, P., Gyasi R. M., Adjei, P., Osei-Wusu., Agyemang-Duah, W., Emmanuel Mawuli Abalo, E. M. and Kotei, J. N. A. (2018) 'Religion and health: Exploration of attitudes and health perceptions of faith healing users in urban Ghana. *BMC Public Health*, 18, p.1358 Retrieved from https://doi.org/10.1186/s12889-018-6277-9.

Puckree, T., Mkhize, M., Mgobhozi, Z. and Lin, J.(2002) 'African traditional healers: What health care professionals need to know', *Intern J Rehab Res*, (25), 247–251.

Rosenberg, D. (2020) 'The air movement group'. Retrieved from https://www.rosenberg-gmbh.com/en/infocenter/news/349-covid19-update-06112020.

Russel, R. J. (2002) 'Dialogue, Science and Religion'. In, Giuseppe Tanzella-Nitti & Alessandro Strumia (eds.). *INTERS—Interdisciplinary Encyclopaedia of Religion and Science*. Berkeley: The Center for Theology and the Natural Sciences. Retrieved from http://inters.org/dialogue-science-theology.

Salinas, D. (2018) 'Transhumanism: the big fraud-towards digital slavery', *Int Phys Med Rehab J*. Volume 3 (5), 381–392. DOI: 10.15406/ipmrj.2018.03.00131.

Sanda, D. C., Smarandoiu, L. A. and Munteanu, C. (2017) 'The dialogue between science and religion: A taxonomic contribution', *Religions* (8) 35. Retrieved from https://www.mdpi.com/journal/religion.

Sanneh, L. O. (1983) *West African Christianity: The religious impact*. Maryknoll, NY: Orbis Books.

Smith, A.K., Ayanian, J. Z., Covinsky, K. E., Landon, B.E., McCarthy, E. P., Wee, C.C.,& Steinman, M. A. (2011) 'Conducting high-value secondary data set analysis: An introductory guide and resources', *Journal of General Internal Medicine*,28(8), 920 - 929. doi: https://doi.org/10.1007/s11606-010-1621-5.

Stone, L. *(2020) Practical theology says care, sacrifice and community as vital as ever*. Retrieved from https://www.researchgate.net.

Stenmark, M. (2010) 'Ways of relating science and religion'. In, Peter Harrison (Ed.). *The Cambridge companion to science and religion*. Cambridge: Cambridge University Press, 278–95.

Tapfumaneyi, R. (2020) 'Church groups urge alcohol-based sanitizers amid coronavirus Threat', *Herald*. Retrieved from https://www.herald.co.zw.

Taylor-Coleman, J. (2020) 'How the new coronavirus will finally get a proper name', *BBC News*. Retrieved from bbc.com/news/world-asia-china-51371770.

Tazira, Y. (2020) 'COVID-19: Churches comply with government directive', *Herald*. Retrieved from https://www.herald.co.zw.

Wadman, M. (2020) 'Abortion opponents protest COVID-19 vaccines' use of foetal cells', *Biology Health Coronavirus*. Doi:10.1126/science.abd1905.

WHO. (2019) 'Naming the coronavirus disease (COVID-19) and the virus that causes it', *World Health Organisation*. Retrieved from https://www.who.int/emergencies/diseases/novel-coronavirus-2019/technical-guidance/naming-the-coronavirus-disease-(covid-2019)-and-the-virus-that-causes-it.
(2020) 'COVID-19 advice for public', *World Health Organisation*. Retrieved from https://www.who.int/emergencies/diseases/novel-coronavirus-2019/advice-for-public.

Wilson, J. (2020) 'The right-wing Christian preachers in deep denial over Covid-19's danger', *The Guardian*. Retrieved from https://www.theguardian.com/us-news/2020/apr/04/america-rightwing-christian-preachers-virus-hoax.

Zimmerman, R. K. (2004) 'Ethical analyses of vaccines grown in human cell strains derived from abortion: arguments and Internet search', *Vaccine*. Oct 22 Volume 22, 31-32.

Chapter Eleven

Exploring African Women and Girls' Experiences During the Coronavirus Pandemic: A Gendered Framework Perspective

Hatikanganwi Mapudzi, Collin Kamalizeni, Ntandokazulu Siwela & Memory Muteeri

Introduction

As the world tries to make sense of the unprecedented impact of the coronavirus disease (Covid-19) on humanity, it is a fact that the impact of the pandemic is not gender neutral- there is a discrete impact on women and girls, one which is already aggravating the pre-existing gender inequalities among African societies. Women and young girls are carrying an excessively higher socio-economic burden than their male counterparts. Among other things, the pandemic has seen a lot of women losing their economic grip, yet their role in food security cannot be underestimated. It is a fact that most women are among the frontline workers in the fight against the pandemic and many of them have lost their lives while on duty, yet they have also assumed the role of facilitating online learning to their children as most schools have migrated to this practice in a way to save the academic calendar. There are reports of increased domestic and sexual violence due to the lockdown restrictions imposed by many governments, while young girls are at high risk of teen pregnancies and sexual abuse due to school closures. In view of these and other factors, this chapter highlights the trials and tribulations being experienced by African women and girls, indicating how their livelihoods are being jeopardised during the Covid-19 pandemic. In discussing these, we tackle women and girls' experiences from these main perspectives: socio-economic, health and education. Essentially, we deliberate on the role of women in the fight against the spread of the virus, arguing for the need for a gender lens to ensure that their rights and dignity are also protected. In an effort to contribute to the Covid-19 response and recovery, we argue for a gendered framework in this regard, one which addresses the differentiated effects of the pandemic on African women and girls.

Women as frontline workers in the fight against the Covid-19 pandemic

Another chief area of concern is the medical frontline, where women make up an estimated 70% of the world's global health and social sector workforce (Dhatt 2020). It is also estimated that 70% of African nurses are women who require support, protection and empowerment (Folorunsho 2020). While many of them have lost their lives while on duty, others are risking their families' safety as their jobs entail being in contact with high-risk environments and sometimes working without the necessary personal protective equipment (PPE). In the Eastern Cape Province of South Africa, a female doctor from Mdantsane infected her whole family with the virus, allegedly other two nurses from the same clinic had tested positive (Dube 2020). Another female doctor who worked at the Victoria Hospital in Alice town succumbed to the virus while responding to the call of duty. Being among the frontline workers, most of them are dealing with a "silent battle for mental well-being", as they are getting overwhelmed with coping with the pressure of their job, as well as the anxiety of possibly getting infected by the virus and in turn infect their own families (eNCA 2020). Not only that, they are also dealing with a unique kind of stigma from the communities, "When they see you in a uniform, people will say you are working with a COVID patient, don't come near. This really frustrates us because we are here to help them…We don't just put this uniform on to come to work and play. We are here for the public. When they see us, they should not be afraid of us," these were the sentiments of one nursing manager from the Limpopo Province of South Africa (eNCA, 2020). There are some unconfirmed reports of some of the frontline workers being evicted by their landlords for the fear of getting infected by these essential services providers. In one of his 'So what now?' episodes on eNCA, Gareth Cliff tackled the topic of whether it is safe to sleep with a frontline worker in the Covid-19 era. These are some of the challenges that impede women's efforts to save the citizens of their countries in the fight against the invisible enemy called Covid-19.

Women as economic providers

According to Forbes Africa (2020) the economic value of women is multifaceted but is currently placed under siege due to the deepening COVID-19 pandemic with work-life being seriously compromised. Most women have always been operating in dual roles, in both domestic and professional settings. As economic providers for their households, many women found themselves not being able to fend for their families after the lockdown restrictions came into effect, affecting most of them working in the informal sector. Phumzile Mlambo-Ngcuka reports that the outbreak seems to have hit hard those organisations with a high rate of women employees, for instance, the hospitality industry (UN Women and the African Union 2020). Losing their sources of income put a strain on them as most of them could not afford to keep their households afloat.

Despite efforts by some governments like South Africa and Namibia to provide social grants and relief funds, most women still struggled to provide for their households. With the easing down of the conditions of the lockdown, women became more exposed to the virus now more than ever, as they go about their daily routine offending for their households. In the process, they are also exposing their families to the virus as they get into contact with many people in the streets. Most of those who worked in the hospitality industry had to lose their jobs in the face of Covid-19, while a few continue to provide essential services in various sectors of the economy. As the rate of unemployment is high in the region, most young men are wholly dependent on their partners and spouses. This inverted status quo of the known socio-cultural and traditional hierarchy, in the eyes of men, seems to have been usurped with women becoming the household protagonists as they threaten the family decision making framework. Some men become infuriated as the traditional ways of masculinity are withdrawn, thereby turning to domestic violence to recover their lost dignity in power and authority (Ballard 1998; Abrahams, Jewkes, Martin, Mathews et al. 2009). These incidents are becoming more prevalent during the Covid-19 lockdown restrictions and are likely to increase, given the repetitive isolation and confinements.

Poor access to basic hygienic amenities, antenatal care and reproductive health service

Media reports have indicated limited access to on-site sanitation for girls and women with confirmed or suspected Covid -19 in quarantine centres, as well as in refugee centres. Lack of piped water supply, on-site sanitation, hand washing facilities and soap has made the lives of women and girls miserable. In Bangladesh, women in refugee camps highlighted the risks of having limited access to these amenities and health services, pointing that "We are afraid because we have nothing...As we live in a very congested area, if there is limited access to medical treatment and the virus comes here, we will all die. So, we need sufficient hygiene materials like soaps and masks, along with doctors and nurses" (UN Women 2020).

According to the World Health Organisation (WHO), water, sanitation and hygiene are key elements in fighting against the spread of this coronavirus (Hara, Ncube & Sibanda 2020). In South Africa, ever since the beginning of the national lockdown to curb the spread of the Covid-19 virus came into effect, reports indicate that the lockdown may have worsened the already existing inequalities in water and sanitation services in townships, informal settlements and among the homeless. In one instance in Cape Town, a homeless community was moved to a temporary tented shelter where the lack of water and sanitation posed as a major challenge. In an interview, a Dunoon resident in Cape Town posited, "While we are grateful for the tents, we still do not have access to water for hygienic purposes" (Hara *et al.* 2020)

The current coronavirus pandemic has disrupted access to life saving reproductive and sexual health services for women worldwide. The COVID-19 has worsened the already poor access to quality maternal health services in most parts of the African continent. According to Abajobir (2020:11), "The ongoing transmission mitigation strategies such as lockdown and curfews may intensify the dire consequences brought on by the lack of access to quality health services and by pre-existing maternal health problems." The already struggling health systems, particularly in Africa have proved not to have adequate capacity and space to attend to the routine health care needs of women.

The lives of expectant mothers have been put at high risk too, as most of them are being subjected to harsh conditions. For instance, the Namibian Broadcasting Corporation (NBC) reported that several pregnant women at public hospitals and clinics in Windhoek are waiting in long queues from as early as 02h00 for antenatal care. Several times they are returned home without being assisted because the health officials only attend to ten mothers per day, no matter how long one has been waiting in the queue (NBC 2020). In a related story, in South Africa, a video went viral on social media, whereby expectant mothers were found lying on the floor in the corridors of Dora Nginza Hospital in Port Elizabeth, apparently due to shortage of beds because the available space was reserved for Covid-19 patients (IOL 2020). It is also a fact that expectant mothers are among the vulnerable people to the pandemic, hence, most of them are afraid to go to healthcare centres for fear of getting contaminated in the process. Others are missing out on routine and emergency care due to strained health services and lockdown restrictions. Dlamini (2020) reported that Zimbabwean women in most rural areas cannot travel to clinics which are usually many kilometres away from their places of residence, for reproductive and antenatal health services, due to the in-country travel restrictions. Another challenge is that of the public transport system which has been banned from moving from one region to the other. In Zimbabwe and Namibia, expectant mothers have been struggling to get clothing for delivery preparation since clothing shops were closed. As a result, the Namibian government considered this as an essential service that should be provided, and this saw clothing shops like Ackermans and Pep operating during the lockdown periods. Similarly, Mitch (2020) profiled a story on how the Covid-19 pandemic has affected maternal health in the Democratic Republic of Congo (DRC). She highlighted how expectant mothers are hesitating to seek medical attention because of anxiety and the high risk of exposure to Covid-19 in the healthcare centres. Confirming the high risk of exposure to Covid-19 by expectant mothers, a gynaecologist Dr. Mukendi Richard pointed that "… pregnant women may sometimes be more exposed to viral respiratory infections insofar as there is a physiological decrease in natural immunity during pregnancy to enable the pregnant women to support the father's foreign cells present in the foetus…In fact, we are seeing a significant drop in the number of pregnant women attending public hospitals because of the fear of easily contracting the virus. But also because of the fear of being held in isolation in case of suspicious symptoms or a positive COVID-19 result" (Mitch 2020). In light of these and other realities, Henrientta Fore, the UNICEF Executive Director pointed that, "it is hard to imagine how much the coronavirus pandemic has recast motherhood." (Vishwanathan 2020). It is common that during crises, resources are funnelled away from sexual and reproductive health services towards targets perceived to be more important. The UNFPA vowed to fight this tendency, noting that "safe pregnancies and childbirth depend on functioning and accessible health systems" (Beech 2020). This implies that if the health facilities are inaccessible, the lives of mothers and the unborn babies are at risk and may be lost in the process.

In settings where the poorest women and girls use disposable materials during menstruation, financial stress has led families to prioritise other needs such as food or essential utility bills over purchasing menstrual hygiene materials (Gupta 2020). The dignity of women and girls in the informal communities, as well as the refugee centres, has been undermined. This has seen many individuals and nongovernmental organisations mobilising resources to at least provide the basic feminine sanitary ware to women and young girls who are sometimes forced to abscond school due to lack of these important products. The homeless women and girls are housed in refugee camps and other shelters, where they are exposed to ill regard for their rights to privacy, as both men and women share the same places where social distancing is difficult to practice as well. In these shelters, access to general sanitation is an issue such that most of the rely on relief packages from NGOs and governments, but these charitable organisations mainly focus on food relief, but not products like sanitary pads, bath towels, roll on and soap to help women maintain a healthy hygienic lifestyle under their living conditions.

Related to the above is the lack of access to contraceptives during this period. Because of the Covid-19 pandemic, health facilities are becoming overrun by patients with the virus, resulting in fewer resources or time available for women and girls seeking out medical attention for their sexual or reproductive health. The prioritisation and reallocation of resources towards the pandemic has seen many women and young girls being unable to access contraception, thereby experiencing unintended pregnancies (United Nations Population Fund (UNFPA) report. Dr Natalia Kanem, the UNFPA Executive Director, reiterated that "The pandemic is deepening inequalities and million more women and girls now risk losing the ability to plan their families and protect their bodies and health" (cited by Godin 2020). Newly released data shows that millions of women could lose access to contraception, resulting in unplanned pregnancies if the pandemic continues for a long period of time (UNFPA 2020). A disruption in supply chains due to lockdown regulations has resulted in shortages of contraceptives, particularly in Africa where people have low income. Static and mobile clinics, as well as community-based care outlets have been closed because of the outbreak. According to the International Planned Parenthood Federation (IPPF 2020), "The Africa region has seen the largest number of mobile clinics closed, with 447 shut." The longer these mobile clinics stay closed, the greater the cost to the lives of women and girls who will experience the greatest care burden. Santos (2020) reported that the Philippines are experiencing baby boom after lockdown hits family planning, as the women are confined to their homes and finding it difficult to access family planning services.

In Namibia, the lack of access to contraception has become a threat to women's life. Ipinge the Secretary General of the People's Democratic Movement (PDM) of Namibia argues, "The absence of contraceptives can lead to an increase in baby dumbing and women turning to unsafe abortions." Unsafe abortions can lead to the death of the mother. With many governments restricting people's movements to stem the spread of the virus, and providers forced to suspend some sexual and reproductive health services that are not classified as essential, such as abortion care, antenatal and contraception services, women are denied this time-sensitive and potentially lifesaving service. Indeed, the Covid-19 pandemic has worsened the gender-based and other health disparities.

Increased responsibilities

The Covid-19 containment measures have resulted in the closure of many services including schools, basic health care, and day care centres. This has shifted responsibility for their provision to households. While this could offer an opportunity for gender roles to shift within the home, emerging evidence suggests that care roles continue to be assumed disproportionately by women during this pandemic. Nesbittt-Ahmed and Subrahmanian (2020) assert that even before the pandemic, globally, women and girls carry out on average three times the amount of unpaid care and domestic work of men and boys. With the emergence of the Covid-19 pandemic, these responsibilities have increased, with new health and hygiene requirements such as hand washing and taking care of sick family members. Moreover, self-quarantine and curfew measures have made these tasks more challenging, as many women have to care for children, the elderly and those who suffer from disease or other disabilities. This has placed additional stress on women. As argued by Garijo (2020) "The disproportionate impact of unpaid caregiving on women and girls is one of the key facets of gender inequality." More often than not, women and girls are juggling among responsibilities: being the teachers of their children, caregivers for the sick and elderly and providing for their household. In the process of taking care of their family members infected by the virus, many women are also putting their own lives at risk. As caregivers, some women are dying while nursing their Covid-19 positive relatives. In the Eastern Cape Province of South Africa, a woman contracted the virus while nursing her mother in law (eNCA 2020), resulting in both of them losing their lives. What is making most women vulnerable is that they do not have access to the personal protective equipment (PPE), as well as lack of awareness on how to care of their infected relatives.

In an attempt to prevent the spread of coronavirus, schools and universities have been closed all over. Home schooling, the new parental chore brought about by coronavirus lockdown regulations, is being handled disproportionately and has worsened the burden of women and the girl child. This has impacted negatively on women who have to spend more time providing care and educational support to children. Evidence has shown that more women had to sacrifice their jobs so that they assume the role of facilitating teaching and learning at home, while also taking care of their little ones whose day care centres' doors have shut. Surrounded by a lot of tasks to do, women have to make sure that the children are not distracted and remain focused. Sadly, as many women assume the role of teacher at home, most of them lack the necessary education or support to ensure the effectiveness of online learning. This has a negative effect on the children's own performance as they struggle to negotiate meaning with parents who have not received the necessary training or support. Online learning means more reliance on technology to keep children learning, but not all women have the necessary knowledge and skills to take the children through online classes. Not only that, many parents had to squeeze their already pressed budgets to provide the necessary tools for online learning, the laptops, tablets, as well as the internet connection. The notion of e-learning has presented women with the challenge of up skilling to learn to become teachers, while at the same time they have to acquaint themselves with the technological applications to help facilitate the e-learning.

While some have successfully gotten around their new roles as e-facilitators, some mothers have had to surrender and simply resort to traditional means of teaching their children in a bid to stay abreast of the syllabus. Some have totally surrendered to the idea of schooling their kids at all this year, meaning that their children are already lagging in this regard. The inability to send their children to school has become another source of anguish.

Increased violence against women and girls

Presently, the economic value of women is gradually eroding due to the emergent new cases of gender-based violence, femicide, sexual violence and harassment and other forms of gender discrimination (Reid & Walker 2005; Kiss et al. 2012; Houtino & Lindgarge 2020). GBV, an increasingly human rights violation, has become a great public concern which is far from ameliorating and is likely to compromise efforts to combat the pandemic. In one of his Covid-19 addresses, the South African President Cyril Ramaphosa regretted the rise of femicide, confessing how the nation is dealing with a double pandemic, the Covid-19 virus, as well as gender-based violence (eNCA 2020, Smith 2020). As men joined their women counterparts at home, as a result of the lockdown regulations, stress levels escalated perhaps due to the condition of being confined in the homes and most of them not being able to fend for their families, and so did the violence. South African media reports indicated that gender-based violence has raised by 500% in the midst of Covid (IOL 2020). One could argue that the rising cases could be escalated by the strain caused by the ban on selling of cigarettes and alcohol which are often used as escape routes to dealing with stress levels.

The girl child has not been spared by gender-based violence. The confinement as a result of the lockdown, has brought about a total unfamiliar environment particularly for the girl child (UN Women East and Southern Africa 2020). The temporary closure of schools has thus put the adolescent girls at risk. Anne Rob (2020) is a Tanzanian journalist who noted that the school closures due to the Covid-19 exposed young girls to the harmful practice of female genital mutilation (FGM). She indicated that school holidays in Tanzania offer parents an opportunity to subject their daughters to FGM. Quoting one of the girls, the young girl indicated that: "I never wanted to go because I knew I risked being cut. For several times my parents wanted me to undergo the FGM cut…When I arrived home,

I was received well and took time studying at home but after a week, I started seeing some changes with lots of visit, an FGM cutter at my home and a week after I was cut early in the morning". This scenario indicates how schools are a safe haven for many of the young Tanzanian girls who underwent the cutting during the Covid-19 break from school. The practice in Tanzania is that after being circumcised, the young girls are forced to drop out of school in order to be married off, apparently the parents tend to secure a higher dowry when their daughter gets circumcised. The UNFPA and United Nations Children Fund (UNICEF) indicated that due to the Covid-19 pandemic, it is going to be impossible to achieve the Sustainable Development Goals of eliminating female genital mutilation by 2030 (Rob 2020).

The World Bank (2020) highlighted that about 1.6 billion children got deprived of their right to education by the Covid-19. There is thus a possibility that millions of these children, particularly girls from marginalised communities, might not be able to return to school due to forced marriages, unwanted pregnancies and other forms of abuse (Sigsworth 2009). Tshuma (2020) noted how Zimbabwean girls have become vulnerable to child marriages due to school closures caused by the Covid-19 pandemic. Quoting the Girl child advocate and Parliamentary Portfolio Chairperson on Education, Ms Priscilla Misihairambwi Mushonga, she indicated that child marriages and teenage pregnancies in Zimbabwe were being worsened by the Covid-19 pandemic: "It is also problematic that our systems are not very flexible for our young girls to access contraceptives. So more free time without school commitments may mean more time to engage in risky behaviours, so by all means, unwanted pregnancies will be on the rise. I am however particularly worried about the child brides because they are being robbed of their future because of this Covid-19. Teachers and the rest if the school community are nowhere near at such a time to notice if a member of the class is missing so that they investigate, so many child marriages will happen successfully and quietly," (Misihairambwi, cited by Tshuma 2020). The sentiments clearly indicate that violence leads to high risk of sexual behaviour which may lead to unintended pregnancies and sexually transmitted diseases. These behaviours may create some form of tendencies to continually indulge in such practices. The issues highlighted here indicate how the pandemic will cause gender inequality in education, as many girls are dropping out of school due to the reasons outlined earlier.

In the Kingdom of Eswatini, GBV cases are also on the rise during the Covid-19 pandemic. Gass, Stein, Williams and Seedat (2010) argue that economic dependence among women is cause for GBV. Women tend to stick to abusive spouses due to their economic dependence. Heise, Ellsberg and Gottmoeller (2002) accentuate that there is a strong relationship between GBV and poverty, although poverty may not be the single trigger. With the Covid-19, the loss of jobs and economic strength by women and in some cases, their spouses, mean a reduction in the living standards, thereby creating some level of poverty and infidelity. Sokanyile (2020) profiled the following incident involving a woman being abused by her partner, "People from the outside looking in think it is easy to just pack up and leave an abusive partner. It is not...Until you are in a situation like that you always tell yourself that if something like that would happen, you would leave. But at that very moment leaving becomes the furthest thing from your mind". This is just one example of GBV occurrences which often remain unreported but are kept behind scenes. Such incidences are often repetitive and therefore continuous.

The few incidences cited above are fundamental in the design of strategies that are useful towards creating preventative measures for women but also ensuring that such a breeding ground is not allowed to take precedence. As evidenced in the preceding discussion, the ongoing Covid-19 pandemic is affecting men and women differently, yet most governments have failed to take these differences on board when responding to the situation. Analysing how the pandemic affects gender not only helps to improve understanding of the epidemiology, but it also helps in the prevention and control efforts. In other words, integrating a gendered response is not only an issue of gender equality, but also critical in ensuring effective and sustainable interventions. In view of this, in the sections that follow, we argue for an inclusive gender lens in the fight against the invisible enemy called Covid-19.

Arguing for a Gender Lens to protect and empower women during the COVID-19 pandemic

While the conversation on life after the lockdown due to Covid-19 continues, there is the growing need to ensure that girls and women are protected as the former are vulnerable to the current hostile domestic environment that treats 'out-of-school' young girls as family commodities (UN Women East and Southern Africa 2020; Flore 2020). While this concept has been in existence time unmemorable, there is the likelihood that this will exacerbate given the harsh effects of the pandemic. Figure 1 illustrates the life trajectory of a woman in two case, represented as Case A, normal and Case B, resulting from the lockdown restrictions.

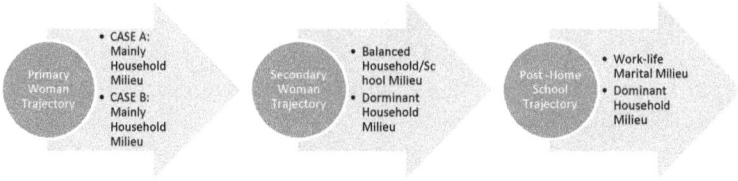

Primary Woman Trajectory
- CASE A: Mainly Household Milieu
- CASE B: Mainly Household Milieu

Secondary Woman Trajectory
- Balanced Household/School Milieu
- Dorminant Household Milieu

Post-Home School Trajectory
- Work-life Marital Milieu
- Dominant Household Milieu

Figure 1: A Woman's Changed Life Trajectory
Source: Authors' own

Figure 1 depicts a women's trajectory presented in three phases: primary, secondary and post-home school trajectory. Two cases, Case A for a normal women life cycle is offered as uninterrupted, while Case B portrays that which is disturbed due to the pandemic, characterising social delays and inadvertently proffering a new order of life susceptible to the societal pangs of the Covid-19 pandemic. These forces emerge as strange dynamic effects of life emerging within the Covid-19 lockdown and confinement. In the process, the girl child inexplicably falls prey to unscrupulous practices that have overtaken the missed school opportunities as a result of the lockdown, further exposing them ordinarily to high level of gender-based violence. This therefore calls for carefully developed programmes that would break the new trajectory.

One major aspect of empowering women to combat the Covid-19 pandemic points to the role of technology, an area in which most women appear to be generally deprived, as depicted in Table 1.

Table 1 illustrates that African women have an inverse relationship to men when it comes to accessing the internet, leaving the former group vulnerable to the effects of Covid-19, as its mitigation measures are widely published through various technologies. The figures demonstrate women gross deprivation of effective strategies towards protection and prevention measures. While total accessibility appears not far away from masculinity, they still lag behind, thereby disadvantaging them. With the low numbers of women in formal employment, the cost of accessing internet may not be within their realm, posing further damages to their welfare (UN Women and the African Union 2020). These figures suggest the limited use of technological innovations by most women, with little options to learn in the Covid-19 era.

Table 1: African Women's access to Technology

African Women Exposure to Technology	% Rate	+/- to men
Accessing the internet	27	-
Affordability	15	-
Total accessibility	**42**	-

Source: UN Women and the African Union, 2020

Addressing the issue of GBV during the Covid-19 pandemic

The cultural-traditional beliefs recognise that absolute power rests with masculinity. This denies shared control of household resources from a gender perspective, resulting in limited access to domestic income, for example, making it difficult for women to possess savings. The UN Women and the African Union (2020) urge governments and other stakeholders to contemplate providing socio-economic support for women in key issues requiring a gendered response to Covid-19. As the same report observes, women are often excluded from leadership positions and may not participate in the decision-making process, as experienced during the Ebola calamity. A further proposal advanced towards addressing GBV during theCovid-19 pandemic seeks to institute a comprehensive approach such as public-private-partnerships (PPP's) that brings all relevant players in the socio-economic contract to the dialogue table, placing gender equality in the forefront (UN Women and the African Union 2020). In this report, AUC Chairperson, Moussa Faki, maintains that the pandemic aggravates disparities and prejudices directed towards the vulnerable population, further heightening the presence of GBV in poor societies. The pandemic has drawn several factors such as social, economic, psychological, cultural and spiritual-religious influences on GBV. The effects of confinement and social distancing are being felt the world-over, as most people are no longer actively engaged in productive employment, thus increasing the incidents of GBV. While most women and girls remain in lockdown, either for lack of work or closed schools, these are brought into proximity to abuse, further embellishing cases of GBV.

In providing a supportive environment for women, a special attention should be made where specialised hotlines are made available to send immediate reports for any suspicious threats to their welfare (Bhana & Pattman 2011). While points receiving GBV are usually confined to law enforcing authorities, these could be extended to include other social welfare departments such as community development offices, schools, hospitals and other offices of public concern. A major strategy to combating the pandemic relates to confinement and social distancing which, if implemented carefully, results in a transformed household likely to become a haven of peace. Unfortunately, the opposite often reins, where the risk of GBV is highly a human rights issue. The UN Women (2020) warns against making the household a breeding milieu for GBV, but instead one that promotes respect and dignity for women, as impartiality and harmony in gender becomes fundamental in the fight against the effects of the pandemic. If not comprehensively determined, the impact of the pandemic is likely to reach similar trends as that experienced during the Ebola, playing havoc particularly on women. The threats of this pandemic as a result of confinement and social distancing have already been adversely felt in Kenya, Rwanda, Tanzania, Uganda, South Africa and other countries in East and Southern Africa where increased cases of gender-based violence have been reported (Human Rights Watch 2020).

In dealing with the strategies, it is important to secure both short and long-term solutions which may not necessarily be a panacea but will serve as collaborative arrangements towards harmonious feminine-masculine equality for the present and generations to come. Human Rights Watch (2020) proposes interventions that point towards prevention and responses against violence in the East and Southern African Region, as constructed upon rapid mapping processes involving the communities themselves to present solutions through a series of conversations. The diverse representation seeks to ensure a wide representation of different stakeholders likely to close gaps emerging from the effects of pandemic.

The search for effective mitigation strategies to combat the challenges being faced by the African women and girls during the

Covid-19 pandemic could meaningfully be implemented by making a thorough analysis of the trends in the region and the surrounding factors that influencing the challenges. This implies addressing the major ills from a multifaceted approach focusing on the relationships that exist from the perspectives in health, socio-economic, legal, psychological and spiritual factors that affect women and girls. According to Human Rights Watch (2020), at the epicentre of authority plans to respond to the pandemic includes their involvement in decision making processes. Addressing the COVID effects of the pandemic would require an all-inclusive focus that takes into account the cultural-historical and intergenerational dimensions that colour society. For instance, Newham and du Plessis (2020) accentuate the involvement of persons experiencing GBV, either as victims or perpetrators, as the basis towards understanding the root cause of GBV and its significance in guiding gender professionals to a well-structured supportive environment. By establishing the needs and wants of both stakeholders helps to develop a solid framework of ideas from which future cases are constructed. A major facet in establishing the GBV problems may be examined by exploring its existence in different locations.

While governments are battling to provide survival kits for Covid-19, disadvantaged women may benefit from emergency life-saving response services. For instance, many individuals and NGOs have been handing out food parcels as relief to hunger, since many households which live on hand to mouth could not afford to go out looking for food. In the same way, the UN Women (2020) argues that the assessments towards GBV cases should not only confine to inclusive policy frameworks that seek to repair and eliminate identified cases, but should also address social norms and cultural beliefs that promote the behavioural patterns that lead to GBV. This is made possible if proper plans are put in place right from inception, which use a participatory approach where all stakeholders are included and participate in different influential roles.

Conclusion

This chapter outlined the threat of a new economic paradigm confronting the society today, presenting immense social and economic problems on women and girls. The economic value of women was put on the spotlight, revealing their deteriorating condition in the face of the Covid-19 pandemic. It was indicated how the pandemic has created robust socio-economic challenges that require addressing. in doing this, we argued for a gender lens in trying to combat the effects of the pandemic. While women empowerment was conceived to be an attractive strategy, the technological options were considered a necessary tool worth exploring. This entails strengthening a gendered framework in which women are included in all programmatic development areas, including the decision-making process. We therefore recommend that since the pandemic has been universally experienced, robust efforts and resources should be invested into regional and national research to collectively establish relevant strategies for addressing the harm being caused by the pandemic. Furthermore, strategies should be explored that are empirically validated to be implemented as a matter of urgency. While these efforts are being attempted, we advocated for a Public-Private-Partnership (PPP) approach to be employed to lobby international/regional and inter-sectoral stakeholders to play a synergistic role against the pandemic. In conclusion, it should be noted that the pandemic is not gender neutral as such, as both men and women are affected, with women who nurture mankind being hardest hit. This therefore requires an all-inclusive approach with gender as a fundamental unifying element in addressing the pandemic in the short and long-term process.

References

Abajobir, A. (2020) *The Conversation: Africa can't let maternity care slide during the coronavirus pandemic.* African population and Health Research Center. Retrieved from https://theconversation.com/africa-cant-let-maternity-care-slide-during-the-coronavirus-pandemic-136424.

Abrahams, N., Jewkes, R., Martin, L.J., Mathews, S., Vetten, L. & Lombard, C. (2009) 'Mortality of women from intimate partner violence in South Africa: A national epidemiological study,' *Violence and Victims* 24(4): 546–556

Beech, P. (2020) *The Covid-19 pandemic could have huge knock-on effects on women's health, says the UN.* World Economic Forum . Retrieved from: https://ewn.co.za/2020/04/02/un-the-covid-19-pandemic-s-huge-impact-on-women-s-health.

Ballard, T.J., Saltzman, L.E., Gazmararian, J.A., Spitz, A.M. Lazorick, S., and Marks, J.S. (1998). Violence during pregnancy:

Measurement issues. *American Journal of Public Health* 88(2): 274-276.

Bhana, B. & Pattman, R. (2011) 'Girls want money, boys want virgins: The materiality of love amongst South African township youth in the context of HIV and AIDS,' *Culture, Health and Sexuality: An International Journal for Research, Intervention and Care* 13(18): 961–997

CEDAW/C/GC/35 paras 12 and 29(c)(i) *Committee on the Elimination of Discrimination against Women (2017)* General recommendation No. 35 on gender-based violence against women, updating general recommendation No. 19

Daily Nation (2020) Sexual *violence cases rise amid virus curfew.* Retrieved from https://www.nation.co.ke/news/Sexualviolence-cases-rise-amid-virus-curfew/1056-5522346-vd87a4z/index.html.

Dhatt, R. (2020) *Opinion: Global health security depends on women. Global Health News.* Retrieved from https://www.devex.com/news/opinion-global-health-security-depends-on-women-96861.

Dlamini, N. (2020) Zimbabwe: Coronavirus - Lockdown Puts Pregnant Zim Women at Risk. Retrieved from https://allafrica.com/stories/202004270656.html.

Dube. C. (2020) *Mdantsane doctor infects her whole family with COVID-* Retrieved from https://savannanews.com/mdantsane-doctor-infects-her-whole-family-with-covid-19/.

Ellsberg, M.C., Pena, R., Herrera, A., Liljestand, J. and Winkvist, A. (1999) Candies in hell: Women's experience of violence in Nicaragua. *Social Science and Medicine.*51(11):1595-1610. doi:10.1016/s0277-9536(00)00056-3.

eNCA (2020) *COVID-19 frontline workers fighting silent battle for mental well-being.* Retrieved from https://www.enca.com/news/covid-19-frontline-workers-fighting-silent-battle-mental-well-being.

Folorunsho, F. (2020) *Covid-19: 70% Frontline nurses in Africa are women.* United Nations. Retrieved from https://healthwise.punchng.com/covid-19-70-frontline-nurses-in-africa-are-women-un/.

Forbes Africa (2020) Op-Ed: *Why African women in agriculture face the greatest double burden of covidcovid-19 and food insecurity.* Retrieved from https://www.forbesafrica.com/agriculture/2020/06/05/op-ed-why-african-women-in-agriculture-face-the-greatest-double-burden-of-covid-19-and-food-insecurity/.

Fore, H. (2020) Pregnant mothers and babies born during COVID -19 pandemic threatened by strained health systems and disruptions in services. *Unicef.*

Gareth Newham & Anton du Plessis (2020) 'ISS today: how might the covid-19 lockdown affect public safety in SA?' *Daily Maverick.* Retrieved from: https://www.dailymaverick.co.za/article/2020-04-06-howmight-the-Covid-19-lockdown-affect-public-safety-in-sa.

Garijo, B. (2020*) Covid-19 highlights how caregiving fuels gender inequality.* World Economic Forum. Retrieved from https://www.weforum.org/agenda/2020/04/covid-19-highlights-how-caregiving-fuels-gender-inequality/.

Gass, J.D., Stein, D.J., Williams, D.R. and Seedat, S. (2010) 'Intimate partner violence, health behaviours, and chronic physical illness among South African women,' *South African Medical Journal* 100(9): 582–585.

Godin, M. (2020) *Pandemic causing shortage of contraceptives and will impact women's reproductive health.* United Nations Population Fund (UNFPA) report. Retrieved from https://time.com/5828383/covid-19-threatens-womens-sexual-reproductive-health/.

Gupta, P. (2020) *Pandemic disrupts women's access reproductive services.* United Nations. Retrieved from https://www.aljazeera.com/news/2020/04/un-pandemic-disrupts-womens-access-reproductive-services-200407152321464.html.

Hara, M., Ncube, B and Sibanda, D. (2020) *Water and Sanitation in the face of Covid-19 in Cape Town's townships and informal settlements.* Retrieved from https://www.google.com/search?rlz=1C1FGGD_enZA500ZA544&q=Hara,+M.,+Ncube,+B+%26+Sibanda,+D.+(2020)+Water+and+Sanitation+in+the+face+of+Covid19+in+Cape+Town+townships+and+informal+settlements.+PLAAS&sa=X&ved=2ahUKEwi3oeCE8P7qAhWjuXEKHbgQBV8Q7xYoAHoECAsQJw&biw=1366&bih=625.

Heise, L., Ellsberg, M. and Gottmoeller, M. (2002) 'A global overview of gender-based violence,' *International Journal of Gynecology and Obstetrics* 78(1): S5–S14.

Houinato M. and Lindgarde P. (2020) *Covid-19 outbreak and lockdown: addressing impact on women, girls.*" Retrieved from http://www.newvision.co.ug/new_vision/news/1518223/Covi dCovid-19-outbreak-lockdown-addressing-impactwomen-girls.

Human Rights Watch. (2019) 'Don't punish me for who I am": systemic discrimination against transgender women in Lebanon'. Retrieved from https://www.hrw.org/report/2019/09/03/dont-punish-me-who-i-am/systemic-discrimination-against-transgender-women-lebanon#3a465f.

Human Rights Watch, Burma. (August 7, 2017) *National commission denies atrocities*, August 7, 2017.

Human Rights Watch, Burma (February 6, 2017) *Security forces raped Rohingya women, girls,*.

Human Rights Watch. (2017) *Sexual violence against Rohingya: Women and girls in Burma*. Retrieved from https://www.hrw.org/sites/default/files/report_pdf/burma111 7_web_1.pdf.

International Planned Parenthood Federation (IPPF). (2020). 'COVID-19 pandemic cuts access to sexual and reproductive healthcare for women around the world'. Available at: Retrieved from https://www.ippf.org/news/covid-19-pandemic-cuts-access-sexual-and-reproductive-healthcare-women-around-world.

Kiss, L., Schraiber, L., Heise, L., Zimmerman, C., Gouveia, N. and Watts, C. (2012) 'Gender-based violence and socioeconomic inequalities: Does living in more deprived neighbourhoods increase women's risk of intimate partner violence?' *Social Science and Medicine* 74(8): 1172–1179.

Mitch, G.N. (2020) *COVID-19 affecting maternal health in DRC*. Retrieved from: https://genderlinks.org.za// COVID-19-affecting- maternal- health- in- DRC.

Namibian Broadcasting Corporation News. (2020) Retrieved from https://www.facebook.com/www.nbcnews.na/posts/pregnant-women-waiting-in-long-queues-from-as-early-as-02h00-for-antenatal-careh/3215876671796840/.

Newham, G. and du Plessis, A. (2020) 'How might the Covid-19 lockdown affect public safety in SA?' Retrieved from https:// www. dailymaverick.co.za/article/2020-04-06-how- might- the - Covid-19 lockdown- affect- public- safety- in-SA/.

Nesbitt-Ahmed, Z. & Subrahmanian, R. (2020) 'Caring in the time of Covid-19: Gender, unpaid care work and social protection', UNICEF. Retrieved from https://blogs.unicef.org/evidence-for-action/caring-in-the-time-of-covid-19-gender-unpaid-care-work-and-social-protection/.

Reid, G. and Walker, L. (eds.) (2005) *Men behaving differently.* Cape Town: Juta.

Santos, A.P. (2020) 'Philippines faces baby boom after lockdown hits family planning'. Retrieved from https://www.aljazeera.com/news/2020/07/philippines-faces-baby-boom-lockdown-hits-family-planning-200714063035071.html. Retrieved 18 July 2020.

Sathiparsad, R. (2008) 'Developing alternative masculinities as a strategy to address gender-based violence,' *International Social Work,* 51(3): 348–359.

Sigsworth, R. (2009) 'Anyone can be a rapist… An overview of sexual violence in South Africa'. Braamfontein: Centre for the Study of Violence and Reconciliation.

Smith, E. (2020) 'South Africa's Ramaphosa blasts 'despicable' crime wave during coronavirus lockdown', *CNBC.* Retrieved from https://www.cnbc.com/2020/04/13/south-africas-ramaphosa-blasts-despicablecrime-wave-during-coronavirus-lockdown.html.

Sokanyile, A. (2020) 'Brendan Magaar', *African News Agency* (ANA).

Tshuma, A. (2020) 'Girls' vulnerable as covid-19 drives child marriages'. Retrieved from https://genderlinks.org.za/girls'-vulnerable- as- COVID-19- drives- child- marriages - .

UN Women East and Southern Africa Policy Brief (2020) 'COVID-19: Ending violence against women and girls. Key priorities and interventions for effective response and recovery'. Retrieved from https://cieg.unam.mx/covid-genero/pdf/recomendaciones/ending-violence-women.pdf.

United Nations (2020) 'Africa's responses to COVID-19 must be gender responsive'. Retrieved from https://www.un.org/africarenewal/news/coronavirus/africa%E2%80%99s-responses-covid-19-must-be-gender-responsive.

Vishwanathan, P. (2020) 'Coronavirus: Health system overload threatens pregnant women and newborns', *UN News.* Retrieved from https://news.un.org/en/story/2020/05/1063422.

WHO. (2020) 'Gender equity in the health workforce: Analysis of 104 countries'. Retrieved from https://apps.who.int/iris/bitstream/handle/10665/311314/WHO-HIS-HWF-Gender-WP1-2019.1-eng.pdf.

Chapter Twelve

Fourth Industrial Revolution and the Emergent Electronic Commerce – Convergence of ICT and Financial Sectors in Africa and Lessons from other Continents: The Question of Jurisdiction

Pilisano H. Masake & Lizazi E. Libebe

Introduction

Globally, and Africa is not an exception, there is an ongoing convergence of various sectors – this, include sectors such as, the financial sector, information and communication technology sector, and energy sector, to mention a few. Central to this chapter, is the convergence of the financial and telecommunication sectors. The scope, choice of the sectors under review, is premised on the practical design that informs consumers' reality on daily basis – that is, the ability and demand to electronically transact through technological devices like as cell phones, and internet. The pinnacle of the convergence of the sectors under review, is operability and the exigencies of the industrialisation and artificial intelligence – which affords, as it is discussed in detail below, the consumers and businesses the opportunity to trade conveniently.

Converging the telecommunication and financial sector entails merging or combining the two sectors with object for such converged sectors to provide services above and beyond what they were originally designed to offer (Haung, Guo, Xie & Wu 2012: 35). This convergence has been mainly driven by the forces of globalisation and technological advances that has in turn accelerated electronic commerce or ecommerce. Due to technological advances, legal systems are forced to meet the contemporary demands of an evolving society through legislation and judicial decisions. According to Ward, Sipior and Volonino (2016), in the field of technology, the laws and principles are often reactively developed, rendering these laws to lag the technological advances. The implication, among others, include that the traditional laws on issues related to jurisdiction are adopted and applied to arbitrate electronic commerce disputes that occasion in cyberspace. Scholars have identified various legal implications wrought by the convergence of the telecommunication and financial sectors ranging from "[l]icencing, interconnection, jurisdictional issues in cyber space (Ward, Sipior & Volonino 2016: 8) management and security issues" (Munyimvua 2013: 29; Masamila 2014: 58).

The 21st century Africa, has witnessed, progressive development in information and communication technology (ICT), ICT infrastructure and the inevitable inception of the 4th Industrial Revolution (4IR). These developments have significantly challenged and defied the orthodox approaches to commerce – consumers, have an option to transact and conduct business electronically or remotely. With the stir of the communicable diseases like the Ebola and Covid-19, and similar viruses to come in the future – with the gravamen engraved by the advocacy on the "new normal", social distancing theory and practice, ecommerce have been ordained as one of the practical solutions to curbing the spread of the virus. These developments in ICT are indeed necessary and good milestones achieved thus far, however, they are bedevilled by unsolved economic, social, and legal challenges, specifically, jurisdictional challenges.

It is argued in this chapter that, by explication, the jurisdictional issues presuppose that the consumers are not effectively protected from unscrupulous online service providers. Further that, with globalisation and the industrial revolutions, the lack of effective protection, transcends beyond the designs of the unscrupulous service providers to systemic faults within the design and legal apparatus (ICT legal framework) on the protection of consumers and e-commerce activities. The chapter also reflects on ICT and e-commerce in Africa and examines EU and US jurisdictional approaches on e-commerce. It is uncontested that the basic requirement for executing online commercial transaction is e-commerce laws, telecommunication laws, provision of sectoral convergence, and internet coverage. From the e-commerce and telecommunication laws perspective – the objectives are to regulate and afford consumers and businesses with the necessary legal protection and to place e-commerce transactions on equal footing with the traditional paper-based exchanges.

A snapshot on the progression of the e-commerce laws, as published by the United Nations Conference on Trade and Development (2020), revealed that, worldwide about 158 states representing 81 per cent have adopted the e-commerce laws. The distribution of this milestone depicts that in Europe about 98 per cent of the countries have adopted e-commerce laws, 91 per cent in the Americas and about 61 per cent in Africa. From the African context the 61 per cent represent about 33 countries out of the 54 African sovereign states that have adopted, in one form or another, the e-commerce laws. With this margin of statistics on adoption of e-commerce laws, Africa stands to be vulnerable to the exigencies of the Fourth Industrial Revolution and e-commerce. The dearth of the African legal framework on e-commerce renders Africa to be susceptible to the economic imperialist, which in turn robs Africa's economic sovereignty.

Notwithstanding this graphic reality, the chapter provides niche areas for improvement and reform of the current African legal framework on e-commerce. The premise here is clear: Africa is one common village and e-commerce respects no physical boundaries – thus, the weakness in legal framework of any of the African States has great potential to render the well-regulated States weaker.

Globally, issues related to jurisdiction continues to rapidly evolve, encumbering any attempt that contemplates to meet the standards of the ever-changing social constructions of time, space, and mobility (Zekos 2015). It is worth noting here that the determination of jurisdiction lays within the powers of a given sovereign state. Primarily, it is entirely the decision of a country to adopt or otherwise, the e-commerce legal framework – in its own interest. However, there is legitimisation and unification agenda advanced by the international communities, which may greatly influence the development of the legal framework of states. For example, in the context of e-commerce: the United Nations Model Law on Electronic Commerce of 1996 is one of the legal instrument that contemplate to advance the unification of e-commerce legal framework. Further it is relevant to elucidate that notwithstanding the political, social and economic aspersions wrought by e-commerce, there is no doubt that the convergence between the financial and telecommunication sectors has defied the traditional set-ups and functions of these sectors globally and has various implications on e-commerce in Africa.

Jurisdiction, the internet, and e-commerce

Theoretically stating, cyber jurisdiction is perceived as a new form of jurisdiction and as such it raises many challenges. Ward, Sipior, and Volonino (2016: 2) observed that cyber jurisdiction "[i]s an area of increasing concern to e-commerce because of the growth in cross-border re-tailing, and therefore the need for a global solution is also growing". The issue of global solution, from the African context, brings to the fore further questions: what is the role, if any, of Africa in the contemplated global solution? To what extent does Africa influence the global solution on electronic commerce? From the rate of development of the electronic commerce legal framework, it is agreeable that Africa stands in a consumer arena ready to consume the droplets from Europe and the Americas. This is evident from the way, in which, the European laws on e-commerce are transplanted and adopted in African legal systems – in most of African states that adopted e-commerce laws, they mirrored, borrowed, hybridised, etcetera, the conception of e-commerce as understood from the European and the Americas perspective. The indiscriminate transplant of these e-commerce legal framework into Africa, as will be demonstrated below, has the potential of relegating the African conception of e-commerce to the periphery of the 'Other'. With the glitches of cyber jurisdiction, the working assumption, as expounded by Ward et el, expanded here, is that "[e]ngaging in electronic commerce, inevitably, presents legal risks to both electronic businesses (e-businesses) and consumers." (Ward, et el. 2016: 2-3.) Legal actions relative to cyber jurisdiction, among others, include censorship, computer crime, contracts, copyright, defamation and libel, discrimination, fraud, hacking, harassment, intellectual property, obscenity and pornography, privacy, taxation, trade secrets, and trademark. It is agreeable that this list is by far not exhaustive, and that the issues raised are undeniable in the realm of e-commerce. Further, as a jurisdictional fact, prior to hearing a matter – courts have to ascertain if they have the requisite authority to adjudicate over the matter/ dispute, in the context of ecommerce, this could either be: authority over the individual or the business (defendant) and or subject matter.

The concept of jurisdiction is contentious. Jurisdiction often refers to the authority or power vested in a state or institution of the state, including to regulate, enforce and adjudicate over a matter. Generally, jurisdiction refers to the state's authority to prescribe, adjudicate and enforce the law over a subject or person (Gladstone 2003: 144). Kumar (2009) defines jurisdiction with reference to "the practical authority to interpret and apply law, or to govern and legislate". Dugard (2011: 146) posits that the concept of jurisdiction "refers to the authority that a state has to exercise its governmental functions by legislation, executive and enforcement action, and judicial decrees over persons and property". Jurisdiction often becomes indistinct when electronic commerce cross borders. Most scholars agree that the cyber space laws related to jurisdiction is unsettled thereby exposing consumers to risks, (see Trammell & Bambauer 2015 cited in Ward, Sipior & Volonino 2016: 4).

Historically, the concept of jurisdiction was tied to the territory of the state and the physical presence of the subject in such a state. For instance, "a court could only exercise personal jurisdiction over persons present in the state in which the action was brought" (*Pennoyer v Neff* 95 US 714, 722: 1877). However, owing to various factors like globalisation, industrialisation, transnational activities, and etcetera, most states started expanding their jurisdictions beyond their territories – a phenomenon which came to be known as extraterritoriality. Among the objects of extraterritorial jurisdiction is to accord the necessary protection and equally regulate the conduct of citizens when such citizens are abroad. However, these forms of jurisdictions fail to adequately regulate activities within the cyberspace such as electronic commerce. In this context, the inception of electronic commerce has also changed the dynamics on jurisdiction.

According to Jobodwana (2009: 287) e-commerce refers "[t]o all forms of commercial transactions that are conducted through Internet – and may involve individuals and organisations". Fraser *et al* (2008: 8) defined e-commerce to entail "[t]he use of the Internet for the exchange of information of value. More specifically, orders and payments between businesses and between business and consumer. Otherwise stated, e-commerce is the secure trading of goods, information, or services and, in the main, conducted using Internet technologies". Understood from the business world's perspective, e-commerce consists of "any net business activity that transforms internal and external relationships to create value and exploit market opportunities driven by new rules of connected economy" (Damanpour & Damanpour 2001).

From diverse research on both jurisdiction and electronic commerce, what is apparent is that, at the exigence of electronic commerce and artificial intelligence (the fourth industrial revolution), it became increasingly difficult for states to effectively exercise jurisdiction over transnational borderless transactions based on traditional principles of jurisdiction. The traditional principles of jurisdiction hinges on, among others, attributes such as territoriality and physical presence of persons within the territory of a given state. Cognisant of these challenges, Kumar (2009) argued that for the state to effectively assert its authority and to deal with or regulate e-commerce, such a state must exercise its cyberspace jurisdiction. Cyberspace jurisdiction is defined with reference to "real world government's power and normally existing court's authority over internet users and their activities in cyber world" (Kumar 2009). The cyberspace jurisdictional issues may be exemplified in the following hypothetical scenario: 'Imagine, a Namibian entity with its server in Jamaica concludes an agreement with a Tanzanian entity whose server is in Cuba through internet for the provision of a service in Zimbabwe and Canada'.

In this hypothetical scenario, the question is, which country may exercise jurisdiction over the matter? Of course, this presents a daunting task in as far as the question of the choice of law is concerned. It is apparent that to apply the traditional rules of jurisdiction in matters related to e-commerce, especially electronic transactions that traverses territorial boundaries is devoid of any justice or it may lead to irreparable injustice. To circumvent these types of jurisdictional challenges wrought by e-commerce, the international community has developed different strategies or approaches. These divergent views are discussed below.

Divergent schools of thought on jurisdiction in a virtual world

Governments and courts have for long grappled, inconsistently, on the question as to whether they should apply the laws applicable to physical world (jurisdiction based on territory, extraterritoriality or physical presence) onto the virtual (formless) world. There are competing and divergent schools of thoughts on this question. There is a contrasting debate on whether virtual and physical world, in the context of e-commerce jurisdiction are distinct. The pro-distinct thesis presupposes that the physical world is distinct from virtual world – therefore, these two cannot apply the same laws. Rather, separate legal regimes must be applied (Kumar 2009). We refer to this school of thought as the 'liberal school of thought'. The premise for the liberal school of thought is that with cyberspace the world's physical borders have vanished or is non-existent, rendering the physical form of the world, formless. In contradistinction, the other school of thought argue that there is a link between physical world and virtual world – therefore, there is no need to advocate for separate legal regimes. We refer to this school of thought as the 'conservative school of thought'.

The premise undergirding the conservative school of thought is well reflected in Kumar's (2009) works who posits that "though in cyber world there are no geographical boundaries but netizens (cyber users) who are citizens of some countries and are governed by the national laws of these countries. Therefore, physical and cyber world are connected." The conservatist concede that indeed physical and cyber world are different – however, this does not justify abandoning the settled rules applicable to physical boundaries on jurisdiction nor invoking new legal regime. Rather, what is required is to effect minor modifications, as the circumstances may require, of the settled laws of physical world on jurisdiction to virtual world – whereof e-commerce is not an exception (Moore 2002).

The rationale here is simplified by the fact that a person who concludes an electronic transaction, at the material time when such a person acted (i.e. clicked the web wrap) he or she was in a given locality (location/place). Thus, the fact that such a person was physically present at a given geographical place, is sufficient to link such a person's virtual activities to physical world. These schools of thoughts, as will be demonstrated below, have much influenced the courts in the world when developing the principles on jurisdiction in e-commerce matters. These influences are noted in the debate below, that reflects the international and domestic approaches to the questions of cyber space jurisdiction.

International law on jurisdiction and e-commerce

Notably the 21st century has witnessed tremendous growth or increase in cross-border electronically conducted commercial transactions. However, there is little or absent any legal framework at international law level that regulates jurisdictional issues that may arise in cases of disputes related to electronic transactions. Wang (2008: 233) mooted this dearth of regulatory framework by noting that both the "UNICITRAL Model Law on Electronic Commerce and the United Nations Convention on the Use of Electronic

Communications in International Contracts fails to expressly provide for a clause on jurisdictions".

In terms of the United Nations Conventions on the Use of Electronic Communications in International Contracts of 2003 (UNCUECIC), one may argue that the jurisdictional regulatory framework is implied, although not expressly stated, in article 6 which deals with the presumptions related to the location of the parties as well as article 10 which provides for the time and place of dispatch. In terms of article 6 of UNCUECIC the location of the parties is a significant indicator as to establishing the place of business – which in turn may be required in determining jurisdiction. In a nutshell, article 6 of UNCUECIC brings to fore presumption related to various tests, namely: place of business, habitual residence, and closest relationship test (Feria 2006: 689). Notwithstanding the implications of the tests laid down in article 6 above – article 2 of the UNCUECIC makes it clear that the Convention does not apply to certain class of contracts.

At continental level – such as Europe, Asia, and the Americas – based on the UNCTAD statistics above, there has been some progression in terms of legal framework that regulates e-commerce jurisdictions (UNCTAD 2020). Of course, the reason for such progression is because these continents are, by far, the larger producers and consumers of e-commerce. Important to note that these developments are persuasive and to some degrees instructive – in the sense that they provide for various forms (types) of e-commerce jurisdictions ranging from: general, special and specific jurisdictions, and therefore may not well be suited for Africa.

Perloff-Giles (2018: 223) suggest that the ecommerce disputes should not be tied to the competence of national courts, rather the presence of the international courts, for example: the international criminal court (ICC) or international court of justice (ICJ) has the potential to alleviate the cyber space jurisdictional issues. This suggestion resonates on the premise that these international courts are in a better position in as far as cross border evidence collection, collaboration, and enforcement mechanism, to mention a few when compared to domestic courts.

The World Economic Forum (WEF 2019) and the International Trade Centre (2020) reveals that there is great potential for e-commerce growth in Africa – which growth is inevitably suggested to procure impact on various services and goods. The assumption is that electronic commerce presupposes availability of significant employment opportunities, with online marketplaces anticipated to create over 3 million employment opportunities by 2025 (WEF 2019).

Premised on the assumption of availability of significant employment opportunities, African states, through the African Action Agenda, appear to continue to encourage policymakers to undertake as a matter of priority the development of ecommerce enablers, such as laws and policies on e-commerce – of which the question of jurisdiction is not an exception. The African Action Agenda further places an emphasis on African states to adopt the ecommerce enablers during the negotiations on the African Continental Free Trade Area (AfCFTA) and adoption of bilateral and multilateral agreements on issues related to ecommerce (WEF 2019) and ecommerce dispute resolution mechanisms. The object of these efforts is to facilitate effective ecommerce transactions, within and across the borders. More so, to alleviate the question of ecommerce jurisdiction challenges. The question on the status of e-commerce and its implications in Africa is discussed later in this chapter. However, the next section examines jurisdictional approaches in e-commerce in Europe and the United States.

European jurisdictional approaches on e-commerce

Under the European Union (EU), issues related to jurisdiction may be approached or resolved, among others, in three ways, namely: through the instrumentality of the Brussels Convention; Council Regulations/ Directives; and or through, the application of common law. The Brussels Convention, however, was repealed by Council Regulations/ Directive 44/2001 which is comprehensive (Razmpa 2011: 1-2). E-commerce jurisdiction is expressly provided for under the EU Directive on E-commerce, in contrast it was not expressly and directly stipulated under the Brussels Convention. On this observation, e-commerce jurisdiction is understood to have been incorporated in Article 23(2) of the Brussels Regulation 44/2001 which stipulates that: "any communication by electronic means which provides a durable record of the agreement shall be equivalent to writing". Here, the fact that electronic agreements are recognised renders them to be justiciable in any of the courts in the Member States. By explication, this entails that e-commerce jurisdiction disputes, though not expressly provided for in Brussels Convention, may be entertained by courts and may fall either under general, special, or exclusive jurisdiction as contemplated in the Council Regulations.

The primary instrument in the EU in as far as issues related to jurisdiction arising from commercial contracts, including e-commerce, may be resolved by the *Brussels Convention on Jurisdiction and Enforcement of Judgments in Civil and Commercial Matters* of 1968 (Brussels Convention). The Brussel Convention provide for various forms of jurisdiction, namely: general, special, exclusive, and non-exclusive. The general jurisdiction affords courts to have jurisdiction over persons who are domiciled in a contracting State notwithstanding the nationality of those persons. Brussels Convention article 2 provides that, "Subject to the provisions of this Convention, persons domiciled in a contracting state, shall whatever their nationality, be sued in the courts of that state."

This provision has been retained in terms of Chapter II Section 1 article 2 of the *Brussels Regulations* 44/2001. Under the general jurisdiction rule, the court may only exercise its jurisdiction if it is clear that the person sued is domiciled in the forum State. Notably, this provision applies to both natural and juristic persons. What constitute domicile is not defined in the *Brussels Convention* nor *Brussels Regulations* – however, in determining whether the person is domiciled in a member state – the courts give effect to the laws of such a member state. Article 59 of the Brussels Regulation stipulates that, "In order to determine whether a party is domiciled in the member state whose courts are seized of a matter, the court shall apply its internal law."

The general jurisdiction incorporated in the Brussels Convention supplemented by the Brussels Regulation also applies to juristic persons (corporations). Similarly, the test to determine whether a court has general jurisdiction is based on domicile. In relation to juristic persons article 60(1) of the Brussels Regulation provides for certain guidelines that may be used to decide the domicile of a juristic person, namely: "a place where the juristic person has its statutory seat, or its central administration, or its principal place of business" (see Wang 2008).

The other form of e-commerce jurisdiction is the special jurisdiction. The special jurisdiction affords the courts with the jurisdiction over a person who is domiciled within the EU member states to be subjected and or be sued in any of the EU contracting state. For example, a person may be domiciled in state "A" but sued in state "B" provided both these states are members within the EU.

Parties to an electronic contract within EU have the right to choose the law that would govern their contract, and equally they have the right to choose a court in which the dispute arising from such a contract may be determined. Razmpa (2011) observed that "in terms of Council Regulations, the consumer has a right to choose a competent court – which could be a court where the defendant is domiciled or where the plaintiff is domiciled." If the litigants concur on the court – then such court has jurisdiction to adjudicate over the dispute. In other words, where there is a choice of forum, then jurisdiction is exclusively exercised by such a chosen forum. This exercise of choosing or nominating a court by the parties is known as the prorogation of jurisdiction. In as far as jurisdiction disputes are concerned – all other disputes which fall outside the general, special, and exclusive jurisdiction – may be dealt with in terms of the English common law. The English common law mainly regulates issues pertaining to jurisdiction "where the contracts are concluded with persons domiciled outside EU member states or states which are not subject to the Brussels Convention or Regulations" (Singleton 2009). The process of determining jurisdiction, under English common law, involves several factors that should be taken into consideration, among others, (a) there must be substantial connection between the forum state and the matter; (b) it must be convenient for the forum to adjudicate over the dispute; and, (c) the place where the parties are domiciled and the law that governs such contractual relationship (see *Spihada Marine Corp v Cansulex Ltd* [1987] AC 460). All these factors, depending on the matter, may be taken into consideration when determining the e-commerce jurisdiction dispute.

US jurisdictional approaches on e-commerce

The USA has two forms of personal jurisdiction that may be applied when an e-commerce jurisdiction dispute arises, these are general and specific jurisdiction. General jurisdiction refers to "the jurisdiction of the USA courts over a person for any cause of action, whether or not related to the defendant's contact with the forum state" (see Wang 2008). The crux of the general jurisdiction is that the person on whom the court intends to exercise its jurisdiction should have, in one way or the other, had some form of contact with the forum state (in the USA). By explication – a person should have, at the moment when the cause of dispute occurred that led to the determination of e-commerce jurisdiction, had "continuous and systematic contact with the forum state" (see *International Shoe Co. v Washington* 326 U.S. 310 (1945) at 320, 66 S.Ct). This may, among others, include activities done in the USA such as: hoisting a server, actively sending, and receiving or concluding electronic transactions – without regard to nationality of such a person – whilst in the USA, etcetera. Seemingly, the precepts of the exercise of general jurisdiction is predicated on three components, that is, "the relationship among the defendant, the forum, and the litigation" (*Shaffer v Heitner* 433 U.S, 186 (1977). This form of jurisdiction is not without flaws. There has been some negative criticism against the application of general jurisdiction, for instance: it contemplates to include activities that are "unrelated to the defendant's contact with the forum state".

There are burgeoning, yet unsettled, questions from academicians as to what "amount of unrelated contact is needed to subject a defendant to personal jurisdiction?" (Scoles et al. 2000: 348). On proper construction of the principles related to general jurisdiction, it appears that its application involves a duo-step inquiry, namely: "first, the interpretation of the concerned state's *long-arm statute* to establish if such statute provides for the exercise of jurisdiction, and secondly, to apply the principles of due process." (Gladstone 2003: 145). Equally, it is apparent that the court may not invoke this form of jurisdiction or a person may not be amenable (court may not exercise jurisdiction) "when the individual's relationship to the state is so attenuated as to render the exercise of jurisdiction unreasonable" (see *Helicopteros Nacionales de Colombia, S.A. v Hall* 466 U.S. 1984: 408).

Besides general jurisdiction, the other form of jurisdiction that comes into play, is the specific jurisdiction. With the specific jurisdiction, the determination centres on "when the underlying claim arise out of, or are directly related to, a defendant's contacts with the forum state" (Wang 2008). Here, the question is whether a person's contact with the forum state is related to the cause of action. If the answer to this inquiry is positive, then it may be enough for the court to invoke its jurisdiction over the dispute. Wang (2008: 238) argues that specific jurisdiction, just like in the process of determining general jurisdiction, can be examined in several ways, for example: (a) interpret the long-arm statute to establish if there is statutory basis to sue; (b) to examine the contacts that are related to the dispute: whether they satisfy the requirements for minimum contact theory;

and, (c) to analyse it in the context of the principle of fair play and substantial justice.

The discussion above, partly demonstrates that courts have indeed been at the forefront in as far as developing the principles related to e-commerce jurisdiction. The principles developed in US courts, among others, include: the minimum contact, the effect test, the reasonableness test and targeting test (see Wang 2008; Gladstone 2003; Boone 2006; *International Shoe Co. v Washington* 326 U.S. 310 1945: 320; *Zippo Manufacturing Co. v Zippo Dot Com*, Inc 937 F. Supp. 161 C. Conn. 1996: para 1124).

The USA approach to cyber jurisdiction has been criticised – citing inconsistency and lack of sufficient standards to adjudicate over ecommerce disputes (Ward, Sipior, and Volonino 2016: 14). With these criticisms, the call is that the development of the standard principles on cyber space jurisdiction should not be limited to the club of few, but rather it should be embraced at international level. This noble call is exacerbated by the fact that ecommerce respects no physical boundary – as it presents challenges, among others, on the identification of the exact place of transaction. The consequence is clear: the traditional conception of jurisdiction that was limited to geography is challenged. The other issue that illuminates from this consequence, is the determination of which rules may be applied to borderless transactions. The fact that there is lack of appropriate legal instruments to handle borderless ecommerce disputes – exposes the business owners and consumers to electronic transactions shocks and risks.

The USA has put in place legislation that assists in determining the e-commerce jurisdictions. These e-commerce jurisdictions, at state level, are governed – among others, by the Long-Arm Statutes. For example, the State of Florida, the *Florida Long Arm Statute* contemplate to vest the courts with the jurisdiction over conduct which started or whose harm was felt in Florida (see Section 48: 193). This include conduct authored by non-state-residents. Equally, at federal state level there are several legislative instruments that encourage states to adopt measures to ensure an effective prosecution of e-commerce disputes. For example, the adoption of the *Uniform Computer Information Transactions Act* as well as the *Uniform Electronic Transaction Act*. These instruments function as model laws for states to emulate.

Regulatory frameworks on e-commerce in Africa

Research show that laws, principles, and policies related to ecommerce lags far behind digital developments, especially on the African continent. Deduced from United Nations reports, it is estimated that about 32 of Africa's 54 states adopted ecommerce legal framework, (online exchange). From the same statistics, its apparent that about 23 states had legal framework related to data protection and privacy. Further that about 20 states had effectively included policies and legislative framework that directly contemplate to protect online consumer (WEF 2019).

Notably, when one speaks about consumer protections – it is noted that there are various dimensions that may be elucidated, among others: options of payments, consumer data treatment, and dispute resolution mechanism, to mention a few. Therefore, when policies and laws are adopted pursuant to consumer protection – such policies contemplate to affect a wide range of activities: business environment, cooperation, intellectual property rights, privacy, etc. In this view, the adoption of effective ecommerce policies increases business and consumer confidence (WEF 2019). The contrast hold that where there is a deficit in ecommerce laws, the chances are that the consumers stands to be exploited. The World Economic Forum (2019) observed that notwithstanding strategies that has been put in place, Africa lag in as far as adoption of ecommerce laws is concerned – as a consequence, there is legal uncertainty which places the issue of ecommerce jurisdiction to illuminate.

In the context of regulatory framework, the World Economic Forum revealed, among others, that half of the African states had incorporated, in their legal systems, data protection frameworks with intermittent enforcement mechanism. Against this observation, the World Economic Forum has proposed a plan of action that contemplate to include the pan-African perceptions on digital economy (WEF 2019).

In view of the data above, it is arguable that, notwithstanding the paradigm shift from traditional commercial transaction to ecommerce as well as the fast-growing ecommerce activities in Africa, the laws that supports ecommerce lacks the robust effects which it deserves (Ewelukwa 2011: 563). It is worth noting that the African legal framework on ecommerce has been to a great extent influenced by the UNCITRAL Model Law on Electronic Commerce of 1996, and the United Nations Convention on the Use of

Electronic Communications in International Contracts of 2005. These instruments have been adopted by African states and implemented varyingly: ranging from modifying and domesticating these instrument (Ewelukwa 2011: 564). It is argued that these international instruments play a vital role in harmonising the legal framework that addresses the issues pertaining to ecommerce, including questions of cyber space jurisdiction. However, from the African perspective, there are questions that lingers: how does Africa substantively benefits from these instruments? Are these instruments a proof of continued hegemony and economic dominion over African businesses? Ewelukwa (2011) observed with a concern that "even if African countries can successfully enact laws to regulate e-commerce, or adopt model laws already formulated by various harmonizing institutions and organizations, it remains to be considered whether these laws will actually facilitate the growth of e-commerce transactions in Africa or will merely decorate the statute books without having tangible impact on commercial transactions" (pp. 570-1). The observation made by Ewelukwa goes beyond the question of adopting ecommerce legal framework and it include the issues related to capacity to implement these legal frameworks. On this note, Ewelukwa (2011) noted a number of impediments that has the potential to derail the full realisation of, and implementation of the adopted ecommerce frameworks, citing among others, the: issue of lack of proper ecommerce infrastructure; lack of expertise in the field of ecommerce; and ignorance on the part of consumers.

In its bid to harmonise the ecommerce and related matters in Africa, the African Union (AU) in June 2014 adopted a Convention on Cyber Security and Personal Data Protection (AUCCSPDP), during its Conference that was held in Malabo, Equatorial Guinea. Mindful of the need to regulate an evolving technological domain, the Convention, among others, contemplate to include provisions that enables effective consumer protection and rules that legitimises the option for a credible digital environment – which is a precursor of electronic transactions, namely: ensuring data protection, and waging war against cybercrimes. The inclusion of the provisions on the proscription of cybercrimes is a calculated attribute made after the realisation that ecommerce may be encumbered by cybercrimes and related security issues.

The AUCCSPDP makes clear that state parties must put in place effective legislative framework that enables personal data protection and prevention of cybercrimes. In this context, activities that pertains to ecommerce are required to be regulated by the state parties, for example: a state party in whose territory such activities were conducted. However, few countries (19 states) have ratified the AUCCSPDP due to various reasons, among others: political, social, economic, or legal reasons, to mention a few.

Notwithstanding a mix of advances and challenges stated above – the question that comes to the fore includes: why discuss ecommerce in Africa? What is the relevance of this discussion? A snap view at the development agenda of the African continent, particularly in the areas of information and communication technology, and online transaction activities cannot be overstated. For instance, it is worth noting that according to the 2019 Report of the World Bank Group on the assessment of Kenya' digital economy, it revealed that ecommerce was progressing well in Africa and as such the progression required effective ecommerce regulatory framework.

An overview on the ecommerce legal framework in African states depicts a noteworthy effort. At national levels, Kenya adopted the Communications Act of 1998 and its subsequent amendment to make provision for ecommerce transactions. As early as 2000 Tunisia promulgated the Electronic Exchanges and Electronic Commerce Law. In 2004 Egypt promulgated Law No 15 of 2004 the Electronic Signature Act designed to regulate the electronic contracts and transactions. Ghana promulgated the Electronic Transactions Act of 2008. In Ghana, this instrument created a conducive electronic transaction environment for consumers and businesses, as it, among others, proscribed a series of cybercrimes, and it provided not only the regulatory scheme but enforcement mechanisms as well. Zambia promulgated the Electronic Communications and Transactions Act 21 of 2009. Uganda enacted the Electronic Transactions Act 8 of 2011 – which specifically regulates electronic transactions, and it provides basic requirements such as effects of an electronically transacted records, electronic signature, and consumer protection (Ewelukwa 2011). In 2014 Botswana promulgated the Electronic Communication and Transaction Act 14 of 2014 Namibian promulgated the Electronic Transaction Act of 4 of 2019.

These legislative developments are observed to increase progressively across African states, and it is a hopeful endeavours for various reasons, for example: ecommerce disputes has no regard to physical borders – as such a weakness in the legal framework of any of the African states places the entire African continent at peril. By extension, the weakness in the ecommerce legal framework of any

282

country could negatively affect the entire globe – i.e. countries with weaker ecommerce legal framework could be used as launching pads by cyber criminals, thereby compromising all ecommerce businesses and exposing consumers to risks.

The role of regional organisations on e-commerce in Africa

The role of regional organisations on e-commerce in Africa cannot be underestimated – ranging from harmonisation of ecommerce, implementation of ecommerce projects, monitoring of ecommerce, facilitation of transportation of goods, and services and provision of ecommerce education. Ewelukwa (2011: 560) conducted a study and identified various organisations that has the potential to play vital roles in the development and progression of ecommerce in Africa, some of the cited organisations, include but not limited to: "[U]niversities, the International Chamber of Commerce, the International Institute for the Unification of Private Law (UNIDROIT), Comite Maritime International (CMI), the United Nations Commission on International Trade Law (UNCITRAL), and the Organisation for the Harmonization of Business Law in Africa (OHADA)".

In Africa, at the forefront of ecommerce harmonisation, is primarily the AUCCSPDP. This instrument implores the African member states to ensure that there is effective legal framework that forestall cybercrimes for purposes of enabling conducive ecommerce, and equally for effective personal data protection. The quest to harmonise the legal framework related to ecommerce is not limited at the AU level, rather, it extends beyond AU and include the UN. For example, the adoption of principles contained in the UNCITRAL Model Law – is undeniably one of the instruments that promotes and advocates for harmonisation in the field of ecommerce.

The UNCTAD Report on Review of ecommerce legal framework on harmonisation in the Economic Community of West African States of 2015, shows that there are several projects that has been adopted to advance the harmonisation agenda – inking the efforts towards thwarting cybercrimes. This is exemplified by the continued efforts at the instance of the Organisation for the Harmonisation of Business Law in Africa (OHADA) through its works, specifically the adoption of the OHADA Treaty in 1993. Other significant OHADA inroads include the adoption of the Uniform Acts which elucidates on various aspects such as secured transactions, and processes of arbitration (Beauchard & Kodo 2011). The other initiative that advances harmonisation that may be mentioned is the African E-Trade Group. The object of E-Trade Group is mainly to facilitate effective ecommerce and promotion of private public partnership in commerce, intra Africa trade, etc, with view to fast track ICT solutions for ecommerce (A-e Trade Group 2019).

The digital divide and some constraints on e-commerce in Africa

The historical injustice suffered by the colonies at the hands of their colonial masters continue to wag its tail in the present independent states. This historical injustice is clearly visible in today's conception of digital divide – which presupposes the substantive and material differences related to the ICT infrastructure development observed between the developing and developed states. Digital divide, according to Ndonga (2012: 250-251) refers to "the inequality of access to the internet, the gap between those who do and do not have access to computers and the internet, the divergence of internet access between industrialized and developing societies, the unequal distribution of computers, internet connections, technological devices and so on between countries and an inequality in access, distribution, and use of information and communication technologies between two or more populations" (see, Norris 2001: 4).

It is common cause that digital divide exists between the developed and developing countries, globally and regionally – ranging from access to internet services, level of technology literacy, capacity to optimise the benefits of ecommerce and access to market information, to mention a few. The impact of digital divide includes that those who are technologically well vested emerges richer and those who are situated at the periphery of technology remain poor. (Okoli & Mbarika 2003: 46) argue that,

> ...developed nations with the resources to invest in and develop ICT infrastructure are reaping enormous benefits from the information age, while developing nations are trailing along at a much slower pace. This difference in rates of technological progress is widening the economic disparity between the socio-economic regions that the development literature commonly refers

to as the North (referring primarily to Canada, the United States, and Western Europe) and the South (primarily Latin America, Africa, and Southeast Asia), thus creating a digital (that is, digitally fostered) divide.

From the African perspective, there are several factors that has been identified as hindrance to effective ecommerce, among others, is the digital divide phenomenon. Ndonga (2012: 245) argues that the African ecommerce is restrained by factors such as "lack of adequate ICT infrastructure, limited ICT knowledge and threat of cybercrimes in Africa". To close the gap caused by the digital divide boundary, the African states and governments are implored to adopt effective legislative framework that enables effective measures against cybercrimes, improving the budget systems thereby investing in ICT infrastructure and ICT education (Jobodwana 2009: 294).

Other issues include language and cultural barriers. Language is a tool and means for communication that is necessary for effective service delivery, formation of business partnership, and a means of production. As Jobodwana (2009: 295) observes "for inter-country trade to flourish a common means of communication should be developed and adopted in Africa such as computer networks and programs, and e-business platforms." However, currently the African continent is much of a consumer continent to an extent that the consumed products, technology, makes no provision for services in local indigenous languages.

The 4ᵗʰ Industrial Revolution and its ramifications for Africans

The Fourth Industrial Revolution (4IR), in the context of ecommerce, is "an umbrella term for 3D-printing, artificial intelligence (AI), big data, industrial Internet of things (IIoT) and robotics" (Sutherland 2020: 232). The impact of 4IR is distributed differently on states, and corporations/business. For business, the 4IR invokes reconsideration of business strategies, calibration of instrument and modalities of conducting businesses. Whereas, for states, 4IR means adjusting regulatory frameworks to keep up with the times and making provision for a conducive business environment capable of attract investment.

Sutherland (2020) perceives 4IR as "the consequences of neoliberal efforts aimed at the destruction of jobs, depress wages, and increase inequality and ordination of coloniality" (see Benioff 2017).

Given that e-commerce is at the centre of the fourth industrial revolution, one stands to wonder if Africa stands to benefit from the digital economy given its travails. The 4IR needs government to act, among others, to provide for data protection, consumer protection, improve cybersecurity levels, make provision for ICT education, installation of robust ICT infrastructure, enforcement mechanism and most all a formidable dispute resolution system that is not riddled with unresolved jurisdictional questions.

An anecdote, expose, of e-commerce in the context of coloniality illuminates – is e-commerce a manifestation of coloniality? It is uncontested that the African states endured colonialism and achieved political independence from the colonial masters. However, it largely remains to be concretely accepted that the African states, with the attainment of political independence, equally achieved the economic and knowledge/ intellectual independence. The question of economic independence become more relevant when faced with borderless e-commerce. What are the effects of borderless e-commerce on African state sovereignty? Is e-commerce a disguised tool for economic imperialist? These questions though differently located to the question of legal jurisdiction in e-commerce issues: they retain relevance in as far as sovereign autonomy of African states which appears to continue to lose its essence at the instance of e-commerce. The presumption here is that if the African states are decentred through e-commerce, the net implication is that African states would lose sovereign powers and would ultimately lose their hard-earned political independence.

The consequence is clear, that is: when African states lose their sovereignty and independence, they become subject to the empire of e-commerce or what Dean and Passavant (2004) call communicative capitalism. According to Dean and Passavant (2004) the empire, in the context of commerce, is seeking to adorn new clothes – by the economic apparatus, such as e-commerce, to decentre the African states. The concerns of the destruction of the African states through commerce are not new: historically, Africa has been colonised through commerce. Initially, as a tool of colonialism, the empire set up trading posts in precolonial Africa and then it used these trading posts to launch the colonial projects. This include but not limited to the deployment, by the empire, of business entities such as the British East India Company, the German West Africa Company, and the British South Africa company, etcetera (Roy 2014). These companies were used as fronts for colonialists in the same way Dean and

Passavant (2004) are apprehensive that the ongoing communicative capitalism and the attendant fourth industrial revolution are part of the empire's new clothes. With this background in the hindsight, the question for Africa then is: how would the law protect African states and institutions from being decentred and desovereignised?

In principle, the law can afford the states with necessary protection. Through the e-commerce legal framework, states can prescribe the issues related to jurisdiction, the authority to adjudicate and enforcement of the law. In other words, the organically created laws may ward off the pervasive empires' ongoing communicative capitalism. However, as was depicted from the UNCTAD (2020) statistics, African states are trailing behind their former colonial masters in as far as the adoption of e-commerce legal framework is concerned. In cases where the African states have adopted the e-commerce legal framework, the African states, instead of adopting organically created e-commerce laws, they opt to borrow, mirror, or transplant or hybridise the European and American conception of e-commerce. The obvious characteristics of these transplanted e-commerce laws include that such laws are delinked from the social, economic, and political environment of Africa – therefore, they may not be or cannot be the ultimate solution to the African e-commerce challenges.

Conclusion

Undoubtedly, the convergence of ICT in financial sectors has boosted e-commerce particularly in industrialised nations. While e-commerce makes provision for opportunities, for various developing economies, the benefits of e-commerce has not fully penetrated many African economies like in the West. This chapter explored some jurisdictional challenges in e-commerce and the implications of internet jurisdiction on e-commerce. It examines regulatory frameworks, efforts, and constraints in e-commerce in Africa, the US and EU, and the role of the AU, African states, and regional organisations in e-commerce. The forces of globalisation and 4IR imply that those countries that are prepared for and understand the many facets of the internet will likely end up on top in the digital economy including aspects of e-commerce. It is evident from the discussion, that the EU and Americas' have adopted diversified approaches to e-commerce jurisdiction. These diverse approaches are not limited to the EU and America, rather, they can extend to other countries and Africa can draw lessons. However, given its travails, Africa must support and develop an inclusive pan-African paradigm or framework for e-commerce and the digital economy - in an age of globalisation, technology, and industrial revolutions. The role of the AU, African states and regional organisations is vital for transforming and contextualising e-commerce in Africa. Lastly, various dimensions of the cultural and political contexts of Africa could hinder the implementation of e-commerce. E-commerce in Africa cannot simply involve the application of e-commerce and information technology diffusion principles developed in the Western context – rather, the e-commerce legal framework should be adopted taking cognisance of the independent sovereignty, social, economic and political context of Africa.

References

A-e Trade Group (2019) 'Joint Press Release'. Retrieved from https://au.int/sites/default/files/pressreleases/37015-pr-pr-hosting-aetrade-july-7.pdf.

Benioff, M.R. (2017) '4 Ways to Close the Inequality Gap in the Fourth Industrial Revolution'. Retrieved from https://www.weforum.org/agenda/2017/01/4-ways-to-close-the-inequality-gap-in-the-fourth-industrial-revolution/.

Bhanu, B. (2016) *Extreme Automation and Connectivity: The Global, Regional, and Investment Implications of the Fourth Industrial Revolution.* Geneva: UBS.

Bingi, P., Mir, A. and Khamalah, J. (2000) 'The Challenges Facing Global E-Commerce', *Information Systems Management*, 17(4), 22-30. DOI:10.1201/1078/43193.17.4.20000901/31249.5.

Boone, B.D. (2006) 'Bullseye! : Why a targeting approach to personal jurisdiction in the E-commerce Context makes sense internationally', *Emory International Law Review*, 20, 241-258.

Damanpour, F. and Damanpour, J. A. (2001) 'E-Business E-Commerce evolution: perspective and strategy', *Managerial Finance*, 27(7), 16-33.

Darley, W. (2003) 'Public policy challenges and implications of the Internet and the emerging e-commerce for sub-Saharan Africa: A business perspective', *Information Technology for Development*, 10(1), 1-12. DOI: 10.1002/itdj.1590100102.

Dean, J. and Passvant, P.A. (2004) *Empire's New Clothes: Reading Hardt and Negri*. Routledge Publishers - ISBN: 978-0415935555.

Dejo, O. (2009) 'Cyber-Crimes and the Boundaries of Domestic Legal Responses: Case for an Inclusionary Framework for Africa', *Journal of Information, Law and Technology* (1) 4. Retrieved from http://go.warwick.ac.uk/jilt/2009_1/olowu.

Dugard, J. (2011) *International Law, 4th Edition*. Cape Town: Juta.

Ewelukwa, N. (2011) 'Is Africa Ready for Electronic Commerce - A Critical Appraisal of the Legal Framework for Ecommerce in Africa', *European Journal of Law Reform*, 13(3-4), 550-576.

Fraser, J., Fraser, N. and McDonald, F. (2000) 'The strategic challenge of electronic commerce', *Supply Chain Management: An International Journal*, 5(1), 7-14.

Gladstone, J. A. (2003) 'Determining jurisdiction in Cyberspace: The Zippo Test or the Effects Test?' *Informing Science*, 143-156.

Hathaway, M.E. (2014) 'Connected Choices: How the Internet Is Challenging Sovereign Decisions', *American Foreign Policy Interests*, 36:5, 300-313. DOI: 10.1080/10803920.2014.969178.

Huang, I., Guo, R., Xie, H. and Wu, Z. (2012) 'The convergence of information and communication technologies gains momentum', *The Global Information Technology Report*, 35-45.

Jobodwana, Z. N. (2009) 'E-Commerce and mobile commerce in South Africa: Regulatory Challenges', *Journal of International Commercial Law and Technology*, 4(4), 287-302.

Kuner, C. (2009) 'Internet jurisdiction and data protection law: An international legal analysis', *International Journal of Law and Information Technology*, 18(2), 176–193.

Masamila, B. (2014) 'State of mobile banking in Tanzania and security issues', *International Journal of Network Security & Its Applications,* 6(4), 53-64.

Moore, E. (2002) 'Cyber jurisdiction', *Litigation Features,* 28-33. Retrieved from http://euro.ecom.cmu.edu/program/law/08-732/Jurisdiction/Cyberjurisdiction.pdf.

Mwinyimuva, H. T. (2013) 'The emergence of mobile banking and its legal implications in Tanzania'. Unpublished LLM Mini-Thesis, Open University of Tanzania, Tanzania.

'Nairobi Manifesto on the Digital Economy and Inclusive Development in Africa'. (2018) Retrieved from https://unctad.org/meetings/en/SessionalDocuments/Africae Week2018_NairobiManifesto_en.pdf.

Ndonga, D. (2012) 'E-commerce in Africa: Challenges and Solutions', *African Journal of Legal Studies*, 5, 243-268. Retrieved from https://www.researchgate.net/publication/270534490_E-Commerce_in_Africa_Challenges_and_Solutions.

Norris, P. (2001) *Digital Divide: Civic Engagement, Information Poverty, and Internet Worldwide*. Cambridge: Cambridge University Press.

Okoli, C. and Mbarika, V.A.W. (2003) 'A Framework for Assessing E-Commerce in Sub-Saharan Africa', *Journal of Global Information Technology Management*, 6(3), 44-66. DOI: 10.1080/1097198X.2003.10856355.

Perloff-Giles, A. (2018) 'Transnational cyber offenses: Overcoming jurisdictional challenges', *Yale Journal of International Law*, 43(1), 191-227.

Razmpa, F. (2011) 'Electronic Transactions: Jurisdictional issues in European Union', *International Journal of Economics and Management Engineering*, 5(5), 1-3.

Roy, T. (2014) 'Trading firms in colonial India', *Business History Review*, 88, 9–42. doi:10.1017/S0007680513001402.

Scoles, E. F., Hay, P., Borchers, P. J. and Symeonides, S. C. (2000) *Conflict of laws 3rd edition*. London: ST. Paul.

Singleton, S. (2009) *E-Contract*. Bloomsbury: Tottel Publishing.

Sutherland, E. (2020) 'The Fourth Industrial Revolution – The case of South Africa', *South African Journal of Political Studies*, 47(2), 233-252.

Wang, F. Y. (2008) 'Obstacles and solutions to Internet jurisdiction: A comparative analysis of the EU and US laws', *Journal of International Commercial Law and Technology*, 3(4), 233 -241.

Ward, B.T., Sipior, J.C. and Volonino, L. (2016) 'Internet Jurisdiction for E-commerce', *Journal of Internet Commerce*, 15(1), 1-17. DOI: 10.1080/15332861.2015.1109988.

World Economic Forum (WEF). (2019) 'Africa E-commerce Agenda, Roadmap for Action'. Retrieved from http://www3.weforum.org/docs/WEF_Africa_EComm_EN.pdf.

Zekos, G. (2015) 'Cyber versus conventional personal jurisdiction', *Journal of Internet Law*, 18(10), 3.

Chapter Thirteen

Theorising vulnerabilities in a context of the Fourth Industrial Revolution and COVID-19

Oliver Mtapuri

Introduction

The transformative speed induced by the Fourth Industrial Revolution (4IR) is omnipresent for the good or bad. As with all revolutions, a revolution disrupts the status quo, dislodges, displaces, destroys the old order and in its place a new order is established. Similarly, COVID-19 is revolutionary in terms of its impact – disrupts, dislodges, displaces, destroys the old order to usher in a new order in a pandemic milieu. Industrial revolutions have gone through transformational stages since their existence from the mid eighteenth century leading to the slow release of physical and mental activities to more technical achievements which have tremendously impacted the economy [for the good or bad](Prisecaru 2016). For instance, the Fourth Industrial Revolution brought about challenges such as replacement of workers by machines and greater inequalities as labour markets were disrupted (Xu, David and Kim 2018, Brende 2019). Disruptions come with speed, consequences, vulnerabilities as well as attendant costs which are of a socio-economic including psychological nature. According to Xu et al. (2018), the Fourth Industrial Revolution differs from other forms of revolutions in terms of speed, scale, complexity, and transformative power. Unemployment has significantly increased because of the wholesale deployment of artificial intelligence and robots, requiring new ways to reduce vulnerabilities, inequality of all sorts including social unrest (Lee, Yan, Pyka, Won, Kodama, Schiuma, Park, Jeon, Park, Jung and Jan 2018). As the revolutions could transform people's lives, the challenges associated with various inequalities are also possible with the 4IR (Lee *et al.* 2018). Sae-Lim and Jermsittiparsert (2019) state that in response to high unemployment that is likely to be driven by the 4IR, individuals will be forced to obtain strategic skills commensurate with future needs in the world of work. Re-skilling inevitably comes with a cost to an unemployed person. Disruptions to routines such as routines of work cause anxiety and uncertainty among retrenched workers and the unemployed. Despite the new opportunities that the 4IR creates, Mpofu and Nicolaides (2019) state that those who will benefit from the growth of 4IR will be few. It is on this basis that scholars like Azhar (2017) endorse the need to ask the fundamental questions around 'distribution' and 'inequality' in this new digital age. This is because understanding how these 'corporate restructures' would potentially impact the lives of workers is imperative. Using a panoptic lens, the prospects for African countries are bleak as 4IR represents a misfit as it ignores current conditions and contexts. The question is: should Africa embrace or not embrace 4IR. Under what conditions should 4IR be embraced to benefit Africa?

Oke and Fernandes (2020) in particular raise the importance of understanding employability and its requirements as it is envisioned that job specifications and the required professional competencies will evolve as 4IR continues to grow and change the nature of work. This is because the adoption of technological optimism easily makes people susceptible to accepting that casualties are a necessary part of any revolution. Revolutions should not leave people worse off than when the revolution began. Revolutions should be life enhancing and transformative. According to the United Nations Department of Economic and Social Affairs (UNDESA) (2017: 18), the current narrative is that "job-destroying effects of new workplace technology are counterbalanced by job creation effects". This depicts the idea that jobs are lost, as part of the revolution, but these knock-on effects would be counter-acted by the jobs created. However, the reality is that more jobs have been lost so far than those that have been created. UNDESA (2017) warns against such optimism which has the power to deflect attention from other pressing challenges. As pointed out, "simply extrapolating current trends of technological acceleration could be misleading, as not every temporarily accelerating growth path turns into exponential growth" (UNDESA 2017: 7). Moreover, reliance on findings based on data collected in affluent countries could be context-specific and therefore misleading. While job losses are said to be inevitable, the awareness of the implications and how to mitigate the social and economic challenges is critical to government's ability to respond appropriately (Manda and Dhaou 2019). With 4IR in its infancy, there are limited studies that offer an appreciative inquiry as a base of how to mitigate and manage the adverse implications. Although Mpofu and Nicolaides

(2019) acknowledge that 4IR will progressively alter how we live and work, and caution that this revolution is unlike previous revolutions as it brings with it increased volatility, chaos, disruption and uncertainty. For this reason, Mpofu and Nicolaides (2019) assert that changes brought by 4IR need to be heeded given their rapid pace. The World Economic Forum (2016), observes that change which may result in massive job losses, or the coming of new opportunities, needs to be managed with targeted action to achieve the desired results. However, this revolution and its aftermath present a blurred picture, making planning increasingly difficult. To complicate matters, the COVID-19 pandemic hit the world at the beginning of 2020 with revolutionary characteristics of equal measure as the 4IR.

Owing to the rapid infections in a short space of time, on 11 March 2020 the World Health Organization declared COVID-19 a pandemic (Lone and Ahmad 2020). In response, governments the world-over began implementing lockdowns as they were promoted as an effective COVID-19 management tool to saving lives (United Nations 2020). While necessary, the measures to curb the spread of COVID-19 quickly demonstrated the reality that this pandemic would go beyond being a mere health crisis. The same disruptions caused by the Fourth Industrial revolution could be said about the COVID-19 disruptions. The disruptions did not affect all businesses in the same way. Those services that were considered to be essential remained open, while most were forced to close due to government-sanctioned lockdowns. Some businesses managed to shift employees to work remotely from home, while others could not manoeuvre out of the conundrum (Bartika, Bertrandb, Cullenc, Glaeserd, Lucac, & Stanton 2020). The conundrum affected businesses with physical plant and equipment that is operated on site. At the beginning of April 2020, the rise in unemployment was bigger than during the Great Depression – as poor workers were hardest hit as firms closed down to curb the spread of COVID-19 - employees in the bottom 20% of earners were the most affected (Elliott 2020). It is clear that even those firms and countries that had embraced the 4IR were also affected by COVID-19. While the biological origins of COVID-19 are not clear, its emergence as a consequence of the 4IR manipulation shows how both can be parasitic and destructive. The next section looks briefly at country experiences.

An overview of country experiences: United States, Germany and France

In the United States of America, many small businesses encountered dislocations before the promulgation of the Coronavirus Aid, Relief, and Economic Security (CARES) Act. Bartika, Bertrandb, Cullenc, Glaeserd, Lucac and Stanton (2020) reveal that about 43% of businesses shut down their operations because of COVID-19 reduced demand for products and concerns by employees of their health. The sectors, which recorded most job losses above 50%, were in the arts and culture, retail, personal services, hospitality and food services sectors while finance, real estate and other professional services managed to shift to remote production (Bartika et al. 2020). Their study also found out that many of these small firms did not have cash at hand revealing their fragility as they were forced to seek for loans or face bankruptcy. This also underscores the precarious positions and vulnerabilities, which many firms faced.

Germany's unemployment rate was lower than that of the United States because the government implemented a scheme called the Kurzarbeit (short-time work programme) which subsidised wages (Elliott 2020). Towards the end of April 2020, the scheme was assisting about 10 million people while the country posted an unemployment rate of 5.8% (Kretchmer 2020). The same measures were applied in France from April to June 2020, whereby about 10 million workers from the private sector were receiving government support through a scheme called chômage partiel (partial employment or short-time working) representing one in two employees (Kretchmer 2020: 10). This figure represents a large proportion of the French workforce affected by the vicissitudes of COVID-19. This also highlighted the precarity and vulnerability of work in circumstances of uncertainty.

African experiences

In South Africa, the percentage of unemployment was higher than that of the European countries reviewed here. With the coming of the pandemic, many businesses were closed and consequently, affecting many people especially the youth. This resonates with the observation that millions of workers will be jobless because of COVID-19 (International Labour Organization 2020b). In many

African countries' borders remained closed from March to September, 2020. As such, people who engage in the import and export businesses were paralysed as they waited for the lockdown to be removed hence remained jobless. For instance, Botswana, like other countries in the region, was locked down for six months affecting both private and public sector entities, schools, the self-employed, small businesses and disrupted the social lives of people.

According to information provided by Commission for Conciliation, Mediation and Arbitration (CCMA) of South Africa, there were 1800 retrenchment cases at the end of March 2020 during the South African lockdown period (Smit 2020). Between April 2020 and June 2020, a total of 98 818 workers were subjects of retrenchments (Smit 2020). This unprecedented 156% increase in retrenchment cases (Smit 2020) demonstrates the massive job devastation that came with COVID-19. The South African labour market had started to feel the effects of new technologies and automated services in the workplace as Standard Bank announced the closure of 91 branches, equating to 1200 jobs lost (Mzekandaba 2020). In addition to this unemployment plight, the economy of South Africa is anticipated to contract by 7.2 per cent because of the pandemic (Government of South Africa 2020). In his 2020 Budget speech, the Finance Minister Tito Mboweni confirmed that unemployment would be the biggest challenge that the country would face in the short and immediate future (Government of South Africa 2020). With unemployment comes destitution and desperation as indicative of a dual blow inflicted on society by 4IR and COVID-19.

As confirmed by Altman and Group (2020: 2), "the balancing act of managing COVID-19 while also sustaining livelihoods and overall human welfare is especially challenging in the context of SA's extreme inequality, unemployment and poverty". When South Africa entered the pandemic, it had an unemployment rate of 29 percent (Altman and Group 2020) and according to Statistics South Africa (2020), this had since increased to 30.1 percent. Apart from increased unemployment, COVID-19 significantly changed the nature of work at the workplace. Owing to the lockdown restrictions, businesses were encouraged to adopt the working from home norm. Even as South Africa eased out of level 5 to level 3 and then level 1, businesses continued to implement measures which promoted working from home. This new '(ab)normal' has pushed various industries and society as a whole to rely on executing everyday duties remotely (Golinelli, Boetto, Carullo, Landini and Fatntini 2020). While somewhat incredibly helpful in keeping industries and teaching and learning operational and reducing exposure to the virus, moving into the 4IR realm through technology adoption came with unemployment which negatively affected livelihood strategies and the economy as did COVID-19. The International Labour Organization (2020a) reports that the youth were already vulnerable before the outbreak of COVID-19 and this has brought great hardships among them across the globe. The economic crisis induced by COVID-19 will result in dislocation of the youth from the labour market in the foreseeable future (International Labour Organization 2020b). The reverberations related to unemployment may persist in the short and long hauls. Both 4IR and COVID-19 conspired and dislodged, displaced, disrupted and destroyed lives, livelihoods, dreams, professions and jobs and embodied a hierarchy of vulnerabilities – these vulnerabilities are illustrated later.

Finding solutions to the unemployment crisis caused by the 4IR and Covid-19

Ferreira, Reitzle, Lee, Freitas, Santos, Alcoforado and Vondracek (2015) argue that Governments alongside institutions like universities should come up with solutions for mass unemployment induced by both COVID-19 and the 4IR both in the short and long terms. They also observe that the crisis is complex because of different contextual and personal factors present in this new population of the unemployed. The implications are that new practices and policies have to be formulated to ameliorate the profound vulnerabilities and precarity induced by the two phenomena.

David, Blusteina, Ryan Duffyb, Joaquim, Ferreira, Valerie Cohen-Scalid, Cinamone and Blake 2020) suggest a research agenda that analyses each individual by circumstance, their prospects of re-employment, the size of their family and their living conditions to ascertain targeted interventions which may include psycho-social support, temporary government assistance; re-training and relocation and so on. For Bende, due to these huge transformations occasioned by COVID-19 and the 4IR, up-skilling and re-skilling are a necessary part of transformative education system that is required going forward (Brende 2019). As such, for career development, promoting collective empowerment and raising consciousness among the youths about a transforming landscape would be of critical importance in the near and immediate future. The job losses because of COVID-19 and 4IR mutually reinforce the vicious cycle of poverty.

Based on the shares of their patented technologies; China, Taiwan, The United Kingdom, the United States, France, Japan, Germany, the Republic of Korea, Switzerland and the Netherlands (UNIDO 2020) own the means of production. This makes these 10 economies the digitally-ready countries that are enjoying unprecedented economic prosperity (Department of the Presidency 2020) as creators and sellers of new technologies (UNIDO 2020). As the frontrunners, this has already set up a precedent of the unequal gains that will benefit these countries. With global access to the internet and continued reliance on technologies, third-world countries are an untapped market as a significant portion of the population remain without internet-access (Azhar 2017). Therefore, the idea that a developing country like South Africa could benefit its workforce by employing 4IR is entirely refuted because the means of production are owned by other economies which profit from promoting new technologies as the key to progressive change. This is confirmed by Azhar (2017: 104) who revealed that "estimates already suggest that the global digital economy represents a staggering $4 trillion industry, accounting for over 5% of the GDP in rich countries". This not only contextualizes the economic disadvantage which acts as a barrier for the prosperity of all countries, but illustrates how the retrenchments caused by the 4IR are an extension of the underlying capitalist system which continually benefits the narrow elite located in a few advanced capitalist economies (Azhar 2017). It is evident that not only do these disruptions affect work, they also disrupt ways of life of ordinary citizens, including indigenous ways of life and their production systems through the theft and plunder of raw materials found in Africa that prop the production of 4IR technologies and gadgets.

For South Africa, the labour market is key to ensuring social inclusion because employment secures financial means (National Planning Commission 2019). The financial means in turn provide access to a broad range of socioeconomic needs which satisfy individual well-being like education, housing, healthcare and so on. However, with the rising unemployment due to these factors, citizens will find themselves in a situation of disadvantage, vulnerability and precarity. South Africa is known for having the highest inequality rate in the world (National Planning Commission 2019) and the long-standing unemployment crisis adds immense vulnerability to an already dire situation as the COVID-19 -triggered retrenchments exacerbate further the unemployment and inequality situation.

For instance, COVID-19 is a biological challenge that is affecting the global population. Altman and Group (2020) are of the view that creative ways must be found to contain the virus while pursuing other critical socio-economic imperatives. This is in line with the argument by the World Health Organisation that the determinants of individual health are influenced by access to power, money and resources at the local, individual and global levels (World Health Organization 2020). Furthermore, one's socio-economic class, ethnicity and gender also mediate these factors to entrench inequities (NEJM Catalyst 2017). For example, Denmark managed to handle the pandemic better because its social protection policies played a role in curbing the severity of the impact of the pandemic due to low inequality, favourable governmental policies and availability of healthcare (NEJM Catalyst 2017) which were instrumental in finding the 'right' balance. Because South Africa is not yet in the league of Denmark, it is evident that the embedded inequalities and poverty juxtaposed with rising unemployment complicate matters further. Demirbaş, Bozkurt and Yorğun (2020: v) note the impacts as follows:

> The epidemic has made almost all of us equal spiritually, physically and socially at a global level. It has created a new awareness in all areas including health, education, income inequality, poverty, unemployment, migration, the climate crisis, and access to basic human needs. The epidemic has nourished selfishness in one sense, and reduced solidarity. It has caused loneliness, medical as well as psychological problems, and information pollution. The epidemic has taken the fear of death from the individual and spread it through society. On the other hand, it has increased the need for solidarity and strengthened our common sense of fate. Therefore, our need for understanding based on social cohesion has gained more importance.

With the high inequality in South Africa (National Planning Commission 2020) notes the skewed access to healthcare and employment, and suggests that when addressing the pandemic attention should be paid to the severity of its impacts at the grassroots. For example, with the COVID-19 outbreak, a black vendor who supports herself and her family, without qualification, was most affected by the lockdown. With retailers having offered the option to shop online and/or via WhatsApp for groceries, even with the ease of restrictions, this vendor may have reduced income because of the convenience that has come with increased digitization. This income constraint reduces her ability to access even public healthcare should she fall ill because she does not have money for transport, medication and food which further increases her hardship (NEJM Catalyst 2017). Struggling to survive, she is unable to match the service offered by big retails chain stores. And as a woman who is self-employed in the informal sector, she receives no relief form the stimulus package. Like others, she is expected to apply for the COVID-19 grant from the government which is not enough to cover living expenses, particularly with the rise in food prices. Cases of theft from the grant were also reported in the media.

Despite the government providing relief and stimulus packages for businesses, many employers were protecting their interests to maximize accumulation of profit in an economic crisis (De Klerk 2020). The same author observes that Cosatu requested the government to introduce a moratorium on retrenchments by private firms that receive bail out from the Government during COVID-19 crisis. This demonstrates how more attention needs to be paid to the grassroots because the intended support may not be reaching them. This is in sync with the Altman and Group (2020) who opine that financial support to firms in distress is necessary to reduce the damage. Very little support was provided to the informal sector during the lockdown and as the unemployment swelled, Altman and Group (2020) are of the view that economic recovery is likely to be very difficult. It thus makes sense to establish a livelihood strategy and economic stimulus based on current circumstances of disruption of the status quo, dislodgement, displacements and destruction of the old order for the new '(ab)normal'. After all, it is the citizens in the informal economy that will be expected to support themselves and their families and contribute to the economy, while firms in private businesses put their bottom-line interests over the workforce. Without the means to improve the economy, the rate of unemployment could permanently increase (Altman and Group 2020). Altman and Group (2020) argue that new ways and strategies have to be found to address the variegated vulnerabilities and precarities that exist in circumstances of COVID-19 and 4IR.

While the 4IR may revolutionize lives, it also displaces human beings from their livelihood strategies and deprives them inadvertently of opportunities for subsistence and social mobility as COVID-19 did. As remarked by Mpofu and Nicolaides (2019: 13), "technology will increasingly replace the human employee so that in reality, there is more likely to be far greater inequality than there is today with enhanced discrimination". The disruption of labour markets and displacement of employees by new technologies increases the personal, social and economic apprehensions that employees have about surviving without their employers (Mpofu and Nicolaides 2019). As observed by Van Drie (2019), in previous industrial revolutions there has been a separation between capital and labour, and this allowed for the exchange of labour for income. With automation, 4IR demonstrates that capital no longer relies on human labour, causing increased precarity. As estimated, this precarity will 'affect 1.1 billion workers (49 percent of jobs) and taking away US\$12.7 billion in wages' (Balliester and Elsheikhi 2018: 12). About 67 percent of jobs will be made redundant in developing countries and little is known regarding the new jobs to be created in the new industrial landscape (Balliester and Elsheikhi 2018). Furthermore, as cautioned by Mpofu and Nicolaides (2019:14), "half of today's work activities might be automated by 2055, but this could also occur much earlier or later depending on the several factors, in addition to other economic conditions". Mpofu and Nicolaides (2019) state that technology is crucial if it supports enhancing standards of living of citizens. This illustrates how automation threatens not just jobs, but also the material well-being of people, such that a critical understanding of these kinds of effects and threats is imperative.

Manda and Dhaou (2019) observe that recent trends show how technological change is increasing wage inequalities between both workers and firms. Van Drie (2019) observes that large firms are transforming production and the movement of goods by using autonomous robotics. As such, computers and robots may command an absolute advantage when compared to labour (Balliester and Elsheikhi 2018). Apart from being a cheaper form of labour, the use of robots by the international business community has been implemented because their use also significantly reduces the reliance on human beings since robots do not fall ill or take bathroom breaks (Van Drie 2019). And because of this automation, "developing countries can no longer depend on their comparative advantage of having an abundance of cheap labour. Hence, one can argue that the development strategy by way of industrialisation may become unworkable" (Van Drie 2019: 5). Under such circumstances, firms from developed countries may relocate to their home countries where a majority of their consumers stay (Van Drie 2019). Such a process is called reshoring and usually ends up with a loss of jobs in developing countries leading to greater informality (UNDESA 2017). The perpetuation of job losses have been a hallmark of 4IR and COVID-19 thus far.

While noted that it is impossible for jobs to be completely overhauled by automation, these labour-saving technologies have contributed to higher levels of under-employment (UNDESA 2017). This increased competition for new technologies, makes employees less valuable and as the reliance of these automated processes and robotics increase, the greater the likelihood that the conditions of service for the workforce may worsen. With the changing nature of work impacting the type and quality of work available, it follows to question what this will mean for the security of workers in respect to the retirement provisions. UNDESA (2017) remarks that indeed flexible, insecure and precarious work comes with fewer work benefits and welfare protection. Trade unions have traditionally organised workers and bargained on their behalf however, it is unclear if unions will be able to continue doing so with a declining workforce. Because of the social costs, central to responding to 4IR is figuring out the ways in which humans can be placed at the centre of all transformations, particularly in developing countries or the non-digitally-ready countries. A large portion of the South African population is found in the informal sector and the problem with job losses that technology causes is that more people become vulnerable to exploitative working conditions and corresponding job insecurity.

Without the frontrunner advantage, adopting these technologies might be futile especially because "the quantity of jobs, disruptive changes to industries and business models will also affect the quality, skills requirements and day-to-day content of virtually every job" (World Economic Forum 2016: 17). UNDESA (2017) warns against excessive pessimism regarding the perceived socioeconomic impacts of 4IR as it would give the impression that it goes beyond the capacity of decision-makers. The world economic system has largely benefited privileged nations, which have the capacity to produce and distribute products (Christofis 2019). UNIDO (2019) reports on this trend by observing that technological breakthrough (4IR) is once again driving the world between leaders, followers and laggards. In the development and diffusion of innovations, patenting and exporting activities become important (UNIDO 2019). The 10 economies listed earlier are likely compete among each other for further economic advantage and domination (Christofis 2019). With the core concentration and weak development of new technologies in emerging economies likely to compete (UNIDO 2019), it is clear these countries will face challenges related to the adoption of the 4IR. Based on this observation, it is important to pause and reflect on 4IR enthusiasm and interrogate its value (Department of the Presidency 2020). Simply mobilising resources to promote 4IR with limited corresponding evidence to what it actually means; how it affects countries in its different stages of development; and how countries can maximise its benefits and not be harmed is a critical component in humanizing this transformation (Department of the Presidency 2019). This is particularly important for developing countries where poverty, inequality and unemployment rates are relatively high against a backdrop of inadequate provisioning of basic services such as electricity, housing, education, health including water and sanitation. The following questions are pertinent: what role will 4IR play in context of COVID-19; and what are their combined effects on society, health, water and sanitation?

While ICT indices measure the digital developments of countries over time, South Africa has ranked consistently poor (Department of the Presidency 2020). A major concern noted by UNIDO (2019) is the integration of countries still developing basic industrial capabilities. Many firms in developing countries are still using 3IR technologies comprising basic ICT and automation making it difficult to exploit 4IR technologies (UNIDO 2019). While South Africa performs well in the infrastructure development indices, it performs poorly with respect to internet usage, skills and digital awareness, (Department of the Presidency 2020). It is for this reason that UNDESA (2017) suggests the necessity of governments to create an environment which ensures development, adaptation and diffusion of new technologies that are country-context specific. For example, part of the reason why South Africa scores poorly is because the 'untapped markets' are situated in rural areas and as reported by the Department of the Presidency (2020), only less than half of the rural population in South Africa are connected to the internet. In both rural and urban areas, those that are connected are unable to use the internet due to data unaffordability (Department of the Presidency 2020). This is why understanding the impact of technology is important. Therefore, policy measures must go beyond infrastructure provision to supporting the use of these technologies

(UNDESA 2017), and it is critical to stimulate the opportunities for home-based enterprises at a time when many people are being displaced. UNDESA (2017) observes that adoption of technological advances is not easy in the informal sector because of the preponderance of women and young people who are engaged in informal activities particularly in rural areas. As reported by the Department of the Presidency (2020), digital inequality is high among rural dwellers, particularly rural women with low education and income levels. In effect, the introduction of 4IR without the due diligence affects not just formal employment, but also jeopardises the livelihood strategies of the informal sector and its contributions to GDP. The above calls into question the state of readiness of South Africa and African countries for 4IR. Moreover, it illustrates how precedence has been placed on the promotion of 4IR technologies through infrastructure development with little priority being given to the capacitation and development of people. Investment in SMME development would be critical in creating jobs and addressing vulnerability.

Discussion

The 4IR and COVID-19 revolutions have disrupted the status quo, dislodged, displaced, destroyed the old order and in their place a new order of despair, vulnerability, fragility and precarity in a pandemic milieu. The opportunities are not yet clear to the retrenched workers has despair and vulnerability take hold. For Mpofu and Nicolaides (2019) only a few have so far benefited including the corrupt ones. It is not a convincing premise to accept casualties as workers despair as a necessary part of the revolution given the devastation. The job creation effects of 4IR have not been evident as much as the retrenchments. Similarly, the layoffs because of COVID-19 are as pronounced as economic depressions.

Business closures are rampant due to reduced demand for products and services affecting mostly the arts and culture, retail, personal services, hospitality and food services (Bartika et al. 2020). Similarly, there is evidence suggesting that many small firms did not have cash at hand mirroring their fragility as they were forced into bankruptcy or debt. Small businesses in the import and export of goods were paralysed under the lockdown, as they remained jobless. Before COVID-19, the youth were already vulnerable. This massive joblessness among the youth has serious repercussions as it may cause restlessness and violence. The shattered lives, livelihoods, dreams, professions and jobs can be heaped into a hierarchy of vulnerabilities as exemplified in fig 1 below. What is clear is that the crisis has many dimensions related to different contexts and personal factors requiring new ways to address vulnerabilities and precarity. What is clear is that the job losses from COVID-19 and 4IR mutually buttress the vicious cycle of poverty, entrench the inequalities and deepen unemployment. In turn, the enduring unemployment crisis exacerbates the vulnerabilities and inequalities brought by COVID-19 and 4IR. The disruption of labour markets destroys livelihood strategies and lives. It is evident that the widespread introduction of robots not only threatens jobs, but the lives of people as they succumbed to COVID-19 under Covid-1 COVID-19 ventilators, which are products of the 4IR. At the same time, for those still working, insecure and precarious work has fewer benefits and little welfare protection. People's vulnerabilities increase because many of them work in the informal sector where incomes are not always guaranteed and hence vulnerable to the vicissitudes of endogenous factors such as tight cash and lack of skills as well as exogenous factors such as COVID-19 and 4IR.

Theorisation on vulnerability

I define vulnerability the absence of a proportionate shield against threats and risks (whether real or imagined) posed by natural and man-made stimuli such as earthquakes, storms, strong winds/hurricanes, tsunamis, technology, diseases/pandemics (like Covi-19). Vulnerability results in multiple effects. I categorise the effects based on their properties to induce vulnerability. The effects are both positive and negative. I will present the negative effects first. The *Helplessness effects* represent circumstances in which subjects have limited options to whom to turn for assistance as systems are overwhelmed. These systems include systems of governments, in communities, of Non-Governmental Organisations and firms in the private sector that fail to respond to the equally overwhelming needs and multiple wants, for instance, for medicines and jobs, from vulnerable citizens – vulnerable to disease such as COVID-19, which did not have a cure and 4IR technologies, which displaced them from work.

Hopelessness effects involve losing confidence in the above institutions and their systems to deliver food, jobs and vaccines in the wake of the onslaught of the pandemic and new technologies arising from the 4IR. *Stress effects* represents the pressures and strains induced by diminishing prospects to work and redundancy of current skills and the need to re-skill and re-learn when opportunities are dwindling and context in which prospects of hospitalisation are real in a COVID-19 milieu. *Depression effects* staying in isolation and observing engenders feelings of misery and despair which may result in depression and withdrawal due to inability to see prospects of normality as was present in the old status quo. *Inequality effects* result from the inequalities and inequities created by the new status quo or new '(ab)normal' in which the well-off are cushioned from the negative impacts of the pandemic as well as the technologies of the 4IR as they enjoy uninterrupted quality lifestyles with little disruptions against which they are cushioned by the availability of multiple resource streams of a technological, asset and monetary nature. *Poverty effects* represent the impoverishment of the masses of the people as a consequence of disruptions arising from both 4IR and the legacy of COVID-19 – of retrenchments and job losses, loss of incomes, hospitalisations, loss of assets including houses, increasing debt and so on.

Paralysis effects this represents a status of dysfunctionality of systems and individuals to function with expected normalcy leading to inaction and widespread failure to act. *Corruption effects* manifest in the emergence and surge in corruption cases arising from the procurement of personal protective equipment in circumstances of wholesale desperation. *Governance effects* – the role of government was elevated. This was evident from the imposition of laws and regulations, norms and standards of conduct and behaviours of citizens during state-imposed lockdowns. *Ventilation effects* represent circumstances in which individuals, communities and countries cannot breathe and require ventilators to assist in breathing as a 'solution' to the effects. Breathing here represents the state of being operational or to function properly. *Co-morbidity effects* denotes how each individual manages to cope with COVID-19 and manage their communities to prevent infecting oneself and others. This also applies to countries, how well they managed the pandemic was predicated on their state of (un)readiness. *Death effects* – all above singly or in combination conspire to cause death. *Fear effects* result from death that looms from the totality of effects from COVID-19 and 4IR. *Uncertainty effects* represent the absence of vaccines and a scenario shrouded in ambiguity and insecurity, which nurtures further uncertainty. *4IR effects* manifest when others are left behind in terms of technology adoption (for the good or bad) and the increase in digital inequality and other inequalities rooted in industrial revolutions. I will now present the positive effects.

Oneness effects – people in their fears rallied together in oneness as they came together to face the scourge of COVID-19 and used technology to connect as humanity. This is aligned to *technology adoption effects*, which was evident in circumstances where there was widespread use of technology to buy goods and services and for communication purposes. *Recovery effects* these manifested in the show of empathy, care, love, belonging and affection to each other and the recovery rates from COVID-19. Sources of vulnerability include a poor asset base at the individual level, prevailing inequalities in society, poor social protection policies and weak health care systems at the state and sub-national levels, which also acted as accelerators and decelerators of vulnerability. The legacy of COVID-19 and 4IR are socio-economic in nature as both individuals, businesses and communities are affected physically, economically and socially, for the good or the bad. I shall paint a picture of three hypothetical cases to illustrate the impact of 4IR and COVID-19 on people in society. The first case is that of an elderly woman who relies on a state awarded social grant and for her grandchildren who also receive child support grants. She has no additional sources of income. She is not on a private medical scheme as the others in the hierarchy of vulnerabilities. In a context of COVID-19, she needs soap, sanitisers, and masks and to social distance when she stays in a cramped and overcrowded two-roomed shack where soaps and sanitisers were already a problem before COVID-19. Electricity was a challenge since they relied on illegal connections, which are often busted by the Energy supplier. She has no internet connectivity, which jeopardises her grand children's education because they cannot participate in online learning which the 4IR beckons. She belongs to Third Order vulnerabilities as shown in Fig 1 below, which I named the *Ordering of vulnerabilities/Hierarchy of vulnerabilities framework*. It has a wider base representing her vulnerabilities.

The second case is that of a teacher or lecturer or a police officer or nurse who belongs to the Second Order Vulnerability category. They are all on stated-supported medical schemes; own decent housing comprising four bedrooms in a suburban area while their children attend private schools. Their vulnerabilities increase or reduce depending on individual circumstances and tend to narrow as they have command over the resources to ward off vulnerability as this group generally can afford sanitisers and masks including the opportunity to self-isolate, and their children being able to participate in online learning and themselves online teaching (in the case of teachers).

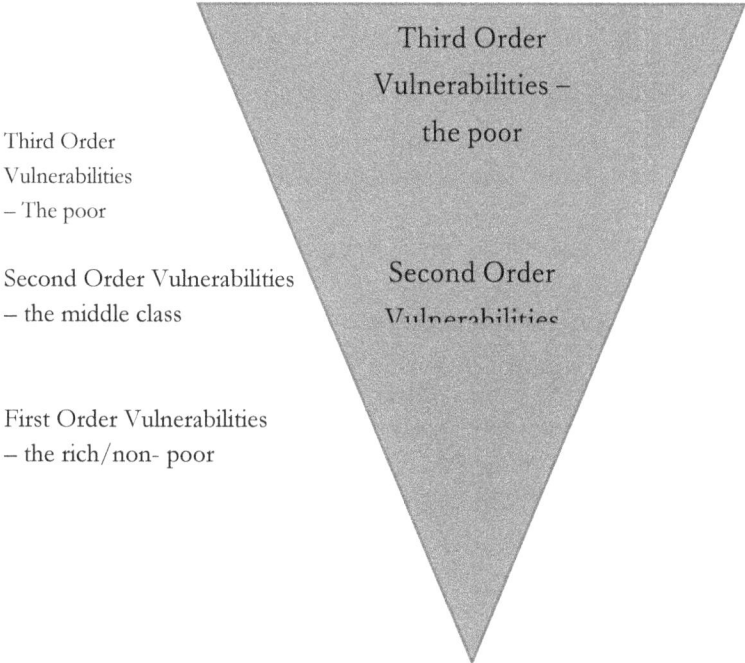

Third Order
Vulnerabilities
– The poor

Second Order Vulnerabilities
– the middle class

First Order Vulnerabilities
– the rich/non- poor

Third Order
Vulnerabilities –
the poor

Second Order
Vulnerabilities

Fig 1: Ordering of vulnerabilities/Hierarchy of vulnerabilities framework

The third case is case is that of a rich person who has cash, assets in the form of expensive houses and cars both locally and abroad, who is on a private medical aid scheme and the children are receiving home schooling. Instead of facing the vulnerabilities of COVID-19, they migrate to their Island home where there were very few reported cases of COVID-19. They went with their children's tutors and enjoyed the benefits of 4IR undergirded by internet connectivity as their lives were largely uninterrupted by COVID-19, save for the travel restrictions that they had to comply with and the local social distancing regimes in their safety havens. These belong to First Order Vulnerabilities, which reduce to close to zero based on available resources – which include money, medical and educational facilities and houses in safe havens. However, this does not mean that they and their staff are not prone to contracting COVID-19 in the safe havens because COVID-19 affects all including presidents and the rich and famous people following exposure. This Hierarchy of vulnerabilities which is also called Ordering of vulnerabilities applies in both rich and poor countries where inequalities exist on a continuum of rich and poor people as defined in that society.

Given the foregoing, I identify the following properties of vulnerabilities. These include:

Cost factor/affordability - Vulnerability comes with costs in both monetary and material terms. It depends on the member's status and endowments in terms of how they fare in managing their vulnerabilities.

Severity – vulnerability hits others harder than some in society. Some people are more likely to face more vulnerabilities than others. Some groups of people do better than others as shown in Ordering/Hierarchy of Vulnerabilities Framework.

Intersectionality with gender – vulnerabilities affect women more they do to men as there was an upsurge in cases of Gender Based Violence during the times of COVID-19 pandemic lockdowns.

Omnipresence – vulnerabilities are always there or are always present.

Magnitude – vulnerabilities differ in magnitude, scale and depth with respect to their impacts.

Potency – the strength of each episode differs by circumstance or event. Some events affect everyone as the COVID-19 but with differences by status of either being rich or poor.

Propensity – some people may be predisposed to certain events than others based on underlying circumstances.

Avoidability – some vulnerabilities can be cushioned against by assets and resources and effective policies and systems.

Aversion some people are more averse to vulnerability than others are and build appropriate mechanisms to mitigate vulnerability such as subscribing to medical aid schemes and insurance.

Understanding the properties of vulnerabilities is important to inform both policy and practice in the formulation of migratory interventions at the individual, household and community levels. For example, *propensity* allows the identification of individuals or communities predisposed to certain events than others based on underlying circumstances.

Conclusion

This Chapter looked at COVID-19 and 4IR and their effects on the workplace and workforce. Both assumed revolutionary omnipresent with severe disruptive effects to the status quo by dislodging, displacing, and destroying the old order as a new order emerges. Both phenomena make planning increasingly difficult because of these disruptions and increase the precarity and vulnerability of workers and jobs. With unemployment comes destitution and desperation as indicative of a dual blow inflicted on society by 4IR and COVID-19. 4IR as with COVID-19 threatens not just jobs, but also the material well-being of people. This pertinent in developing countries where poverty, inequality and unemployment rates are relatively high. Some of the effects of the two phenomena include helplessness effects; hopelessness effects, stress effects, depression effects, inequality effects, poverty effects, paralysis effects, corruption effects, uncertainty effects and others. The Chapter also posited a Hierarchy of Vulnerabilities Framework as well as some properties of vulnerabilities as its key contribution to knowledge.

Acknowledgement

The author received funding from the Department of Science and Innovation and National Research Foundation-funded South African Research Chairs (SARChI) Initiative at the University of KwaZulu-Natal. The views expressed in this Chapter are not necessarily the views of the Department of Science and Innovation and the National Research Foundation or its management or governance structures.

References

Altman, M. and Group, C.E., (2020). 'Top Covid-19 policy priorities for protecting employment'. Retrieved from: https://covid19economicideas.org/wp-content/uploads/2020/05/Priorities-to-Protect-Employment_in_Covid_Altman_020620.pdf .

Azhar, S. (2017) 'The Fourth Industrial Revolution and Labour: A Marxian Theory of Digital Production', *Review of Socio-Economic Perspectives, 2(1),* 103-124. DOI: 10.19275/RSEP011.

Balliester, T. and Elsheikhi, A. (2018) 'The future of work: A literature review', ILO Research Department Working Paper, 29. Retrieved from: https://www.ilo.org/wcmsp5/groups/public/---dgreports/inst/documents/publication/wcms_625866.pdf.

Bartika, AW, Bertrandb, M., Cullenc, Z., Glaeserd, EL., Lucac, M. and Stanton, C. (2020) 'The impact of COVID-19 on small business outcomes and expectations', *PNAS*, 117 (30), 177656-17666.

Blustein, D. L. (2019) *The importance of work in an age of uncertainty: The eroding work experience in America.* New York: Oxford University Press.

Christofis, N. (2019) 'World-Systems Theory', In: Romaniuk S., Thapa M., Marton P. (Eds.), *The Palgrave Encyclopedia of Global Security Studies.* New York: Palgrave Macmillan.

De Klerk, A. (2020) 'Cosatu calls for moratorium on retrenchments', 01 May 2020, *TimesLive.*

Retrieved from: https://www.timeslive.co.za/politics/2020-05-01-cosatu-calls-for-moratorium-on-retrenchments/.

Department of the Presidency. (2020) 'Digital futures: South Africa's Digital readiness for the Fourth Industrial Revolution'. Retrieved from https://www.tralac.org/documents/resources/by-country/south-africa/3902-draft-digital-futures-south-africas-digital-readiness-for-the-fourth-industrial-revolution-npc-july-2020/file.html.

Demirbaş, D., Bozkurt. V. and Yorğun, S. (2020) *The Covid-19 pandemic and its economic, social, and political impacts.* Istanbul: Istanbul University Press

Elliott. L. (2020) 'Unemployment due to Covid-19 is surely worth more than a footnote'. Retrieved from https://www.theguardian.com/business/2020/may/10/unemployment-due-to-Covid-19-is-surely-worth-more-than-a-footnote.

Ferreira, J. A., Reitzle, M., Lee, B., Freitas, R. A., Santos, E. R., Alcoforado, L. and Vondracek, F. W. (2015) 'Configurations of unemployment, reemployment, and psychological well-being: A longitudinal study of unemployed individuals in Portugal' *Journal of Vocational Behavior, 91*, 54–64. https://doi.org/10.1016/j.jvb.2015.09.004.

Golinelli, D., Boetto, E., Carullo, G., Landini, M.P. and Fantini, M.P. (2020) 'How the Covid-19 pandemic is favouring the adoption of digital technologies in healthcare: a rapid literature

review'. Retrieved from:
https://doi.org/10.1101/2020.04.26.20080341.

Government of South Africa. (2020) 'Minister Tito Mboweni: 2020
Supplementary Budget Speech'. Retrieved from
https://www.gov.za/speeches/minister-tito-mboweni-2020-
supplementary-budget-speech-24-jun-2020-0000.

International Labour Organization (2020a) 'World Employment
and Social Outlook – Trends, 2020'. Retrieved from:
https://www.ilo.org/global/research/global-
reports/weso/2020/lang–en/index.htm.

International Labour Organization. (2020b) 'Young workers will be
hit hard by COVID-19's economic fallout'. Retrieved from:
https://iloblog.org/2020/04/15/young-workers-will-behit-hard-
by-Covid-19s-economic-fallout/.

Kretchmer, H. (2020) May. 'How coronavirus has hit employment
in G7 economies'. Retrieved from
https://www.weforum.org/agenda/2020/05/coronavirus-
unemployment-jobs-work-impact-g7-pandemic/.

Lee, M., Yun, J.J., Pyka, A., Won, D., Kodama, F., Schiuma, G.,
Park, H., Jeon, J., Park, K., Jung, K. and Yan, M.R. (2018) 'How
to respond to the fourth industrial revolution, or the second
information technology revolution? Dynamic new combinations
between technology, market, and society through open
innovation', *Journal of Open Innovation: Technology, Market, and
Complexity, 4(3)*, pp.21-40.

Lone, S.A. and Ahmad, A. (2020) 'COVID-19 pandemic – an
African perspective, Emerging Microbes & amp', *Infections*, 91,
1300-1308, DOI: 10.1080/22221751.2020.1775132.

National Planning Commission. (2019) 'South Africa's
Implementation Of The 2030 Agenda For Sustainable
Development: "solving Complex Challenges Together".
Retrieved from:
https://sustainabledevelopment.un.org/content/documents/23
402SOUTH_AFRICA_RSA_Voluntary_National_Review_Repo
rt_Final__14_June_2019.pdf.

NEJM Catalyst. (2017) 'Social Determinants of Health (SDOH)'.
Retrieved from:
https://catalyst.nejm.org/doi/full/10.1056/CAT.17.0312.

Manda, M.I. and Dhaou, S.B. (2019) 'Responding to the challenges
and opportunities in the 4th Industrial revolution in developing
countries. In Proceedings of the 12th International Conference

on Theory and Practice of Electronic Governance' (ICEGOV2019), Melbourne, VIC, Australia, Retrieved from https://doi.org/10.1145/3326365.3326398.

Mpofu, R. and Nicolaides, A. (2019) 'Frankenstein and the Fourth Industrial Revolution (4IR): Ethics and Human Rights Considerations'. Retrieved from: https://www.ajhtl.com/uploads/7/1/6/3/7163688/article_71_vol_8_5__2019_unisa.pdf.

Mzekandaba, S. (2019) 'Technology: The political response'. Brainstorm Magazine, 3 May 2019. Retrieved from: http://www.brainstormmag.co.za/technology/14559-the-political-response.

Oke, A. and Fernandes, F.A.P. (2020) 'Innovations in Teaching and Learning: Exploring the Perceptions of the Education Sector on the 4th Industrial Revolution (4IR)', *Journal of Open Innovation Technology Market and Complexity, 6(2)*, 31-48. DOI: 10.3390/joitmc6020031.

Prisecaru, P. (2016) 'Challenges of the fourth industrial revolution knowledge horizons', *Economics*, 8(1), 57-75.

Sae-Lim, P. and Jermsittiparsert, K. (2019) 'Is the fourth industrial revolution a panacea? Risks toward the fourth industrial revolution: Evidence in the Thai economy', *International Journal of Innovation, Creativity and Change*, 5(2), 732-752.

Smit, S. (2020) 'Possible lockdown retrenchments are already soaring'. Retrieved from https://mg.co.za/business/2020-06-29-possible-lockdown-retrenchments-are-already-soaring/.

Statistics South Africa. (2020) 'Improving lives through data ecosystems'. Retrieved from http://www.statssa.gov.za/?p=13411#:~:text=According%20to%20Statistics%20South%20Africa,the%20first%20quarter%20of%202020.

United Nations. (2020) 'Shared responsibility, global solidarity: Responding to the socio-economic impacts of COVID-19'. Retrieved from: https://unsdg.un.org/sites/default/files/2020-03/SG-Report-Socio-Economic-Impact-of-Covid19.pdf.

United Nations Department of Economic and Social Affairs. (2017) 'Frontier issues: The impact of the technological revolution on labour markets and income distribution'. Retrieved from https://www.un.org/development/desa/dpad/wp-content/uploads/sites/45/publication/2017_Aug_Frontier-Issues-1.pdf.

United Nations Department of Economic and Social Affairs. (n.d). 'Sustainable development'. Retrieved from https://sdgs.un.org/goals/goal9.

United Nations Industrial Development Organization. (2019) 'Industrial Development Report, (2020). Industrializing in the digital age'. Retrieved from https://www.unido.org/sites/default/files/files/2019-11/UNIDO_IDR2020-MainReport_overview.pdf.

Van Drie, O.R.J. (2019) 'The relevance of Marx and social economic policy in addressing the socioeconomic disparities emerging from the Fourth Industrial Revolution'. Unpublished MA thesis, Leiden University. Retrieved from: https://openaccess.leidenuniv.nl/bitstream/handle/1887/68426/VAN%20DRIE%2C%20Oscar%20-%20MA%20IR%20GPE%20Thesis%20-%20Marx%20Relevance%20in%20Light%20of%20the%204IR%20-%20FINAL.pdf?sequence=1.

World Economic Forum, (2016) 'The future of jobs: Employment, skills and workforce strategy for the fourth industrial revolution'. In, *Global challenge insight report. Geneva: World Economic Forum.* Retrieved from: http://www.hsrc.ac.za/uploads/pageContent/9352/WEF_Future_of_Jobs%20(002).pdf.

World Health Organization. (2020) 'Social determinants of health'. Retrieved from: https://www.who.int/social_determinants/sdh_definition/en/.

Xu, M., David, J.M. and Kim, S.H. (2018) 'The fourth industrial revolution: opportunities and challenges', *International Journal of Financial Research,* 9(2), 90-95.

Chapter Fourteen

Re-imagining Teaching and Learning in the Context of the COVID-19 Pandemic: Lessons for African Higher Education Institutions

Hatikanganwi Mapudzi, Christopher Chikandiwa &
Memory Muteeri

Introduction

The coronavirus disease (COVID-19) has presented unprecedented challenges to almost all aspects of the world's economy. Higher Education Institutions (HEIs), both public and private, have also experienced unparalleled yet unique challenges, which forced them to temporarily close while mapping out measures to respond to the pandemic. One of the main areas affected is teaching and learning, following the lockdown regulations put in place by many governments in Africa and abroad. This literature review chapter thus highlights some of the pertinent issues that emanated because of the outbreak of the pandemic. The chapter discusses the HEIs' experiences of the epidemic: the unanticipated disruptions, opportunities, challenges and responses, from an African perspective. The chapter also discusses the impact of COVID-19 on students' learning experiences in the universities, as well as its impact on curriculum design and delivery. Also, the chapter highlights the measures that were unveiled to save the academic calendar and more fundamentally, the implications for the future of learning during and post COVID-19.

In view of the above, the chapter proceeds as follows: we provide an overview of the COVID-19 pandemic and how it reshaped the HE sector in particular, we critically assess the concept of e-learning, some of its benefits and in particular, how the concept was adopted by HEIs as a way of course delivery to ensure the continuation of the academic calendar. Essentially, we also analyse the perceptions of students from various African HEIs, with regards to the implementation of e-learning in their various institutions. In doing this, we rely on secondary data from various sources as indicated herein. Additionally, we also deliberate on the challenges, as well as opportunities presented by the move to online learning. In presenting the opportunities, we discuss the lessons learnt by HEIs, as well as the implications for the future of HE.

Conceptualising e-learning in the context of the Covid-19

The COVID-19outbreak caught the global community unawares and up to now, the world is grappling with efforts to respond to the pandemic. In the African region, the first case of the COVID-19was reported in Egypt in February 2020, followed by Algeria in the same month (WHO 2020). Following this were many cases and at the time of writing this chapter, South Africa was leading with more than 600 thousand confirmed cases in August 2020 (National Institute for Communicable Diseases 2020). The fast spreading of the virus saw many governments laying down some lockdown restrictions, despite the negative effects that the restrictions imposed on the economy and the general populace. The education sector, at all levels, has not been spared by the effects of the pandemic. The lockdown restrictions imposed by governments meant that face to face teaching and learning had to be suspended for an unforeseeable future (OECD 2020). The risk-control decision to close schools and universities presented inconveniences, while at the same time educational institutions were presented with an opportunity for educational innovation. The education sector was forced to temporarily close while various institutions mapped the way forward to ensure the continuation of teaching and learning. Unsurprisingly, HEIs swiftly adopted online delivery models- popularly known as e-learning. In this chapter, remote and online learning, online learning and e-learning, will be used interchangeably. As institutions worldwide adapted to the situation presented by the COVID-19 by moving to e-learning on a full-time basis, this dynamic educational landscape has become of great interest amongst various stakeholders including governments, information technology and online experts, researchers, academics and policy makers, to mention a few. On that note, the section which follows describes the concept of e-learning.

Online learning occurs partly or entirely on the Internet and is made possible through the use of digital technologies. It occurs in various ways which include CD-ROM-based, network-based, intranet-based, as well as Internet-based, while it can also be presented in various formats like audio, video, text and virtual environments which allows for interaction or participation between the students and their tutors (Gilbert 2015). This means that the learning can take place in two ways: synchronously or asynchronously. In the former, learning is facilitated lively through seminars, or meetings via various platforms like Moodle, Blackboard, Zoom or Microsoft Teams and the participants should be available simultaneously. An instance of this is how the Namibia University of Science and Technology's faculty has been facilitating learning through its e-learning platform MyNust, Zoom and Microsoft Teams during the COVID-19 pandemic. The main advantage of the synchronous learning is that it allows for the participation of both the students and the lecturer and feedback can also be provided instantly. When e-learning happens asynchronously, this implies a web-based version of computer-based training (CBT), often CD-ROM based or network-based. This allows students to access course material at their own convenient time (Tarus, Gichoya & Muumbo 2015), they do not have to be online at the same time with their tutor, but they are able to engage with the learning material provided online. The key benefit of the approaches identified above entails accessibility, time and place-based flexibility (Tarus *et al.* 2015). The learning process can take place while both the lecturer and the student are geographically apart, sometimes they can engage in the comfort of their homes.

One of the main advantages of e-learning is that it encourages or forces students to take responsibility for their own learning, while at the same time it helps them to develop self-confidence and self-knowledge (Tarus *et al.* 2015). E-learning has also been hailed for promoting collaborative, constructive and lifelong learning among students, it motivates students to learn, increases students' access to learning material, hence, increased knowledge, as well as shared work resources. In doing this, e-learning helps students improve their thinking and they tend to engage more creatively (Tarus *et al.* 2015; Bowers & Kumar 2015).

Having said the above, it is equally important to indicate the fact that e-learning is not just about using technology for learning and teaching, it also extends to pedagogical issues which highlight the use of digital resources, communication tools, as well as the collection of learning data to effectively support the learning process, to effectively encourage engagement and promote pedagogical decision-making (Gebre, Saroyan & Bracewell 2014; Kong 2017). Interestingly, Hodges, Moore, Lockee, Trust and Bond (2020) distinguish between online learning and emergence remote teaching (ERT), which we can argue that many institutions adopted in the wake of the COVID-19 pandemic. They argue that while online learning is carefully planned and designed, ERT on the other hand is a temporary measure of instructional delivery designed as a result of a crisis and would return to the face to face format as soon as the crisis has abated. According to Hodges *et al.* (2020), ERT's main objective is to ensure temporary access to instructional support during a crisis, for instance, the implementation of models like mobile learning, television and radio educational programmes, as well as blended learning. If Hodges *et al.'* s (2020) distinction is anything to go by, one would therefore argue that what most HEIs have implemented is ERT, where university staff have received immense support in online course design, content development, as well as training in learning management system. Indeed, the move to ERT means that lecturers become more competent and take control of the implementation process. This is very important because if not carefully done, the rapid shift to ERT may deteriorate the quality of the delivery process. This means that more time and effort should be invested in developing quality courses. In this view, Hodges *et al.* (2020) suggest that the universal design for learning (UDL) should be integrated in the discussions on teaching and learning. The main principles of the UDL highlight the importance of designing inclusive, flexible and student-centred learning environments to ensure equal access to learning materials by students (see UDL on Campus)[1].

In view of the above, it is important to discuss HEIs' readiness to effectively support the e-learning process, or rather the ERT described above, in the context of the COVID-19 pandemic. The following discussion highlights the measures put in place by various institutions to ensure their readiness to roll out e-learning in an effective way.

HEIs' readiness for remote online teaching and learning

For many HEIs, remote online teaching became the only alternative, but the viability of the strategy depended on a number of issues, it was not just an automatic move from face to face to online teaching. Before the implementation of the digitisation of teaching and learning, a number of modalities had to be put in place, which was not a smooth-running process for many institutions, especially those that had not been traditionally using the e-learning platform for teaching. For instance, institutions had to run webinars to train and equip the faculty members and students with the necessary knowledge and skills to use the e-learning platform (Peicheva & Milenkova 2017; Milenkova & Manov 2019). The information technology and online experts in various institutions provided crash programmes for faculty to learn how to navigate the e-learning platforms with ease while providing virtual lessons and assessments to the students. It is undeniable to say that most faculty members were wary, as they were suddenly thrown into the deep end of the online pool. Naidu (2020) reported that some concerned academics from the South African HEIs called for a halt to online learning, as they argued that the process could result in an "academic disaster" and add to the effects of the COVID-19 pandemic. Amongst the reasons for the call included the widening digital divide, as well as the differences in resourcing for which they called for "state-level intervention in resourcing and infrastructure development; academic, financial and accommodation protection for students; and labour protection for education workers" (cited by Naidu 2020). Despite the efforts by the information technology and online experts to provide training to the faculty, the process requires skills, new ways of thinking, more time than face to face instruction, of which some faculty of certain ages grappled to adapt to these requirements. It is also imperative to highlight that one of the important issues in e-learning is content management. In order for the e-learning environment to be effective, instructional designers ought to master the theoretical foundations underlying instructional design, while at the same time they should be able to identify the relationship between theory and practice.

Students' perceptions of remote and online teaching

Studies have indicated mixed views about students' perceptions of e-learning. Buzzetto-More and Sweat-Guy's (2006) study found that students enjoyed using course website as they felt that the web stimulated their desire to learn. In their study, students were found to be content with the quantity as well as the quality of their e-learning experiences. In another study, Batalla-Busquets and Pacheco-Bernal (2013) noted that in comparison to virtual learning, face-to-face training is perceived as more motivating and beneficial. What can be derived from these contrasting findings is perhaps the notion that the students' perceptions could be influenced by various factors like educational, social, financial or cultural backgrounds. For instance, the way a course is designed, developed and delivered can highly influence the students' involvement in the course. A course might fail to meet the students' needs and or expectations, which would then affect how they perceive the mode of delivery. Sometimes the way students perceive the mode of delivery is also based on the instructor- accessibility, approachability, the degree of fairness, enthusiasm, mastery and delivery of content, as well as the inspiration and knowledge imparted.

Other reasons for the differences in perceptions could be issues of infrastructure availability and exposure to them. Asunka's (2008) study in Ghana highlighted the issues of inadequate resources and institutional problems as affecting students' perceptions of e-learning. The students studied indicated that online learning offers no advantages over face-to-face learning. Similarly, Tagoe's (2012) study in Ghana revealed that students preferred the blended mode of learning- online and face to face. At this juncture, it is imperative to discuss how students in African HEIs have been experiencing e-learning since the mode was adopted following the outbreak of the COVID-19. The discussion is based on the literature reviewed in this regard.

In addition to the training provided to faculty, necessary training was also provided to the students alike. For instance, from our observation at the Namibia University of Science and Technology, students were given orientation on how to navigate through the learning management system, as well as how to interact with the content and their lecturers or tutors. Overall, we also observed that students did not like the idea of e-learning, and this seems to be the case with many students across the continent, as indicated in the discussion that follows. The students' reasons for not showing any enthusiasm towards online learning were valid and genuine, among them being unfamiliar with online delivery, lack of the necessary devices such as smartphones, laptops, as well as the limited access to internet bandwidth. In the main, the students' argument was that online learning would not be inclusive and thus excludes the marginalised who are disadvantaged by poor infrastructure. It also became clear that most students preferred face to face interaction with their lecturers and peers. In discussing students' experiences of e-learning, what follows are some sentiments highlighted by students from different parts of the continent.

Nganga, Waruru and Nakweya (2020) reflected on the Kenyan situation. The Kenyan students from the University of Nairobi (UON) expressed their dismay on Twitter (#UONboycottonlineclasses), where they protested against the announcement by the university management that they would continue their learning online. Some students took their time to register their frustrations in this regard: 'You want me to take online classes. I live in Turkana (in far-off remote northern Kenya). Does this university even care that I obviously can't access [the] internet? It is University of Nairobi, not University for people of Nairobi'- Jared Washington Ochako (quoted by Nganga *et al.* 2020). Another student, Uon-Mzee Mzima opined: 'Training is an inevitable part of any business but, depending solely on an e-learning platform can make learning less personal, less engaging, and in the process, less effective. We urge comrades to boycott such shenanigans' (cited by Nganga et al. 2020).

From the sentiments presented above, the main argument from the students is that e-learning is unaffordable and to some extent elitist, hence, impractical.

In Zimbabwe, the government also proposed online learning, an idea which was rejected by the student body, the Zimbabwe National

Students Union (ZINASU) (Mukeredzi, Kokutse & Dell 2020). The reasons put forward for the rejection of e-learning was that, the union argued, most of the students have no access to reliable mobile network connections, expensive data tariffs, while the country itself lacks reliable electricity supply. According to the World Bank (Trading Economics 2020), less than half of the Zimbabwean population (41,4%) had access to electricity in 2018. One of the private universities in the country, Ezekiel Guti University, ordered students to register for online learning only after they had paid fees for the first semester, or they were being excluded from accessing the e-platforms (Mukeredzi, Kokutse & Dell 2020). In response to the online learning proposal, ZINASU Secretary General Tapiwanashe Chiriga argued:

> We express our concerns over how such platforms have only become accessible to students who have paid up full fees…While we recognise the need to continue with learning during this terrible time and the need to embrace innovation and technology, it is our position that learning at all material times should be accessible and affordable to all students. (quoted by Mukeredzi *et al.* 2020: para 7)

State universities like the Great Zimbabwe University and the Midlands State University opted for the use of Google class and WhatsApp respectively, to conduct classes. This again was regarded as elitist by some student movement, Economic Freedom Fighters-Zimbabwe, represented by Everton Mutsauri, who pointed that, "It is important for policy makers and the universities to look at the very high data tariffs. Only the elite will be able to attend all online lectures. This is an example of policies being enacted by the elite for the elites". (quoted by Mukeredzi *et al.* 2020: para 9).

One of the effects of the COVID-19 pandemic is that many students were forced to defer their studies in 2020, as they could not cope with the economic hardships associated with the suspension of face to face teaching and learning. In view of this development, the Namibia University of Technology offered students the option to decide whether they wanted to continue with their studies or not. The University Registrar, Mr Maurice Garde (2020a), indicated that students were given time to familiarise themselves with online learning and then decide whether to cancel their studies. He also indicated that those who decided to cancel their studies would be granted a credit of 75% on tuition fees.

The Namibian student unions also chastised their government's decision to embark on e-learning amidst the COVID-19 pandemic. The Students Union of Namibia (SUN) was prepared to "seek an urgent court interdict against forced online education, as well as persuade and spearhead mass cancellation of higher learning" (Jantze 2020). The argument for calling for the cancellation of e-learning was that more than 50% of the network coverage by the mobile telecommunication companies MTC and TN Mobile was limited to 2G, which would not be effective and efficient for e-learning. Another student body, the Namibia National Student Union (NANSO) also demanded that the management of the University of Namibia (UNAM) suspend e-learning. Commenting on the situation, the Acting Secretary General of NANSO, Patience Masua argued:

> We firmly hold the opinion that the halting of online learning and the adjustment of the learning calendar is the best possible solution that will ensure all students have an equal opportunity. We echo a clarion call for all other higher learning institutions to join in the fight to ensure learning is equal. We equally recognise and appreciate the efforts of academic staff whose efforts with online learning do not go unnoticed (quoted by Jantze 2020: para 13)

From this discussion so far, it is clear that the main reason against the e-learning proposed by many governments is the fact that many students do not have the necessary "tools of trade" for the success of the e-learning project. In the case of the Namibian students, if they continue with e-learning while not having the adequate resources, the chances of failing their courses are increased, which would then put them at risk of losing funding from the government agent, the Namibia Student Financial Assistance Fund (NSFAF).

In South Africa, the South African Students Congress (SASCO) called for a national boycott of online learning, citing the reason that it is not available to all students (Mukeredzi, Kokutse & Dell 2020). In an effort to successfully roll out e-learning, Wits University lent 5000 laptops to disadvantaged students, in addition to 30GB of data which was provided to all student for a month (Wits Covi-19 Update 2020). In August 2020, the University of Zululand, as well as the University of Fort Hare, received their first batches of laptops and modems to distribute to students who do not have the means to access online learning (Lindeni 2020; Unizulu student notice 2020).

It is clear that the transition to online education as a result of the COVID-19 was unsettling to the students who experienced some kind of discomfort in it. Focal to this tension is the real and enduring issue of the digital divide which has visibly been aggravated by the pandemic, thereby exposing the existing inequalities faced by the marginalised members of the society (Whitley, Benson & Wesaw 2018; Vogels, Perrin, Rainie & Anderson 2020). In addition to this sad reality is the fact that some students hail from disadvantaged households which do not present the comfort (as compared to the hostel accommodation) that enhance academic learning (Fischer 2020). The lack of physical distance between home and private spaces for studying (library) may result in poor concentration among students. Despite having access to online learning material, some students find library sites as cumbersome to navigate as they are used to the traditional way of borrowing learning material from the library. Thus, the abrupt transition to a new mode of instruction makes the learning experience more distressing among students. In some instances, students deferred their studies as a result of the hardships presented by the e-learning mode. Notably, Tamrat and Teferra (2020) highlighted that close to 10 million African students discontinued their studies as a result of the impact of the COVID-19 pandemic. At the Namibia University of Science and Technology, the Registrar, Mr Maurice Garde (2020b) noted that: "NUST is proud to state that 78% of students have transitioned successfully to online learning and progressing well with their studies and the transition to the online mode of studies", while the remaining 22% experienced various challenges in the COVID-19 environment. A study by the UNESCO Institute of Statistics (2020, Learning through radio and television in the time of COVID-19, para 2) indicated that, "Some 826 million students (50%) kept out of classrooms by the pandemic do not have access to a computer at home…Around 706 million students lack internet access and 56 million live in areas not covered by mobile networks…"

The notion of moving from face to face to remote online teaching was faced with resistance from students across the continent, for the reasons cited earlier in this section. On that note, it is also essential to deliberate on some of the challenges associated with the e-learning mode, in the context of HE.

Challenges faced by African HEIs

The outbreak of COVID-19 resulted in many governments laying down some lockdown restrictions, which meant that face to face teaching and learning had to be suspended for an unforeseeable future. Starting the school year late or interrupting it completely disrupts the lives of many students, parents and teachers. Remote learning strategies can reduce the impact of the crisis imposed by COVID-19, yet this is not without risks and challenges. For many of the institutions, remote online teaching was the only alternative, but the viability of the strategy depended on a number of issues, it was not just an automatic move from face to face to online teaching.

The situation is very mixed and if not managed appropriately, the inequalities that exist in opportunities will be amplified. For instance, some students from disadvantaged families cannot afford books or a desk, let alone internet connectivity or laptop. It is of great importance to make sure that the variances in opportunities are minimised to a greater extent such that the present crisis will not aggravate adverse effects on the already disadvantaged poor student's learning. Many ministries of higher education are concerned that total dependence on online learning methods suggest that only students from families that are well-off will benefit.

Limited access to internet and electricity

As reiterated in the students' sentiments discussed earlier, online learning is unaffordable to most of them due to the highly priced internet connections, unreliable network and unavailability of electricity. As indicated earlier, Zimbabwe is amongst the countries in the continent which has very costly mobile data tariffs. The institutions of higher learning, together with schools were instructed to shut down in March to control the spread of COVID-19. It is clear that there are substantial disparities in the provision of higher education through online education. These inequalities manifest in universities, the academic community and in most African countries. There are significant variations in how distance education is received. In many lower-income countries there is shortage of broadband, unreliable or mostly absent, as evidenced in the case of Zimbabwe described earlier (Mukeredzi et al. 2020). In addition, electricity supply is a big challenge. Less well-endowed universities in general have not developed the technical, curricular or other infrastructures necessary for quality online education. Thus, virtual learning is far from being inclusive, given these circumstances: "Online classes are good; they help compensate virtually the time lost away from class. However, imposing it on the students in the most remote areas of the country without good network coverage and electricity is not logical" (Mutinda quoted by Nganga *et al.* 2020: para 20).

The sentiments echoed above are very critical and this is one of the reasons why some students opted to defer their classes. The idea of connecting on Zoom or MS Teams for online classes is just a far-fetched dream, due to connectivity issues.

Inappropriateness of the e-learning mode to some practical courses

Noteworthy is the fact that there are a number of subjects and courses that are difficult to teach or deliver through online teaching methods, for instance, those courses with practical components like from the engineering, medical and pharmaceutical, as well as journalism fields. For instance, in the field of sciences, laboratory-based courses pose so many challenges that are almost impossible to be addressed online. Students need to use chemicals, conduct experiments and in general get the feeling of lab work. Accordingly, Esther Ngumbi, assistant Professor of Entomology maintains that:

> The transition to online learning was likely to be easier for both lecturers and students in the social sciences, humanities and business disciplines compared to those in sciences. I think a teaching science class is more complicated especially where you need science labs. However, given the circumstances, I think we will see useful innovations that can

326

help guide future teaching of science labs (quoted by Nganga et al. 2020: para 24).

Subjects in the humanities such as dance, music and drama also do not lend themselves to online instruction. In line with the above argument, if not effectively managed, online learning can provide a limited sense of community. Students learn a lot and sometimes understand better from their peers (peer learning). Vygotsky's (1978) sociocultural theory of learning emphasises the importance of active involvement of peers in the learning process, indicating that as learners engage with their more knowledgeable peers, the process of co-construction of knowledge also takes place. Large traditional undergraduate lecture courses do not often afford deep intellectual pursuits, but the use of discussion groups can be quite effective. Online teaching and learning may not easily cater for collaborative learning like group work, community building (students get isolated in their homes and have no one to discuss with) or much communication, either among students, as well as between students and their lecturers. Although there are new technological tools, as well as pedagogical inventions that can assist, these are often unavailable and sometimes demand significant investment by HEIs, together with training on how to effectively use them, for both students and staff.

Compromised remote examination process

A major problem with online learning is how to examine students. Written assignments can be done online, as well as theses, including their presentations and defences. But in the case of examinations (the most common form of assessment, in particular at the undergraduate level and for large cohorts), there are concerns about fraud and privacy (through the use of software used to check online dishonesty during examinations. Altbach and de Wit (2020: para. 16) "Are we at a transformative moment for online learning?" They further noted that according to the Dutch Student Union,

There are serious privacy concerns about the use of algorithms by Google, Facebook and the leading European provider, Proctor Exam, in invigilating exams. If students are denied permission by the software, they will be unable to take their exams and will be delayed in their studies.

Even though lecturers are putting an effort to improve, a particular group (the majority of the elderly faculty members) lack the understanding and the determination to acquire the new and complicated approaches and technologies. The fact is that developing high quality online courses requires skill, new ways of thinking about pedagogy and money. In the current rush to quickly adapt to online teaching requirements, these are all in short supply. Furthermore, most academics posit that in virtual learning more time is required as compared to deliberations that are done face to face, or else the outcomes are less satisfactory.

Lessons learnt and implications for the HEIs

The dawn of the COVID-19 pandemic brought the whole world to a halt and the main lesson learnt from this experience is that we ought to get used to uncertainty and the change brought about in many aspects of our lives: business and economic perspective, changing work environments, income uncertainty, technology and innovation, as well as in law and politics. From a societal and individual perspective, work has increasingly become less location-specific and more network oriented. For HEIs, this is the time for them to show their capacity to adapt very quickly to the challenges posed by the pandemic in the education system, with lots of flexibility. However, such type of a crisis had not been anticipated, and none had put sophisticated risk management measures in place. The question that needs to be answered therefore, during and beyond the crisis, is how we can turn these quick fixes into more sustainable approaches. There are definitely lessons to be learnt to improve institutional resilience in HE. Having highlighted the experiences of the staff and students alike during the pandemic, as well as the challenges and opportunities presented by the pandemic, it is also important to further the discussion by highlighting some pertinent issues, moving forward. Scientists in the medical field have reiterated that the faceless Covid-19 enemy is going to be among us in the unforeseeable future (WHO 2020). What this means is that we have to adapt and learn to live with the virus. Consistent with the situation, academic institutions have been forced to adopt online educational delivery modalities. While this transition might be possible in developed countries, it has proven to be a huge challenge in the African context whose ICT infrastructure, systems, expertise and policies still need to be upgraded. Although it might sound premature to predict how the pandemic will permanently affect the education system in general, there are signs of permanent imprints on the path of digitisation and learning innovation. Here, we discuss some of the lessons learnt by HEIs, as well as implications for the future.

Need for investment in technological innovation

The discussion highlighted earlier clearly indicates that some revolutions in the education sector are imminent. It is a fact that the COVID-19 has accelerated technological development and what we are witnessing is a race between technology and education (Goldin & Katz 2008). This could be the opportunity for African universities to demonstrate that they can be reservoirs of expertise and knowledge, thereby gaining new legitimacy in society. One can argue that the rate at which HEIs are moving with technological innovation is lamentable, as evidenced by the way they (the HEIs) halted academic activities as a result of the COVID-19 outbreak. With their traditional lecture-based approaches to teaching and learning, HEIs were forced to search for innovative technological solutions within a short space of time, which in some instances meant investing a lot of money in training the information technology and online experts, as well as procuring licenses for some sophisticated software to use for educational purposes, since the outmoded classrooms were not accessible anymore due to social distancing and other regulations put in place to contain the virus. The traditional classroom learning was quickly replaced by new learning modalities- for instance, some countries dedicated certain television and radio stations for educational programming. UNESCO (2020: para 4) reiterates that:

> Considering this technological divide, most countries around the world are also using television and/or radio-based programmes to implement distance education. Africa seems to be the most active in the

efforts to leverage either TV or radio (70%), some combining both (34% of countries)...The value of educational broadcasts through television and radio also goes beyond the needs of students alone. In some countries, these programmes are conceived to provide intergenerational learning, including in local languages. They also include issues such as health and psychosocial well-being, both of which are important in supporting populations affected by the threat of COVID-19.

Synchronous online learning tools have become the norm since the outbreak of the pandemic- Zoom, Microsoft Teams and Google classrooms are being implemented around the world to help pre-empt academic institution closures. However, from a technical perspective, these have proved to be inadequate in the long run, particularly in the African context where we are seeing governments making efforts to help students get the necessary devices to ensure effective e-learning, as in the case of the South African and Namibian governments. In the meantime, practical-based courses have proven difficult to do remotely, such that some institutions like the University of KwaZulu-Natal, Wits University, as well as the Namibia University of Science and Technology, had to make arrangements for students taking certain practical courses (e.g. medical, journalism and engineering students) to go back to the campus in order to do the practical which require the use of specialised laboratories and equipment (eNCA 2020). What this means is that ideally, e-learning platforms should be designed to integrate multiple learning activities and modalities to ensure active learning and broader interaction. This calls for a dedicated budget to ensure the availability of the requisite expertise and infrastructure. It also means that the students and online instructors are equipped with the technical know-how and skills. What is currently imperative are new modalities of delivering education. The fact is that the current situation presents the opportunity to develop unique forms of personalized education, there is need for innovation in terms of students assessments, meaning that there is need to go beyond the usual traditional assessment strategies, particularly for large undergraduate classes. Another common practice is that the current online teaching and learning still assumes the most basic format, which is more or less the same with the traditional face to face. Perhaps we could argue that the pandemic which caught the world by surprise did not afford HEIs the chance to rethink pedagogy. As a response to the pandemic, the ERT could have been poorly planned, badly executed and has excluded many disadvantaged students who found themselves involuntarily having to postpone their studies. This is therefore the time to innovate in this instance, for example, academics need to closely work with professional instructional designers to develop purpose-built teaching and learning materials. While reflecting on this, the use of indigenous languages in teaching and learning is becoming more and more vital and trans-languaging will work in this instance. HEIs can benefit from Open Educational Resources[2] (OERs) which allow adaptations like translation. Mobile devices have also become handy in translating languages in speech. It is therefore evident that there are many opportunities and there is a place for online learning in the face of the COVID-19 pandemic, but the major concern is that the lack of infrastructure is a massive impediment to this aspect of socio-economic development.

Having said the above, HEIs still need to adapt to the specific needs of individual students, if the online learning is to be effective. This entails the need to provide sustainable strategies to enable the quality delivery of teaching and learning. Of course, adapting to the new normal of e-learning is not an easy process, but it is imperative and urgent to mitigate the effects of the pandemic in the education fraternity. On that note, the key drivers include the institutional management, the course facilitators, students, as well as the learning resources. It has to be noted that just migrating to the online mode is not enough. Indeed, at the height of the pandemic, many HEIs rushed to the inevitable stop gap- online. It has been indicated that while digital technologies can potentially change teaching and learning interactions, they are highly unlikely to directly bring the required change (Education Endowment Foundation 2019). What we can therefore learn is that technology should rather supplement, but not replace teaching. Just investing in new technology does not automatically translate into achievement. Instead, the effective use of technology is premised by realistic teaching and learning goals, and not a certain technology (Bettinger, Fairlie, Kapuza, Kardanova, Loyalka & Zakharov 2020). The point to note here is that the COVID-19 pandemic forced many institutions to quickly roll-out

ERT, without enough opportunity to put in place the necessary pre-conditions for such a move. Thus, the effectiveness of the migration to online learning still needs to be evaluated.

The need for public-private partnerships and collaboration

The previous sections of this chapter indicated how the use of technology-mediated learning in HEI has been limited across the African continent, due to limited access to the necessary resources. For instance, compared to its counterparts, South Africa is a technologically advanced country in Africa, but the nation has been experiencing load shedding for many years now. With the e-learning becoming the norm, the power cuts experienced by the country are surely a barrier to the successful implementation of online education. From an economic perspective, the use of mobile technology in Africa still poses some challenges. Commenting on this, Tamrat and Teferra (2020: para 7 & 8) noted that:

> A mobile handset and 500MB of data cost 10% of an average monthly income in Africa, which is double the 5% threshold recommended by the UN Broadband Commission...This harsh reality will continue to affect the business of academia conducted through online platforms in a meaningful way by inhibiting students' capacity to access available resources from their own institutions or other external sources.

Following the outbreak of the COVID-19 pandemic, some alliances are becoming mandatory, in an effort to navigate through the challenges presented by the pandemic. It is high time the private sector works more closely with HEIs and governments to improve innovation, as well as the production of relevant skills. Organisations and indeed industries' future success is highly dependent on developing digital skills, artificial intelligence and automation, alongside intangible abilities such as emotional intelligence, problem-solving, adaptability and resilience. Different stakeholders including the government, educational specialists, information technology specialists, as well as health professionals, are coming together to help provide temporary solutions to the challenges. For instance, the

South African and the Namibian governments envisaged to help students with devices and mobile data packages to enable students to access online learning. This involved negotiating with telecommunications network operators like MTN, Vodacom and Cell C (South Africa), as well as MTC and TN Mobile (Namibia) to provide reasonable and affordable data packages so that students could access digital learning platforms at a lower cost. Mobile operators are also increasingly bringing in lower priced mobile devices on the market, as in the case of South Africa's MTN, in partnership with China mobile: '…MTN released a "smart feature phone," the Smart S, in a number of African markets including South Africa, Nigeria, Uganda and Rwanda…as a partnership with operating system maker, KaiOS, China Mobile and chipmaker Unisoc to bring affordable 3G smart feature phones to the African market' (Gilbert 2019: para 6).

This could become a prevalent and significant trend to future education, even after the COVID-19 era. While such initiatives are still limited in terms of scope, much large-scale and cross- industry partnerships can be formed towards a common goal-educational. This calls for a broader cooperation in order to address the challenges posed by the pandemic. It is a fact that the African continent has been receiving international support from high profile institutions like WHO, the World Bank, Gates Foundation, to mention a few (eNCA 2020). However, the support has mainly been geared towards the health and economic sectors, while the education sector has not been given the same consideration. This highlights the need for governments and the private sector to also provide the necessary support to the education sector, particularly by providing technological infrastructure to the less privileged students, ensuring interconnectivity among HEIs, as well as improving digital skills. This is critical and urgent in the face of the pandemic which is thought to be around for the unforeseeable future. This could be the time for African HEIs to take major steps in building their ICT profiles, in partnership with the private sector.

Aggravation of already existing inequalities

The COVID-19 pandemic has exposed the already existing inequalities in African communities. With many losing their jobs in the wake of the pandemic, this resulted in income shocks which saw many families struggling to keep their children in school. In this situation, persons with disabilities, girls and the marginalised were disproportionately affected (World Bank, 2020). The governments that are expected to help such groups seems to be also strained and becoming cash strapped as they tend to prioritise and channel funding towards managing the pandemic: procuring the personal protective equipment and other equipment like ventilators, building more facilities to accommodate COVID-19 patients, as well as hiring more health workers to boost the frontline workers' capacity, both locally and abroad, as in the case of the Cuban doctors who were deployed to South Africa to help fight the pandemic (eNCA 2020). The education sector seems not to be receiving similar attention as the focus is on the global pandemic. However, despite many HEIs temporarily migrating to online teaching and learning, not all students are privileged to participate, due to their socio-economic circumstances.

As highlighted earlier in this chapter, e-learning highly depends on the extent and quality of access to the necessary technologies. Statistics by UNESCO have indicated how many students were forced to defer their studies due to lack of the necessary e-learning infrastructure. While virtual classrooms have become the norm the world over, many students in developing countries have been denied the opportunity and access to education, this is engendering social inequalities and marginalisation. This is a barrier to achieving the sustainable development goal of inclusive education for all by 2030. The issue of inequality is succinctly summarised by Rodrigues and Biag (2017), who noted that students from low socio-economic backgrounds are disadvantaged when it comes to accessing education.

For instance, since the closure of schools and universities, the Namibian government promised to provide devices and data for connectivity, in order to enable disadvantaged students to participate in e-learning (The Namibian 2020). Five months after the closure of institutions, this has not yet materialised and the affected students are still patiently waiting. Instead, some institutions like the Namibia University of Science and Technology resorted to arrange for face to face classes in order to allow those students who did not have devices and connectivity to also do their assessments (Garde 2020b). While this happened, other students opted to suspend their studies and hope to continue when the disaster has abated. Unfortunately, not all of them might be able to return to school, due to varying circumstances. There is so much uncertainty as to when life will return to normalcy and when HEIs will open their gates and classrooms for the students. Until then, this means that these members of the society are lying idle, unless a practical political decision is made to subvert some of the challenges presented by the pandemic, some of which include subsidizing for students to have access to devices and data for them to continue with their studies. An important intervention needed at this point is that the access costs should be decreased, while the quality of access should be increased. Very little is known about the existence of any alternatives for those students who do not have internet access, but this is an area that can be investigated to establish alternative measures which do not necessarily need internet connection. For instance, some countries have resorted and dedicated some television and radio stations for educational programming for primary and secondary schools (UNESCO 2020). This option could also be explored for HEIs However, it is also important to highlight their low effectiveness, particularly for those marginalized communities like persons with disabilities who are at higher risk of being left behind- if remote learning is to be effective for them, it has to include the necessary accessibility features. For instance, students with sensory impairments like eyesight challenges or hearing are highly likely to be left behind as they would not be having access to their learning support which is often provided in their learning institutions, for instance, the hearing impaired are often assisted with sign language, the blind learn with the help of Braille teachers, to mention a few. Thus, providing emergency learning modalities is less likely going to work for such students.

Quality assurance is imperative

The e-learning intervention that has become popular following the COVID-19 outbreak has been received with mixed feelings by different stakeholders. Among other issues discussed earlier include the fact that the approach lacks wider interaction and engagement, does not cater for lab-based activities and is also costly in terms of connectivity. Sharing the same sentiments, Perris and Mohee (2020: para 7) argue that, "Online learning requires institutional vision and investment, proper pedagogical training, thorough (contingency) planning, varied instructional design, technology-oriented learning outcomes, reliable infrastructure and ample learner support".

The point being raised in the above sentiments is that e-learning requires a viable quality assurance intervention. The quality assurance processes should ensure the safeguarding of the quality of the content design, development and delivery, adequate infrastructure, well-trained faculty, as well as reliable student support, among other things. For HEIs, this implies the need to engage a comprehensive exercise of designing an institutional quality assurance review instrument for e-learning, which is aimed at subverting any flaws in the e-learning initiatives. Essentially, internal reviews should be conducted at certain intervals, to assess HEIs' readiness for online education. This would help in identifying the necessary improvement plans.

In the quality assurance processes, caution should be taken by institutions not to adopt a "quick fix" to e-learning. There could be a misconception that e-learning is about posting *Youtube* videos, uploading PDF files, giving quizzes and providing discussion forums. In fact, online delivery requires much more and needs to be learner-centred, while at the same time being integrated with student support. Perhaps the question that should be answered is how do we implement performance-oriented, student-centred and competence-based teaching in the context of e-learning? This question highlights the need to engage and train the staff being involved in the online education processes - the faculty, administrative, as well as the information technology staff.

Disaster capitalism

The COVID-19 pandemic has presented a health crisis in which some individuals and organisations are capitalising on to fulfil their own agendas, a concept which Klein (2007) calls "disaster capitalism". During disasters and turbulent times, it is important to understand that some people will always view the situation differently. They recognise the crisis as an opportunity, not necessarily to benefit the total well-being of society, but rather to exploit the circumstances to benefit specific groups and agendas. Klein's theory of disaster capitalism explains that, " During the shock of disasters, whether economic, natural wars, capitalists, corporations and others see the opportunity to implement their policies and agendas, exploiting the fact that societies are too disoriented and distracted to resist (Abdulmark 2020).

The coronavirus pandemic is nothing short of a disaster that has shocked the world. As Klein puts it, both natural disasters for instance, the tsunamis and human made like terrorist attacks put the entire population into a state of collective shock. In the midst of the collective shock, neoliberals grab the opportunity to push forth their free market ideas. The COVID-19 pandemic has afforded some individuals and institutions an opportunity to manipulate the situation in their favour, and the general populace have not been left with an option but to accept without comprehending the full implications of the ideas. For instance, Turner (2020: 2) noted that, "The Donald Trump administration has wasted no time pushing through a profit-driven right-wing agenda that will decimate the environment and leave millions at risk". another instance is that of the Cuban government which deployed its medial professional around the world on a medical aid mission and it is estimated that the government racks in about $6 billion from exporting medical services (Nasongó 2020). Nasongó further highlights how the pandemic presented an opportunity for many governments to employ "austerity measures", "deregulation" and the "privatisation of public property" (Nasongó 2020: 4).

In the education fraternity, the closure of schools and HEIs presented an opportunity for a boon for cyber- education- providers of internet technologies have been making unprecedented profits since the beginning of e-learning, apparently through the provision of "free" education apps like Google, yet in the end the profiteer from the data that are essential for their advertising strategies (Nasongó 2020). Indeed, many other companies have swiftly responded to benefit from the pandemic (Trucano 2020: para 3). Trucano indicates that:

> Many ministries of education are working with mobile operators, telecom providers, ISPs and other companies to increase access to digital resources while schools are closed. Drawn from the World Bank's tracking of edtech and remote learning during the COVID-19 pandemic in specific countries, here are 10 practical examples of what is happening in this regard around the world… zero rating .. .bandwidth shaping… distributing devices in communities… public hotspots, and lighting up old services and devices … free sim cards.

Ironically, this presents as philanthropical acts to help deal with the pandemic, yet the main objective is profit making.

Stewart (2020: 3) argues that the sudden decision by most HEIs to move to online learning was also a result of "capitalistic concerns and not pedagogical or curricular ones", as some institutions did not consider the marginalised students who did not have the necessary tools to engage in online learning, faculty were not given the necessary time to prepare for the shift to online learning. Stewart thus argues that this whole;

> …illogic of capitalism robs us of our capacity to recognize that we are in crisis and despite the lip-service of our prepared sentiments/ statements about how we are all "in this together"; in the midst of this chaos our responses have actually been about organizational continuity, capitalism, and reducing our value to what we are able to sustain and what our bodies are able to produce (Stewart 2020: 4).

The point being made in the above sentiments is that there is need to interrogate how and why we operate the way we do, otherwise failure to do so might lead to oppression and further affect our ability to live a balanced life.

Concluding remarks

The purpose of this chapter was to highlight how the COVID-19 pandemic has disrupted the HEI life, as well as the measures implemented in response to the global pandemic. We indicated the unique challenges posed by the pandemic to different stakeholders of the HEIs, while at the same time playing their part to ensure continuity of instruction. In the main, we argued that the COVID-19 pandemic intensely underlined the need for change in HEIs, by exposing the fragility of the education system, as well as their inherent inequalities. We particularly noted that the closure of institutions as a way of managing the spread of the pandemic resulted in exclusion and inequality which are highly likely to aggravate if action is not taken to exonerate the marginalised and vulnerable groups. Having said that, we believe the pandemic will soon become a thing of the past. Going forward, we believe that the pandemic has presented a platform to re-imagine higher education, as well as addressing issues of inequality. The end of the pandemic should not signal the need to simply return to the traditional ways of teaching and learning. Instead, online learning should rather become part of the HEIs' skills set. The fact is that online teaching and learning is the future of education at all levels. The investments that have so far been made in remote learning should be a launchpad for better and more personalised, as well as sustainable way of education provision. This entails the need for effective online learning strategies to provide continuity in learning even when institutions open their doors for face to face teaching and learning. Other stakeholders described earlier should also play their part in implementing the necessary actions to drive learning both in and out of the classroom.

Endnotes

[1.] Universal Design for Learning (UDL) is a set of principles for curriculum development which provides all individuals equal opportunities to learn. It is a framework for creating instructional goals, methods, materials, and assessments that accommodate everyone--not a one-size-fits-all solution, but instead, a flexible approach that can be customized and adjusted for individual student needs.

² . Open Educational Resources: "Are freely and publicly available learning resources that reside in the public domain or have been released under an intellectual property license that permits their free use and re-purposing by others. They include full courses, course materials, modules, textbooks, streaming videos, tests, software, and any other tools, materials, or techniques used to support access to knowledge." - Hewlett Foundation.

References

Abdulmalik, A, L. (2020) 'The dangers of disaster capitalism during virus crisis'. Retrieved from https://www.zawya.com/mena/en/economy/story/The_dangers_of_disaster_capitalism_during_virus_crisis-SNG_178445986/.

Altbach, P.G. and de Wit, H. (2020) *Are we at a transformative moment for online learning?* Retrieved from https://www.universityworldnews.com/post.php?story=20200427120502132.

Asunka, S. (2008) 'Online learning in higher education in Sub-Saharan Africa: Ghanaian University students' experiences and perceptions', *International Review of Research in Open and Distance Learning,* 9(3), 1-23.

Batalla-Busquets, J.M. and Pacheco-Bernal, C. (2013) 'On-the-job e-learning: workers' attitudes and perceptions', *International Review of Research in Open and Distance Learning,* 14(1), 40-64.

Bettinger, E., Fairlie, R.W., Kapuza, A., Kardanova, E., Loyalka, P and Zakharov, A. (2020) 'Does EdTech substitute for traditional learning? experimental estimates of the educational production function', National Bureau of Economic Research, Working Paper No. w26967. Retrieved from https://publications.hse.ru/en/preprints/357673279.

Bowers, J. and Kumar, P. (2015) 'Students' perceptions of teaching and social presence: a comparative analysis of face-to-face and online learning environments', *International Journal of Web-Based Learning and Teaching Technologies,* 10(1), 27-44.

Buzzetto-More, N., & Sweat-Guy, R. (2006) 'Incorporating the hybrid learning model into minority education at a historically black university', *Journal of Information Technology Education*, 5, 153-164.

Education Endowment Foundation (2019) 'Digital technology moderate impact for moderate cost, based on extensive evidence'. Retrieved from https://educationendowmentfoundation.org.uk/evidencesumma ries/teaching-learning-toolkit/digital-technology.

Fischer, K. (2020) 'When coronavirus closes colleges, some students lose hot meals, health care, and a place to sleep', *The Chronicle of Higher Education*, 11 March 2020. Retrieved from https://www.chronicle.com/article/when-coronavirus-closes-colleges-some-students-lose-hot-meals-health-care-and-a-place-to-sleep/.

Garde, M. (2020a) 'Student credit during COVID-19 period', Memorandum for staff and students. Namibia University of Science and Technology, 26 June 2020.

Garde, M. (2020b) 'Student credit during COVID-19 period', Memorandum for staff and students. Namibia University of Science and Technology. 30 June 2020.

Gebre, E., Saroyan, A. and Bracewell, R. (2014) 'Students' engagement in technology rich classrooms and its relationship to professors' conceptions of effective teaching', *British Journal of Educational Technology*, 45(1). DOI: 10.1111/bjet.12001.

Gilbert, B. (2015) 'Online learning revealing the benefits and challenges'. Unpublished Master's thesis, St John Fischer College. Retrieved from https://fisherpub.sjfc.edu/education_ETD_masters/303/.

Gilbert, P. (2019) 'MTN is launching a $20 smartphone'. Retrieved from http://www.connectingafrica.com/author.asp?section_id=761& doc_id=753391.

Goldin, C and Katz, L. (2008) *The race between education and technology*. Harvard University Press. Cambridge.

Hodges, C., Moore, S., Lockee, B., Trust, T. and Bond, A. (2020) 'The difference between emergency remote teaching and online learning'. Retrieved from https://er.educause.edu/articles/2020/3/the-difference-between-emergency-remote-teachingand-online-learning%C2%A0%C2%A0 .

Jantze, Z. (2020) 'Student unions demand cancellation of e-learning', *Informante*, 8 April 2020. Retrieved from https://informanteweb.na/student-unions-demand-cancelling-of-e-learning/.

Kong, S. C. (2017) 'Partnership among schools in e-learning implementation: Implications on elements for sustainable development', *Journal of Educational Technology & Society, 22*(1), 28-43.

Lindeni, A. (2020) 'Distribution of laptops and modems for UFH students'. Retrieved from https://www.ufh.ac.za/news/News/DistributionLaptopsandModemsUFHstudents.

Milenkova, V. and Manov, B. (2019) 'Mobile learning and the formation of digital literacy in a knowledge society. International association for development of the information society', 15th International Conference, Mobile Learning, 2019.

Mukeredzi, T., Kokutse, F and Dell, S. (2020) 'Student bodies say e-learning is unaffordable and elitist'. Retrieved from https://www.universityworldnews.com/post.php?story=2020042207507312.

Naidu, E. (2020) 'Concerned academics call for halt to online learning'. Retrieved from https://www.universityworldnews.com/post.php?story=2020042306443818.

Nasongó, W.S. (2020) 'Disaster capitalism in the age of the Covid-19'. Retrieved from https://www.theelephant.info/ideas/2020/04/17/disaster-capitalism-in-the-age-of-covid-19/.

National Institute for Communicable Diseases (2020) 'Latest confirmed cases of Covid-19 in South Africa' (21 aug 2020). Retrieved from https://www.nicd.ac.za/latest-confirmed-cases-of-covid-19-in-south-africa-21-aug-2020/.

Nganga, G., Waruru, M. and Nakweya, G. (2020) 'Universities face multiple challenges in wake of COVID-19 closures'. Retrieved from https://www.universityworldnews.com/post.php?story=202004 07162549396.

OECD (2020) 'Education responses to COVID-19: Embracing digital learning and online collaboration'. Retrieved from https://www.oecd.org/coronavirus/policy-responses/education-responses-to-covid-19-embracing-digital-learning-and-online-collaboration-d75eb0e8/.

Peicheva, D. and Milenkova, V. (2017) 'Knowledge society and digital media literacy: Foundations for social inclusion and realization in Bulgarian context', Quality of Life, (1018-0389)/*Calitatea Vietii*, 28(1), 50-74.

Perris, K. and Mohee, R. (2020) 'Quality assurance is key to sustainable blended learning'. Retrieved from https://www.universityworldnews.com/post.php?story=202006 18085512381.

Rodrigues, M. and Biagi. F. (2017) 'Digital technologies and learning outcomes of students from low socio-economic background: An Analysis of PISA 2015', Publications Office of the European Union, Luxembourg. Retrieved from https://ec.europa.eu/jrc/en/publication/eur-scientific-and-technical-researchreports/digital-technologies-and-learning-outcomes-students-low-socio-economicbackground-analysis.

Stewart, T.J. (2020) 'Capitalism and the (il)logics of higher education's covid-19 response: a black feminist critique', *Leisure Sciences*. DOI: 10.1080/01490400.2020.1774011

Tagoe, M. (2012) 'Students' perceptions on incorporating e-learning into teaching and learning at the University of Ghana', *International Journal of Education and Development using ICT*, 8(1), 91-103.

Tamrat, W. and Teferra, D (2020) 'The shift to online learning calls for global cooperation'. Retrieved from https://www.universityworldnews.com/post.php?story=202004 13115722610.

Tarus, J. K., Gichoya, D. and Muumbo, A. (2015) 'Challenges of implementing e-learning in Kenya: A case of Kenyan public universities', *The International Review of Research in Open and Distributed Learning*, *16*(1), 120-141.

Trading Economics (2020) 'Zimbabwe - access to electricity (% of population)'. Retrieved from https://tradingeconomics.com/zimbabwe/access-to-electricity-percent-of-population-wb-data.html.

Trucano, M. (2020) 'How ministries of education work with mobile operators, telecom providers, ISPs and others to increase access to digital resources during COVID19-driven school closures (Coronavirus)'. Retrieved from https://blogs.worldbank.org/education/how-ministries-education-work-mobile-operators-telecom-providers-isps-and-others-increase.

Turner, E. (2020) 'Disaster capitalism and Covid-19'. Retrieved from https://newschoolinternationalaffairs.org/wp-content/uploads/2020/05/Disaster-Capitalism-COVID-19.pdf.

UNESCO (2020) *Learning through radio and television in the time of COVID-19*. Retrieved from https://en.unesco.org/news/learning-through-radio-and-television-time-covid-19.

Vogels, E.A., Perrin, A., Rainie, L. and Anderson, M. (2020) '53% of Americans say the internet has been essential during the COVID-19 outbreak'. Retrieved from https://www.pewresearch.org/internet/2020/04/30/53-of-americans-say-the-internet-has-been-essential-during-the-covid-19-outbreak/.

Vygotsky, L. S. (1978) *Mind in society*. Cambridge, MA: Harvard University Press.

Wits Covi-19 Update (2020) [COVID-19 UPDATE 25] 'Wits VC wishes students well as online learning begins'. Retrieved from https://www.wits.ac.za/news/latest-news/general-news/2020/2020-04/covid-19-update-25-wits-vc-wishes-students-well-as-online-learning-begins.html.

Whitley, S.E., Benson, G. and Wesaw, A. (2018) 'First generation student success: a landscape analysis of programs and services at four year institutions'. Retrieved from https://firstgen.naspa.org/2018landscape-analysis.

World Bank. (2020) 'The World Bank education global practice guidance note: remote learning & COVID-19'. Retrieved from http://documents.worldbank.org/curated/en/53168158595726

4427/pdf/Guidance-Note-onRemote-Learning-and-COVID-19.pdf

World Health Organization (2020) 'Q&A on coronaviruses' *(COVID-19)*. Retrieved from https://www.who.int/emergencies/diseases/novel-coronavirus-2019/question-and-answers-hub/q-a-detail/q-a-coronaviruses#:~:text=symptoms

www.ingramcontent.com/pod-product-compliance
Lightning Source LLC
Chambersburg PA
CBHW022134020426
42334CB00015B/892